Street Smart

RICHARD A. BLAKE

STREET
SMART

THE NEW YORK OF LUMET,
ALLEN, SCORSESE, AND LEE

THE UNIVERSITY PRESS OF KENTUCKY

Publication of this volume was made possible in part by a grant
from the National Endowment for the Humanities.

Scholarly publisher for the Commonwealth,
serving Bellarmine University, Berea College, Centre
College of Kentucky, Eastern Kentucky University,
The Filson Historical Society, Georgetown College,
Kentucky Historical Society, Kentucky State University,
Morehead State University, Murray State University,
Northern Kentucky University, Transylvania University,
University of Kentucky, University of Louisville,
and Western Kentucky University.

Editorial and Sales Offices: The University Press of Kentucky
663 South Limestone Street, Lexington, Kentucky 40508–4008
www.kentuckypress.com

All photographs are courtesy of Jerry Olingher's Movie Materials Store in New York, N.Y.

09 08 07 06 05   5 4 3 2 1

Library of Congress Cataloging-in-Publication Data
Blake, Richard Aloysius.
  Street smart : the New York of Lumet, Allen, Scorsese, and Lee / Richard A. Blake.
    p. cm.
  Includes bibliographical references and index.
  ISBN 0-8131-2357-7 (alk. paper)
  1. New York (N.Y.)—In motion pictures. 2. Lumet, Sidney, 1924—Criticism and
interpretation. 3. Allen, Woody—Criticism and interpretation. 4. Scorsese,
Martin—Criticism and interpretation. 5. Lee, Spike—Criticism and interpretation. I. Title.
  PN1995.9.N49B63 2005
   791.43'627471—dc22   2005007622

This book is printed on acid-free recycled paper meeting
the requirements of the American National Standard
for Permanence in Paper for Printed Library Materials.

∞ ✪

Manufactured in the United States of America.

 Member of the Association of
American University Presses

Contents

Illustrations follow page 144

Acknowledgments

A special note of thanks is due to several colleagues at Boston College. First of all, thanks to John Michalczyk who, as department chair and founder of the Film Studies program within the Fine Arts Department, urged completion of this project and by creative accommodation made it possible. With his support I was able to obtain a generous grant from the Boston College university research fund that enabled me to secure professional assistance to complete the manuscript preparation.

Thanks too to Karen Klein McNulty, Mark Caprio, Eugenie M'Polo, Coleen Dunkley, and their student assistants in the Media Center who managed to locate the films and make them available as needed. Finally, a note of appreciation to the students of the two classes who took a preliminary tour of New York City neighborhoods in American Directors, FM 389, and who asked the important questions, as tourists often do.

Prologue

Over a week had passed since the collapse of the World Trade Center. The afternoon of September 11, I managed to contact a cousin who lives in our old neighborhood in Brooklyn but works near Ground Zero. (I'll call her Jean, even though it isn't her name.) She was safe. In fact, while running a bit late that morning, she heard a confused news bulletin on the radio about a fire in the area and further postponed her departure to avoid the possible inconvenience of a subway delay. Within minutes of the initial news flash, television pictures began to reveal the extent of the horror. Our conversation that afternoon was hushed and monotone, like mourners gathered at a funeral, wanting to strengthen each other but finding our words hopelessly inadequate, empty.

During the next few days, we lost contact. The phone company temporarily rerouted its ruined lines from commercial centers near the disaster area through residential sections in Brooklyn. As a result, the circuits in some neighborhoods became hopelessly overloaded, and some areas were virtually inaccessible to outside callers. My initial anxiety about Jean's safety gave way to worry about her coping with the transfigured geography of her life.

After a week or more had passed, workers toiling day and night gradually managed to restore service. By the time we spoke again, the merciful numbness was beginning to wear off as we, like most Americans, started to feel the pain of the wound that had not yet begun to heal. Our voices seemed more brittle and our sentences more edgy. Jean described her persistence in calling coworkers and her relief in learning that no one from the office had been injured. Their building was still standing, with apparently only minor damage, but of course the area had been closed off while rescue crews went about their sickening task of sifting through the smoldering rubble. Electric lines were out. Even if they could reach the office, what could they do without phones, elevators, computers, lights, and ventilation? They were instructed to stay home until power could be restored.

Bereavement, the sense of helplessness, and boredom during this unexpected layoff from work took its toll. It was a long, empty, frustrating, and anxiety-ridden week. Like many people in those first days, Jean was torn between the desire to return to a normal routine and the dread of facing the area whose grotesque transformation had become eerily familiar through television. During our conversation, she described filling the time with long walks through the neighborhood in the glorious September sunlight. Each sentence unearthed a long-buried childhood memory for me: sights, smells, and sounds as vivid today as they were at midcentury: the neighborhood shops on Third Avenue, the schoolyard, Owl's Head Park. Time past fuses into time present. Will historians continue to describe those days of crew cuts, penny loafers, and black-and-white television, of Ike and Lucy, as a gentler, simpler era? What of McCarthy, Korea, and air raid shelters in the basement? Yes, they were frightening and exciting then, especially to a child, but in comparison to the present, they seem gentler, simpler indeed.

A View from the Footbridge

Jean's description of one walking tour in particular brought me back through the decades as though I had never left home. It begins at the old Brooklyn–Staten Island ferry slip, now a recreational pier at the foot of Sixty-ninth Street, turns left, and goes up a short hill along tree-lined Shore Road toward Fort Hamilton. On the right are three baseball diamonds and a playground. On the left are Marist High School and several private houses perched on rocky bluffs overlooking the harbor. I see it clearly. At Eighty-third Street one can turn right, enter the park, cross a footbridge over the Belt Parkway, which connects the City to the South Shore of Long Island, and descend to a bicycle-and-pedestrian path at the water's edge. The concrete treads on the water side of the bridge are deep enough that a skillful thirteen-year-old can bounce a Schwinn down the steps and keep pedaling all the way to Coney Island, whose parachute ride and Ferris wheel were once visible in the distance.

In her walk that particular afternoon, Jean crossed the bridge, intending to stroll back along the water to the ferry slip. It was a natural route to follow. On a cloudless late summer afternoon, the path provides a spectacular view of the Statue of Liberty and the Battery at the tip of Manhattan. At this point, Jean hesitated in her narrative. "I crossed the bridge. When I looked over toward Manhattan, they were gone," she gasped. "There was nothing there. Only brown smoke." Her voice trailed off into silence. Perhaps I heard a gulp or even a muffled sob. My own throat swelled shut and my eyes watered at that stark observation, so brief in the telling, yet so poignant in the hearing; so empty of poetry, yet filled with anguish, like the smoldering void itself.

Like everyone else, I had spent most of the previous week sitting stupefied in front of the television, obsessively watching the obscene events replayed again and again. I read the newspapers and listened to the commentators, trying to grasp the enormity of the crime, seeking some plausible explanation amid the torrent of reports and rumors. Like many others, too, I remained in a state of emotional denial. Somehow, possibly because of shock, possibly because of the numbing repetition, I had somehow managed to keep the atrocity at a distance, as though it were an earthquake in some distant land. No longer. A telephone conversation, a walk taken in imagination and memory through a park in Brooklyn that I had not seen since adolescence, opened the path to tears and, one would hope, healing. It was my world that had been violated.

Why? How? I had left Bay Ridge, Brooklyn, nearly fifty years ago, before the low-lying horizon of Staten Island became bracketed by the Verrazano Bridge at the mouth of the harbor on the left and on the right by the World Trade Center at the tip of Manhattan. Neither had been built by the time I left Brooklyn, and the Dodgers had not yet moved to Los Angeles. I had not lived in any part of New York for fully sixteen years before September 11, and on periodic visits, I began to feel progressively more the visitor. Family had scattered, and most friends and associates had moved on. Even the subways had been rerouted because of endless work on the Manhattan Bridge, and I have been in the astounding situation of having to ask strangers for directions on a transit system that had been part of my life since beginning high school. Even so, Jean's words reminded me that it was my psychic landscape that had been defiled, as surely as if my home had been ransacked by strangers. Despite the distance of miles and years, I am a New Yorker.

A View from the Movies

The experience of that telephone conversation also had another, totally unexpected impact on my life. It added a human dimension to an academic project about New York City and its place in American films, especially by filmmakers whose lives, like mine, have been inextricably woven into the fabric of the City. For several months I had been reading, gathering notes, and trying to organize my thoughts about them. In what way did the experience of growing up in the neighborhoods of the City influence their artistic imagination and consequently color the films they put on the screen? Is their New York different from Hollywood's New York? The project seemed then, and now, an interesting topic to explore through a book-length study. After September 11, the project suddenly gathered an immediacy, a personal emotional investment of the kind that rarely intrudes into academic inquiries, which, by their nature, tend to be scientific, objective, and dispassionate.

But in my own visceral reaction to this act of unspeakable violence, I discovered a personal validation of my postulate. Imagining the destruction from a particular point of view, from a footbridge in a park in Bay Ridge, made a difference. In a very real sense, I had never left Brooklyn; I was still connected and still viewed great events of the world from that psychic vantage point. If in the weeks following September 11, 2001, I realized how much the cityscape was still part of my perceptual and emotional life, then the same might be true of the New York filmmakers: Woody Allen, Sidney Lumet, Martin Scorsese, and Spike Lee. Are their lenses tinted with the New York experience, and more to the point, are their films? How could they not be?

Of course, these four filmmakers provide a mere sampler. Many others come from New York, and countless directors from all parts of the country—indeed, from around the world—have at some time used the City as a backdrop for their work. There's no great trick to creating an authentic New York atmosphere on a California soundstage, as the industry has proved again and again. These four artists, however, add something to Hollywood's skillful but artificial "authenticity." Each grew up in one of those ethnic neighborhoods that form the backbone of New York City. What is more, each of these four has set several major works within the metropolitan area, and each is at home shooting and doing postproduction in the City.

What makes the study of these four particularly interesting is that each traces his roots to very different backgrounds within the vast metropolitan area. One need not be a sociologist to appreciate that ethnic residential areas of the City, of any city, are wildly diverse. They remain mysteries to outsiders, a category that includes people who live on the next block as well as in distant cities. My middle-class, mostly Irish Bay Ridge, Brooklyn, for example, might be on another continent than Spike Lee's African American Brooklyn or Martin Scorsese's Italian Lower East Side of Manhattan, and this in turn is a world apart from Sidney Lumet's Jewish Lower East Side a few blocks away or Woody Allen's affluent, artistic Jewish community on the Upper West Side. But none of these neighborhoods has much in common with the glittery worlds of show business, high finance, and violent crime that come to mind when one thinks of the popular movie presentations of New York.

As a result, native New Yorkers live the paradox of being extremely small town and provincial while inhabiting one of the most cosmopolitan areas in the world. Like my cousin and like me, we stand securely rooted in a neighborhood and look across the water (actual or metaphorical) at the wonders of a distant city. The New York of skyscrapers and champagne might as well be Katmandu, Shangri-la, or Oz. Most of us have never spent New Year's Eve in a swank nightclub, nor do we mingle with celebrities backstage. Most families working in New York understand that only rich people and tourists can afford theater, concerts, and elegant restaurants. These things are not for those of us who ride the subway to work. We learned that this world exists not from personal experience, but from the movies. Still we took comfort, and perhaps even pride, from knowing that they are close by, parts of our city.

Even today, the Brooklyn I remember may be subtly filtered through childhood experiences, and the Manhattan I imagine never really existed except in the movies I saw from the balcony of Loew's Bay Ridge or the RKO Dyker. My mind may have concocted an artifice: a Brooklyn of nostalgia and a midtown Manhattan that stirs both admiration and resentment. How could it be otherwise for one who has grown up in New York? Midtown and neighborhood alike have of course been recycled many times in the movies. The relationship between the two is symbiotic, especially, I suggest, on the part of the four filmmakers under discussion. Their New York is as real as the smell of the neighbor's onions in the stairwell of their apartment building, but it is as artificial as the Midtown they saw in the movies and tried to recreate in their own films. They turned their experience of life and movies into art, into more movies, and these in turn now shape *our* understanding of New York.

In the chapters that follow, I look at four extraordinary American filmmakers with New York eyes. We will look at a few "New York" films, not to evaluate accuracy of detail, but rather to try to trace the strands of authentic New York experience that give these films a particular texture. In the process, I address the larger issues of their artistic sensibilities, social perspectives, and even philosophical questions. I try to locate their own neighborhood footbridge that provides their perspective on the City, and consequently on the human drama they have recorded through their films.

The pages that follow will deal with films rather than personalities or urban history. The introduction will sketch some of the key concepts in the relationship between New York, its filmmakers, and their films. In this section, I sketch out some generalizations that can be later examined in light of the films. Although the analysis of the films necessarily involves some discussion of the setting, the geography and architecture are far less important than the effect the material world has had on the filmmaker and his creation. Looking at the films with awareness of its New York origins merely provides another critical tool, much like reading the films with the conscious awareness of one's ideological perspective as, say, a postmodernist, Marxist, feminist, or Christian. Each perspective offers its own vantage point from which to view a central reality.

The subsequent four chapters that focus on individual filmmakers are a convenient, and I hope useful, organizational strategy to deal with a complex topic. This does not pretend to be an auteurist treatment of each of the four. Auteur criticism, which emphasizes the role of the director to the near exclusion of collaborators, has been largely supplanted in recent years as critics have become more self-consciously sensitive to the complexity of the filmmaking process.[1] As a result, these chapters examine individual filmmakers, but they do not attempt the "complete works" treatment used by classical auteur critics. Rather, they are limited to only those few films that best illustrate the directors' relationship to New York City. Those who find the arguments convincing should try to validate them in their studies of other films as well. Seeing these films through lenses ground in New York neighborhoods has provided me and my students with a new appreciation of both the films and the filmmakers.

Cinema City
All Around the Town

Common wisdom, an articulation of the obvious, may not be all it's cracked up to be. One might presume, for example, that a fish would be the world's greatest expert on water, but Marshall McLuhan, that highly perceptive but enigmatic media theorist of the 1960s, challenged this common belief. Instead, he thought that a fish would be the worst possible source of information on the topic.[1] The fish lacks perspective. As far as the fish is concerned, water is simply there, a part of its natural environment that cannot be questioned or explained. No decent fish would ever take the time to reflect on it. A school of chemists, physicists, meteorologists, sailors, and bartenders would do a much better job telling us about water. They can stand back from their subject and be coolly analytical about their inquiry.

Turning to outside experts or trying to view a subject from their perspective has much to commend it. In what has long ago become a rhetorical cliché, when a speaker wants the audience to stand back and view a familiar topic with a lens of wider angle, he or she might use this ploy: "Imagine an alien landing in a spaceship and looking at our backyard. What would it see?" The assumption is that the transgalactic visitor brings fresh eyes to the situation and thus enjoys a perspective impossible for a native. The outsider can observe details and see connections lost on one whose familiarity has bred, if not contempt, then at least blurry vision, like that of one trying to read a newspaper pressed

1

firmly to the tip of the nose. According to the same logic, outside evalu-
ators and auditors serve this useful function in the corporate and academic worlds, and their observations can be most illuminating,
constructive, and at times embarrassing. Unlike insiders, auditors might
be more alert to financial fraud, accrediting agencies to educational fraud.

Still, outsiders can also be dead wrong at times. Despite the advantage of freshness, the observer may be just as likely to miss the point
entirely. Consider the visitor from outer space, who might perceive jog-
ging as a form of corporal punishment for unspecified crimes and the
golden arches of McDonald's as a ubiquitous religious totem. The trav-
eler from beyond the sun lacks context, experience, and a feel for the
subject matter. That's the point. The alien observes precisely as an outsider; he's not immersed in the culture under scrutiny. He can bring
fresh perspectives, of course, but he might also bring presuppositions
from his own native planet. Perhaps he simply believes without question what the guidebooks say or what other travelers have told him.
Perhaps he mistakes what he saw in the movies for the real thing.

The challenge for any observer is to bring both the perspective of
the outsider and the sensitivity of the insider to the project. New York
filmmakers flavor their work with an insider's awareness of the pulse
and social patterns of City life in ways that may elude even them. This
is obviously the case not only when they use New York as a setting, but,
I would maintain, even when they make films that have nothing to do
with New York. The characters and situations in their films are, for
them, simply the real world; nothing need be added consciously to the
stuff of life. Critical viewers cannot let the matter rest there. Looking at
the films with the zeal of outside auditors, who strive for some manner
of objectivity, they want to understand and explain the numbers in the
balance sheet. How in fact has New York left its mark on artists like
Sidney Lumet, Martin Scorsese, Woody Allen, and Spike Lee? Are the
results predictable, like an ear for street talk and an eye for setting? Or
does the City work its magic in subtle and strange ways that may surprise even the artists themselves?

The Phantom City

New York has appeared in more movies than Michael Caine, and as a
result of overfamiliarity, it poses a problem for critical natives and visi-

tors alike. New Yorkers, both artists and audiences, take the atmospheres for granted, as fish do water. Aside from those eight million people who may be living there at any given time, everyone else drops in on a tourist visa from someplace else. In fact, even those who have never visited the Big Apple at all feel a certain sense of awareness of the city because of the movies. Audiences from Malibu to Miami, from Karachi to Capetown, know all about New York from seeing its images on the screen in all sorts of films, from Edison's turn-of-the-century vignettes of city life to the latest episode of *NYPD Blue* on television, from period dramas like Martin Scorsese's adaptation of Edith Wharton's *The Age of Innocence* (1993) to Steven Spielberg's apocalyptic future fiction *AI, Artificial Intelligence* (2000).

Knowing New York from the inside as well as the outside may not be as easy as it seems. In his famous short story, "Only the Dead Know Brooklyn," Thomas Wolfe argued that even longtime city dwellers still had a lot to learn about their home turf. Writing in a phonetic transcription of his North Carolinian's version of the Brooklyn accent, Wolfe concludes that the one borough of Brooklyn bristles with such complexity that a lifetime of study would be inadequate to the task of mastering it: "Dere's no guy livin' dat knows Brooklyn t'roo and t'roo (Only the dead know Brooklyn t'roo and t'roo) because it'd take a lifetime just to find his way aroun' duh goddam town."[2] And Brooklyn is just one of the five boroughs of New York. Many of these two million inhabitants of Brooklyn might work or shop in Manhattan, but rarely would they be motivated to visit the other boroughs.

The limits on knowing New York "troo and troo" are even more obvious for visitors. Far more New Yorkers live in Brooklyn than in Manhattan (that's a fact), but relatively few visitors travel across famous bridges or through murky subway tunnels to visit them. Nor do they ordinarily visit Staten Island, Queens, or the Bronx, unless they venture up to Yankee Stadium, which sits on the northern edge of the Harlem River, scarcely beyond the upper reaches of Manhattan. The overwhelming majority of the citizens of the real flesh-and-blood city live in what is condescendingly called the "outer" boroughs, while visitors think New York consists of a few visually recognizable sections of Manhattan.

Even those who do live in Manhattan actually inhabit a cluster of neighborhoods as diverse as Harlem, Central Park West, Chinatown, Washington Heights, and Gramercy Park, and their perspective is just

as limited as it is for those who live in Bensonhurst, Brooklyn. Each local-
ity lays claim to being New York, yet each has a character of its own.
Many of the visual, external images may be familiar because of location
shooting or studio-constructed and often reused sets, yet the ethos and
feel of these neighborhoods remain virtually unrecognized by natives (the
fish principle) and unknown to visitors (the spaceship principle). New
York has a virtually undetected, complex, spiritual identity as well as a
physical look, and that holds especially true for its neighborhoods.

The familiar sights and sounds that create the concept of New York
in the popular imagination are preponderantly located in the commercial districts of Manhattan: Radio City and the Rockettes, the Empire
State Building, the Waldorf Astoria, Central Park, Times Square, and
Bloomingdale's. These universally recognized scenes—stock footage,
location shooting, or back-lot reconstructions—provide an instantly
accessible shorthand to outline a setting of place and time for filmmakers, and as a result they are used again and again. In fact, these
well-known icons appear with such frequency in films that they have
created the concept of New York throughout the world. Without the
movies, the term *New York* would have a different content. In this
sense, New York is as much an artificial construct of the movies as
John Ford's Old West or Tarzan's Africa. They never existed, but we
like to believe they did, and as a result, we generally prefer them to the
more pedestrian actuality.

This movie version of New York is pure fantasy, a Disneyland for
cynics, a theme park for the hyperaggressive, and a spectacle that fascinates as it horrifies. It has, however, little relationship to the reality experienced by people who live in the neighborhoods and ride the subway
to work each morning. Their destination, as a rule, is not the glamorous
movie New York, but some bleak, impersonal office building in Manhattan, which is still called simply "New York" by natives, as a linguistic
relic of the days before the boroughs were incorporated into Greater
New York in 1898.

Few citizens claim New York as home. They identify themselves as
coming from Sheepshead Bay, Inwood, Kingsbridge, Tottenville, or
Sunnyside, names that visitors rarely hear. Little matter. Tourists for the
most part do not visit not the real thing, because they are not aware that
it exists. Instead, they search for the idea of New York that they have
gotten from the movies. Similarly, filmmakers, if they are outsiders, tend

to shoot the idea, the phantom that their audiences expect, even when they are most concerned with providing documentary realism. The natives, on the other hand, can't shoot anything but the real New York, even when the fictional setting of the scripts leads them far from the hometown of their imaginations. For them, the spiritual New York remains in their work, even though the physical New York is far removed. Separating the real thing from the phantom in an artist's work can pose a challenging but ultimately rewarding critical perspective on the films.

A Parisian Spaceship

The conflation of a phantom New York with the real thing is perhaps most starkly expressed by the French philosopher and social critic Jean Baudrillard (b. 1929). He serves quite well the role of the legendary visitor from outer space who offers an alien's perspective of this strange territory. Following a long line of French intellectuals that reaches back to Jean Jacques Rousseau (1712–1778) and Alexis de Tocqueville (1805–1859), Baudrillard finds America a fascinating topic for reflection. After several tours through the United States, he compiled his observations in a volume entitled simply *America,* which appeared in English in 1988. He finds equally intriguing the vast open spaces of the American deserts and, more to the point in this context, the American city. Without apology, he matter-of-factly acknowledges his debt to the movies in his conception of both, and in particular in his idea of New York City.

Baudrillard contrasts his experience of an American city to that of observing a Dutch or Italian city after visiting an art gallery. In Europe, he is astonished that the paintings have captured the look of the city. In New York, he reverses the process: He is amazed that the City actually has the look of the movies. He admires the way European painters capture the light and architecture of their surroundings. In America, he delights in his discovery that the light and architecture of the metropolis do justice to the movies. He writes: "The American city seems to have stepped right out of the movies. To grasp its secret, you should not, then, begin with the city and move inwards to the screen; you should begin with the screen and move outwards to the city."[3] In an amazing fashion, he suggests that for him the reality is embodied in the movies, and the real city excites his admiration inasmuch as it replicates the movies.

With this unusual but intriguing perspective, Baudrillard's selection of various details in city life become revealing of himself as observer more than of the City. As a visitor, he notes with some apprehension "the terrifying diversity of faces, their strangeness," yet he adds a note of admiration: "The beauty other cities only acquired over centuries has been achieved by New York in fifty years."[4] This from a cosmopolitan Parisian, who would certainly be accustomed to an ethnically diverse population from the former French colonies! For some strange reason, he has been conditioned to notice diversity in New York in a way that he does not in his own city. He does not explain this phenomenon. Perhaps in Paris he is a fish swimming in overly familiar waters, unaware of other fish, whereas while he is in New York, he is an observant tourist from an alien planet. Perhaps, too, crime dramas may have conditioned him to believe that racial diversity inevitably leads to tension, excitement, and even violence.

His time frame is also puzzling. Does he believe that the "terrifying diversity" that adds a note of "beauty" began only in the 1930s, or does his point of reference indicate the advent of sound movies, or does it mark the beginning of his own viewing of American films as a child? He could be suggesting, however indirectly, that for him, with his unique perspective, the history of New York began only with its first appearances of talking New Yorkers in the sound movies. Thus for him, his concept of New York could not exist before the movies, nor can it exist today without them. This explanation would at least be consistent with his thesis. And can it be that his awareness of its "strangeness" as terrifying had been heightened by the movies, where the huge images on the screen have forced him to observe the ethnic physical characteristics that would go unnoticed among living people passing by on a busy Parisian boulevard? In any event, although New Yorkers might agree that his perception of diversity holds true for crowded streets in midtown Manhattan, they would add with some vigor that it does not at all describe most of the aggressively homogeneous ethnic neighborhoods where a good many native New Yorkers actually live.

As a visitor, and thus a stranger by definition, Baudrillard is captivated by the impersonal nature of life in the central city, shaped as it is by his predispositions formed through the movies. Limited in the scope of his observations, he clearly misses the sense of community that thrives in the residential areas that he has no reason to visit or imagine. He muses: "Why do people live in New York? There is no relationship between them. Except for an inner electricity which results from the simple fact of their being crowded together."[5] What he sees as a faceless crowd, however, in fact consists of people temporarily in transit in public places who lead private lives somewhere within the city. Many people, and Baudrillard would surely be among them, seemed almost surprised to discover that many of the firefighters and stockbrokers who died on September 11 actually had families in other parts of the City, on Long Island or in the New Jersey suburbs, and these bereaved felt a grief that is common to the human condition. Most of the apparently disconnected individuals Baudrillard observes on congested sidewalks likewise have homes, families, churches, schools, friends, and civic organizations that demand a personal investment and provide a sense of belonging, but at home, not where Baudrillard examines them.

Again, if his perception of the reality has been shaped by the movies, as he claims, then of course he sees the city streets as two-dimensional, like a movie screen. He misses the textures of single-family houses on tree-lined side streets or tenements whose very crowding creates a town square of the stoops that spill into the sidewalks. Here, everyone knows everyone, just as though they were in a small town. From this perspective, New York consists of thousands of small towns, each with its own personality. Furthermore, in a darkened theater, a viewer like Baudrillard sits in absolute solitude, unaware of other spectators, concentrating on the flat images on the screen. In a movie house, he is a perfectly objective, passive observer, who could not establish a personal interaction with the characters on the screen even if he should want to. Being engrossed in a film is by its nature an exercise in loneliness, and according to Baudrillard, visiting the real city as a moviegoer is very much the occasion for reliving and reconstructing the filmic experience. Walking the city streets is like watching a movie. Seeing faceless, yet vaguely menacing pedestrians on the street is like watching shadows on a flat motion picture screen.

Any possibility for survival in this harsh urban universe, Baudrillard asserts without explanation, depends not on the family, but on "tribes, gangs, mafia families, secret societies, and perverse communities."[6] He continues by contrasting New York to Noah's Ark, because in the City people must survive as individuals, not couples, and work out their own means for lasting through the night, which he finds populated with the mad who have been "set free," the "punks, junkies, addicts, winoes [*sic*] or down-and-outs." Again, this may indeed be the population familiar to both moviegoers and visitors slumming for an evening's adventure. It is the image Baudrillard has fashioned from seeing too many movies set in New York. This segment of New York life can be found easily enough by any visitor looking for it. The heart of the city, however—those endlessly varied and fascinating middle-class residential areas—might be more likely to feature ordinary working people, of varied skin color and language, leading their own gray, monotone lives of suffocating respectability. These New Yorkers rarely provide material for flashy movies or quirkily perceptive and highly entertaining but imaginative essays about "America" as seen though the bloodshot eyes of an inveterate moviegoer from Paris.

Baudrillard presents an insightful portrait of life in New York, but it must be read on its own terms. Like any travelogue, his essay tells only part of the story, and that part includes the quirky and odd, the horrifying and repugnant, the menacing and terrifying. Of such details are interesting essays fashioned. Yet in this partial account, whether he intended it or not, he has produced a caricature, a cartoon, filled with thought-provoking social analysis, but a picture few native New Yorkers would recognize as their home. They can spot outsiders. They look with amusement at tourists cringing in terror at street corners, awaiting permission from the green "walk" sign before they venture into the crosswalk of a deserted street, and asking with a mixture of fear, adventure, and embarrassment if the subways are safe enough for a midday trip to Wall Street with the children. They have grown patient with misperceptions of visitors, much like Aleuts or Samoans, who endure the relentless curiosity of anthropologists, who drop in for a few weeks, ask silly questions, and publish learned analyses of their culture.

Not all New Yorkers are "punks, junkies, addicts," and the like, even though the movies have made a good number of people believe that, among them apparently Jean Baudrillard—at least in the persona he adopts in his witty travelogue. Observing or reading about the reactions of visitors, most longtime residents readily turn upside-down the old bromide about their city. For them, New York is a great place to live, but I wouldn't want to visit. The travel writer notices the oddball, the ominous, and the intriguing, as though looking for settings in a film. The native has made a private truce with reality and calls it home.

Film: Painting or Window?

Jean Baudrillard's conception of New York as a entity perceived through previous experience of movies raises in concrete form the classical dilemma of film criticism. Stated in its most theoretical terms: When viewers look at a screen do they contemplate the film itself or the objects reproduced by the film?[7] In other words, is the film an object viewed in itself, or is it the medium through which other objects are viewed? As Baudrillard describes his perception of New York, he easily passes from one to the other without acknowledging a difference. When he looks at the City, he seems to be watching a movie playing before his eyes. Conversely, when he looks at a movie screen, he seems to believe he is seeing the reality in the moving lights and shadows on the screen. In what sense does the film provide access to the entity that exists outside the theater? For him they seem interchangeable. The real New York City and filmic images of New York become for him two facets of his unified perception, the proverbial two sides of a coin. Baudrillard's conflation of objects of his perception—the City and films about the City—may be a tribute to the artistry of generations of American filmmakers, but it poses a challenge to critics who want to understand the spiritual, urban context of individual films created by New York filmmakers.

As a visitor, he describes his mode of perception as progressing from the outside to the inside; from the films he has seen, toward the City itself. Hollywood writers, directors, scenic designers, and dialogue coaches as a rule follow this process. Their perception of New York and its people, and their presentation of it in the artifacts they create are conditioned as much by previous films as by the reality. Previous films shape their notion of the real City, which they in turn present to audiences through their own set of movie images. Thus the cycle continues. If their film is to present an authentic image of New York to audiences, it must be a New York that audiences recognize by having seen other movies about New York. The artistic process involves producing new films by recycling old films. It does not produce new films from current sociological data. The concrete and asphalt, the real cab drivers and cocktail waitresses, reside only on the peripheries of the artistic horizon.

Similarly, when audiences view a film set in New York, their interpretations of the signs on the screen grow from their prior experiences of films about the City. People who have never even visited Manhattan feel confident that they are familiar not only with the landmarks but even more, with the social patterns and characters of the personalities that people the screen. New York, the object of the movie camera, assumes its own unique identity precisely because of the many cameras that have been turned upon it. In turn, a film that is shot in New York (or that is about New York) is both an entity in its own right and a lens or medium through which one views the City. We can't have a film about New York without the real New York; and at least for people like Baudrillard, we can't have the real New York without films about New York. The perceptual loop closes.

A series of comparisons may help to clarify the question. A painting, drawing, or sculpture provides an experience entirely different from that of a movie. Despite the painter's striving for photographic verisimilitude, these works clearly consist of a series of gestures by the hand of an artist. One looks at a painting as a skillful arrangement of color and brushstrokes on canvas, or a statue as an inspired arrangement of mass and texture. Paradoxically, the actuality represented by the work of art becomes immaterial; the artistic construct of the actuality clearly becomes the center of attention. One looking at a painting of an apple, for example, has no interest in the piece of fruit that inspired the work. Observers have no doubt that they contemplate an artifact, not the real thing. The thing observed is not an apple, but an arrangement of lines and color that captures the artist's interpretation of what an apple inspired at one particular moment. Van Gogh's crows in a wheat field have long ago perished and the field has in all likelihood become a housing development. Both have passed from the scene unmourned; for one looking at the painting, they are unimportant. His painting, however, remains and continues to attract interest and admiration.

Photography changes the equation dramatically. A strip of light-sensitive paper (or today a digital memory card), when placed behind a perfectly transparent lens, immediately and mechanically captures an image of whatever material object is placed before it. Camera and film do not select or edit what they record, any more than paints and brushes do. Both sets of instruments merely provide possibilities for the artists using them. A painter may exercise a greater degree of freedom: the apple could be blue, or square, or grinning. Photographers work within more clearly defined limitations. They may introduce brilliant innovations in the use of lights, filters, and printing, but they still must rely on the physical object in front of the lens at the moment they trip the shutter. After the picture is made, the artist may digitally enhance or alter the image, but at that point, the work becomes much like that of the painter.

A simple experiment helps point out the difference. Asked to identify an object in a museum, few students would identify a painting of an apple as "an apple." It's clearly a painting. In contrast, many would at first identify a photograph as "an apple," and only after a moment of reflection would they agree that the object is a sheet of paper, stained with emulsions that suggest the shape of an apple.

In photography, a chemical or electronic process allows the image to emerge on the paper as a permanent record of the light patterns that were reflected from the material object in one moment of time. Looking at a photograph of an apple involves seeing two objects at once: the actual piece of fruit as it once existed, and the photograph created by one who both selected the object to be photographed and controlled the instrument that shot it. The French philosopher Roland Barthes expresses the duality of the photographic image: "A specific photograph, in effect, is never distinguished from its referent (from what it represents), or at least it is *not immediately* or *generally* distinguished from its referent."[8]

This observation does not compromise the notion that photography, for all its reliance on mechanical reproduction of images, is indeed an art form, and a very demanding one at that. The artist selects not only the object and its setting, but the shutter speed, lights, aperture, film quality, and position of the object within the frame. Even so, the object is an actual, material apple, not conception in the artist's mind suggested by a material entity. The artifact is not a collection of colored oils smeared on canvas by hand, but a series of chemically induced stains on a piece of paper. If the painter eats the apple, what remains without question is only the painting. If the photographer eats the apple, then what remains is not only a photograph but also the historical record of one unique apple captured in one place at one historical point in time. Barthes again is helpful: "In photography, I can never deny that *the thing has been there*," while in contrast he notes, "no painted portrait . . . could compel me to believe its referent had really existed."[9] It could be simply the product of the painter's visual imagination.

Cinematography raises the stakes appreciably by adding the dimension of time. The photographer's apple is fixed in an infinitesimal moment without duration. It removes the object from its history. Unlike the actual piece of fruit, it has no past or future. The photograph holds no record of blossom, bud, sour green unripe fruit, or, finally, decaying core. The photographer may have eaten it immediately after taking the picture, but no one will ever know. The record of its existence, frozen at one instant and captured on film, is all that remains. Because all physical reality is situated in the movement of time, catching the apple at one given moment necessarily introduces a level of artificiality to the finished product. A material object insulated from time cannot exist.

Cinema, by contrast, adds the dimension of time and thus pushes the artifact one enormous step closer to actuality. The motion picture camera, for example, could show the photographer actually eating the apple. Time-lapse cinematography could show its development from blossom to decay. The margins between artifact and reality thus become progressively blurred—still distinguishable, of course, but appreciably closer to each other.

A newspaper photograph of a city street, for example, provides an artificial image of activity frozen in an instant of time. This motionless image never existed. Cars and people and pigeons move continuously. A motion picture adds the time dimension and thus creates the ever more convincing illusion of actuality, but it is still only an illusion. When it shows a city street with all its vitality, even a street reconstructed on a soundstage, a viewer believes it is the real thing, not merely the play of light and shadow on a reflecting surface. The reality lies elsewhere. But where? In memory? Imagination? Experience? Or all of these?

Where Is New York, Really?

In the climactic shootout at the end of *The Lady from Shanghai* (1948), Michael O'Hara, played by the director Orson Welles, looks on in horror as the estranged couple, Arthur and Elsa Bannister (Everett Sloane and Rita Hayworth) confront each other in a hall of mirrors. He stands by helplessly as they begin shooting at each other. With each report, the images of their respective adversaries crumble into cascading glass shards. O'Hara, the shooters, and the viewer cannot be sure which image is real and which a mere mirror reflection. For the Bannisters, discovering the reality among the images is quite literally a matter of life or death. In the meantime, they fire wildly, hoping to hit something.

For viewers of film, finding the real New York amid the images on the screen may not hold such dire consequences, but it can influence their understanding of the artifact they perceive in the darkened theater. Surely the real heart of New York is not discovered merely in the stock footage of the skyline, nor is it in the streets, stoops, and tenements so carefully constructed on Hollywood back lots, nor in the ersatz Brooklyn accents adopted by actors to indicate that they are criminals. The New York that shapes and colors the films of these four directors is the spiritual entity that tourists like Baudrillard often misconstrue, and that natives, like fish, often fail to notice.

One method for uncovering the real New York and its influence on several key filmmakers, I suggest, involves beginning with the films themselves. The process parallels that of a good diagnostician, who begins with the phenomena of the symptoms and works back toward an understanding of its etiology. The first step involves knowing what to look for and where to look for it. It is the contention of the pages that follow that the works of certain New York filmmakers—notably but not exclusively Woody Allen, Martin Scorsese, Sidney Lumet, and Spike Lee—bear the marks of the City in their bones. The hypothesis assigns the origin of these marks to the artists' memory and experience of living and working in the city.

Although they have been re-creating the City, the City has been creating them as observers and filmmakers. These marks on their psyches make their work qualitatively different from those tourist-filmmakers who compose a portrait of city life entirely from their imaginations, which in turn are shaped by earlier movies set in the City. They remember the subtle give of July asphalt under their high-top Keds and the exhilarating pop of a Spaldeen leaping off a broom handle and soaring over two sewers for an extra base hit. This is not the kind of stuff one learns in film school or by watching old movies about New York. But it cannot be forgotten and left behind. It resurfaces in the artists' work with relentless consistency.

Although Jean Baudrillard—and many filmmakers, especially film school graduates steeped in the study of earlier films—use their experiences of previous movies to shape their understanding of the City, these four New York artists have used their inside knowledge of the City to shape the images and characters they put on the screen. They reverse the process Baudrillard described so well. Although visitors deliberately use their memory of earlier films to heighten their sense of the City, the natives, consciously or not, use their memory of the City to color their movies, even those that are not shot in New York and do not have New York themes. Like ethnicity, race, or class, New York leaves an indelible impression on the artists that in turn leaves its mark on their films.[10]

These four filmmakers provide a good cross section of viewpoints—Jewish, Italian, African American—but of course they hold no copyrighted monopoly on successful and insightful films about their city. Many different New Yorks, both actual and mythical, have appeared on the screen from the earliest days of film. Some offer incisive observations of various segments of city life; others bear only a marginal relationship to reality. A city, any city, offers endless possibilities, each of them valid within the artistic world that the film constructs. As fiction, these representations—caricatures, if you will—function as perfectly acceptable artistic tools, but at the same time, many of them are patently absurd when compared to the reality.

This point is important. Mythic, imaginative, and fictional representations of New York are perfectly legitimate. It is not my intention to criticize them for lapses in accuracy. As artifacts, films legitimately select and reconstruct various settings as arenas of activity for their characters.[11] *West Side Story* (1961) never pretends to be a documentary about Puerto Rican neighborhoods, and no one should fault it for presenting the Jets and Sharks doing a ballet as a prelude to a rumble. Fiction movies need not adhere to the standards of sociological or architectural documentaries, even when they pretend to be "realistic."

The movies, made by natives and tourists alike, create fantasy worlds, even though they may be based on real-life locales. In fact, precisely in these fantasies, New York as a spiritual entity emerges most clearly. Here, I would offer as an obvious example the disturbing images of the nightlife around Times Square in Alexander Mackendrick's *Sweet Smell of Success* (1957). In this masterpiece of the film noir style, cinematographer James Wong Howe distorts physical images in order to probe the moral landscape. Incidentally, Mackendrick was born in Boston, studied film in Scotland, and began his career in England. Howe came from Canton, China. Clifford Odets, the author of the play and screenwriter for the film version, was born in Philadelphia but grew up in the Bronx,

New York. In combination, they developed a brilliant study of personal corruption as imaged in the lightless, almost airless canyons of midtown Manhattan. Examples of using New York imagery to provide a moral context could be multiplied a hundredfold.

The native directors, however, provide yet another perspective on the relationship between New York and the movies. Like the tourists, they use the images for settings and moral contexts. They assume that audiences already have some familiarity with the geographic and architectural icons on the screen. What I suggest here, however, is that an understanding of New York, their New York, can add to an understanding of their work as a whole.

Establishing Shot through a Wide-Angle Lens

Putting the number of New York movies in the hundreds may be an overly conservative estimate. Certainly, if television programs were included, the list would reach many thousands. With so many different takes by diverse filmmakers, the stunning variety of images is overwhelming, each with its own meaning. Park Avenue and Wall Street suggest one thing; Harlem and the Lower East Side the opposite; Schubert Alley and Broadway something entirely different.

Other cities have similarly achieved iconic status, just like New York, but they tend to connote a single, more narrowly focused personality for moviegoers. New Orleans, the Big Easy, has its Bourbon Street, jazz, Mardi Gras, and steamy, menacing underworld. San Francisco's hills outnumber Rome's, and they provide a perfect setting for police car chases with the Golden Gate Bridge in the background. Chicago offers gangsters from the Depression era, but they are quite different from Miami gangsters, who are drug traffickers and wear pastels and ponytails. Hollywood's Tinseltown image comes naturally enough from its leading industry; Beverly Hills with its shops on Rodeo Drive redefines the term *conspicuous consumption.* The neighborhoods of greater Los Angeles, however, provide dreary anonymity for petty criminals and alienation for lovers amid its palm tree–lined streets, slightly run-down stucco houses, and endless tangles of freeways. A mention of Boston with its Beacon Hill or Philadelphia with its Main Line immediately suggests American aristocracy and old money, even though the vast majority of the citizens of both cities is neither aristocratic nor monied.

And movie Washington seems populated exclusively by attractive young professionals who constantly prowl the corridors of power and stop for casual liaisons when they are not saving the republic from its sinister enemies, foreign and domestic. Each of these cities has a movie identity, which reflects a fragmentary, distorted rendering of the real city, but one recognized by moviegoers around the world. What appears on the screen fulfills the artists' vision and the audiences' expectations of the city as a setting for the story, not the city itself.

New York, however, can legitimately stake a claim to primacy as a movie locale, if not for its variety of meanings that it projects, then certainly because of its lengthy history as a movie capital and the sheer number of movies made in it or about it. From the earliest days of the industry, New York has always been a movie town.

This relationship began in the birth of both the City as we know it today and in the birth of the film industry in the last years of the nineteenth century and the first years of the twentieth, before the term *Hollywood* had entered the American vocabulary. The peep-show era, featuring Edison's hand-cranked Kinetoscope, is commonly thought to have begun in Andrew Holland's converted shoe store on Broadway on April 14, 1894. The first commercial demonstration in America of the new gadget that produced projected moving pictures with Edison's Vitascope took place at Koster and Bial's Music Hall on Thirty-fourth Street and Broadway, on April 23, 1896.[12] Weeks later, the Lumière Brothers from Paris opened a show with their own apparatus at Keith's Union Square Theater on June 29, 1896. Almost immediately, the fad spread, and single-reel movies became a commonplace novelty act in vaudeville houses throughout the country.

During the years that the film industry was emerging, profound changes were taking place in New York as well. After the opening of the Brooklyn Bridge in 1883, the cities of New York and Brooklyn became linked by an elevated train crossing the new span. Soon politicians began the process that cobbled together Greater New York from its preexisting entities. These included New York City, which stretched to the rural uptown reaches of the Bronx, the City of Brooklyn, and scattered towns and villages in Queens County and Richmond County, popularly known as Staten Island. During this period, these varied and distant communities were being woven together into a single tapestry by the steel threads of an urban rail system. This network eventually went underground as the subway, which opened for business in 1904. As a result of its ubiquitous rapid transit system, New Yorkers have lived with tension between these local identities growing out of their neighborhoods and a cosmopolitan sense of the self that comes from being simply a New Yorker. This geographic schizophrenia will appear in its movies—and, as we will see in subsequent chapters, in the artists who made them.

While New York was reaching undisputed eminence for its status among American cities, the movies were making the transition from technical novelty to a highly lucrative medium of mass entertainment. The two entities grew to maturity together. As it became the unchallenged American center of arts, trade, and finance, New York provided a natural home for innovations like the movies. This happened for a number of reasons.

First, the earliest equipment was designed and manufactured by Edison's laboratories in West Orange, New Jersey, a short ride by commuter train to Manhattan. Although Edison's actual role in developing the apparatus has been traditionally overstated, he owned the factory, financed the project, and hired the technicians, especially William Kennedy Laurie Dixon, who, more than any other American, can claim to be the inventor of the motion picture. In the earliest phase of the industry, Edison lent his name and prestige to the technology and eventually approved the manufacture and marketing of various forms of early motion pictures as the latest miracle from Menlo Park.[13] The strategy for making money from the new invention involved actually making the films to be shown with it, which the Edison crew did on the factory grounds in a backyard studio which they called the Black Maria because of its tar-paper walls.

Before long, as audiences looked for films that did more than demonstrate the wonder of seeing pictures moving on a screen, the bustling streets of New York provided endless opportunities for enterprising camera operators, like William Heise and Billy Bitzer, the German-born photographer who eventually gained a permanent place in film history as cinematographer for D. W. Griffith. The ride from West Orange to New York City in search of more marketable subject matter became progressively more impractical, especially because Edison's battery-powered apparatus weighed over half a ton. It made good business sense to locate their production facilities, such as they were, near the scenes they were shooting. Edison's pioneers moved into a loft building on Twenty-eighth Street and soon found their neighborhood hosting their rivals American Mutoscope and Biograph on Thirteenth Street. Thus the first "factories," as the studios were known at the turn of the twentieth century, clustered in and around the commercial center of Manhattan.[14]

Then as now, rents were prohibitive, and as plots for story films became more elaborate, the factories needed more space than they could afford in the congested and expensive locations in Manhattan. Economic considerations then led the industry to consider the outer boroughs, which provided open lots, warehouses, and loft buildings at lower rents while still providing an easy connection by trolley car and elevated railroad to talent and audiences in Manhattan. By 1905 Vitagraph had moved to Brooklyn, and Edison and Biograph moved to the Bronx in the following year.[15] Other companies soon sprang up on the west bank of the Hudson, at Fort Lee, New Jersey. In 1920 Famous Players–Lasky (later to become Paramount) opened its magnificent new facility in Astoria, Queens, and Fox built two studios way uptown in the West Fifties of Manhattan.

With astonishing rapidity, however, Hollywood began to supplant New York as a production center, even though business offices remained on the East Coast near the country's financial center. In the late 1920s, the introduction of sound brought a temporary stay of execution to East Coast filmmaking because New York was home to the music industry, to sound technicians, and to hundreds of actors who could actually speak lines. Ironically, however, before long, it was sound that put the final nail in the coffin for New York. Soundstages require exclusive use of studio space for a single production. Rehearsals and simultaneous shooting of multiple scenes for several silent movies in the open, barnlike space of the early studios were no longer possible. The image of the director in riding boots shouting instructions through a megaphone over the din of the busy studio became an icon of film history. The chaotic noise of moviemaking was soon replaced with the cry "Quiet on the set" over a the speaker system and the snap of the black-and-white clapper board used to synchronize sound and image in the editing room.

Even if a production could afford adequate space, another problem remained. With the art of soundproofing and recording in its infancy, New York's ambient urban traffic noise posed a seemingly insurmountable problem. Cost-conscious studio heads inevitably set their gaze west-ward, toward the vast tracts of cheap land around Los Angeles, where they could build huge complexes of soundstages out in the country, far from the rumble of traffic. Thanks to the rural quiet and predictable weather patterns, much of the sound shooting could even be done out-doors on a back lot, with sunlight and reflectors replacing expensive electric lighting equipment in the dreary, windowless New York facto-ries.[16] And no passing trolley cars would ruin the shot.

Over the years, Hollywood and the movie industry have become synonymous in the public vocabulary, but it is important to remember that the industry took its initial shape and movies developed their style in New York.

Second, a cheap, popular form of entertainment requires a dense population if it is to be economically successful. Rural areas and small towns could not bring together enough customers eager to pay only a nickel for a few minutes of primitive entertainment, at least not on a regular basis. The teeming streets of New York, with its huge non-En-glish-speaking populations, provided an ideal market for silent films. These earliest films could be shown for a profit right where they had been shot, and audiences loved the home-grown product. Films provid-ing familiar scenes and situations were a treat for local audiences and set the look of films that audiences in other parts of the country would soon accept as part of the movie experience. If they couldn't live in the Big City, then at least they could savor the energy and excitement vi-cariously. Going to the movies offered a sense of adventure, and New York, along with the Wild West or exotic Turkish harems, provided it. Even after the industry moved to Hollywood, it had to reconstruct New York in its studio to provide an atmosphere of urban sophistication that its audiences craved.

Finally, New York boasted the country's densest concentration of theaters, and these provided a ready-made venue for exhibition.[17] At the turn of the century, movie theaters as such had not been invented, and entrepreneurs of the new industry were still trying all kinds of sites, including barbershops and barrooms, for their equipment. A function-ing live-entertainment theater proved ideal, both for the filmmakers seeking a steady source of income and for the theater owners who could add a few moving pictures as a novelty act and pay far less for them than they would for a live performer. For a short period, between the time the novelty of seeing anything in motion wore off and the emergence of the photoplay or story film emerged as an attraction in its own right, theater owners used movies as "chasers"—that is, as the act that would "chase" patrons of one program out of their seats to make room for the next shift of paid admissions. Again, movies were cheaper than jugglers and trained dogs.

As the industry became more dependent on story-based films, filmmakers could tap into the theater's vast supply of skilled but chronically unemployed technicians: set painters, costumers, lighting experts, makeup artists, and the like. The public's appetite for new products became insatiable, and in New York, there was no shortage of actors and writers eager to satisfy it and to gain a most welcome paycheck, even if it meant demeaning themselves by working for the movies. Naturally, they brought a New York "look" to the early films.

The reaction of one struggling actor, whose feelings were probably typical, has been preserved. Although his prospects as both actor and writer appeared bleak at the time, he still hesitated to work for Edison despite the promise of $5 a day because, as he put it, "I'll lose standing as an actor with theater people if they see me in a movie."[18] He chose to try his luck as a screenwriter instead, a role that he could pursue with anonymity and thus do less damage to his reputation. He failed as a writer, however, eventually overcame his pride, accepted a few acting roles with Edwin S. Porter at Biograph on Fourteenth Street, and eventually moved into directing, using his real name: D. W. Griffith.

From Documentary to Cartoon

In the earliest days, before, say, 1900, when the movies were still considered a miracle of technology, people went to the movies for the thrill of seeing the gadget in operation. They would turn the crank on one of Edison's peep-show machines or sit on benches in a darkened room to see flickering images projected on a sheet. Before long the novelty of moving pictures wore off. At first, audiences especially enjoyed seeing familiar sights twitching on the screen, even though they might have been photographed only a few yards from the theater. The delight of recognizing the images on the screen might be compared to thumbing through a family photograph album and finding Dad in his high-school graduation class.[19] The discovery of the familiar in a photograph can be great fun for the relatives, and it was for City dwellers who knew the territory from daily experience. Almost immediately, the films also began to be shown in other parts of the country, and indeed in other parts of the world, where audiences had no such direct experience of the cityscapes presented to them on film. They enjoyed them nonetheless. Seeing the sights of New York became an integral part of the movie experience. For many audiences, going to a movie meant a vicarious visit to New York, and sights of the busy city streets were what movies were supposed to look like. As a result, early audiences became familiar with the look of New York simply because of the movies.

By way of a momentary digression, it is interesting to recall that primitive cinema went through much the same development in Europe. The Lumière Brothers, Auguste and Louis, unveiled their cinématographe in Paris in December 1895, and their program consisted of unrehearsed scenes from the lives of ordinary citizens, like *Workers Leaving the Lumière Factory* and *Boys Sailing Boats in the Tuileries Gardens*. Of course, there was no editing. They simply turned the crank on the camera until they ran out of film. The surviving films from Paris, no less than those from Manhattan, have the look of an amateur's first ventures with a new video recorder on Christmas morning, immediately after tearing through the wrapping paper but before reading the instruction booklet. Nonetheless, the images moved, and audiences were captivated by them, just as they were in New York.[20] People in rural France—and throughout the world—became familiar with the sights of Paris through the movies.

This fascination with moving images of city streets soon waned. Once one had seen the invention in operation, there was little motive to return and pay more money to see it again. It became clear that the medium in itself was not enough to ensure a steady income, and audiences had to be lured back into the theater by a different kind of content. To answer the demands of the marketplace for novelty, Edison's top filmmaker, Edwin S. Porter, created one-reel adventures like *The Life of an American Fireman* (1902), *The Great Train Robbery* (1903), and *Rescued from an Eagle's Nest* (1907), starring D. W. Griffith and a stuffed bird on a string. In Paris, Georges Méliès, a magician, turned to fantasies like *Voyage to the Moon* (1902) and *The Impossible Voyage of 20,000 Leagues under the Sea* (1907). Both of these immensely popular filmmakers rejected the familiar urban settings in favor of exotic locales that opened the imaginations of their audiences to world of adventure more akin to today's comic books than to anything the viewers could have experienced personally.

The rise of the story film in both Paris and New York necessarily brought with it a shift from documentary reproduction of sights familiar to audiences to a more artificial or stagy reconstruction of the settings to support the atmospherics of the plot. Filmmaking moved from street to studio. The imaginative studio staging of the action applied not only to distant, exotic locales, but to the very street scenes beloved by the earliest audiences. Not only were the now-familiar architecture and look of the city re-created artificially, but the characters and the communities introduced into the scenes had to provide the feel that the story demanded and that audiences expected. Gangsters, socialites, and Broadway entertainers assumed characteristic personalities that grew out of the ambiance of New York City. They became recognizable types, cast in their predictable settings, even though the tenement kitchen, the socialite's boudoir, or the criminal's dark alley might actually consist of a few painted images on a canvas backdrop. In order to provide the appropriate cues for their audiences—especially those whose idea of the City came exclusively from the movies—film artists had to make a New York that was more New York than New York.

The trend asserts itself in the works of D. W. Griffith. His popular *Musketeers of Pig Alley* (1912) features an innocent young wife, played by Lillian Gish, who attracts the attention of a notorious gangster with disastrous and violent results. As Richard Schickel has so well explained, this was a period in New York history when people feared that criminal gangs had gotten out of control.[21] Audiences found the themes timely, and although they might be repelled by the characters and situations they saw on the screen, they loved the films. Then as now, violence and danger sold tickets. With the fervor of an evangelical preacher, Griffith painted the moral dangers of city life in their starkest colors. He used authentic on-site locations for his outdoor shooting, but of course the sites were selected and the studio sets designed to show that crime run rampant posed a threat to innocent citizens, especially to women who worked outside the home and to men who fell under the influence of loose women. As a Kentuckian who had found life in the City the antithesis of the values he cherished growing up on his family farm, Griffith showed a pro-rural, antiurban bias through much of his work.[22] For him, the city, especially New York, assumed a symbolic, even moral, dimension. In his autobiography Griffith gave this assessment of his adopted city: "New York never seemed like a melting pot to me, it seemed like a boiling pot . . . the flesh of these women was of every color known. . . . I learned early in life that for all the scheming, busy humanity, money was the king, the devil king."[23] His explicit reference to women "of every color known" relates the evils of city life to interracial intimacy as the epitome of moral degradation, a preoccupation he explores at great length in his masterpiece, *The Birth of a Nation* (1915).

The same year as *Musketeers of Pig Alley*, Griffith also made *The New York Hat*, starring Mary Pickford. The story is set in a small town, but the catalyst of the action is a hat that symbolizes the moral laxity that the local people associate with New York. At the death of her mother, Pickford's character lives out a joyless girlhood with her overly strict father. Captivated by a beautiful hat in a milliner's window, the emotionally impoverished young girl confesses her girlish longing for the hat to her clergyman. A sensible, compassionate man, he believes that she deserves some frivolous joy in her life, and he buys the hat from funds left by the deceased mother. When the heroine suddenly appears wearing the expensive hat and it becomes known that the minister gave it to her, the people in the town and the father immediately assume the worst of both of them. Retribution comes swiftly. The father destroys the hat, but before he can take further steps, the minister produces the dead mother's will.

The very presence of an alien element associated with New York in this small town precipitates a chain of events that leads to the brink of tragedy. Even though Griffith in fact condemns the unfounded suspicions of the town dwellers, he still uses the convenient shorthand of "New York" in the title, rather than, say, "Parisian," to help audiences grasp the point of view of the townspeople immediately. In later films, like *The Mother and the Law*, the modern-day segment of *Intolerance* (1916), and *Way Down East* (1920), the heroines, played by Mae Marsh and Lillian Gish, respectively, find their virtue compromised once they move into the sinister surroundings of the big city.

Griffith was not alone in portraying the dangers of life in the big city. Oscar Micheaux, the foremost African American filmmaker of the silent period, uses the city as the arena for degradation for Isabelle (Julia Theresa Russell), the heroine in *Body and Soul* (1925). The city that embodies her fall is Atlanta, but in fact Micheaux shot the film in New York. Micheaux, the a novelist turned filmmaker from South Dakota, consistently used his work to urge black Americans to avoid the snares of city life and commerce.[24] An admirer of Booker T. Washington, he equated progress with farming and skilled labor, a theme that frequently appeared in his films. This ideology, along with his unflinching por-trayals of black criminals and the pretensions of the black middle class, brought no small amount of criticism from reviewers in the black press, who feared that these negative images would foster a poor self-image for African American audiences and reinforce the destructive stereotypes of black people all too common among many European Americans.[25] For Micheaux, staying close to home and learning a trade were far safer paths to follow than seeking one's fortune amid the dangers of city life.

A Nation in Transition

In the opening decade of the twentieth century, the assumption of the moral superiority of rural areas and small towns was not limited to the premier moviemakers. The belief in agrarian utopianism has been con-stant in American culture since the seventeenth century, when the first settlers left what they perceived as the tired, corrupt cities of northern Europe to search for a new Eden in the unspoiled wilderness of North America.[26] The concept of Jeffersonian democracy was built on the con-viction that America's future would be based on farms and plantations of the vast open spaces of the interior rather than on urban industries. To this end, Jefferson believed a population of ten citizens per square mile ought to stir Americans to move on to less congested areas.[27] The westward movement in the eighteenth and nineteenth centuries rein-forced the myth that the genuine American heroes, from Lewis and Clark and Daniel Boone to Buffalo Bill, were products of the frontier, not the perceived squalor of the cities.

By the time the movies arrived on the scene at the turn of the twen-tieth century, American suspicion of cities had intensified. Small won-der. During the latter half of the nineteenth century, the United States underwent the most stunning transformation of its short history. The Civil War ended the plantation system in the South and sent both freed slaves and displaced whites, like D. W. Griffith, streaming toward the cities in search of work, where they were joined by wave after wave of immigrants from Ireland and then southern and central Europe. On the heels of the booming war economy, the country was emerging as a major industrial power. Factories and urban populations grew together in a reciprocal relationship: cheap labor attracted industry, and factories attracted people looking for jobs. Thus the rapid growth of industry brought an explosion of urban centers and a simultaneous dramatic, proportionate decline in farm populations, thought at one time by people like Griffith to be the backbone of not only the American economy but of the American way of life.[28]

Immigration not only swelled the populations of American urban centers, which now rivaled those of Europe, but it brought a drastic change to the composition of the American people. In this respect, industrialization in America differed from the nineteenth-century European version. The influx of immigrants to American cities had a different dynamic than the urban migrations in Europe, where the newcomers came from within the country. Workers flocking from the farms to the mills in Sheffield, Leeds, or Manchester were British or Irish. By contrast, the strange people who landed on American shores brought with them their odd un-American—and thus suspect—languages, religions, values, and customs. Americans from the more landlocked regions of the country found the cultural mix of the city streets unsettling at best and at worst dangerous, as witnessed by the testimonies of dissimilar figures like D. W. Griffith and Jean Baudrillard.

Little wonder, because this mixing of diverse people challenged earlier concepts of American diversity. According to the common consensus, the United States was to be a white, Anglo-Saxon, Protestant republic. The vast continent, however, offered space for every deviant religious or ethnic group to settle in its own region—Dutch in New York, Germans in Pennsylvania, Puritans in Massachusetts, Catholics in Maryland—without intruding in the lives of the other. Thus the early colonies tended to be exclusivist, an ideal that was unspoken but nonetheless real. Tolerance was construed as freedom for anyone to found a new settlement somewhere else, where the founders and followers could think and worship as they pleased. Coexistence, much less accommodation among diverse groups in the same space, was not considered part of the contract. During the nineteenth century, the rise of the cities in postcolonial America created a rupture with that tradition.[29] In urban areas, most notably in New York, everyone from the founding families to the newest immigrants occupied the same territory. Groups had their own neighborhoods, to be sure, but living elbow to elbow in the same city, they could not avoid one another. Right through the early decades of the twentieth century, multiculturalism was not universally embraced as a value in the more traditional areas of the country.

The new story movies contributed to America's cultural vertigo. In 1908, over half the films shown in American theaters were made in Europe, and their major markets were the cities.[30] The American film industry organized itself quickly, and by 1913 that statistic had dropped to 10 percent, but the early popularity of foreign films, playing to native urban audiences as well as to immigrants, left a lasting association between the cities, the movies, and the undermining of traditional American values by foreign elements. Both the films and the mixed audiences they catered to seemed to represent a dilution of American culture.

The growing cosmopolitan tint of American urban society was not limited to the working classes; it cut across class barriers. The steamship and increased commerce made cultural exchange with the Old World commonplace, and the transatlantic cable began operations in 1866. Museums and opera houses featured artists from around the world, and American aristocrats were expected to make the grand tour of Europe to complete their education. The Spanish-American War in 1898 gave the United States an empire—and gave Americans a clear signal that the new century would not be free of foreign entanglements. As the Atlantic Ocean narrowed, the ideal of a distinctly American, isolationist society was severely challenged, and New York, already recognized as a haven for newcomers, provided the gateway for foreign ideas.

Paradoxically, as New York became less "American," it exerted a greater influence on American life. Banks and huge corporations centered in New York controlled, or at least seemed to control, the destinies of millions in the interior. Power shifted from the traditional ideal of self-determination through the open town meeting to deals struck in closed boardrooms on Wall Street, where decisions came from industrial barons who had been elected by no one and who represented their own self-interest above all else. Monopolies were a fact of life, and as they grew through the nineteenth century, the government seemed unwilling or unable to stop them. For many, especially workers and farmers, the American dream of self-determination became a nightmare of control by big business, and the nightmare had its point of origin in New York.

Scapegoating, even demonization, in the midst of such dramatic change was inevitable. In the popular imagination, country and small town represented stability and the past, pristine values shaped by an Anglo-Saxon Protestant heritage. These represented everything that was the opposite of New York City. The turn-of-the-century small town, with its soda fountains and white picket fences, entered into the myth of American identity, even though as a social force it provided a statistically insignificant stopping point in the migration from farm to city. Social historian David J. Russo explains the internal migrations of Americans:

> In the twentieth century most Americans came to live in these relatively few urban centers, which became the standard location for a population that had been dispersed in rural settings for the last three centuries. Neither before nor after did most Americans reside in towns: at first they moved out to the country-side, then they swarmed into the cities. Most of them have never been town dwellers, but they have always needed towns, even if they have not lived in them.[31]

Ironically, this mythical nostalgia for small town America has been most effectively maintained through the movies, that most urban and urbanizing of media. No one has "needed towns" more than Frank Capra, who built an entire career out of Americans' affection for small towns—an affection that seemed to grow even as more Americans migrated to the burgeoning urban centers.

Even if Capravilles never existed—at least to the extent Americans like to think they did—they still represent the myth of a more manageable, more moral universe. Even before the trauma of World War I, no thinking person could escape the fact that that era, in whatever form it existed, was clearly passing away and another, more exciting and less predictable era had begun. The city was coming into the ascendancy, but it embodied the dangers that came from a mixing of cultures, classes, and races. An antiurban resentment, always present in the American psyche since the first immigrants abandoned the inhospitable cities of northern Europe, grew even more pronounced at the turn of the century as the cities, especially New York, came to dominate the American landscape. In the popular imagination, the city was everything America was not.

Film historian Garth Jowett describes American reaction to the "the combined assault on the existing social order" caused by industrialization, urbanization, and immigration as focusing directly on the city as the source of all that endangers the American way of life:

> So vast and far-reaching were the transformations they set in motion that ultimately they were considered by many the cause of all the harmful, antisocial influences that threatened to destroy the basis of traditional American society. Thus for a great many Americans the city had always been symbolic of all that was evil. The sociologist Anselm Strauss has noted that this attitude had two related, but different aspects: "The city destroyed people who were born there or migrated there. The city also imperiled the nation itself."[32]

In this psychic environment the city became both symbol and scapegoat, and no city was more notorious than New York

A decade of viewing one-reel street scenes photographed around Manhattan by Bitzer, Heise, and a score of other, less-known early camera operators gave people a visual context for their concept of urban life. And as such, it provided a specific locus for their fear, anger, and resentment as well as their fascination with the New World coming to life with the new century. The actual city, as documented by the earliest filmmakers in their one-real vignettes of street life, became irrelevant. In the space of a very few years, the familiar imagery on the screen developed into a network of symbolic references that *meant* something, and as such could be manipulated by makers of story film to further the work of fiction. Thus the New York of the movies took on a life of its own. Reality provided only the raw material; artists and audiences collaborated on the meaning: decadence, danger, excitement, glamour, squalor, and unimaginable wealth. New York was frightening and exciting in equal measure. Movie audiences loved the movie version almost as much as they resented the real thing.

New York, California

In the period of transition from documentaries of street scenes to studio-shot story films, the reconstruction of the urban landscape took place in New York studios and was executed by artists who actually lived there. They were re-creating an artificial, symbolic universe on the set, but the congeries of sights, sounds, smells, and characters that underlay the symbols had to be addressed each morning on their way to work. Their walk to the "factory" provided both an artistic inspiration and a wholesome check on their creative impulses.

Then that link to the real world was severed. The move to California took the artistic process one giant step further from the reality. With its advantages of space and weather, Southern California quickly and decisively supplanted New York as the nation's movie capital. By 1915 the Los Angeles Chamber of Commerce boasted that fully 80 percent of American movies were made in the area.[33] As a result, the actual brick-and-asphalt New York receded from the collective consciousness of the filmmaking community as artists from all sections of the country congregated amid the newly developed orange groves to contribute to the second founding of the motion picture industry. This new generation of artists knew that New York looked different than Chicago or Pittsburgh, other filmmaking cities of the period, but their sense of the difference came not from the personal experience of living there, but from seeing the movies that were made in the original movie capital. For them, the screen was not a lens that provided access to the real thing; the images on the screen *were* the real thing. Mesmerized by the work of their forebears in the industry, they might not have realized that movie New York verged, if not on the status of a cartoon, then certainly that of a cliché. Creating an image of New York in the movies meant reproducing what had been put on the screen before. It involved reconstructing on a lot in Hollywood what had been created in a loft in New York, which was in turn a re-creation of what filmmakers saw in the neighborhood. In the Hollywood era, artist and audience alike knew without a doubt what the city looked like because they saw it in the movies—whether the scene was shot on a street corner in Manhattan or painted on a plasterboard set in Burbank. But they didn't live there, so they lacked a reality check.

Thus, filmmakers in Hollywood had to provide visual cues for audiences that had never visited New York themselves. The familiar architecture could be easily reproduced on the set, even though the collection of designer skyscrapers sketched on a backdrop and seen through an office window or the plywood stoops of a tenement house were an "interpretation" of the actuality that might in fact bear little resemblance to the real thing. The process of artistic re-creation extended beyond visual constructs of buildings to caricatures of the City's living inhabitants. These have entered into popular culture through the movies. New York cab drivers, chorus girls, or bus drivers, for example, probably differ very little from their counterparts in other major American cities, but the movies gave them a reputation that far outstripped the real thing.

Expatriate New Yorkers contributed more than their share to the transformation of New York from a documentary setting to a series of Hollywood icons. Ever eager to follow the cash, experienced filmmakers from New York soon joined this vast westward industrial hegira and began to reconstruct their memories of home in a new setting. Perhaps in a fit of nostalgia and homesickness, they began to create an idealized movie version of reality. Memory and distance embellished the real thing.

The sound era accelerated the process of caricature. When the movies learned to talk, writers who could write dialogue and actors who could speak lines became prized commodities to be lured to Hollywood. The hunt for talent began in the obvious places. The twin centers for drama in the English-speaking world were then, as now, London and New York, and actors bore the traces of their origins on their vocal cords. From the moment movies began to speak, upper-class or highly educated American characters spoke with a tinge of an English accent, while poor people and criminals had a pronounced New York tinge to their voices (or "verses," as a gangster would say). To this day, everyone recognizes a New York accent as it sounds in the mouth of a character actor, but few would readily identify a Chicago accent—and many deny that such a thing even exists. In the movies, Chicago gangsters like James Cagney in *The Public Enemy* (1931) boast about their origins on the tough stockyard area of the South Side, but they sound as though they came from the East Side of Manhattan, as Cagney did. Thus while real New Yorkers were colonizing Hollywood, Hollywood was reconstructing the symbolic nature of New York with the eager collaboration of the expatriates from theater and publishing. One could call this development the Hollywoodization of New York, a transformation accomplished mainly by expatriate New Yorkers.

Ironically, these transplanted New Yorkers lured to Hollywood not only failed to preserve some vestige of authenticity, but they even helped accelerate the descent into caricature. They suffered the effects of culture shock, and one might argue that they reproduced for the screen a city that they remembered as somehow much better and much worse, but in any event more exciting, than it actually was. Bored by palm trees and oil wells, they romanticized the crowded streets, the shops, the crime, and the elegant restaurants of their homeland. James Sanders describes the influx of sophisticated writers who left the literary salons and sophisticated night life of Manhattan for what they considered a wasteland in Southern California: "In memory, New York nights seemed one long glide into the small hours on a cloud of conversation and music and dancing among the hundreds of nightclubs, hotels, cabarets, and after-hours boîtes that filled midtown Manhattan. Los Angeles's nightlife, on the other hand, was notorious—for barely existing."[34] New York, for them, offered everything that the Los Angeles of the 1920s could not, and perhaps their chauvinist impulses got the better of them as they tried to show their colleagues as well as their audiences what a real city was like. Movie New York became an Art Deco Shangri-la.

As James Sanders further observes, these transplanted Manhattanites contrasted the low-rise horizon of Los Angeles—a form of architecture imposed because of the ever-present fear of earthquakes—with the soaring towers of their home country. For them, the core of skyscrapers in midtown embodied the energy latent in the more modestly built outer boroughs. The office towers at the center seemed to energize the perimeters, so that a neighborhood in Brooklyn or the Bronx radiated a kind of vitality not found in other fictional movie locations in other cities. One might not be able to see these towers from the neighborhood, but it meant something to know they were there, a mere subway ride away. In the movies, the customary visual landmarks, like the Empire State Building, the Statue of Liberty, or, until lately, the World Trade Center, make New York appear as the quintessential vertical city, even though most of its citizens spend their days much closer to the ground. Taller is bigger and bigger is better, something all New Yorkers can relate to, regardless of their own personal elevation. This sensibility—some would call it arrogance—arises from the dual citizenship held by all native New Yorkers, who owe allegiance to a neighborhood they call home and at the same time to "the greatest city in the world," which somehow makes their modest homeland different from an outwardly similar neighborhood in Philadelphia or Baltimore.

East Side, West Side

In the 1940s and 1950s, when the classic New York directors who will occupy my discussion in subsequent chapters were watching movies on Saturday afternoon rather than making them as a life's work, audiences in Loew's Pitkin in Brooklyn or the RKO Fordham in the Bronx recognized the symbolic content of New York imagery and responded to it much like moviegoers in other parts of the country or even of the world. Although native New Yorkers might have had a unique delight in identifying several location shots of familiar territory, they visited fantasy worlds of penthouses, nightclubs, office towers, and Broadway dressing rooms much like audiences in the Bijou on Main Street out there on the far side of the Hudson. They understood how the shorthand of setting and character was supposed to work, and like audiences around the world, they responded to the magic.

But there were several key differences. For them, the City was more than a network of symbols; it was their hometown, the place where they lived, went to church or temple, played stickball, and fell in love. They appreciated that Humphrey Bogart, for example, represented in look and sound the archetypal tough guy, and they could respond appropriately to his symbolic persona on the screen, but as a native New Yorker himself, he sounded like the neighborhood grocery man or the parish priest. The dark stairwells and foggy waterfronts Bogie crept through were menacing, of course, but they were not very different from the look of their own neighborhood. Because New Yorkers perceived these images, which were pure fantasy in other parts of the world, as arising from their familiar surroundings, they responded with a certain degree of ambiguity. They could grasp a menacing presence, but this did not transfer over to the City as a whole. New York was not all that dangerous: for them, the fantasy was thus tempered by reality. The images induced a form of visual schizophrenia.

Similarly, the presence of foreign-born or minority characters in the films created a predictable sense of the exotic, decadent, or sophisticated, but for the natives, it was not all that strange. It was familiar psychic territory. A young Martin Scorsese or Sidney Lumet would not react to Italian criminals, corrupt Irish detectives, venal Jewish merchants, or African American hustlers as threats to traditional American values. Ethnic mixing was neither good nor bad; it was simply the way things are, and certainly it was nothing to fear in itself. Many residential neighborhoods might be ethnically homogeneous, but the schools, subways, and shops certainly were not. Then as now, people had different reactions to diversity, but for good or ill, it was a simple fact of daily life. It was not, as some outsiders might believe, a strange phenomenon peculiar to a distant city with a foreign way of life. For audiences in New York, Dorothy's lily-white Kansas or Longfellow Deeds's sweetness-and-light Mandrake Falls were the real fantasy. These worlds bore little similarity to the real America as experienced by the city dwellers who flocked to see Oz or Tara as an evening's escape from the everyday world of their own neighborhood.

The movies' adulation of small-town America and corresponding apprehension with city life—read New York—was more than a mindless and inevitable reflection of a majoritarian viewpoint. It represented a partially conscious effort on the part of the industry to create its own version of life in the United States. Hollywood studios were controlled by outsiders, immigrants, and former city dwellers, mainly Jewish, who somehow conceived of America as a world that represented everything they strove to leave behind. They idealized the images of their new homeland as a statement of their own American orthodoxy, even though this sanitized "American" world still found restricted clubs and professional quotas quite acceptable. At the same time, the city in which they found prosperity, their fulfillment of the American dream, was to a great many Americans suspect at best and dangerous at worst. They found the mythic America they created more palatable to audiences and to themselves than the real America where they made their fortunes.

In his fascinating study of the dynamics of Hollywood, film historian Neal Gabler documents the roots of this small-town fantasy America as stemming from a small group of immigrant Jews from Central Europe. Many of the names are familiar: Sam Goldwyn, Jack Warner, Harry Cohn, Jesse Lasky, Adolf Zukor, Louis B. Mayer, Carl Laemmle. According to his thesis, these perennial outsiders to both European and American elites tried to prove their allegiance to their new country by extolling in their movies the nation they thought existed and that they aspired to be accepted into. He comments: "What is amazing is the extent to which they succeeded in promulgating this fiction throughout the world. By making a 'shadow' America, one which idealized every old glorifying bromide about the country, the Hollywood Jews created a powerful cluster of images and ideas—so powerful that, in a sense, they colonized the American imagination."[35] Having experienced poverty in the slums, they created a world where hard work inevitably brought success. Having escaped ghettoes on both sides of the ocean, they created a town where everyone is accepted as equal. Having tasted city life at its harshest, they preferred town life at its most pastoral and urban life at its most idyllic. Their own tastes reinforced the agrarian, antiurban strain already present in the American psyche centuries before the invention of the movies.

Filmmakers who were not Jewish shared the vision of the moguls and cashed in on it quite successfully. Frank Capra, an immigrant from Sicily working for Harry Cohn at Columbia, probably rivaled Norman Rockwell, the famous illustrator of covers for the *Saturday Evening Post,* as the godfather of mythic America. In contrast to the moguls, when European directors, like Eric Von Stroheim and Joseph Von Sternberg, arrived in Hollywood and brought their dark urban images and sophisticated themes with them, they merely confirmed Americans' worst suspicions of foreign and big-city decadence.[36]

The classic films of the sound era created fantasy versions of both small-town and urban environments. The exaggerated qualities of the one highlighted the mythic qualities of the other. If the movie version of small towns represented the best in American values, then the city, especially New York City as the archetypal city, represented the worst. No one protested this cinematic black eye. On the contrary, New Yorkers watching these films took delight in affirming the image of their city as the toughest, most corrupt, noisiest, dirtiest, gaudiest, most violent town on earth. This is consistent with their feelings about their town. Perversely, New Yorkers take special pride in boasting that their subways are more dangerous and their cab drivers more sociopathic than in any other city in the world. Survival in this environment simply adds to the cachet of being a New Yorker: "If I can make it there, I'll make it anywhere," as Frank Sinatra tells us so forcefully in "New York, New York." He never has to sing the unspoken conclusion for New Yorkers: "And baby, I made it big."

Home Sweet (and Sour) Home

The myth provides a weirdly satisfying sense of self-identity, even if it strays from the truth a bit. New Yorkers know that, even if they won't admit it. Those living in the tough neighborhoods of New York surely harbor few illusions about the reality of violence, corruption, and degradation in their hometown. Even people in comfortable middle-class areas read the *Daily News* and the *New York Post,* tabloid papers that leave no local stone unturned if there is any hope of finding something slimy underneath it. The facts are undeniable. Even so, it's not the whole truth.

The movies, like the tabloids, present only one part of the picture, but lived reality is something far more complex. Although the streets provided threats to physical and moral well-being in abundance for any youngster, just as the movies proclaimed, fear was balanced by a sense of security, of being at home. Hollywood movies frequently miss this. The neighborhoods included the churches and synagogues, the schools and candy stores, the delis and movie houses that gave the young person a sense of belonging to a comfortable, living community. Friends played stickball in the playground, or if there was no playground, in the street, despite the intrusive interruption of cars. The block was a small town, and the street, as the focal point surrounded by stoops, formed a village square. The building was something like an extended family. The odors in the stairwell revealed what the neighbors were having for dinner. Unlike the movie version, which stresses the impersonal nature of living in high-rise apartments in Manhattan, the ethnic neighborhoods, especially in the outer boroughs, create a small-town atmosphere within the megalopolis. The longtime British correspondent in America Alistair Cooke once referred to New York as "the biggest collection of villages in the world."[37]

Village life brings its own consequences that mitigate the impersonal life of movie New York. New Yorkers have a complex relationship to their city that involves balancing the tension between two lives: one among the strangers of the vast metropolis, and the other among acquaintances in the neighborhood. The one encourages paranoia for survival's sake. It explains in part the legendary aggressiveness of New Yorkers toward strangers: Why be polite to someone who intrudes on your space and who you will never see again? At the same time the other side of New York life fosters ferocious loyalty to the block, the neighborhood, or the borough. (People in Brooklyn still seethe at the departure of the Dodgers nearly fifty years ago and hate the Yankees more than Bostonians for their annual ritual of defeating those magnificent Brooklyn Dodger teams in the years immediately before the perfidy.) Living among hordes of strangers can be both exhilarating and intimidating; living among family, friends, and acquaintances in familiar settings can be reassuring. Native New Yorkers have it both ways.

Jane Jacobs, a pioneer apologist/advocate of city life, writes insightfully about the personal experience of the streets in any city, but her comments have a particular pertinence to New York street life. In their quest for order, urban planners like her nemesis, the storied Robert Moses, see only chaos and clutter on the streets and miss the humanizing effects of ongoing personal contacts in crowded neighborhood: "The sum of such casual, public contact at a local level—most of it fortuitous, most of it associated with errands, all of it metered by the person concerned and not thrust upon him by anyone—is a feeling for the public identity of people, a web of public respect and trust, and a resource in time of personal and neighborhood need."[38] Visitors like Jean Baudrillard lack this experience. They find the impersonal crowds on the streets intimidating, if not terrifying, and this is the city that tourists and movie audiences are most familiar with. New Yorkers realize that the cold but frenzied world that Baudrillard complains about exists somewhere in the City, but it certainly does not reflect life on their block. Hollywood versions of city life leave little room for church socials, local taverns, or Laundromats. In a New York created by moviemakers from California, no one visits a beloved family doctor or argues baseball with the barber or buys fruit from the store on the corner.

In the movies, everyone lives in Manhattan, unless the script calls for some local color from another borough: Brooklyn or the Bronx for criminals, Queens for cops. Staten Island rarely appears. It did in *Working Girl* (1998), where it represents a crude, cartoonish world that stands in contrast to the sleek office towers of Manhattan. Its main character, a secretary named Tess (Melanie Griffith), longs to make the symbolic ferry trip away from her roots and to a new life in Manhattan. Its director, Mike Nichols, was born in Berlin, Germany, and grew up in Chicago, so his parody of the least-known borough and its residents is understandable.

To risk a broad generalization that will be nuanced in subsequent chapters, New York directors do not have to construct their sense of the City from previous films with their limited and highly imaginative perspectives. Thus they have a more catholic vision of the City in its entirety and an awareness of the regional differences that thrive in different areas of the megalopolis. As a result of having grown familiar with the City through years of living there, they present a complex tapestry of the City life woven of strands of many colors and textures, each making its contribution to the whole.

In his remarkable study of the streets and architecture of New York through the history of commercial filmmaking, James Sanders points out that the authentic New York look is something quite different from the Hollywood version:

> New York based film makers would view things differently, not only casting their gaze across the full breadth of the city's landscape, by seeing it as a patchwork of urban villages. . . . Under the guise of conventional storytelling, locations-shot features would examine New York's neighborhoods with an almost anthropological precision and care, exploring their local ways of life, observing their streets, shops, houses and gathering places, and ultimately revealing them to be not merely background settings, but powerful sources of narrative conflict and tension.[39]

For these filmmakers, the City assumes the role of an actor, or rather a whole cast of character actors, that further the story. It is not merely the glitzy or sinister setting that allows stereotypical characters to perform their highly predictable functions.

Sanders's work is cited frequently in these pages because his analysis of the visual contributions of the actual city (or its re-creation in Hollywood) forms an invaluable basis for further reflection on the film themes and styles that emerge from the complex interaction between New York filmmakers and their native city. In the pages that follow, the analysis of the films and filmmakers will move beyond the physical surfaces of the City and attempt to penetrate the ethos of the specific neighborhoods that gave the filmmakers their own particular sense of New York.

Simply by looking thoughtfully at the films, with a conscious awareness of their New York neighborhood roots, one can offer several observations about the artists, and these in turn provide, it is hoped, an added appreciation of their work. They are at home in areas that others, even other New Yorkers, find alien. They know about the dangers of urban life, but they balance the threat of an impersonal city with the security of a familiar neighborhood. They prefer to live and work close to home. They have strong ethnic identities themselves and deal with other groups every day. They realize that being foreign or diverse is not alien to the American way of life, but in fact is constitutive of it. They know tourist Manhattan, but they are aware that the City is much larger than a few iconic areas of one borough. Like most New Yorkers, they harbor ambivalent feelings about midtown. It is both the rich and famous neighbor they resent, and yet it represents a promised land they envy. When New Yorkers boast that theirs is a city one loves to hate, they mean midtown Manhattan. It is alien and oppressive, but it gives an added identity even to the neighborhoods native New Yorkers call home.

Sidney Lumet, Woody Allen, Martin Scorsese, and Spike Lee have felt at home in New York to the extent that they have kept making their films there, and the overwhelming majority of them have New York settings. The City is the story they keep telling, over and over again. It's hard to imagine a circumstance that would lead them elsewhere for very long. Yet even on those occasions when they move their cameras away to some distant locale, they take the City with them. New York is so much a part of their artistic and psychic sensibility that wherever they are, their characters retain the traits of New Yorkers. They cannot leave town, even when they try. Why should they? It's home.

Sidney Lumet

Filmography

Find Me Guilty (2005)
Beautiful Mrs. Seidenmann, The (2000)
Gloria (1999)
Critical Care (1997)
Night Falls on Manhattan (1997)
Guilty as Sin (1993)
Stranger among Us, A (1992)
Q & A (1990)
Family Business (1989)
Running on Empty (1988)
Morning After, The (1986)
Power (1986)
Garbo Talks (1984)
Daniel (1983)
Verdict, The (1982)
Deathtrap (1982)
Prince of the City (1981)
Just Tell Me What You Want (1980)
Wiz, The (1978)
Equus (1977)
Network (1976)
Dog Day Afternoon (1975)
Murder on the Orient Express (1974)
Lovin' Molly (1974)
Serpico (1973)
Offence, The (1973)
Child's Play (1972)
Anderson Tapes, The (1971)

King: A Filmed Record . . . Montgomery to Memphis (1970)
Last of the Mobile Hot Shots (1970)
Appointment, The (1969)
Sea Gull, The (1968)
Bye Bye Braverman (1968)
Deadly Affair, The (1966)
Group, The (1966)
Hill, The (1965)
Fail-Safe (1964)
Pawnbroker, The (1964)
Long Day's Journey Into Night (1962)
Vu du pont (1961)
Fugitive Kind, The (1959)
That Kind of Woman (1959)
Stage Struck (1958)
12 Angry Men (1957)

Lower East Side
Sidney Lumet

"I was born in Philadelphia and had the good sense to leave when I was four," Sidney Lumet once said in a television interview.[1] How New York! Brash, arrogant, caustic, and totally oblivious about how his remark would play in the vast wilderness beyond the Hudson! Despite his immigrant status, Lumet is the quintessential New York director, both in his own estimation and in the minds of his critics and biographers. He sets his films in the City with the native's unfailing sense of locale. He knows which architecture or neighborhood fits the atmosphere. Walls and lampposts work as silent bit players. His characters, like cab drivers at a red light, twitch with the edgy impatience that at any moment may explode into violence. They fulfill every fantasy about what a New Yorker should be. His is a dark city, inhabited by people who make their livings amid the shadows, unseen by tourists sequestered in the warm neon cocoons of theaters and midtown hotels, unnoted by those who comment in the guidebooks on restaurants with the best wine lists.

To call Sidney Lumet a New Yorker, however, says nothing about him or his work. *New York* is too vague a term; it encompasses too much to provide any useful information about him or clues to his work. Like all natives and child immigrants from Philadelphia and elsewhere, Lumet is the product not of New York but of a particular village within that vast urban complex. "New York" is an abstraction. The Lower East

Side is a real neighborhood with its own characteristic sounds and sights and scents.

What is more, his relationship to this specific place was conditioned by his living in a unique moment of time. Born in 1924, he experienced the Lower East Side as the Great Depression colored his childhood world. As he reached adulthood, global war and a stint as a radar technician in the army opened his horizons to an outside world in ways that he neither expected nor wanted. The experience deepened his sense of Jewishness in a world that could be very hostile and very, very dangerous. A bright young Jewish man from the next door might predictably have gone uptown to study at Columbia University, as Lumet did, and become spiritually assimilated into the mainstream of politely secularized, white-bread society. Lumet never made that transition. Despite his success in mass entertainment, he never left home, and that is a blessing for all of us. Roots nourish the blossom, and the works he created over the decades bear the unmistakable genetic code of his origins.

His return to New York and the theater after the war coincided with the arrival of television. This infant industry, a stepchild of radio, took its first tottering steps in New York before migrating to the underutilized soundstages of post-television, post–studio era Hollywood. Lumet was in the right place at the right time, and both place and time made him a New Yorker surrounded by several subordinate clauses.

Jewish New York

We get ahead of ourselves in the narrative and must fill in a few details. When Baruch Lumet moved his family from Philadelphia to the Lower East Side of Manhattan, he brought them into an aggressively Jewish world. In the late 1920s, this region could be characterized as an urban melting pot before the pot did much melting. Recent immigrants of varied tongue and hue settled into low-cost housing, near their low-paying jobs, and at least for a time stayed close to their familiar transplanted cultural surroundings. Well past midcentury, a stroller would still pass easily within a few blocks from the Jewish Lower East Side to Chinatown to Little Italy. These and other ethnic groups re-created the old world as they struggled to gain a toehold in the new. Languages and cuisine varied from street to street. The neighborhood, as horrific as conditions often were, provided a safe haven until the new arrivals learned enough English and gained the confidence to sail into the open seas of Uptown, Brooklyn, Queens, or the Bronx. Only later would their children commute by PATH (Port Authority Trans-Hudson) trains to northern New Jersey, by Long Island Railroad to Nassau County, or, if they really made it, by New Haven Railroad (now Metro North) to the comfortable suburbs of Westchester County and Connecticut.

This intercity long-distance commuting would come later. By 1928, much had changed from the earlier days of Jewish immigration, but much remained the same. The coming of the subways at the turn of the century allowed the workforce to disperse uptown and to the other boroughs, but as the partially assimilated rode the IRT (Interborough Rapid Transit) into the middle class, the newest arrivals continued to come to the Lower East Side, at least until they were able to function in English. For the second generation, the old neighborhood still provided the most authentic food and the best opportunity to preserve a sense of ethnic roots through native-language newspapers, churches and synagogues, social clubs, and contact with newcomers bringing news from the old country. Of course, in many Jewish communities, the rise of National Socialism in Germany and the political climate of Central Europe would be a matter of concern. What was it really like for family and friends back home in the 1930s? The new arrivals brought more stories to explain their flight from the old country.

Baruch Lumet's career provides a perfect example of the immigrant's movement from the ethnic neighborhood to the mainstream. Trained at the Warsaw Academy of Dramatic and Musical Arts, he debuted on the Polish stage in 1918, spent a brief time in London, and then moved to Philadelphia.[2] At first he sought his livelihood in the thriving cultural world of Yiddish theater. By 1926, he began to work for Maurice Schwartz's Yiddish Art Theater in New York and soon after, the family took up residence on the Lower East Side. His was a familiar voice on Yiddish radio. Before many years had passed, Baruch Lumet had English-language roles on Broadway, toured Mexico and Canada, and after World War II became a pioneer in the new medium of television. He appeared in several of his son's films, most notably as Mendel, the dying father of Nazerman's mistress, in *The Pawnbroker* (1965). From 1953 to 1970 he served as director of the Dallas Institute of Performing Arts. He died in 1992.

Sidney Lumet followed his father's footsteps from ethnic theater to the mainstream, but at the accelerated pace typical of the second generation. As a toddler he made the trip from Philadelphia to the Lower East Side, and by the age of four, he made his own debut in the Yiddish theater.[3] Following his father, he appeared as a child actor in Yiddish-language radio as well as theater, and he made his Broadway debut in the original production of *Dead End* in 1935. Through the following years, he had several parts in English-language plays with Jewish-related themes, like *The Eternal Road, Journey to Jerusalem,* and *Morning Star.* During these years, he attended the Professional Children's School in New York. Many of his early plays also had notable social-justice themes, like *Brooklyn, USA,* and *One Third of a Nation.* Continually typecast as "the tough Jewish kid," he began to sense the limitations of his career as a character actor and decided to pursue a more academic approach to the theater. World events intervened. After his one-semester career with dramatic literature at Columbia University, he joined the army at the age of seventeen and was assigned to the Signal Corps.

After the war, he returned to the New York stage and appeared in several "problem" dramas with Jewish themes, such as *A Flag Is Born,* about the founding of the state of Israel, and *Seeds in the Wind,* the story of Holocaust survivors who try to found a utopian community. By 1947, he had formed a workshop for actors who had rejected the Method style adopted by Lee Strasberg (1901–1982) at the Actors Studio. (Ironically, Lumet would become noted for his success in encouraging his actors to provide the kind the gritty "naturalistic" performances often associated with Method actors.) During this period he also taught acting at the High School for Performing Arts, which achieved widespread recognition as the setting of *Fame* (Alan Parker, 1980) and its spin-off television series of the same name.[4]

Lumet's work with actors in the workshop led inevitably to directing. During the late 1940s he gravitated toward plays that mirrored his own social concerns.[5] Directors with experience, who needed steady income, found a ready home in the new medium of television, which was—so it seemed at the time—an offshoot of radio, and thus housed near the corporate headquarters and production facilities in New York. One of the earliest television directors at CBS was Yul Brynner, who invited Lumet to join the pioneer venture of live drama on television. Ironically, the career trajectories of the two men crossed for the benefit of both. Brynner the director, whose Swedish accent made him a natural to play the king of Siam, was headed to an extraordinary career in acting. Lumet the actor found his niche as a director, but not without a period of incubation.

Small Screen, Big Opportunities

This period in television, for all its crudeness in staging, has maintained the reputation as television's Golden Age, and deservedly so. Even discounting the inevitable fits of nostalgia we academics suffer as we look back from our present plastic age of MTV, formulaic sitcoms, and moronic "reality" shows, the Golden Age of the Truman-Eisenhower era had more than glitter. In large part, social factors influenced the product. In the early days, television sets were quite expensive. It was an appliance largely owned by the relatively wealthy and thus the relatively well educated. As a result, even though the burlesque comedy of Milton Berle's *Texaco Star Theater* (1948–1953) was the blockbuster champion of the ratings game, drama with some serious content could attract a significant proportion of the television owners of the day. As late as 1954, the year after Bishop Fulton Sheen's *Life Is Worth Living* (1952–1957) effectively put an end to the Berle era, anthology-style drama programs held four of the top ten slots in the ratings: *Studio One, TV Playhouse, Kraft Theater,* and *Ford Theater.*[6] The era was short-lived. By 1961, Newton Minnow, the chair of the Federal Communications Commission of the new Kennedy administration, famously described television as "a vast wasteland."

During the rough-and-tumble days of live television, the production schedules and budgetary limitations were unimaginable by today's polished standards. It was, however, a perfect laboratory for young talent to develop its skills for later work on the stage, in film, or in the next generation of glossier, more technically sophisticated television. Directors learned to improvise with very few sets, to make rehearsal time count, and to adjust to new projects on a weekly or even daily basis. They had no luxury of multiple videotape retakes, and the broadcast schedule allowed no time for flexible deadlines. When the little red light went on, the show went on the air, whether it was ready or not. They had to hold an audience in front of a small black-and-white screen through close-ups of actors performing in highly limited spaces, and they had to bring the viewers back for another act after a commercial break for Kraft cheese or Philco television sets. They had no time to allow actors to develop motivation. A director had to get the best performance out of the cast quickly, a skill that Lumet, a former actor himself, has been noted for throughout his career.

Clearly, the industry recognized Lumet as a director who could get the job done on time and within budget. According to the filmography compiled Stephen E. Bowles, as a staff director, Lumet compiled a prodigious list of credits during this period.[7] These include 150 episodes of *Danger* and 26 installments of *You Are There,* a series of historical reenactments narrated by a young Walter Cronkite. Moving beyond the role of staff director, Lumet went on to more prestigious projects, like *Playhouse 90* for CBS and *Kraft Television Theater* and *Studio One* for NBC.

In time technology brought a remarkable shift in television audiences for network television. In contrast to the Golden Era, today's commercial television tailors its product almost exclusively to the mass audience, and the "marginal" segment of the viewing public—that is, the more affluent and better educated—seeks suitable entertainment on cable, satellite, or public television. When Sidney Lumet was honing his skills, however, working in network television did not hold the stigma for the artistic community that it was to develop later. When it moved to Hollywood, television renounced its parentage in the New York theater and adopted the mores of its new stepparents, the movies, at the very time Hollywood began to tailor its product to the youth market. Lumet sat tight in Manhattan. Even after he had made a reputation as a competent motion picture director, he remained in New York.

New York Forever

Lumet's allegiance to his adopted city can be measured by his rejection of an offer to move to Hollywood to direct *A Raisin in the Sun,* eventually directed by Daniel Petrie and released in 1961. At this point in his career, this would have been a perfect project for Sidney Lumet. At the time he was still known primarily as a television director whose only widely known film to date was his debut effort, *12 Angry Men* (1957), a screen adaptation of a television play. Authored by Lorraine Hansberry, *A Raisin in the Sun* had received the New York Drama Critics Circle award as best play in 1959, a year that included competition from Eugene O'Neill's *A Touch of the Poet,* Tennessee Williams's *Sweet Bird of Youth,* and Archibald MacLeish's *J.B.*[8] This award elevated the screen adaptation of *Raisin in the Sun* to the status of prestige project, a plum for any director. In addition to offering Lumet the opportunity to capitalize on his experience of the legitimate stage, the play dealt with his characteristic themes of racial prejudice and social justice.

What is more, Lumet needed a winner. He risked being branded with the reputation of being a one-shot director who got lucky with his debut offering, which was after all merely a filmed television play. After the success of *12 Angry Men,* he made *Stage Struck* with Henry Fonda and *That Kind of Woman* with Sophia Loren. Both generated less than generous critical and box-office response. Lumet himself referred to the first as "a pancake" and said that in the second, "the best scenes were cut out and the weak ones were left in."[9] Significantly, for Lumet, the postproduction was done in Hollywood after the film was shot in New York. In his eyes, the film had certain virtues when it left New York, and its weaknesses were clearly attributable to the Hollywood studio system.

Bowles records Lumet's own comment about his decision to turn down *Raisin:* "I can improve by staying in the East, and there's always television and Broadway to pay my expenses . . . I'll let Hollywood come to me." He notes that Lumet did not like the "lack of independence, inflated production costs and the less congenial working facilities" he believed he would have found in Hollywood. Taking the Hansberry project could have raised Lumet's reputation as a serious film director to a new level, but he calculated the price for transplanting his New York art to Hollywood was too high. If his parents had the "good sense" to move to New York, Lumet had the good sense to stay. In the events of these early days of his filmmaking career, Lumet reveals a strong conviction—one might call it bias—that his particular brand of filmmaking grew out of the New York experience, which for him was a combination of autobiography, legitimate theater, and television. He found drama in the city streets that he knew through his own experience rather than on the Hollywood soundstage. For him, the drama grew in intensity when it became compressed into the confined spaces and limited mobility of the live stage. Here one found the primacy of the spoken word, brought to life by skilled actors, forced to interact with one another during the spontaneity of the live performance. Even more, television, in cramped New York studios, added the splendid dimension of the close-up, compressed into the margins of a black-and-white screen often no larger than fourteen inches on the diagonal. The medium brought the drama into the real settings of the audience's homes. It created a degree of close visual intimacy impossible in the theater, where the setting fostered a sense of formality, and the location of fixed seating distanced audience and actor, even in the most intimate theater settings. His conviction grew into a vision of what the cinema could be.

A Minority Opinion

Lumet was not alone in this conviction, but his was a minority opinion. During the 1940s and 1950s Hollywood struggled to adjust to television. Although the studios engineered corporate realignments with the infant industry for their own profit and leased out their soundstages and editing rooms for television production, they tried to recapture their own audience by producing ever more spectacular wide-screen, Technicolor blockbusters.[10] "Movies are better than ever" was the slogan that suggested that movies could offer spectacle beyond the capabilities of television. For the major studios, Hollywood thought it could best counter television by becoming more "Hollywood."

Although the California corporations maintained their belief that bigger is better, some segments of the industry, Lumet among them, began to think small, and two factors added credibility to their position. First, Italian neorealism had proved commercially viable with American art-house audiences. These dramas, filmed with the extremely limited equipment available in postwar Italy, took their stories and settings from the streets and for the most part employed nonactors in the principal roles. They dealt with ordinary people trying to survive in the devastation of war and its aftermath. These were quite different from the more self-conscious film noir style that reached its peak of artistic achievement during this period in the United States. Film noir employed a highly stylized use of light and shadow borrowed from the German Expressionist look of the silent era. The neorealists provided a flat, objective newsreel image. Film noir grew out of a world of pulp fiction, with its hard-boiled detectives, gun molls, and corrupt cops, and of course it relied on the box-office power of known Hollywood stars. Neorealism dealt with obscure citizens whose daily routines were disrupted by catastrophic events.[11]

The second factor was clearly American. The success of quality, Golden Age television proved that a significant audience was prepared to accept a small-screen style of drama on the big screen. Rather than needing massed armies in glittering armor, successful movies could show ordinary people facing ordinary situations in extremely realistic settings—often described as gritty—and photographed with near-documentary realism. If honest and authentic, these could attract box-office as well as critical kudos. In this regard, two of the most widely acclaimed films of the mid-1950s can be revisited because of their role in preparing audiences for the arrival and acceptance of Sidney Lumet as a major director.

Symbolic of the legitimization of these small films with their roots in television was the overwhelming success of *Marty* (1955), directed by Delbert Mann and developed from a television play written by Paddy Chayefsky, who also wrote the screenplay for the film. It originally appeared on *Goodyear Television Playhouse* in May 1953. Two years later, the Academy of Motion Picture Arts and Sciences named it the best film of the year and awarded additional Oscars to both Mann and Chayefsky, who had collaborated on the television version two years earlier, and to its then-unknown star, Ernest Borgnine. Betsy Blair was also nominated, but the best actress award went to Anna Magnani in *The Rose Tattoo,* based on the play by Tennessee Williams. Set in the Bronx, not Manhattan, *Marty* was the story of ordinary New Yorkers, a lonely thirty-four-year-old Italian American butcher, Marty Pilletti, and a twenty-nine-year-old schoolteacher, Clara Snyder, who begin a stop-and-start courtship marked with all the awkwardness of teenagers who aren't quite sure how to go about the business of falling in love. The combination of television's intimacy and the Bronx neighborhood setting proved a winner.

Marty followed the success the previous year of *On the Waterfront.*[12] This all-time classic took the Academy Awards for best picture, best director (Elia Kazan), script (Budd Schulberg), actor (Marlon Brando, as Terry Malloy), and supporting actress (Eva Marie Saint, as Edie Doyle). Like *Marty,* the story also involved a romance among ordinary working people in the New York area, specifically Hoboken on the New Jersey waterfront. This bleak, wintery neighborhood with its seedy playgrounds and architecturally dominant Catholic Church shivers on the lip of the

Harbor within sight of movie-and-tourist Manhattan, but culturally it belongs to another universe. In *On the Waterfront,* the love story is secondary. The dramatic center of the film is the conflict between Terry Malloy (Marlon Brando) and Johnny Friendly (Lee J. Cobb), the mob boss, which embodies the internal conflict within Terry as he struggles with his own personal integrity.

Director Elia Kazan learned his craft on the stage and screenwriter Budd Schulberg at Paramount, but both shared a keen sensitivity to social-justice issues. Their collaboration led to a film of conscience. Both flirted with communism during the 1930s[13] and found the New York docks an effective setting for their exploration of the effects of institutional corruption in the lives of the workers. Like *Marty, On the Waterfront* features the tightly confined interior spaces reminiscent of a television setting, but then on occasion opens up to wider outdoor settings around the neighborhood.

In retrospect, the outstanding critical and commercial success of these two films in 1954 and 1955 provides a prelude to the film career of Sidney Lumet, which began with *12 Angry Men* in 1957. Many of the elements in the lineage are obvious, although one must be careful to temper claims of exclusive parentage. The family traits appear in many films during this period and earlier, of course, but these two "prelude" films provide excellent and obvious examples of several trends in moviemaking at the time that converge in the works of Sidney Lumet.

By way of summary, *Marty* and *On the Waterfront* most emphatically reaffirmed New York–based films as having an important place at the commercial table of American cinema. These two films were shot by New Yorkers on location in the New York area and featured stories rooted in neighborhoods outside Manhattan. They had the black-and-white look of tabloids and newsreels, while Hollywood self-consciously turned to wide screen and lurid Technicolor. In a word, they looked something like the television of the day. Both were directed by artists who mastered their craft in local industries—television and the theater—rather than the Hollywood soundstage. They proved that American "neorealism," to use a suggestive but by no means standard description of the style, could be as marketable as the Italian version. In fact, the American films proved even more successful in capturing a vast mainstream audience, whereas the popularity of the Italian films was largely limited to the espresso-bar theaters in major cities.

In addition to documentary style and New York setting, these earlier films also provide a coming attraction to the thematic content that will preoccupy Sidney Lumet for the next forty years. These themes, I maintain, are inseparable from the New York experience. In both of these prelude films, the main characters, Marty and Terry, struggle to identify themselves as individuals in a social subgroup, which in turn struggles for identity within a larger, impersonal community. Individual characters are members of a family, an ethnic community, a neighborhood, a circle of like-minded friends, a union, or the mob. They have to define themselves as individuals within the limitations that their social milieu tries to impose on them.

Marty Pilletti has to work to free himself from the expectations of his tight-knit group of male friends and his immediate family to court a woman who is not Italian. His moving from them to Clara threatens the survival of the group. He must sort out contradictory signals from them. In their loneliness, his friends, bachelors and apparent losers all, continually talk about looking for girls, boast about their conquests (real or imaginary), and even pass around a girlie magazine for amusement. When Marty succeeds in the quest by finding Clara, he threatens the social fabric of his buddies. They try to keep the would-be lovers apart. Marty's mother nags him about providing grandchildren, but when he brings Clara home, she realizes that marriage will end her own nuclear family. She explains to Marty that as a college graduate and working woman, Clara is "one step from the streets." She wants him to stay with her until he finds a suitable Italian girl. Marty struggles for independence from the demands of the group. The two groups, friends and family, realize that Marty's leaving will push them toward disintegration and eventual annihilation. The old song perfectly describes their dilemma: "Wedding bells are breaking up that old gang of mine."

Similarly, Terry Malloy feels the pressure from his brother Charlie (Rod Steiger) and his girlfriend Edie Doyle to go along with mob control on the docks. Charlie doesn't want to jeopardize his own status as chief lieutenant to Johnny Friendly. Edie, whose brother has been murdered, doesn't want Terry to meet the same end. In addition, the members of the longshoremen's union have a stake in maintaining the status quo. Johnny Friendly and his goons extort kickbacks, everyone knows too well, but staying on their good side guarantees steady work. Crossing them could provoke violent reprisal. After Charlie's murder, Terry gradually realizes that his personal integrity demands separating himself from the mob by cooperating with the commission investigating crime on the docks. In the end, he has to become his own man by defeating Friendly by force and destroying his power over the community. Both the mob and the honest union members view Terry's defection as endangering their very existence. They try to talk him out of doing anything to upset the status quo. Like Marty Pilletti's friends, mob and union alike would rather destroy the individual than risk their own disintegration.

This notion of a double conflict provides a useful point of entry into the films of Sidney Lumet. In the pages that follow, I want to propose his experience of the Lower East Side as a helpful starting point for appreciating many of the conflicted loyalties of many of Lumet's most memorable characters. First, a New Yorker of Lumet's vintage is an individual within a relatively closed ethnic neighborhood with its own customs and identity. In order to grow, the individual feels the need to move beyond the mores of the group. The community, however, feels pressure from the larger community to change its ways, to dissolve or assimilate. To survive with its own identity, it tries to persuade individuals to conform to the old ways because it perceives any defection as a threat to its survival. This type of conflict facing Depression-era children of the Lower East Side formed the core of *The Jazz Singer* (Alan Crosland, 1927), the very early sound film that shows Al Jolson torn between his desire to go into show business as Jack Robin and his family's expectation that he will become a cantor as Jacob Rabinowicz. Choosing the stage will be a rejection of the family, his name, and his religion; choosing the temple will be a rejection of his dreams.

The ethical structure of the narrative of many Lumet films involves many variations on this theme as it is developed in various settings from the British Army in *The Hill* (1965) to the New York Police Department in *Serpico* (1974) to the television industry *Network* (1976). In abstract terms, the conflict can be imagined as set of concentric rings. At the center, the individual is torn between loyalty to a group and the need to break out of its constraints to preserve personal integrity. In the outer circle, however, the embattled group itself struggles with its need to maintain its own traditions and values while it is threatened by the wider society. In Marty Piletti's case, the group is relatively benign. His marriage to Clara signifies the assimilation and weakening identity of the Italian American family and his circle of buddies in the neighborhood. They may feel betrayed and express disappointment for a while, but they will eventually come to accept the inevitable breakdown of the old ways in a constantly changing environment. Terry Malloy plays for higher stakes. His challenge to Johnny Friendly and collaboration with the crime commission may send many people to prison and could get Terry killed. The mob will not leave Hoboken quietly.

Preponderantly, Lumet prefers the high-stakes game. His social institutions have grown corrupt through the years, and like cornered animals, they will stop at nothing to ensure their own survival. A Lumet hero is typically torn between the desire to play along with the majority, or to stand up for his personal integrity, challenge the group, and accept the consequences of his actions, which include, most prominently, being left alone, ostracized by the group.

The characters face a serious conflict precisely because of their ambivalent feelings about the institutions. Marty would like to stay with his mother and his friends; they provide security in a frightening world. Terry feels a sense of loyalty to his brother and the other union leaders who have taken care of him; in all probability, they will take care of him in the future even after their differences with Charlie. He doesn't really feel cut out for leadership; he would rather stay in his familiar role as one of the crowd. Put another way: heroes in Lumet's movies are like New Yorkers struggling to rise beyond the confining world of the neighborhood in Brooklyn or the Bronx or Hoboken, but not eager or even capable of soaring so high as to sever the ties to their history. As the old saying goes, you can take the boy out of Hoboken or the Bronx, but you can't take Hoboken or the Bronx out of the boy. Terry and Marty may change their relationship to their old haunts, but they are lifers. And even if they could escape from their neighborhood, flight exacts a terrible price, and they are not convinced it is one they are willing to pay.

This complex conflict of loyalties lies at the root of much of Sidney Lumet's work—and, with some flexibility in interpretation, arguably of all of it. The films chosen for discussion are not only the most familiar and most readily available, but to my mind, they best exemplify the many variations he works on this major theme. Other critics would have picked other titles, and one would hope readers would wish still others had been used. All of them, I would maintain, bear the marks of a Lower East Side childhood, of New York television and theater, of Jewish identity and leftist politics.

12 Angry Men (1957)

In 1956 all the pieces were in place for the by-now-veteran television director Sidney Lumet to join the parade to film, but without leaving New York. Like *Marty, 12 Angry Men,* Lumet's first film, was a product of television. Written by Reginald Rose, also a New Yorker, and directed by Franklin Schaffner, it originally appeared on *Studio One* on CBS in 1954. It drew the attention of Hollywood insider Henry Fonda, who decided to coproduce it as a feature film with Rose. He had been impressed with Lumet's work at the Actors' Workshop, not television, and he invited Lumet to direct the film because, as Lumet recalls, "they could get me cheap."[14] By taking the lead role himself, Fonda was able to secure distribution through United Artists. It was well received critically and commercially. It won no Academy Awards, even though it was nominated as best picture in the year of *The Bridge on the River Kwai.* Reginald Rose was also nominated for best screenplay and Sidney Lumet, in his maiden voyage, was nominated as best director. Although he missed the Oscar, he did receive the best director award from the Directors Guild of America.

The film opens with an exterior of a cold, impersonal courthouse on Foley Square in Lower Manhattan and cuts to the interior, showing an equally cold rotunda, populated by anonymous figures engrossed in the business of the law. The focus of attention narrows further into a courtroom, where the judge (Rudy Bond), exuding a sense of boredom with the tedious legal formalities, explains to the jury that a conviction brings a mandatory death penalty. The defendant (John Savoca) has dark hair, eyes, and complexion. He may be Puerto Rican, the major Latino population in New York in the 1950s; he could also be Italian, or from today's perspective, he could conceivably be Middle Eastern. He might even be the "tough Jewish kid" that Lumet played in his early days on the stage. His status as an outsider generates hostility among the jurors, who refer to him as one of "them" and apply the stereotypical negative images of the group to the young defendant.

Official New York, any site of authority beyond the boundaries of one's immediate neighborhood, can be intimidating, even threatening, in its very impersonality. The dramatic tension feeds on this sense of anonymity. The defendant has no name and consequently, no identity. Neither do the judge or the jurors, who are identified, like robots, only by numbers, yet they are involved in exercising the ultimate power of the state over a young man caught in the gears of the justice system. The sterile, sparsely furnished jury room provides the single setting for the bulk of the film, and its blandness adds to the frightening impersonality of the proceedings. (This is pure television. A more standard movie treatment would have provided flashbacks to the crime or to other past events that explain the behavior of the jurors.) The windows open on the walls of an air shaft, with the sight of several buildings visible to the jurors in the distance. As the deliberations unfold entirely within this room, the walls and ceiling close in, largely because of Lumet's manipulation of the lenses and camera positions. The tension builds through prolonged, forced confinement with potentially hostile strangers in a hot room with no air-conditioning and with a fan that does not work, until dusk approaches and one juror discovers that the fan is connected to the light switch. The approach of thunderstorms adds a suffocating humidity to the atmosphere. New Yorkers of this era know the feeling: being trapped on a stalled, suffocating subway with a rainbow mixture of anonymous riders who represent an irritant at best, and a menace at worst. In the 1950s few subway cars were air-conditioned.

Psychological tension of dislocation adds to the claustrophobia. For defendant and juror alike, the cold marble corridors of the courthouse, the forced confinement in a bare-walled, alien environment away from the familiar neighborhood, block, and building that are home to people who share a common ethnic background represent an unspecified threat. They don't belong here with strangers. Away from familiar surroundings, the young defendant is terrified and alone. In his sole appearance on screen, his face appears in the frame alone, separated from everyone else in the courtroom. Similarly, locked into the jury room, the jurors inhabit equally alien territory, and as a result they become increasingly edgy and irritable toward one another. They enter the jury room in a spirit of jovial, male congeniality. It takes time for them to become twelve angry men.

True to the spirit of democracy and the urban melting pot, these men have little in common other than their duty as citizens. In creating this jury, author Reginald Rose balances demographic realities with dramatic need. On the one hand, he presents a remarkable social and economic cross section of New York's population. Some are skilled and presumably affluent professionals. One is a stockbroker (Juror 4, E. G.

Marshall), another an architect whose name, Davis, is revealed in the concluding scene (Juror 8, Henry Fonda), and a third an advertising executive (Juror 12, Robert Webber). Others are successful in business: one owns a messenger service (Juror 3, Lee J. Cobb) and another sells jellies and marmalades (Juror 7, Jack Warden). Juror 11 (George Voscovec) is a European watchmaker who fled from the Nazis, and Juror 5 (Jack Klugman) identifies with the defendant because of his own background of poverty. Juror 6 (Edward Binns) is a working man who says he lets his boss do all the thinking for him, and Juror 9 (Joseph Sweeney) is a retired senior citizen.

For dramatic purposes, however, Rose has provided an all-white, all-male jury, which is scarcely representative of New York, even in the 1950s. This is diversity, but within one specific stratum of society. This selectivity enables him and Lumet to focus precisely on the dynamics of the group in its internal struggles to arrive at consensus. Adding the jurors' own race and gender issues to the arguments would have complicated the deliberations of these "ordinary citizens" struggling to sift the evidence and find the truth though dialogue within the confines of a ninety-minute television production. They do not, however, ignore ethnic issues. Quite the contrary. The defendant's ethnic identity, defined no more precisely than "one of them," lies at the core of the dramatic conflict. In the process of the jury's deliberation, Rose and Lumet unmask and analyze racial assumptions of this group of white men with regard to the alien group—any alien group. Exposing the unfocussed irrationality of bigotry will mark Lumet's work for decades.

12 Angry Men also introduces the dual conflict that characterizes much of Lumet's later work. At the center, Davis, Fonda's character, struggles for his integrity and individuality as a member of the jury. As the deliberations begin, he stands alone in his convictions, and although the others try to exert pressure on him to change his vote so that they can end their business and go home, the outcome of the conflict is never in doubt. Davis will not budge. In his refusal to yield to the group, Davis threatens its identity. The others needs the reassurance that comes from conformity. At the same time, the group functions as a separate, enclosed world within a larger society. If American democracy is (at least in the ideal order) based on "liberty and justice for all," then the jury with its prejudices must safeguard its own identity within this larger universe. Davis's defection threatens their ability to survive as a sub-group. By opting for justice, the members, with varying degrees of re-gret, will become assimilated into the mainstream. They will have lost their identity as protectors of the notion of justice for "us" and punish-ment for "them." Davis's eventual victory represents the triumph of the individual with his traditional liberal values over a group that thinks like a mob. The victory of reason meant more to Lumet and Rose than a satisfying dramatic conclusion to a courtroom drama. When *12 Angry Men* appeared, it must be recalled, the horrors of the McCarthy era, HUAC hearings, *Red Channels,* blacklisting, and "naming names" still smoldered in the public consciousness, especially among artists in the worlds of film, television, and the theater.

As the "tough Jewish kid" from the Lower East Side, Lumet may well have identified with the defendant, but as a socially conscious art-ist, Lumet inhabits the white linen suit of the fellow artist, the architect Davis. Known throughout the film simply as Juror 8, he reveals his name only in the epilogue, when he introduces himself to Mr. McCardle, Juror 9, the elderly man who first supported Davis in his dissent from the otherwise unanimous and immediate decision to send the young man to the electric chair. These are the only two jurors to reveal their names.

Davis is an extraordinarily polyvalent character. He identifies with the defendant and feels a personal violation at the rush to conviction. In his minority status as the sole dissenter, he experiences the animosity of the majority. As the lone holdout, he separates himself from the jurors as an outside observer of their gradual unmasking of their own biases. In this role, he forms a bond with the audience. Yet as a member of the jury, a righteous citizen among a flawed citizenry, he provides the cata-lyst that leads them to the truth about themselves as they grope their way toward the truth about the case. In this capacity, he becomes the surrogate for Lumet the artist, as he tests the social fabric.

Henry Fonda of course brings a familiar screen persona to the role. In countless roles going back twenty years, he played the slow-speaking man of integrity who wants nothing more than to be left in peace. Al-though reluctant to join in combat, once committed to a cause, he be-comes an implacable enemy of injustice. Fearless in his pursuit of the right, he never loses his temper, sinks to sarcasm, or seeks vengeance or personal vindication. In this regard, Davis is the younger brother of past Fonda heroes like Abraham Lincoln in *Young Mr. Lincoln* (John Ford, 1939) and Wyatt Earp in *My Darling Clementine* (John Ford, 1946). As Davis, he is the New York architect who identifies the Woolworth Building for a fellow juror, but whose speech patterns reflect those distant lands beyond Jersey City. For Lumet the values of Middle America prosper amid concrete canyons as well as in cornfields. As a native himself, Lumet realizes that not all New Yorkers live up to the movie stereotype as fast-talking, belligerent tough guys, gangsters, or showbiz types. The "typical" glib Mad Av advertising executive (Juror 12, Robert Webber), shallow and astutely obnoxious, provides the stereotype and the foil for the Fonda character. New York is big enough for Henry Fonda, and Fonda can do his Middle American man-of-integrity shtick even on Foley Square.

What is striking about the other jurors is their ordinariness. They might be found in any neighborhood, anywhere; they just happen to be from neighborhoods in New York, as a native like Lumet would surely realize. One stakes out a reputation as an authority on baseball. Another discloses that he grew up in a slum and another that he is foreign born. The foreman reveals almost nothing about himself, other than his thin skin when he perceives criticism about his chairmanship. In addition, they bring personal baggage to the jury room. One has had problems with his son, another feels the sting of aging, and a third simply despises "them." By keeping to its narrow focus, the script merely sketches in these details to provide a personality for the jurors. It does not allow their lives to become subplots. The exception to this strategy is Juror 3 (Lee J. Cobb), the last holdout, whose bitter conflict with his son leads him to transfer his anger from his son to the defendant. The point explains his stubborn resistance to the reasoned arguments of Davis and the others.

The final shots reverse the movement of the first. After the verdict, Davis and McCardle meet and introduce themselves by name, and then the camera moves to a position looking down from the facade of the courthouse. In long shot, Davis descends the stone steps of the building and melts once again into the City. In entering the building in the opening shots and occupying the cold interior spaces, these nameless jurors have embodied democracy in the abstract. Their duty done, they reenter the city, enhanced by their achievement, but once again ordinary individuals on the City's streets.

The Pawnbroker

Sidney Lumet's preoccupation with ethnic identities within New York receives its most poignant treatment in *The Pawnbroker* (1965). In *12 Angry Men* he approached the topic as an outside observer, examining the issue from the perspective of the anonymous majority culture as the jurors unmask and confront bias in their own white male peer group. He shows us the representative of a minority, the defendant, only in passing, and thus turns our attention away from the perspective of the one whose minority status might have contributed to his execution after a perfunctory trial conducted exclusively by members of the majority. Other than in a few transparent code words, ethnicity never rises openly in the discussion, but it hovers over the drama like a great unnoticed cloud.

By contrast, in *The Pawnbroker* Lumet moves the issues of ethnic identity to the center of the screen. Sol Nazerman (Rod Steiger), the eponymous hero, emerged from the Holocaust a man broken in spirit. His present life draws its meaning precisely from the fact that he is Jewish. In Europe, although he was a productive citizen, he became a victim as a member of a group. In Spanish Harlem, the neighborhood where he conducts business, he once again plays the role of outsider because of his Jewish background.

Adapted from the novel by Edward Lewis Wallant by screenwriters David Friedkin and Morton Fine, with the collaboration of Sidney Lumet, the film examines the psychological and spiritual scars that deface the soul of Sol Nazerman like so much urban grafitti.[15] Lumet's parents made their way to New York long before the horrors of Nazism, but Sidney Lumet's treatment of a displaced survivor, although not based on personal experience, reflects extraordinary compassion for his hero. In painful, halting steps, Lumet leads us back through Nazerman's history. Wife and children, parents, profession, and home, everything that he loved, was taken from him, and he could do nothing to protect himself from systematic annihilation. History drained the life out of his soul, while his body continues to function with slightly more animation than an automaton. Some huge, unseen weight presses down on his shoulders. Somewhere he has lost his capacity for pleasure; in the film he never comes close to smiling. Mendel (Baruch Lumet, Sidney Lumet's father), the dying father of his mistress, tells him bluntly: "I came out alive; you came out dead." Like most Lumet heroes, Sol Nazerman is not a likable man, yet as one discovers the cruelty he has endured, it is impossible not to forgive him for his cruelty to everyone around him.

The film takes a while to get to the City. The opening sequence, which starts before the titles, provides an idyllic recollection of life in the old country, where Sol Nazerman is a professor of philosophy. He and his beautiful wife have taken the family on a picnic in the country. The memories of family life gain in loveliness as they recede in time. When the scene shifts to present time, reality comes as a genteel shock. The second sequence is set in the backyard of a tract house with the traffic of the Long Island Expressway humming in the background. The strong sunlight casts no shadows, but rather renders the landscape featureless. Nazerman is stretched out on a cheap beach chair, while his teenage niece and nephew engage in typical American banter and his sister-in-law tries to persuade him to finance a trip for her and her husband. Fences hem him in to his own slender patch of property, forming a self-imposed ghetto of confinement. His has become a life of middle-class banality. He has made his life's journey from the idyllic to the mundane by way of the horrific, which will be revealed only gradually as his story unfolds. Conversation comes with difficulty. Nazerman relishes his privacy and does not identify his solitary status as loneliness. His sister wants to take a trip back to Europe, to savor the atmosphere of antiquity. Nazerman describes the atmosphere as "a stink." He has become a cranky old man, but the others in the family seem to accept him for what he is. He pays the bills. He seems satisfied with this arrangement.

After these two introductory sequences, the action moves to Spanish Harlem, the paradigmatic ghetto of urban poverty in the 1960s. The word *ghetto* holds horrific connotations for a Holocaust survivor. In fact, Lumet has been criticized for universalizing the experience of European Jews making the Holocaust a prime analogate among many other instances of ethnic oppression.[16] As an indication of just how dead Nazerman has become, Lumet suggests that he—and in the view of some of Lumet's critics, by extension the Jewish community at large—has learned little from the horrifying experience. Safe in America, he has allowed himself to become again by analogy a "good German," who stands by while Latinos and African Americans live in a state of continual institutional oppression. He deliberately blinds himself to an injustice that is a reflection of the Holocaust itself. Even more, by running his pawnshop and turning a modest profit while asking nothing about the syndicate that supplies his income, he profits from his collaboration. Many of Lumet's harsher critics feel that in this film he compromises the unique, specifically Jewish meaning of the Holocaust.

If the criticism holds any truth—and it does, although I and others believe the conclusions of some may be overly harsh—Lumet's vision of the issue might be best understood by recalling his history on the Lower East Side, where ethnic groups over the past century and a half have arrived, struck roots, and moved out. The ongoing tragedy of New York politics and social history is that established immigrant groups in time forget their experience and repeat the same biases against more recent arrivals: Irish, Italian, black, Latino, Asian. Jews, as Lumet points out especially in *Daniel* (1983), have been at the center of the liberal consensus that sided with other minorities throughout the decades of their own status as "outsiders among other outsiders."[17] The tragedy of Sol Nazerman in the eyes of Sidney Lumet lies in his rejection of the Jewish mission of furthering the interests of social justice in the New World, specifically in New York. His abandonment of the City for the quiet, banal, but comfortable surroundings in Levittown on the Island represents a betrayal. Because Nazerman has deadened himself to the needs of others, he allows inhuman cruelty, something like that of the death camps, to continue into the present. The fact that these atrocities continue in other times and places long after Nuremberg make them all the more horrible. The scars Nazerman bears on his soul disfigure him far more obscenely than the number tattooed on his forearm.

In a similar fashion, some interpreters of the film feel that Lumet has compromised Nazerman's Jewish identity by allowing him to become an actor in a Christian redemption parable. If this is the case, one might conclude that Lumet has found Jewish spirituality inadequate to the task of saving Nazerman from his history.[18] This observation arises during the last scene, in which Nazerman's assistant, Jesus Ortiz (Jaime Sanchez), disrupts the attempted robbery of the pawnshop. When he directs the robber's gun from Nazerman to himself, it goes off and he takes the bullet in his abdomen. He crawls out of the shop, and as he bleeds to death on the sidewalk, Nazerman cradles the head of the dying man on his chest, like an image of the Pietà. He opens his mouth as if to scream, but the only sound that emerges from the sound track is the musical score, not his voice. When Jesus breathes his last, Nazerman returns to the store and impales his hand on the bill spike next to his cash register. In close-up, his face, sweating copiously, shows a combination of disbelief and pain. After his twin ordeals of death of Jesus and self-inflicted pain, Nazerman leaves the store, and in extreme long shot, he disappears into the street, a solitary figure making his way along a busy sidewalk, much like Davis after his ordeal in *12 Angry Men*.

As a New Yorker who lived in the mix of traditions, Lumet seems perfectly comfortable adapting elements of Christian imagery into his Jewish story. A close look at the text suggests that religious critics, both Jewish and Christian, may be fusing several visual fragments into a coherent parable of redemption where Lumet has striven to preserve a troubling, even terrifying ambiguity. Jesus Ortiz, because of his name, clearly suggests a redeemer figure, and his grabbing at the gun during the robbery could conceivably have saved Nazerman's life. But other circumstances must be considered. Jesus has made a career of street crime and has joined Nazerman in the hope of getting rich honestly but quickly. When rewards come more slowly than he expected, he conspired in the robbery and hoped to earn his share of the take. He panicked when he saw Nazerman's resistance, but the robbers were more intent on coercing him to open the safe than killing him. If they killed him, they would have had no chance to get the money. The shooting appears more an accident than an act of heroism.

Furthermore, for the purposes of a coherent parable, Nazerman's actual "redemption" is not quite as obvious as some seem to propose. While Nazerman holds Jesus, who has just died, he opens his mouth as though to scream, but the soundtrack provides only discordant brass. At that point, he may still be incapable of feeling outrage or grief. The disjuncture between sound and image leaves the resolution in doubt. As happens so often in nightmares, he may try to scream, but no sound comes out. Similarly, when he impales his hand (suggesting Christ's pierced hands) he makes no sound. The pierced hand moves the Christ imagery and thus identification from Jesus—who in the Christian reading has given his life to save another—to Nazerman himself, the "saved" who voluntarily assumes the wounds of Jesus (Ortiz/Christ) into his own body, like a compliant mystic taking upon himself the stigmata. He coldly grimaces under the self-inflicted wound, but his moves are impassive, zombielike. It is still not clear that he has recovered normal human feeling through his ordeals, or whether he is still torn between the terrible pain he experiences and the superhuman effort to repress it. Finally, when he walks out onto the street while the camera watches in high-angle long shot from a distance, nothing indicates that he has re-entered the flow of human life with human feelings. He is as alone in his numbness after the events in his shop as he is in his recollections of the Nazi horrors. He has finally left the self-imposed imprisonment of his shop, but to what end? He left Europe and came to America with his burden of suffering scarcely lightened. He may even be, as some have suggested, the Wandering Jew of medieval legend, doomed to roam earth forever in search of a home because of his complicity in the death of Christ.[19] Each day, each act of mindless violence compounds his pain, and his only response is a continuing anesthesia of the soul.

Although Lumet shuffles elements of Christian and Jewish stories into his own syncretistic exploration of Nazerman's inner life, he has created a character that is far from being a mythic hero. Sol Nazerman embodies to a grotesque level the kind of brutal disregard for others that New Yorkers hate about themselves and that provides outsiders with material for cartoon images of crude City dwellers. To survive one has to be tough, perhaps even at the risk of common decency. When Tess (Marketa Kimbrell), his mistress, calls to tell him her father has just died, Nazerman tells her to go bury him and not bother him with her grief. In New York, relentless human misery, screaming out as it does in the midst of the trappings of incomparable wealth and beauty, can be oppressive, overwhelming. Visitors can be visibly shaken at the sight of deranged homeless people wrapped in newspapers and sleeping on ventilation grates outside luxurious boutiques and galleries. They are even more shaken by the ladies in mink and the gentlemen in English flannel who walk around them, pretending not to see—or worse, actually not seeing. It is the only way to survive and function in the City.

Lumet's Nazerman has raised that callous survival strategy to a way of life and finally to a pathology. He builds walls around himself. At home, he separates himself from neighbors with decorative fences. In his car, closed windows protect him from traffic and from the city streets. A curtained partition keeps him from the dying Mendel, the one man who speaks the truth to him. The pawnshop on Park Avenue and One Hundred Sixteenth Street bristles with security fences to protect him from the street. And inside the fortress, a network of steel gates isolates him from the human misery that enters his shop hoping for a few dollars to get through the day: a black woman with candlesticks, possibly stolen; young Latino men with a power mower, certainly stolen; a confused black man, a would-be intellectual longing for conversation with "the professor"; a frantic white drug addict trying to pawn a useless radio; a sad young white man trying to get something, anything, for a high-school oratory trophy; and most horrifying of all, a young, emaciated, pregnant blonde woman, with deep rings under her eyes, offering a worthless engagement ring that her boyfriend said was a real diamond. Nazerman cannot allow any of these stories to touch him. If he did, he would go mad. He hands out a few dollars and pierces the receipts mechanically on the spike next to his cash register.

Nazerman's strategy of isolation serves a purpose, and abandoning it brings grave consequences. Twice, Nazerman faces women without the protective gates. Mabel (Thelma Oliver), a young black prostitute who longs for marriage to Jesus, tries to pawn a necklace. She thinks that the few dollars she raises will help turn her own life around and keep Jesus from reverting to a life of petty crime. Nazerman sits outside his cage, and Mabel offers her body to induce him to increase his offer. As he faces her exposed chest, his mind flashes back to the sight of his lovely wife, similarly naked, forced to serve in a prison camp brothel for Nazi officers. Revisiting memories of her degradation and his powerlessness to help her press hot needles into his soul.

Marilyn Birchfield (Geraldine Fitzgerald) also enters his space. She first approaches him as an eager, well-intentioned social worker trying to raise money for neighborhood youth programs. Safe within his cage, he donates a few dollars, apparently to get rid of her. Not deterred, she invites him to share lunch on a park bench. He meets her outside his shop but rejects her food and any offer of kindness. Finally, after a series of terrifying self-discoveries, he wanders through the City at night, from his Harlem shop, downtown, across the West Side, and over to Lincoln Center. He finds Marilyn's apartment in that huge sterile block of buildings between Columbus Avenue and the Hudson River. Sitting in her airy living room, with a tiny balcony overlooking the West Side rail yards, the then-functioning elevated West Side Highway, and the docks of the riverfront, he tells her about his experiences during the war. Everything he loved was taken away, he recalls, and he could do nothing.

Their conversation has taken place outside Nazerman's shelter of gates and bars, but the barriers remain. She reaches out to invite his touch, but he leaves her hand suspended in midair. He has articulated his pain to her, but he is not able to accept her support. Yet their exchange has loosed another chain of memories. As he rides the "A" train back uptown, in his reverie, the car becomes transformed into the freight car that carried him and his family to the death camps. He recalls fighting off sleep in a standing position, held upright only by the press of the other prisoners around him. To his terror, his son slides off his shoulders and onto the floor of the car, where he will be surely trampled or suffocated. Because of the crowd, Nazerman can do no more to help him than he could to rescue his wife.

A third encounter outside the gated shop takes place in between the other two meetings. Nazerman has complacently remained on the payroll of Rodriguez (Brock Peters), the neighborhood strongman. His shop serves as a front for laundering money from Rodriguez's various criminal operations. After his exchange with Mabel, he admits to himself what he probably knew for some time: that one area of Rodriguez's activity involves a chain of brothels, as well as drugs and extortion. After his encounter with Mabel and his recollection of his wife's forced degradation, he realizes the extent of his own complicity in human traffic. He meets with Rodriguez in his spacious, white-appointed duplex, and asks to be let out. The gangster confirms his suspicions about prostitution and lambastes him for his hypocrisy for suddenly discovering moral scruples after many years of criminal involvement. Like it or not, Rodriguez concludes, Nazerman is complicit in evil and will continue the present arrangement. Devastated by Rodriguez's articulation of his guilt, he leaves the apartment and begins the journey through the City that will eventually lead him to Marilyn Birchfield's apartment.

Why does he end this stage of his journey in Marilyn's apartment, after he has insulted her in his shop and berated her for offering to share her lunch with him during their meeting on the park bench? As in the final scene, Lumet drapes Nazerman's emotional state in ambiguity. Rodriguez's outburst has stung him to the core. Perhaps he goes to Marilyn to gain assurance that he could have done nothing in the past, and by extension can do nothing to better his world in the present. Another explanation is possible. Perhaps his journey is a cry for help, even though when Marilyn tries to respond by offering simple human contact, he is not yet able to accept it. He needs a final trip through the underworld (on the subway) and a confrontation with Jesus's death before he can rediscover his humanity—if he does.

These ambiguous, climactic scenes explain the negative reactions of several Jewish critics. Lumet leaves the film with two possibly objectionable interpretations. Nazerman's identification with a form of oppression little better than the Nazis make him a collaborator in human evil. The comparison, some would say, devalues the Holocaust as a specifically and uniquely Jewish event, and allowing Nazerman to be portrayed as complicit in such evil offends Jewish sensibilities. Second, his inability to respond to Marilyn's attempt to touch him demonstrates the futility of all human efforts to rescue him. It seems, according to this reading, that Nazerman will need a Christlike "redeemer" like Jesus so that he can be rescued from his spiritual death.

Despite his easy shuffling of Jewish and Christian elements in his telling of the story, Lumet offers a particularly keen appreciation of Nazerman's sense of alienation in his adopted homeland. Through Nazerman's interactions with Jesus, Lumet provides an insight into the counterbias that can insinuate itself into the thinking of minorities or self-perceived outsiders in a pluralistic city like New York. In Sol Nazerman, Lumet provides an insight into the thinking of the stereotyped, which leads them to stereotype those they believe are stereotyping them. This reverse bias helps explain the cultural distances that remain even in constricted physical spaces. In one revealing scene, Jesus notices the prison camp number tattooed on Nazerman's forearm. He asks if it represents membership in some club. Clearly, the younger man has not the slightest awareness of the death camps. Nazerman merely grunts at the young man's ignorance. He cannot waste his time explaining the mark to one so benighted.

Jesus does, however, think he understands Jews. Like many New Yorkers of the era, he has grown up in a neighborhood where Jews own many of the small businesses. He deals with them every day, giving them his hard-won money, dollar by dollar. "These people," he reasons, must have a secret for success. As one who has survived on odd jobs and petty crime, he concludes that if he wants to get rich, he should take Sol Nazerman as his mentor. Perceiving the stereotype Jesus has imposed on him, Nazerman lashes back at Jesus's indirect anti-Semitism with a parody of the Shylock image. He tells him he believes in nothing: not

God, not art, not science. He believes only in money: "Money is the whole thing." After teaching him how to assay gold, he describes the fabled business acumen others have created for a people not allowed to own land and who must therefore survive by trade. Seething with bitterness, he concludes: "Suddenly, you make a grand discovery: you have a mercantile heritage. You are a merchant—you're known as a usurer, a man with secret resources, a witch, a pawnbroker, a sheenie, a mockie, and a kike!" [20] This is, after all, merely the sentiment Nazerman feels that Jesus believes about him. Why not say it out loud, because it's what everyone thinks about Jews anyway? His outburst betrays the stereotyped's stereotype of the stereotyper, a common source of friction in interethnic tensions in crowded, pluralistic cities like New York. It may be, as a matter of speculation, that Lumet placed weight on the dialogue because of own his experience in cramped, multicultural spaces of the Lower East Side, as though Nazerman were articulating the prejudice Lumet perceived in many of his friends and neighbors. However it may be explained, it is certainly one of the unforgettable moments in the film.

Nazerman's struggle echoes the double conflict that characterizes many of Lumet's films. He tries to forge his own identity by distancing himself from his heritage and his family, and from his mistress and her family. He finds no solace in the companionship of fellow survivors of the horror. At the same time, his Jewish community struggles to maintain its existence in America, where the danger comes from subtle bias, as it had in Europe, where it eventually led to annihilation. In his later films, Lumet will continue to explore complex urban relationships between individuals and groups, and between groups and the larger society. He will never again focus so sharply on Jewish identities, but race and nationality will continue to color and complicate the lives of his characters wherever they are in New York.

Dog Day Afternoon (1975)

In 1975 Sidney Lumet took up the question of outsider status again, but this time the issue was not so much Jewish identity but sexual orientation. So what? In the film, the hero gradually emerges as a self-aware gay man, but as a live-and-let-live New Yorker, Lumet gives the fact little weight in shaping the audience's reaction to the character. Sonny Wortzik (Al Pacino) is about much more than being gay. In fact, his homosexuality becomes apparent only well into the story, when his likable personality has already made its impression. We know him as a person before we know him as a homosexual. As with *The Pawnbroker,* Lumet stirs up contradictory feelings about his principal character. Sol Nazerman has appropriated into his own life all the brutality that had been worked on him by others. He survived, but at a terrible cost. One can only loathe him for what he has become while sympathizing with him for what life has done to him. Sonny, by contrast, is a nice guy, but he makes inexcusably stupid decisions that wreck his life and the lives of many people around him. Nazerman is an old man who looks back on his life from the edges of the grave; Wortzik is scarcely more than an adolescent who cannot imagine the consequences of his actions.

For all the light touches, in *Dog Day Afternoon* Lumet presents a character that shows even more complexity and ambiguity than Nazerman, whose downward trajectory can be traced through a chain of logically connected biographical links. In contrast, Sonny's life consists of irrational, unconnected leaps. Lumet, however, adopts the posture of the typical jaded New Yorker. He looks at misfit personalities without judgment and allows them to reveal their lives gradually. (A friend, who enjoys needling me about the odd behavior by citizens of my native city, once pointed out an item in a Boston paper about a group of men, protesting something, who had dressed up as yellow butterflies in chiffon gowns and roller-skated around Manhattan. I told him that what was odd was that someone noticed.)

Dog Day Afternoon revels in odd behavior. Lumet directs with a light comic touch—several scenes are truly funny, which is quite unusual for him—while at the same time treating the characters with both affection and respect. Sonny masterminds a bank robbery in the Park Slope section of Brooklyn on one of the hottest afternoons of the summer. Nothing goes according to plan. As soon as they draw their weapons, the youngest robber loses his nerve and announces that he wants to go home. Sonny explains patiently that he has to leave the getaway car and take the subway. When they open the safe, they discover that a few hours earlier, a messenger took almost all the cash to the central bank. Smoke from a burning ledger attracts the attention of outsiders, and soon the flustered robbers and the terrified bank staff, now hostages, find themselves facing an army of police potent enough to invade and annex Staten Island.

The struggle for personal survival within Lumet's customary concentric circles soon begins to take place for Sonny. For all the comic elements in the failed robbery, Sonny is no fool. As a former bank employee, he knows about alarms, surveillance cameras, and marked bills. With one accomplice gone, he is left alone with Sal (John Cazale), who, like Sonny is a Vietnam veteran but who may have become a bit unhinged by the experience. All responsibility devolves on Sonny, who deals quite competently with the hostages, the police, the media, the FBI, and even a pizza deliveryman. Under extreme pressure, Sonny has to formulate a plan in a bank building that has become as stifling as the jury room in *12 Angry Men* once the police cut the air conditioning. Sal is less than useless; he could be a problem. Brooklyn streets are wider, brighter, and airier than the familiar canyons between Manhattan skyscrapers, but on the other hand, the low buildings provide no shade from the summer sun.

Despite his being alone in his leadership role, Sonny builds a community around him. He acts with firmness to ensure compliance with his orders because of fear, but gradually, like a born leader or politician, he builds personal loyalty among the hostages. Sonny shows himself to be a kind man, not a crazed criminal. Howard (John Marriott), the bank guard, has an asthmatic attack and Sonny frees him. In a wonderful Lumet touch that is both comic and chilling, as the guard leaves the bank, the police assume that because he is black he is one of the robbers and pounce on him. When Mulvaney (Sully Boyar), the bank manager, needs insulin for his diabetes, Sonny sends for a doctor to give it to him. At one point he plans to lock the staff in the vault, but he changes his mind when the women want to use the restroom first. Sylvia (Penny Allen), the head teller, in good motherly fashion, rebukes Sonny for his language in front of "my girls" and shows herself fearless in protecting them, but once she perceives that they are in no immediate danger, she becomes an efficient middle manager for Sonny, just as she was for Mulvaney earlier in the afternoon. When given the opportunity to leave, she refuses. To help pass the time, Sonny amuses one of the tellers by giving her his rifle and teaching her to do army drill maneuvers with it. Pretending to be a soldier is more fun than cashing checks; she would never think of trying to use the rifle against Sonny and he knows it. People in the audience as well as in the film begin to like Sonny and hope that he succeeds in his plans.

Sonny's charisma as a leader extends beyond the bank. Once the hostage story hits local television, a huge crowd gathers on the street behind police barricades. When Sonny shows his defiance in dealing with the police, the bystanders rally behind his antiauthoritarian flag. (It may be an overstatement to liken the situation to anarchy because Sonny has established a command center and clearly remains in charge.) When reporters reveal Sonny's sexual orientation in their efforts to sensationalize the story even more in the slow news period of the dog days, the street becomes the center of a gay pride demonstration. Thus his leadership moves outward from his three-man gang of hapless bank robbers, to the bank employees, to the neighborhood, and finally, thanks to the local news teams, to the gay community and to the entire city. A man of modest resources throughout his life, he has risen to the status of folk hero because of the other ordinary people, thousands of them, who conceive of themselves as his allies: little people resentful of the massive institutions of New York, like the banks and the police force.

Sonny is not intimidated by power elites; he shows ordinary citizens how to fight back. In one scene, he throws the bank's money to the cheering crowds. In another, when the police have become a bit too energetic in their reaction, Sonny leads the crowd in a chant, "Attica, Attica," a reference to the brutal suppression of the Attica, New York, prison uprising in 1971 when 1,500 police opened fire on the rebellious prisoners and killed 42 of them. In Sonny they have found their Howard Beale (Peter Finch), a character in Lumet's next picture, *Network* (1976), the crazed television newsman who had the entire citizenry leaning out their windows shouting, "I'm as mad as hell, and I'm not going to take it any more." In this later film, the oppressive institution is the television industry itself.

Like Davis in *12 Angry Men,* Sonny creates a community around himself on the force of his own personality. Sol Nazerman, by contrast, tried to withdraw from any form of community and go it alone. Nonetheless, typical of Lumet heroes, both men wrestle with their identities as individuals in the midst of a community. Sonny also struggles with commitment to a nuclear family. Married to an abrasive, oversized wife, Angie (Susan Peretz), he is father of two children. The police bring her on the scene in the hope that she will be able to remedy the situation. She makes it worse. Sonny considers his real wife Leon (Chris Sarandon), a delicate young man with a soft mannerisms and varnished fingernails.

Leon appears all the more fragile dressed as he is in a flimsy hospital robe and drugged into a near stupor after his latest suicide attempt. Sonny, it turns out, had planned the robbery to get the money to pay for a sex-change operation for Leon. After this is over, he plans to leave Angie and the children and live with Leon. Sonny's position between his two wives has elements of absurdist comedy. Mel Brooks would have made it a raucous farce. Lumet treats it with such sensitivity that despite the outrageous premise, both Sonny and Leon emerge as sympathetic characters, and their romance seems perfectly reasonable. True to the cosmopolitan reluctance to pass judgment on anyone, he respectfully allows both men to tell their stories. Who is Sonny Wortzik? Is he the army veteran, bank robber, and married father of two? Or is he the seriocomic homosexual who leaves his family for an effeminate male lover who wants to be a woman? The crowd outside doesn't care. It cheers him on for being himself and standing up to the establishment.

This "establishment" that Sonny defies as leader of the minorities consists of two distinct parts. The first level of opposition comes from the New York City Police Department, the second from the FBI. Together, they represent that outer ring of conflict that is characteristic of a Lumet scenario. Like the bank staff, the police are a racially and ethnically mixed crew, who as individuals could easily have fit into the crowds that gradually become sympathetic to Sonny's nonconformist, antiauthoritarian agenda. They do not, obviously, because they have become sworn officers of the law, and as such, they have their own agenda. Their job involves providing public order in a city that could sink into chaos if quirky individuals were allow to express themselves without rein. One African American officer, who appears briefly as the bogus chauffeur of the escape van, talks the talk, but streetwise Sonny sees right through the charade. He spots the man in coveralls and huge Afro as one of "them," not one of "us." Sonny knows who his adversaries are.

The officer in charge, Sergeant Moretti (Charles Durning), like Sonny, carries an identifiably ethnic name and also like him uses the vocabulary of the Brooklyn streets. Both his suit and his patience wilt in the afternoon heat. He sets up a command post in a barbershop, but he has no more success in controlling the situation than Sonny had with the robbery. A SWAT team tries an apparently unauthorized commando raid, police on the street seem overly eager to brandish their weapons and torpedo ongoing negotiations, and the press and the crowds continually get in the way. One man, the husband of one of the captive tellers, leaps the barriers and physically assaults Sonny. Moretti's command style involves shouting a string of obscenities at this unruly gaggle, with or without a bullhorn. He plays by the book, but he has trouble with the big words. He lacks the imagination to resolve the crisis. Like Sonny, he is a man of ordinary talent put in circumstances beyond his experience and capabilities, but lacking Sonny's charismatic leadership and talent for improvisation, he makes little progress.

If the police represent ordinary citizens akin to Sonny and the crowds but apart from them, the FBI agents are chilling as utterly alien presences. Their leader, Agent Sheldon (James Broderick), with his appropriately nonethnic name and relentlessly cool demeanor, seems ready to take any means necessary to repress Sonny's challenge to civic order. The agents' tan suits and white shirts remain impossibly crisp in withering heat. Sheldon takes over the case, and when he makes the arrangements for the getaway trip to JFK, one can expect only treachery. Both Sonny and Moretti have done everything possible in their own bumbling ways to avoid bloodshed. Sonny's solution, a flight to Morocco, as unlikely as the scheme appears at first, gradually gains in plausibility as the motorcade pulls onto the tarmac where the plane awaits them. If they had their way, no one would get hurt. As Sonny, Sal, and the hostages exit the van, the driver, an FBI agent named Murphy (Lang Henricksen), an appropriate name for an establishment law officer in ethnic New York (the Irish are now considered with some hostility as mainstream Americans by later immigrant groups), uses a concealed gun to dispatch Sal with one neat shot to the forehead. Agents disarm Sonny, cuff him, and read him his rights. Among the credits we learn that Sonny is now serving a twenty-five-year sentence in federal prison and Leon has had his operation and is living as a woman in New York.

Dog Day Afternoon ends as a tragedy, but a tragedy born not of Aristotelian hubris as much as from the fatalism that touches all New Yorkers to some degree. You can't beat the system. Sonny inspires admiration by daring to be an individual among the eight million and thus gaining his fifteen minutes of fame, but no one doubts that in the end that he will lose. Having escaped with his life is victory enough for anyone to hope for, but as the title assures us, he was swallowed up in the criminal justice system, one more nameless face among the masses dressed in prison drab. The City wins; it always wins.

Serpico (1974) and *Prince of the City* (1981)

The justice system fascinates Sidney Lumet, not especially for its effect on criminals as much as for its impact on those who are part of it. This world of police and prosecutors, Feds and felons, provides a perfect setting for Lumet to explore the complex, ambiguous relationships between the individual and the small, tight social system that forms his own personal community and the larger universe that threatens the survival of both the smaller, self-contained world and the individual. Conflict between straight cops and crooked cops has, of course, become a movie cliché. Lumet, however, is more concerned with the cop caught somewhere in the middle, part of the system yet rebelling against it, longing for acceptance by the group yet defining himself as somehow outside it. He returned to the New York Police Department four times: *Serpico* (1974), *Prince of the City* (1981), *Q & A* (1990), and *Night Falls on Manhattan* (1997). In each film he tempers an idealized notion of what police officers represent for the life of the City with a cynical realization that the reality on occasion fails to match the ideals. He reverses the usual old adage that one rotten apple spoils the barrel. In Lumet's view, one could make a case that it is the rotten barrel that spoils any good apple that comes close to it. His characters straddle the uncertain boundary between hope for reform and despair at the pervasiveness of the corruption they encounter. Of the four, *Q & A* brings together more of the Lumet New York themes than the other three, and for this reason will receive more extensive treatment. *Serpico* and *Prince of the City* are admittedly more significant films, and *Night Falls on Manhattan* holds interest as a reprise of Lumet's still-unresolved questions about personal integrity in a city that can grind down the most idealistic of heroes.

Serpico is an adaptation of Peter Maas's best-selling true story of Frank Serpico, an idealistic young Italian American policeman who, on his first day on the beat, discovers the pervasive culture of corruption that permeates the police department. It touches little things, like a free lunch, but it touches everything. Everybody, it seems, receives favors from everyone. Serpico (Al Pacino) accepts his place as a rookie on the force and says nothing for a while, content to maintain his own personal standards of honesty. But this is not enough. When he does complain, he receives the reputation as a troublemaker and is moved from one job to another. Others in the precinct cannot trust an honest cop because there is always the possibility that he will turn in the others. If everyone is corrupt, then nobody talks. They increase pressure on him to play along and not wreck the system that takes care of all of them. Ever more isolated socially and professionally in his undercover work, his personal life implodes. He adopts the beard and long hair of the 1970s, a look that alienates him even further from everyone else in the precinct in that era of polarization between "hippies" and "hardhats." His girlfriend Laurie (Barbara Eda-Young) exhausts her patience in dealing with his outbursts and leaves him. Superior officers, themselves profiting handsomely from informal payments, bury his reports.

In desperation, he goes to the *New York Times,* which runs a series of articles airing the allegations. In response, the mayor forms a commission to investigate the charges, and Serpico is a key witness.[21] After his testimony, in the opening sequence of the film, before the central story, which is told in prolonged flashback, fellow officers let him enter a drug den alone, deliberately withholding the backup. Serpico takes a bullet to the face and nearly dies at the hospital. In the final shot, Frank Serpico sits alone on a dock in front of the huge featureless hull of the ship that will take him into self-imposed exile in Europe. Like Sonny Wortzik, he challenged this system, had his moment of triumph, but ultimately lost. The City won again. He protected his integrity and individuality, but by doing so, he discovered that the City had no place for him.

Prince of the City, which came seven years later, mined much of the same mother lode of material. The screenplay by Jay Presson Allen and Sidney Lumet is based on the story of Robert Leuci, a member of the SIU (Special Investigations Unit of NYPD) assigned to the narcotics trade. Because of extraordinary citywide jurisdiction and lack of supervision by the normal precinct-based command structure, Leuci and his colleagues in the SIU developed a cowboy approach to law enforcement. Since the epidemic of heroin use reached public consciousness in the 1970s and created a near panic among politicians and citizenry alike, the tactics of the SIU were condoned and perhaps even admired; they got results. If they could arrest dealers on occasion, no one seemed to care about the illegal break-ins, warrantless searches, and phone taps— or worse, the bribery and control of addict-informants with confiscated heroin. With access to this valuable commodity, several of the officers were not adverse to turning a profit on their transactions, and in effect, they became dealers themselves. When the press broke the famous French Connection case, involving 140 pounds of pure heroin that disappeared from police custody, the public demanded an accounting. The police were negligent at best. More likely, it seemed, insiders had taken it for multimillion-dollar resale on the streets, thus making the NYPD one of the largest drug syndicates in the City. Clearly, heads had to roll in the narcotics unit, and because many felt that the department could not be trusted to investigate its own, the federal Department of Justice took over the investigation. Author Robert Daley turned the story into a best-selling book entitled *Prince of the City*, a title given to members of the SIU, who considered themselves as privileged royalty, exempted from the laws that bound ordinary citizens. Lumet was attracted to the story because, as he said, "Nobody told the truth. And everybody was, theoretically, pursuing the truth."[22]

Frank Serpico stands out as a thwarted idealist with no doubts about his mission in life. His enemies are external, and they are mainly his fellow officers, rather than the felons he confronts on the streets. In contrast, Danny Ciello (Treat Williams), the character based on the real Robert Leuci, wrestles with demons that are internal. He is an ambiguous, self-serving character who, after many emotional twists and turns, finally agrees to inform on the men in his unit. His motivation shifts. At first he wants to ease his conscience and restore his sullied ideals, and later to save himself from indictment for his own corruption on the job and perjury during the internal investigations he has conducted for the Justice Department. The story traces his painful descent into this blind canyon of deceit and betrayal, where gradually he has fewer and fewer options.

The opening sequence makes it clear that like his partners in SIU, Danny Ciello lives a comfortable life in the suburbs, surely beyond the salary of a detective, as his addicted brother points out during a family argument. He augments his income by doing occasional favors for his cousin and friends in the Mafia and by sharing in the spoils of the drug trade with his partners. His brother's tirade piques Ciello's conscience, and after three separate meetings with federal prosecutors, he agrees to help gather evidence to break the cycle of corruption in the department, but only on the condition that they will never ask him to do anything that would harm his partners in the SIU. Ciello's boyish naïveté inevitably leads to tragedy. In this web of corruption, everyone is entangled, and his handlers, not he, make the decisions about which connection to pursue and which to ignore. He must do as the prosecutors instruct him, even if it means breaking the sacred blue wall of silence, the unspoken code that condemns any informer on a fellow officer as a "rat" whose life may be forfeit.

The structure of the story echoes the standard Lumet structure of twin conflict. Ciello finds himself slowly sinking in a double vortex of New York life. With adolescent optimism, he thinks he can have it all without paying a terrible price. He wants to maintain his personal integrity within the closed professional and social world of the SIU and the Mafia. He thinks he can be a criminal and a law enforcement officer at the same time. It won't work. Both these worlds, criminal and police, are threatened by outside forces, especially the Department of Justice. Ciello's defection from their local codes of loyalty to a distant authority will endanger their very existence. They can't condone Ciello's disloyalty. Ciello's wife, Carla (Lindsay Crouse), knows that the investigation will soon spin out of control and he will not be able to keep within the boundaries he has set. She warns him repeatedly, but he cannot or will not hear.

This conflict has its tribal element as well. It pits ethnic New Yorkers against the characterless power structure in Washington. The New York police have a sprinkling of suitably ethnic names, like Alvarez, Mayo, Edelman, and Levy, but the group is heavily dominated by Italian names like Bando, Marinaro, and Maccone. Naturally, the Mafia hoodlums are all Italian, and their haunt is Mulberry Street in Little Italy. Ciello's first successful prosecution is Blomberg, a crooked lawyer, and another adversary is known simply as King, an African American. This cast of Italian Americans and other ethnic types constitute Ciello's immediate New York world. The alien world, centered in Washington, is also, and less convincingly, dominated by Italian Americans: Capallino, Polito, Vincente, and the ultimate Justice Department supervisor Sandrocino, icily portrayed by the diminutive Bob Balaban. Yet in all this scrupulously balanced ethnic mix, the only character whose background is explored (at Ciello's prodding) is Brooks Paige (Paul Roebling), who went to Harvard, Andover, and St. Bernard's Academy "for blond boys in blazers," as Ciello characterizes it. In Ciello's world, as in Lumet's, the WASP is no more exempt from stereotyping than a member of any other group.

As adults, the federal lawyers have outgrown their prep-school blazers and adapted neat business suits, reminiscent of the FBI in *Dog Day Afternoon,* while the locals, police and criminals alike, favor the garish polyesters popular in the 1970s. The police conspire in family settings, like horse farms upstate, or in backyards on Long Island or Staten Island. In contrast, the feds deal with Ciello in a lavish apartment overlooking Central Park or in sterile offices in public buildings. The police and the criminals remain rooted in role and place; they have few career options. They have to hang on to preserve their pensions. The federal agents are interchangeable parts. Once they make a deal with Ciello, they move on to higher positions, and when new people come on the scene, the rules change. Ciello has nothing to say about the reinterpretations of past agreements.

Lumet underlines the wrenching ambiguity of Ciello's position in the closing scenes where prosecutors go over the story one more time as they try to reach a decision on whether to prosecute him for his crimes and perjury. Their observations are all true. He is a drug dealer, thug, and liar. To preserve any semblance of equal justice, he must be punished. On the other hand, he is a hero, the model of the police officer doing his duty at great personal risk. To reward his valor and encourage others to come forward in similar circumstances in the future, he must receive amnesty. In the end, the state declines to prosecute the case.

In the final scene, Lumet shows Ciello restored to his position as detective, but in the relatively safe role of instructor in the police academy. When one of the young detectives discovers his identity, he sneers, "I have nothing to learn from you." He walks out of the lecture hall in protest, a clear suggestion on Lumet's part and painful realization by Ciello that perhaps the police have learned nothing from his ordeal and will repeat the same mistakes in the future. Perhaps one person cannot make a difference in any entity as large and complex as New York or in the police department after all. The camera moves slowly into a close-up of Ciello's face staring into the camera and framed the blank background of the chalkboard. Like Serpico sitting by the featureless hull of the ship, he finds himself totally and absolutely alone. Serpico, however, plans to leave the City; Ciello wants to stay, but he has discovered that once he has placed his own personal integrity over loyalty to his group, he stands alone, even in a crowded classroom. In this scene, Lumet states the obvious fact that in New York, without a neighborhood or clan or partners, one can experience a terrible loneliness.

Q & A (1990)

In *Q & A* Lumet returns to the topic of police corruption. As was the case in the earlier two police films, the department provides a concrete setting for the much broader questions of the survival of the individual within the tight-knit urban group and the survival of the group itself, which is threatened by outside forces challenging its long-held traditions. In the first two films, the corruption arose from money and concurrently from the power to control its flow. Ethnic issues lurked in the background, ever present in the identifiable surnames of the characters but rarely foregrounded. In *Q & A* Lumet reverses the priorities. Money from the drug trade underlies the conflict between the Mafia and the Puerto Rican street dealers, of course, but the issue at the center of the script, written by Lumet himself, is ethnic identity. Racism and its more refined manifestation, tribalism, lie at the core of the corruption; the money is incidental.

Among the cast of characters, no one stands above the ethnic mix as a mainstream, old American WASP. Everyone comes from somewhere else. What's more, tribal identity is more than a name; it defines the individual's role in the drama. In the script, references to race and nationality are relentless, at times funny or toxic, but always pointed. This rings true. New Yorkers claim an odd relationship to their mixture of clans. We will immediately identify someone as a member of a group. We speak of an Italian doctor or an Irish priest or a Jewish family upstairs, even though their ancestors may have been in America for a century. We direct good-natured jokes at each other and feel that by living in a cosmopolitan area and being up front about our ethnic differences, we have defused prejudice. Lumet challenges this comfortable assumption of his fellow New Yorkers, and his conclusions are devastating. Racial awareness takes many forms, all of them poisonous.

With the old Protestant power structure kept from the scene, the Irish assume the role of the Establishment, as surely it must seem to more recent immigrant groups. But clearly, the City faces a cataclysmic ethnic shift, and the Irish face their uncertain future with a mixture of fear, resentment, and rage. Mike Brennan (Nick Nolte) prowls the streets in Spanish Harlem, then Park Avenue and One Hundred Third Street, before the gentrification of the Upper East Side leapt over Ninety-sixth Street and continued north. He uses a decoy to summon a witness out of an after-hours club, and when the man appears, shoots him in the head. He cooly plants a .45 in the hand of the dead man and coerces witnesses to swear that they saw the victim aim it at him.

Kevin Quinn (Patrick O'Neal), head of the homicide division of the district attorney's office, summons Aloysius Francis Reilly (Timothy Hutton), a rookie assistant district attorney, to prepare the inquest. The Irish function as perpetrator, investigator, prosecutor, and judge. In other words, they hold all the power. When Reilly arrives, Quinn treats him more as a family member than a protégé. He knew Reilly's father, "one of us," in the old days. The younger Reilly had also been on the force before he became a lawyer. He still wears a patrolman's white socks and black oxfords with his lawyer's gray business suit. When Quinn asks about his credentials, Reilly tells him he had graduated from Brooklyn Law School. Reilly asks why he went there rather than to St. John's. Reilly replies that his father thought the Jesuits were too liberal. This exchange reveals two points. Lumet is not above overdoing his own stereotype of Irish whose alleged illiberal narrow-mindedness extends beyond the racial bigotry he is exploring in the film. Second, as scriptwriter, he betrays a lack of factual information about Catholic culture. St. John's University was founded by the Congregation of Mary, the Vincentians, not the Jesuits. As a workingman, the elder Reilly might have made this mistake, but as an Irish district attorney with political ambitions, Quinn would have had enough dealings with Fordham (Jesuit) Law School graduates and St. John's (Vincentian) graduates to catch Reilly's misstatement. In any event, this trial will be a good, open-and-shut case for a new law-school graduate to gain experience: a decorated Irish detective killing a expendable Puerto Rican drug dealer in self-defense. No problems; no questions.

As he awaits the arrival of the new assistant district attorney, Brennan entertains his colleagues with a story of a Italian suspect who gave him back talk during his fingerprinting. Brennan put him through a window, and in fear of what Brennan might do next, the man soiled himself. Brennan has the Irish gift of storytelling. His constant reference to his adversary as a "guinea" seems perfectly acceptable to his friends. He greets Reilly as "one of us," a reference to his Irish ancestry and to the fact that he was a second-generation police officer. After introducing Reilly to the other officers, two of them exchange racial barbs significantly more pointed than "guinea." Valentine (Luis Guzman), a Puerto Rican, refers to his partner, Chapman (Charles Dutton), an African American, as a "jungle bunny." Chappie, as he is known, responds by calling Valentine a "straight-haired nigger." Everyone laughs at the exchange, even though the captain makes a mock admonition by reminding them that racial epithets violate department policies. Valentine tells the captain that he and Chappie are affirmative action hires, and if they quit, the department would face inquiries and possibly lose funding. They realize they are outsiders to the Irish department. When the court stenographer arrives from Far Rockaway, they call him a "matzoth eater." Again, everyone laughs.

During the formal departmental inquiry, the Q & A, in Quinn's office, Reilly's inexperience shows, and he is clearly intimidated by Brennan and Quinn. With gusto equal to his story of the fingerprinting episode, Brennan describes the events that led to the shooting. While he spins his tale of perjury, the police, prosecutors, and court stenographer exchange ethnic insults in their usual pattern of crude humor. Reilly never interrupts Brennan's statement, not even to ask for clarification or additional details. The official record will consist exclusively of Brennan's story, exactly as he created it. As is fitting in any gathering of an Irish clan, the whiskey bottle stands in the center of the room, another unneeded bit of stereotyping on Lumet's part.

At lunch the next day, Blumenfeld (Lee Richardson), who is near to retiring from his job as a chief prosecutor for the district attorney's office, reluctantly introduces Reilly to an oily defense lawyer named Pearlstein (Fyvush Finkel). When the man leaves, Blumenfeld tells Reilly, "When Jesse Jackson used the word 'hymie,' he meant him." Blumenfeld acts as guru to his younger associate, and based on his experience, he makes an observation about the murder weapon that raises the first question about Brennan's story. Reilly sees Blumenfeld as a man of integrity in a cesspool of corruption in the district attorney's office, but at the end, when he tells Blumenfeld what he has discovered and that he will take the matter to the press, the older man tells him to let it drop. When Reilly insists, Blumenfeld tells him they can rediscover records showing that the elder Reilly took bribes. They can take both his father's reputation and his mother's widow's pension, if Reilly dares to go public. Reilly yields to the enormous pressure and as a result becomes just another cog in the corrupt machinery.

When Blumenfeld shows that his own loyalties rest with the department rather than the law, Reilly is crushed. "You're breaking my heart, Blumie," he sobs. Blumenfeld, the Jew who was capable of a cruel anti-Semitic remark after the meeting with Pearlstein, showed that, like everyone else in the department, he is tainted by ethnic bias, even toward another Jew. This kind of ethnic remark stands as the visible tip of the iceberg of institutional corruption of the department. Racialism, graft, and murder are merely variations of the same pathology.

Blumenfeld may be breaking Lumet's heart as well. Like Sol Nazerman, he should know better. As a Jewish outsider to the corrupt world of Irish police, Italian gangsters, and Puerto Rican drug dealers, he has the perspective to see evil for what it is. He does, but in the last analysis chooses not to oppose it.[23] Despite his impeccable liberal credentials, he is no better than they are. And Blumenfeld does not stand alone in this complex web of crime. When the Puerto Rican drug dealer, Bobby Texador (Armand Assante), needs soldiers as bodyguards and assassins, he hires two Cuban hit men, who are identified as Sephardic Jews and then referred to as "hebes." Again, when Quinn meets with his backers to plan his campaign for attorney general, an office that will vault him into the governor's mansion, the pollster who describes his chances, with slighting references to black and Hispanic areas, is conspicuously wearing the orthodox yarmulke and tzitzit, a square garment with cords that are visible below the waist.

Lumet goes into even more delicate territory in his exploration of the relationship between bigotry and corruption when he enters the world of the gay demimonde. In *The Pawnbroker,* some thirty years earlier, Lumet had Jesus take Mabel to a tawdry club, where a joyless female impersonator did a lackluster dance that reflected the lives of the petty criminals who watched the performance. In *Q & A,* Lumet takes a more direct and incisive look at this subculture not based on ethnicity but nonetheless remaining on the outside of the power structure as represented by the Irish (Catholic, and therefore at least in public perception, openly hostile to gays) police force.

From the opening scenes, Lumet leaves no doubt that Mike Brennan, rogue cop, is a sadistic thug edging ever more closely to psychotic collapse. One of his colleagues observes that Brennan "is not prejudiced.

He hates everybody. He's an equal opportunity hater." Brennan, however, reserves a special hatred for homosexuals, for reasons that are darkly suggested but never explicitly confirmed. He may well be homosexual himself, as one of the female impersonators speculates, and thus his brutality may be a way of proving to himself and his fellow officers how straight he is. He may also be trying to destroy what he most loathes in himself. As he searches for Montalvo, a transvestite who witnessed a crime Brennan is trying to conceal, he tours the notorious vice area of the West Thirties, around the entrance to the Lincoln Tunnel, a section once known as Hell's Kitchen and recently renamed Clinton as part of its gentrification program. He rounds up the streetwalkers to enlist their cooperation in his search for one of their coworkers, but he singles out Sylvester, a transvestite, for a particularly sadistic form of intimidation in front of the others. He has proved to the streetwalkers and to himself his brutal contempt for people like Sylvester.

But Brennan cannot escape this world, even if he wanted to. He is forced to rely on a particularly beautiful cross-dresser, José Malpico (International Chrysis), to lead him to his key witness, whom he intends to murder. Their relationship takes a sexual but loveless direction, as much the result of Brennan's suggestion as of Malpico's seduction. As Brennan waits for Malpico to change costumes for their sexual encounter, he discovers what he wants to know and uses the cord of his victim's robe as a murder weapon before the act is consummated. By strangling his now expendable informant, he can assure himself that he was only using the prospect of sex to gain information, but as we have watched the relationship progress through various stages, we are less certain.

Brennan's ultimate quarry is José Montalvo (Paul Caulderon), another female impersonator. When they finally meet on a yacht in Puerto Rico, Brennan bullies him into providing sex, as though he knows the routine in dealing with male prostitutes. Montalvo realizes that his life is in danger and tries to comply with Brennan's wishes in the hope of prolonging his life, but Brennan murders him, again with the cord of his robe, and again as though convincing himself of this contempt for people like Montalvo: in his estimation, a fairy, a junkie, and a spic.

In the midst of this murderous, self-contained world, Aloysius Francis Reilly searches for his own integrity. When he responds to Quinn's summons, he leaves his own secure bed in his new, sparsely decorated apartment and rides in a patrol car through the dark, rain-soaked streets of

New York. The lights writhe across the windshield, their reflections distorted by droplets of rain and the incessant beat of the wiper. This journey marks the start of Reilly's descent into the underworld. In the tradition of Odysseus and Aeneas, he will discover much about himself during his pilgrimage across grotesque landscapes peopled by monsters and sirens. The denizens greet him as one of their own. He is, in ways he never imagined.

Reilly surely believes himself above the graft, doctored testimony, and casual brutality that he may or may not have appreciated during his years on the force. Before this journey ends, he will discover the truth about his father, and by his coerced silence, he finds himself part of a conspiracy that stretches from Quinn through Brennan and involves several murders. Lumet's plot is complex and admittedly confusing, but its very complexity allows the audience to share the moral vertigo that afflicts Reilly. In short, Quinn, as a tough Irish kid from Queens, took a sadistic delight in joining the Puerto Rican gang wars in Harlem. He enjoyed the excitement and the killing, a propensity he carried with him as a prosecutor who enjoyed witnessing executions. During a rumble, he killed a man, a fact that he cannot allow to surface during his political campaign. He forces Brennan to kill all the known witnesses because he holds the files on Brennan's own murder of a suspect some years earlier. The records disappeared from the district attorney's office. Reilly puts the pieces of this improbable case together piece by piece, scarcely believing what he discovers. Knowing the facts of a felony makes him an accessory. Keeping quiet as an officer of the court makes him an accomplice. Caught in this web of interlocking relationships, Reilly is indeed one of them.

Reilly's self-perceived immunity from police corruption buckles under such intolerable pressure that one is inclined to excuse him as a victim rather than a perpetrator. As an eager young prosecutor on the side of justice, he may have thought of himself as wanting to "make a difference." Instead, he finds himself caught up in a world that is too big, too complex for him to control or even comprehend. It ends up controlling him. His racism, the other face of institutionalized evil, is another matter altogether. His complicity as an Irish cop from Queens, "one of us," is far more nebulous and his innocence far more ambiguous. In this respect, his voyage of self-discovery takes him across rougher waters than he might have expected.

In gathering further information about the Brennan shooting, he calls witnesses to make their statements. Bobby Texador and his common-law wife, Nancy Bosch (Jenny Lumet), were present at the after-hours club during the incident. Reilly recognizes Nancy. He should. In fragmentary fashion, through several conversations between Reilly and Nancy, their story is reconstructed. They were engaged six years earlier, when Reilly was still on the force. He had met her mother, a Spanish-speaking woman from Puerto Rico, but when her father appeared one day, Reilly was stunned to discover that he was African American. She reacted violently to "the look on his face" and broke off the engagement. She aborted their child, and in revealing this detail, she deliberately stirs guilt in Reilly's Irish Catholic conscience, maintaining she is just as Catholic as he is, only not as strict. After their separation, she descended into a life of drugs until she met Texador, who saved her and now generously takes care of her and her mother. Why Reilly never tried to find her in the previous six years is not clear, but he does pursue her quite energetically after their meeting at the precinct house. She tells him that the bigoted cops are at least honest about their feelings. He feigns liberal tolerance, she maintains, but at heart, he is as prejudiced as they. Reilly is shaken, not so much by the angry denunciation as by the realization that she may be right.

The film ends with the matter not quite resolved. Bobby escapes an assassination attempt by the Mafia, but not the relentless pursuit of Lieutenant Brennan. Brennan, for his part, has become completely unhinged. He returns to the precinct to exact vengeance from those who had betrayed him, and after killing Chappie, he takes a fatal bullet himself. Reilly puts the pieces of the twisted case together and realizes he has enough evidence to go after Quinn, who is at the core of this entire series of murders and cover-ups. He is devastated when Quinn laughs in his face, telling him that he is above the law and will be elected attorney general. Blumenfeld, as we have seen, agrees with Quinn's assessment and tells Reilly to drop his quixotic quest.

Reilly visits Nancy's mother, who confirms the perception of deep racism that she, as well as Nancy, discovered in Reilly. The film began with a descent into the night in New York, and it ends on a sparkling beach in the Caribbean, where Nancy and Reilly had once vacationed together. In the opening scene, we see a world hidden in darkness and distorted with rain. But here on the immaculate white sand, everything appears bright and clear. Nancy sits alone in the sun. Reilly approaches and asks for forgiveness, but she tells him to go away. He extends his hand, but like Sol Nazerman rejecting the touch of Marilyn Birchfield in *The Pawnbroker,* she does not respond to his advance. He sits in the sand a few feet from her, and an ocean away from the City, a New Yorker lost in thought about himself and the world that has made him what he is. Has he risen above it, or has it destroyed him?

Night Falls on Manhattan (1997)

Lumet reprises the theme of failed idealism in one of his most recent pictures, which he scripted himself from the novel *Tainted Evidence* by Robert Daley, whose nonfiction story *Prince of the City* Lumet also adapted for the screen. Sean Casey (Andy Garcia) is a latter-day version of Al Reilly. Like him, he is third-generation Irish and a second-genera-tion police officer from Queens. He worked overtime to get through St. John's Law School in Jamaica. (The selection of St. John's may have been Lumet's atonement for the error in making it a liberal Jesuit insti-tution in *Q & A.*) As was the case with Al Reilly, the district attorney Morgie Morgenstern (Ron Leibman), who sprinkles his dialogue with Yiddish, "the language of our people," picks his inexperienced assistant to prosecute a high-profile case of a drug dealer, Jordan Washington (Shiek Mahmud-Bey), who killed two police officers and seriously wounded a third during a drug bust. Morgenstern makes his choice for two reasons. First, Casey's father, Liam Casey (Ian Holm), was the of-ficer seriously wounded in the raid, a factor that would carry enormous weight with a jury. Second, he wants to deny the publicity to his ambi-tious top assistant, Elihu Harrison (Colm Feore), who desperately wants the case. Harrison is a WASP who plans to run against him in the pri-maries, and if he loses, Morgenstern observes, Harrison will return to the "party of his people" and run against him in the general election in November as a Republican. Harrison wears a bow tie. With cutting reverse snobbery, Morgenstern, a graduate of City College, voices con-tempt for his Harvard background.

During the trial, Sam Vigoda (Richard Dreyfuss), a perennial civil rights advocate for the underdog and major annoyance to the district attorney's office, bases his case on the self-defense argument. He never denies that his client shot the officers. He does, however, have reason to believe that Washington and the police in three neighboring precincts had a long-standing agreement on protection that soured over time. Because he knew the police wanted to eliminate him, Washington had no choice, Vigoda argues, but to open fire as the officers approached. The police, of course, claim to know nothing about the payoffs and perjure themselves. Casey deflects the damage to his case by bending the rules of judicial conduct to the extent of provoking Washington into a violent outburst in the courtroom. Washington is found guilty, of course, and Casey becomes the darling of the press for ridding the City of this sociopathic menace. At the height of Casey's notoriety, Morgenstern suffers a debilitating heart attack and cannot run for re-election. With little time for a campaign, the mayor needs a candidate already known to the voters and sees Casey as the obvious choice to replace Morgenstern on the ticket.

As the new district attorney, Casey discovers that Vigoda's allegations will not go away. Lieutenant Wilson (Jude Ciccolella), with his WASP name, cool manners, and impeccably pressed suit, opens an investigation in the Internal Affairs Division (IAD). Joey Allegretto (James Gandolfini), Liam Casey's longtime partner, surfaces as one of the conspirators, not only in the graft but also in the planned assassination of Jordan Washington. In a poignant meeting with both Sean and Liam in the Casey home, Allegretto asks for a break in exchange for incriminating testimony. The request may have been reasonable enough, but IAD has made it clear that it has enough informants; from this point on, it wants not deals but convictions. In addition, Sean believes that Allegretto's making the request in the presence of his father puts undo pressure on him. In a self-righteous rage, Sean excoriates Allegretto, refuses to consider any deal, and even makes his father swear on his mother's grave that he was not part of the conspiracy. Like Al Reilly in his romance with Nancy Bosch, the elder Casey crossed tribal barriers by marrying Maria Nuñez, a fact that holds no significance in the story, but in Lumet's worldview, exogamy holds great moral weight and adds to the probity of Liam Casey, the ideal Irish cop. It may also have been a device to explain the Latin features of actor Andy Garcia.[24]

When Allegretto fails to make a deal, he takes his own life. At this point, Sean sees firsthand the result of his unbending adherence to the letter of the law. He later discovers that his father, although innocent of the conspiracies that swirled around him, had falsified the date on the arrest warrant for Jordan Washington. The raid was simply illegal. This technicality could put Washington back on the street, and it would put an end to Liam's thirty-seven-year career and his pension. Knowing that his father had acted out of zeal rather than malice, Sean decides to destroy the evidence. His love interest in an unsatisfying subplot, Peggy Lindstrom (Lena Olin), who is an associate in Vigoda's office, also learns of the forgery but passes on the opportunity to bring the document to the authorities. In the meantime, Liam, ever on the moral high ground, confesses his forgery to the issuing Judge Impelleteri (Dominic Chianese), who issued the warrant that had expired and been altered. He also presided over the trial and sentencing. He calmly fills out another form with the appropriate date, pretending that the altered document never existed. In effect, police, district attorney, defense lawyers, and judge have conspired to circumvent the technicalities of the law in order to preserve the larger interests of justice.

Once again, Lumet uses his two-step approach to the struggle for survival. Casey tries to preserve some shred of personal integrity, whereas the police try to preserve their own way of life, which involves loyalty to fellow officers even in the face of their criminality. In *Night Falls on Manhattan,* Lumet treats the topic with much greater ambiguity than he had in *Q & A.* In the earlier film, Al Reilly struggled to keep his moral code intact as he dealt with overt racism, drug trafficking, and murder. The issues were clear. In *Night Falls on Manhattan* nothing is clear. In one conversation, Casey, the newly elected district attorney, visits Morgenstern, who is confined to a wheelchair after his heart attack. Morgenstern tells him that the job consists of making deals, and to survive, he must be sure that when people get a piece of him, he must get a bigger piece of them. That's the way the system works. Casey takes this philosophy as his own. In the final scene, he addresses a new class of assistant district attorneys at their first training session. He describes their work as a series of compromises. If they play by the rules, they may lose a case, and it will break their hearts. If they bend the rules, they will win, and it will break their hearts. (Al Reilly, it will be recalled, also referred to a broken heart when Blumenfeld told him that he cannot pursue his case against Quinn.) They will continually operate in a gray area, he tells them, and there they will discover who they are. Sean Casey speaks forcefully of responsibility, but in fact he has become part of a system that functions on the edges of morality according to its own rules.

For Lumet, working in the criminal justice system provides a splendid analog for living in New York, and having lived in New York shapes his perception of police work. It's a tough world that can wear a person down. Outsiders feel that New York by its very size becomes impersonal, but people who have lived their lives there know that's not the case. Everything unfolds in an incredibly complex web of personal and tribal relationships, each of which has its own code. One simply cannot avoid payoffs, however indirect, and do business. Lumet, who has made forty films in New York, knows that fact as well as anyone.[25]

One can pretend to distance oneself from these interlocking and competing loyalties with their own gray moralities and refuse to play by their rules, but as Serpico, Ciello, Reilly, and Casey discover, they cannot. These men gain their identity from belonging to a specific social group, by being "one of us," in their case the criminal justice system, but they want to preserve their individual space at the same time. They try to have it both ways. The group, after all, has its own mores and its own instincts for survival. By trying to define an identity for themselves as apart from the group while remaining in it, Serpico is exiled, Ciello ostracized, Reilly defeated, and Casey compromised. Lumet admires the first three for their idealism but shows them punished for their naiveté. Casey compromises but survives, leaving the nagging question: at age seventy-three, with forty films behind him, has Lumet become more honest or more cynical? For a New Yorker, is there a difference?

The Verdict (1982)

Even when he switches the locale to Boston, Sidney Lumet remains a New York filmmaker making New York films. This makes *The Verdict,* with its script by Lumet and playwright David Mamet, an especially interesting film to use as a test of the analytic tools suggested in these pages. The elements of the conflicts that Lumet's characters undergo have been shaped by a New York consciousness. Frank Galvin (Paul Newman) wants to oppose the social structures, while needing to be part of them in order to survive. The system has its own rules to safeguard its own survival and will take extraordinary measures to protect its own interests, even if it means destroying those who oppose it, even to the point of destroying its own. Galvin's adversaries include both the legal system, as represented by one of the most powerful lawyers in Boston, Edward Concannon (James Mason), who represents Galvin's ultimate adversary, the Catholic Archdiocese of Boston. In this film, as is so often the case in Lumet's films, the WASP elite scarcely exists. This conflict is purely an internal matter for tribal chieftains. The oppressive majority consists of entrenched Irish Catholics, the old guard, and for the first time Lumet makes the official Church part of the mix.

Galvin grew up as part of the system. He's Boston Irish in ancestry and a graduate of Boston College Law School, a Catholic and Jesuit institution that boasts of its Irish origins. He was second in his class and an editor of the *Law Review,* and he began a brilliant career in one of the major firms in town. As a junior associate, he was falsely accused of jury tampering and took responsibility to save one of the partners. The firm reneged on its promises of reinstatement and compensation and released him. Galvin avoided jail time and disbarment, but his reputation was tarnished, his career ruined, and his marriage destroyed. Stereotypically for an Irish American, Galvin sought solace in the bottle. In the grim opening sequence, Lumet shows Galvin at midday, alone in a working-class bar, playing a pinball machine whose random bounces suggest the unpredictable and pointless changes of direction his life has taken. He circles names in the obituary pages and drinks while he waits for the afternoon viewing hours to begin and then makes the rounds of funeral parlors, introducing himself as an old friend of the deceased and giving his card to the grieving widow in case she might need his services. It has come to this. He is worse than an ambulance chaser; he is a hearse chaser. Despite his desperate efforts, he has not had a case in over a year. In the evenings, he returns to the bar, very much at home drinking and exchanging crude jokes with the working men of the neighborhood. Despite his white shirt and necktie, Galvin is still one of the boyos.

An old friend with a suitably Irish name, Mickey Morrissey (Jack Warden), does him a favor by passing along a clear-cut medical negligence case with the expectation that an out-of-court settlement will allow Galvin to collect his percentage without risking the embarrassment of appearing in a courtroom impaired by drink. Kevin and Sally Doneghy (James Handy and Roxanne Hart) have sued to collect damages from a hospital after a botched anesthetic left Sally's sister in a vegetative state. The Doneghys have few resources and need the money for her long-term care. Kevin has the opportunity to take a better job in

Arizona, but without the legal compensation, they will have to stay in Boston and help with the sick woman's care.

A cash, out-of-court settlement, it seems, will suit everyone's best interests: the Doneghys as well as the doctors at St. Catherine Laboré's and the Archdiocese of Boston, which operates the hospital. Avoiding the negative publicity about this tragedy is worth the price, even if the doctors were not negligent, as they claim. Bishop Brophy (Edward Binns) wants to offer the check personally to the Doneghys' attorney as a sign of the Church's compassion for the family after this terrible accident.[26] All Galvin has to do is show up in the bishop's office and accept a check for $210,000, one-third of which he will be able to keep as his fee. Just to go through the motions, as though trying to prove to Concannon that he is still considering going to trial, he interviews a doctor who tells him it was negligence, not an accident. He visits the comatose woman in her grim hospital ward and takes Polaroid photos of her for his files. In a fine cinematic touch, Lumet adopts Galvin's point of view as he watches her image emerge on the film. Galvin's vision suddenly becomes clear as he sees her come into focus as a person and a victim. The price the archdiocese has put on her life seems far too low, and the thought of allowing the doctors and the Church to avoid responsibility irks him. Galvin decides to reject the offer despite the possibility that he and the Doneghys will lose everything if the jury decides against him.

The contest is not fair. Once engaged in battle, the Church's legal team, with its array of bright young associates and researchers, will stop at nothing to cover up the crime. Galvin's key witness, the doctor who first raised the question of criminal negligence, apparently changes (or was persuaded to change) his mind and leaves the country before the deposition, leaving Morrissey to speculate that "Concannon got to him." The judge (Milo O'Shea), ironically named Hoyle after the author of the book on fair play, is a crony of Concannon's and denies Galvin's request for a delay to allow him to track down his witness. During the trial, Hoyle consistently overrules Galvin's objections, disallows testimony, and at one point even joins in the cross-examination that discredits Galvin's only witness, a seventy-four-year-old anesthesiologist of mediocre training and experience, who, as it turns out, supports himself by testifying in malpractice suits. Galvin had found his name in a directory. The witness, Dr. Lionel Thompson (Joe Seneca), is African

American, and when he appears on the scene, Lumet has Morrissey make the stereotypical Irish comment: "At least he's not a Jew."

In a subplot sewn together of improbable coincidences, Concannon successfully plants an assistant on Galvin's team, the beautiful Laura Fischer (Charlotte Rampling), who insinuates her way into Galvin's personal life. Her job is to pass along information about Galvin's case that she gains during exchanges of pillow talk, which flows freely after several rounds of drinks, which she seems to enjoy, or need, as much as Galvin. Concannon has secured her cooperation in this sleazy mission by offering her his help in returning to legal practice after an unsuccessful marriage. Her ethical scruples, such as they are, threaten to surface as she grows in both respect and affection for Frank Galvin, but in the end, they don't deter her. She wants Concannon's check and a job.

Like Sean Casey in *Night Falls on Manhattan*, Galvin is forced to seek justice in the gray area of the law. Clearly desperate after the slick, beautifully coached testimony of Dr. Robert Towler (Wesley Addey), the physician who administered the anesthetic, Galvin rests his last hope on finding the admitting nurse, who has left Boston. The other nurses, like the New York police, have their own white wall of silence to protect their own, the hospital, and their jobs. Galvin, who has posed as "an old friend" of deceased strangers in the hope of getting a job, doesn't hesitate to continue violating ethical standards by claiming various identities as he and Morrissey work through the phone book searching for clues about the former nurse. Perhaps his own brush with disbarment and jail have given him a sense of cynicism about the fine points of the law. At the end, he gains key information by criminally breaking into a mailbox and stealing a phone bill that leads him to the elusive witness. His tactics work. Kaitlin Costello Price (Lindsay Crouse), the former admitting nurse, agrees to testify in court and to produce the altered document, which she has saved in case she had to defend her own innocence one day. In triumph, Galvin leads the witness through the events that led to the fatal procedure and the subsequent cover-up, but because of a technicality that Concannon's high-powered research team presents to the court, Hoyle instructs the jury to disallow Galvin's evidence and the nurse's testimony. Galvin is stunned. He cannot overcome this rejection of his last bit of evidence. In his summation, however, Galvin tells the jury to ignore Hoyle's instructions and follow their own intuitive path to justice, even though it strays from letter of the law.

The jury supports Galvin and the Doneghys. Even in victory, how-ever, Galvin has separated himself from his roots, and ultimately, at best he has fought to a tie. All his adult life, he wanted to be a successful lawyer, but by winning according to his own rules, he has set himself apart from the legal establishment (dominated in Boston by the likes of Hoyle and Concannon) and its client, the Archdiocese of Boston (as represented by Bishop Brophy). To emphasize Galvin's aloneness, Laura Fischer stands on the far side of the courthouse stairwell as he and Morrissey descend the main staircase to savor their victory. She may have some regrets, but she has no words of repentance, nor he of for-giveness. He merely glances up, sees her, and walks on. Lumet knows too much about life in the city to end his story of urban corruption with a movie cliché involving reconciliation. Later, Galvin sits in his cluttered office drinking coffee when the phone rings. Laura lies on a rumpled bed with an open whisky bottle on her night table. The phone rings and rings, but Galvin refuses to answer it. Perhaps at the end of his day of triumph he will find companionship only with the men in flannel shirts who gather in a neighborhood bar. He has chosen to be alone with his moral standards; Laura is condemned to remain alone with hers.

The legal establishment and the Church will go on, as they have for years, despite this temporary defeat. Lumet's Boston, like his New York, is simply too big, too powerful, to change. The best one can hope for is to avoid being ground down by it.

Other Examples

The Lower East Side has left its mark on virtually all of Lumet's work. The sense of ethnic community as a beleaguered minority preserving its own mores provides an overarching context. At the same time, an indi-vidual within that community struggles to achieve a personal identity within the group. The character cannot have solidarity and individual-ity at the same time. This is the typical Lumet conflict. It passes beyond the police department and criminal justice system to provide a portrait of life in contemporary, urbanized America, where individuals try to withstand the pressures of their institutions and the institutions take on a life of their own, more often malignant than benign.

The Hill (1965) exposes the brutality of the military prison system in North Africa during World War II. The camp guard Sergeant Williams (Ian Hendry) and Sergeant Wilson (Harry Andrews), who functions as commandant because of the incompetence of the officer in charge, believe their mission is to break the spirit of the prisoners and thus maintain discipline within the army. To this end, they punish those perceived as insubordinate by forcing them to climb repeatedly up a steep, man-made ramp of sand and gravel while dressed in battle gear with full packs. One soldier dies during the sadistic exercise. The others mutiny and demand the right to make a formal complaint. Before they can, the guards beat Warrant Officer Joe Roberts (Sean Connery) so badly that he is hospitalized. Afraid that this added act of brutality will make the complaint even more damaging to their careers and to the good order of the camp, Williams tries to murder Roberts in his hospital bed. The other prisoners come upon the scene and attack Williams, beating him to death. With his murder, the forces of repression are vindicated, and any reform of the prison system will be impossible. Those in power cannot let the rebels win. The army and prison discipline go on; the individuals prove transient and ultimately expendable.

In *Network* (1976), Lumet presents an unflattering portrait of the television industry as a corrupt and oppressive social institution. In this effort he was reunited with scriptwriter Paddy Chayefsky, a fellow veteran of the New York television during the Golden Age. In the film Max Schmacher (William Holden) represents the old guard in the newsroom. He is one of "Murrow's boys," the veterans of World War II who worked with the legendary Edward R. Murrow at CBS and pioneered the art of broadcast journalism. His personal standards clash with the larger institution of the Universal Broadcasting System, the fourth among the major networks, where survival comes from the barrel of the Nielsen ratings. Diana Christiansen (Faye Dunaway), the executive determined to crack the power of the big three, knows how to attract an audience and build revenue. Naturally, with her initial success, she becomes the darling of the corporate executives and a menace to the old-timers. Hard news, Schumacher style, will be replaced with a psychic offering prophecies of the future, a mad news analyst, Howard Beale (Peter Finch), who threatens to commit suicide on the air, and an audience participation show, oddly prophetic of contemporary "reality" programs, in which domestic Maoists will showcase their politically motivated robberies on videotape. The network decides to use the revolutionaries to get rid of Howard Beale as well—on air, of course. The Communications Corporation of America

(CAA), the conglomerate that owns UBS, is delighted with Christiansen's grand strategies, as long as they build ratings and ad revenue.

Max tries to cling to his life in television by beginning an affair with Diana, who might be a embodiment of television itself; she has no core, no capacity for human emotion. After leaving his wife, he moves in with Diana, but it won't work. "If I stay with you, I'll be destroyed," he says. He cannot save network news, but he might save himself, even if he has to live out his days alone, like Frank Galvin or Frank Serpico. Like New York itself, UBS, itself a mere cog in the relentless machinery of CAA, is too big to consider the well-being of individuals like Howard and Max. Max at least survives; Howard does not.

Daniel (1983) and *Running on Empty* (1988) stand as Lumet's tributes to leftist politics as he looks back in nostalgia while Ronald Reagan was leading the country steadfastly toward the right. Based on the novel by E. L. Doctorow, *Daniel* follows in large part the actual story of Julius and Ethel Rosenberg, executed in 1953 for giving secret information about American nuclear research to agents of the Soviet Union. The film adopts the point of view of their oldest son, Daniel Isaacson (Timothy Hutton), who as an adult pieces together childhood recollections and present-day detective work to try to understand his parents and the impact they made on the lives of him and his deeply disturbed sister Susan (Amanda Plummer). In his recollection, his parents, Paul and Rochelle (Mandy Patinkin and Lindsay Crouse), were enthusiastic social activists, cafeteria Communists in college, who were passionate about defending the rights of the working classes during the Depression, and who, like many of the Jewish old left, were seduced by utopian delusions about the Soviet Union.

Regardless of the degree of their treason, Lumet presents their antagonist, the state, as a pernicious power that sees the Isaacsons as subversive, as they proudly are. The film opens with a reflection on the various means the state uses to take the lives of its citizens, building to a final description of the horrors of the electric chair. Paul's mother required a second jolt before she died. In one of the flashbacks to the 1930s, trade unionists and students ride school buses upstate to attend a political rally, whose added attraction is a concert by Paul Robeson, the magnificent African American actor and singer, whose open commitment to the cause of communism effectively ended his career in the United States. The state police direct the buses down a country road, where the motorcade is assaulted by club-wielding goons protecting the American way of life. Like many a Lumet hero, Paul Isaacson has to find his own integrity within his politically committed family, which in turn must protect its own values in opposition to a regime it finds threatening to the working classes.

Running on Empty moves the story of the Isaacsons into a later generation of political radicals. Like Daniel Isaacson, the hero is caught in the crush of history and has to deal with the illegal activities of his parents. Danny Pope (River Phoenix) is the teenage son of Annie and Arthur Pope (Christine Lahti and Judd Hirsch), who as student radicals in the 1960s set off a bomb at an MIT laboratory that they suspected was being used for military research.[27] Unfortunately, a janitor was blinded in the explosion, and ever since, the Popes have been on the FBI's most wanted list. Survival by flight and disguise has become a way of life for the entire family. The factor of the Jewish identity does not enter into the story, since the Popes appear to be white-bread WASPs. Before her marriage, Annie was Ann Patterson, and after her notoriety, she became known to the press as the "Fugitive Deb." Their outsider status comes solely from their political beliefs. Annie and Arthur have adapted to the fugitive lifestyle; they work odd jobs for cash and gain help, mostly information, from their old network of friends in the "underground." Thanks to these tips and their own observations, they recognize the signs of impending danger, and through many years of experience, they have learned to pack their few belongings into the van within minutes and flee when they suspect the authorities may be closing in.

Although this family, just like an ethnic community, takes extraordinary means to survive within the larger hostile society, Danny has to survive within the family. He never planted a bomb, but he has to live with the consequences of his parents' criminality. Moving from Florida to New Jersey near the end of the school year and entering one more high school while once again concocting flimsy excuses for not having records from the previous school, he longs for a more conventional teenage life and for the opportunity to develop his remarkable musical talent. He approaches graduation, but college applications demand information about family history and resources. Because his family can divulge neither, he has all but given up on the idea of going to college. He also falls in love with Lorna Philips (Martha Plimpton), but he knows that he cannot presume having time to develop a lasting relationship.

Gus Winant (L. M. Kit Carson), a friend from the old days of the movement, appears with a small arsenal in the trunk of his car. Still fighting the radical wars of the 1960s, he plans a bank robbery to support the cause, as well as himself. The Popes recoil in horror at this reminder of their own violent past; unlike Gus, they have grown into mature, responsible adults, but the larger society will not forgive their criminal history. In the end, they must make a series of decisions. The robbery fails, and the authorities have gained evidence linking Gus to the Popes. Annie and Arthur have to flee once more, but they decide to leave Danny behind to begin a new life without his parents. Like so many Lumet heroes, Danny must create his own identity apart from the group that nourished him, but in so doing, he has separated himself irrevocably from his roots. At the end of the film, he faces his future quite alone, without the support of his family.

Critical Care (1997) moves Lumet's characteristic ethical coming-of-age story from criminal justice to the medical-care system. The familiar message appears in this film as a very, very dark comedy, with elements of funny but chilling fantasy. The search for personal integrity begins for Dr. Werner Ernst (James Spader) as he begins his third year of residency. Unlike Lumet's cops, lawyers, and political activists, Ernst could never be mistaken for a naive idealist. Regardless of what he might have written on his application to medical school, he sees his profession as a pathway to money and women. In Lumet's view of ethics, however, idealism is relative. In comparison to the other doctors, Ernst is a moral hero. Dr. Butz (Albert Brooks), chief of staff, suffers from alcoholic dementia, but he has enough grip on reality to prescribe expensive but useless procedures for patients to get as much money as he can from the insurance companies. His incompetence and greed startle even a self-possessed young hustler like Dr. Ernst. Butz's name, of course, suggests both "butt" and "putz," a Yiddish slang expression for penis.

Ernst jumps at the invitation to become an assistant to Dr. Hofstader (Philip Bosco), who directs a prestigious research facility, whose primary goal is to develop machines to replace the human contact between physician and patient. In stark contrast to the greed and mechanization stands Stella (Helen Mirren), the wise, compassionate, and tough nurse who oversees the intensive care unit. A survivor of radical surgery for her own breast cancer, she sees issues of life and death with a clarity denied the others. In this gleaming cathedral of high-tech medicine, one patient is kept alive because the hospital can make money by transplanting livers into him, which he promptly rejects. Another is caught between two daughters, one of whom wants him alive and the other dead, because a quirk in his will determines the heir according to the date of death. Butz sides with the first sister in keeping him alive, since he brings in $112,000 each month from the insurance company. Both patients clearly want to die, and they have visions of an afterlife that is not at all unpleasant.

Ernst is in the middle of these ethical crosscurrents. He allows himself to be seduced by one of the daughters (Kyra Sedgwick), who uses a videotaped record of their liaison to blackmail him into ending her father's life in time for her to get the inheritance for herself. The hospital, much like the one in *The Verdict,* will spare nothing to enhance its reputation and income, and the lawyers will gladly sacrifice Ernst if they have to. Much chastened by the experience with the would-be heiress that threatened to wreck his career, Ernst hits on a clever legal ploy that saves himself not only professionally but also morally. In doing so, he loses the romantic sister and undoubtedly the chance to continue his rise in the hospital's hierarchy. At the end, he is alone with his morals, while Drs. Butz and Hofstader, along with the rest of the hospital, keep doing what they have been doing. In a final scene, Stella points out that the two beds vacated by Ernst's two patients will soon be filled by other revenue-producing human beings. Butz, like District Attorney Quinn, will survive any charges made against him and will remain head of the ICU. Hofstader will continue his research to drain the last bit of humanity from the practice of medicine. Ernst can't change a thing.

Conclusion

A director with over forty films to his credit does not invite simple generalizations that neatly explain each of his works. The films cited provide a reasonable sampling of Sidney Lumet's ideas and, it is hoped, provide one more critical tool for understanding the artist. I hope to suggest that awareness of his New York roots can help scholars and fans alike gain a greater awareness of the unique character of much of his contribution and a greater appreciation of the consistency of his values over a long, productive career.

Sidney Lumet does not stand alone among American filmmakers in his fascination with ethical dilemmas. What does give his films a characteristic New York cast is the ethnic sensitivity rooted in the Jewish community of the Lower East Side. His characters work out their sense of personal integrity as members of a group, which in turn struggles to maintain its own identity, for good or ill, while withstanding enormous pressures from larger society. In Sidney Lumet's New York, everyone bears the traces of ethnic background, and these pervasive tribal associations shape the reactions and values of the characters.

When ethnic groups are not present at all, Lumet invests other institutions with the same dynamic as the urban clans. They have their own mores and fight to protect their way of doing business from outsiders on the one side and on the other side from any of their own who might betray the group ethos for personal reasons, however noble. They try to enforce conformity because any deviation from their norms threatens their very survival. The hero must make a decision—many decisions, in fact—about defining his own space within the community. (The masculine pronoun is appropriate; Lumet rarely places women at the center of his conflicts.) Often the decision leads to isolation. If he survives at all, a man without a clan becomes lonely and extremely vulnerable. For this reason, Lumet seldom provides a happy ending or even a neat conclusion.

As the world becomes more industrialized and urbanized, and as social institutions become more pervasive and intrusive, we all become endangered. Sidney Lumet provides a shrewd analysis of the human condition for all of us, whether or not we happen to live in New York.

Woody Allen

Filmography

Melinda and Melinda (2004)

Anything Else (2003)

Hollywood Ending (2002)

Curse of the Jade Scorpion, The (2001)

Small Time Crooks (2000)

Sweet and Lowdown (1999)

Celebrity (1998)

Deconstructing Harry (1997)

Everyone Says I Love You (1996)

Mighty Aphrodite (1995)

Bullets over Broadway (1994)

Manhattan Murder Mystery (1993)

Husbands and Wives (1992)

Shadows and Fog (1992)

Alice (1990)

Crimes and Misdemeanors (1989)

New York Stories (1989) (segment "Oedipus Wrecks")

Another Woman (1988)

September (1987)

Radio Days (1987)

Hannah and Her Sisters (1986)

Purple Rose of Cairo, The (1985)

Broadway Danny Rose (1984)

Zelig (1983)

Midsummer Night's Sex Comedy, A (1982)

Stardust Memories (1980)

Manhattan (1979)

Interiors (1978)

Annie Hall (1977)

Love and Death (1975)

Sleeper (1973)

*Everything You Always Wanted to Know About Sex * But Were Afraid to Ask* (1972)

Play It Again, Sam (1972)

Bananas (1971)

Take the Money and Run (1969)

Casino Royale (1967)

What's Up, Tiger Lily? (1966)

What's New, Pussycat (1965)

Flatbush
Woody Allen

Allan Stewart Konigsberg drew his initial breath of Brooklyn air on the first day of December in 1935. A social scientist would look at his birth certificate and dump him into the same demographic caldron as Sidney Lumet, born a few miles away into another Jewish family a mere eleven years earlier. A film critic would look at their films and conclude that they had been born on separate planets. Any native New Yorker, comparing biographical notes on the two artists, would immediately side with the film critics. In New York, as everyone knows, the melting pot is a slow cooker; the ingredients retain their own distinct flavor for a long time. As with Sidney Lumet, the category "New York Jewish filmmaker" makes no sense, because "New York" is too vast and amorphous a category to be useful in any exercise in classification, and the Jewish community embraces many distinct subgroups. The East River divides Brooklyn from the Lower East Side as surely as the Atlantic separates the shtetls of Russia from Ellis Island. "One of the longest journeys in the world is the journey from Brooklyn to Manhattan," writes Norman Podhoretz in *Making It,* as approvingly cited by Alexander Bloom in describing the young Jewish intellectual's sense of being an outsider when moving from the "provinces" to the center of New York cultural life.[1]

Although Woody Allen has lived in Manhattan for his entire adult life and for over forty years his films have portrayed life amid the skyscrapers and condominiums with the intimacy of a native chronicler, don't be misled. Despite the trappings of Manhattan urbanity, Woody Allen remains a native of Flatbush; he is not a New York filmmaker, but a Brooklyn filmmaker. He studies Manhattan with the eye of a long-term visiting anthropologist from a distant land. Anyone willing to entertain the plausibility of that minority opinion can gain a useful, critical insight into the workings of the mind of the artist and his perspective on New York City life.

The Death of Brooklyn

People living during Allen's childhood could surely remember, if only vaguely, the day in 1898 when Brooklyn ceased being an independent city and became part of Greater New York. Although always much larger in population than Manhattan, because of accident and zoning, it was destined to become a bedroom community—the biggest bedroom community in the nation.[2] The sign on the Brooklyn side of the Verazzano Bridge puts it well: "Welcome to the fourth largest city in America." Although skyscrapers sprouted like sunflowers across the East River, in Brooklyn, residential structures spread like crabgrass, close to the ground in ever thickening clusters, with the Williamsburg Bank Building as its solitary skyscraper, a clock-studded lighthouse amid the dunes of the westernmost tip of Long Island. Naturally enough, this ancillary status leads to a classic love-hate relationship with "New York," as Brooklynites continue to refer to Manhattan. (The Borough of Manhattan is coextensive with New York County, it is true, but this cannot explain their calling it "New York." Residents of the Borough of Brooklyn never refer to themselves as living in "Kings," an indication of Kings County, which is coextensive with the Borough of Brooklyn. One must conclude that the terminology has historical roots from the nineteenth century. New York was and remains another city, and in fact another world.)

This erosion of Brooklyn's identity accelerated during Woody Allen's student days. *The Brooklyn Eagle*, founded in 1841 and edited for several years by Walt Whitman, closed down in 1955. The shakedown in the local media during this period was spurred on by the rapid growth of local television, and of course all the studios as well as the surviving newspapers and radio stations were located in Manhattan. Two years later, Walter O'Malley, a name that lives in infamy in Brooklyn, took the Dodgers out of Ebbets Field on Flatbush Avenue and moved to the fleshpots of Chavez Ravine in Los Angeles. The blow to borough pride was catastrophic. Without a big-league baseball team, Brooklyn lost what little voice it had in a very noisy neighborhood. More than ever in the world's gazetteer, "New York" meant Manhattan only, and Brooklyn achieved recognition in the national psyche for little more than its mythical accent perpetuated in the movies by generations of gangsters and tough kids in the heterogeneous military units of World War II. The Dodgers' perfidious move to Los Angeles may be one more reason for Woody Allen's abiding dislike of California. The issue was personal as well as civic. Despite his movie persona as an awkward klutz, as a teenager Allen was a passable baseball player in the Police Athletic League and remains an avid sports fan to this day

Known as the Borough of Churches (a stunning discovery to those who know it only from gangster movies), Brooklyn has remained an archipelago of neighborhoods, each with the distinct characteristics of a small town. Unlike Manhattan, where the imposed regimental battalion of north-south, east-west streets marches lockstep from the East River to the Hudson, and northward from Fourteenth Street though Washington Heights and across the Harlem River and into the Bronx all the way to the borders of Yonkers (only Broadway dares to be diagonal, and then only as far as Columbus Circle at Fifty-ninth Street), the streets in Brooklyn form a kaleidoscope of fragmented patterns, each regular within its own boundaries, yet intersecting with other pieces of the puzzle at crazy-quilt angles. The street map reveals a network of old independent villages now fused into contiguous neighborhoods.

With a few exceptions, Brooklynites rarely travel between the villages of their home city. They go into a hole in the ground on the corner of their own neighborhood, take the subway, and go to "New York" for jobs, shopping, restaurants, theater—even for visits to the doctor. In Woody Allen's days in Brooklyn, one could still shop in the several department stores clustered on Fulton Street—Loeser's, Mays, Browning-King, Namm's or "A & S's" (a native will never say "A & S" and never, ever say "Abraham and Strauss")—or see a headliner at the Brooklyn Paramount, but even in the early 1950s, signs of decline were clear. All the big downtown movie palaces, as well as most of the neighborhood theaters, closed after television aerials sprouted on the rooftops of the brownstones. Coney Island, the popular beach and amusement park, had lost its glitter after the war. Old-timers say it never recovered from the fire at Luna Park in August 1944, and they would agree that George Tilyou's Steeplechase Park was bush league in comparison. After Robert Moses's highway program, people who had a car preferred to ride out to "Jones's Beach" on the "Island," scarcely aware that Brooklyn too was on Long Island. Of course, in Woody Allen's time, Brooklyn Heights, Boerum Hill, Cobble Hill, and DUMBO (Down Under the Manhattan Bridge Overpass), sections that cling to the shore of the East River with the Manhattan skyline always in sight, had not yet been gentrified into cosmopolitan urban refuges for yuppies (young urban professionals) and dinks (double income, no kids) fleeing from outrageous rents in Manhattan. The newly trendy areas are not traditional Brooklyn neighborhoods as much as slightly less expensive extensions of Greenwich Village, Tribeca, and SoHo on the other side. Even Park Slope has witnessed the migration of cops and teachers to the "Island" as their homes are condominiumized for midlevel investment bankers, stockbrokers, and publishing executives.

This lack of contact between neighborhoods contributed to the small-town insularity of each individual enclave in the 1950s. Most Brooklynites know their immediate neighborhood and "New York." A glance at a subway map explains this peculiar phenomenon. The various lines converge on Manhattan like spokes on a wheel. To go from one section of Brooklyn to another, one must travel toward New York, perhaps as far at the Atlantic Avenue/Pacific Street/Long Island Railroad stop in downtown Brooklyn or even across the Manhattan Bridge to Union Square in New York, change trains, and travel back into another section of Brooklyn. Public transportation, built to move a huge workforce between the two boroughs, virtually assures the inaccessibility of one section of Brooklyn to another, as though one must journey along the two sides of a pizza slice in order to span the distance of the crust. In Sidney Lumet's Lower East Side, one could move routinely from one ethnic and economic universe to another during an ordinary day's business. Allen's Brooklyn had no such compressed diversity. One lived on a particular block, in a particular neighborhood, with people of similar background, and commuted to and from their small-town enclave to the "City," another world on the other side of the river.[3] Paradoxically, the biggest borough featured the smallest towns.

Woody Allen's childhood world was flavored by his Jewish environment, but one that had advanced one step beyond the Lower East Side of Sidney Lumet. The Midwood area of the Flatbush section of Brooklyn was resolutely middle class, populated by people who had already reached a degree of assimilation into the American context. The conditions were crowded because of the Depression and the housing shortage during the war, but it was an area of small, locally owned shops and apartment houses on the avenues and a mix of private and attached houses on tree-lined side streets. One would scarcely use the words *tenement, teeming, slum,* or *ghetto* in connection with Midwood. Unlike Lumet's Lower East Side, it had nothing to compare with the overwhelming poverty of the Bowery on one side and the ostentatious symbols of capitalism around Wall Street on the other. Such an environment of economic disparity provided a hothouse for leftist political sympathies, like Lumet's. Brooklyn, of course, had its pockets of unspeakable poverty, its Murder Incorporated, gang wars, racial strife, and waterfront crime, but these existed in areas remote and relatively inaccessible to someone from Midwood. These were headlines and photos in the *Daily News,* not reality. In a world where everyone had enough and no one had too much, a sense of outrage at the inequities of the social order would not be a part of the intellectual landscape. Radical socialists and workers did not gather in storefronts to plan strikes or protest police brutality as they might in lower Manhattan. As a creature of relatively comfortable circumstances, Allen has been criticized for his reluctance to deal with socioeconomic issues in his films.[4] Poverty, racial tensions, drugs, and violent crime do not exist, even as a matter of genteel concern, for the conventionally liberal professionals that populate his films. In an early film, *Bananas* (1971), Allen even provides a scathing satire on "cafeteria Communists" and social activists of the City University system, people who would be treated with enormous sympathy by Sidney Lumet in *Running on Empty* and *Daniel.*

Allen's family had a generation's head start on Lumet's, and as a group, they were more comfortably settled into the middle class by the time young Allan became aware of his circumstances. Both his parents were born into Yiddish-speaking families on the Lower East Side.[5] His mother's family, the Cherrys, came from Vienna and the Konigsbergs from Russia, both around the turn of the century. The Cherrys owned a small luncheonette, candy, and newspaper store in the neighborhood and were known as "observant," a factor that explains her young Allan's regular attendance at Hebrew school. Isaac Konigsberg, Allan's grandfather, fulfilled every immigrant's dream. A successful salesman at first, later in life he eventually owned a fleet of taxicabs and several movie theaters in Brooklyn. He had a taste for fine clothes, traveled extensively, and had a box at the Metropolitan Opera. His son Martin, Woody Allen's father, grew up in comfortable surroundings with every expectation of the good life in his new home in Brooklyn. Then came the Depression in 1929, and the dream evaporated. The Konigsbergs, father and son, got by on Isaac's butter-and-eggs business in Brooklyn and on Martin's odd jobs and business ventures, some of which operated on the margins of the law. In tough times they drove taxis, an embarrassment poignantly portrayed in *Radio Days* when the young Joe (Seth Green), the Woody Allen surrogate, who was always curious about his father's occupation, accidentally discovers him behind the wheel of a cab. The Cherrys had also left the Lower East Side, but they went north to the Bronx. After their marriage, Martin Konigsberg and Netty Cherry set up their household in Brooklyn.

The neighborhood was overwhelmingly Jewish, to the extent that no one thought of being Jewish as something extraordinary, any more than an African living in an inland rural village would be concerned about being black.[6] Because the neighborhoods were self-contained and isolated, ethnic or religious groups were not driven to define themselves as different from some other group, nor did they feel obliged to engage in turf wars, subtle or violent, in order to define their space. On the Lower East Side, by contrast, where many different immigrant groups squeeze themselves into tiny plots of land within highly limited borders, a group naturally finds its identity in being different from the others. It's a world of us and them, and defending one's heritage becomes crucially important. At times, the differences lead to friction and occasionally to conflict, especially as ethnic boundaries shift through time. Having grown up in such an atmosphere, Sidney Lumet seems obsessed by race and ethnicity. A child of Flatbush, Allen seems oblivious to it.

For Allen, the issue of ethnic tension occasionally percolates under the surface as an unspoken complication, but only rarely does it function as a major catalyst of the plot or motivation of the character. What constitutes "major catalyst" remains open to question because many of Allen's characterizations are self-consciously Jewish and often refer to their origins as contributing to their status within the narrative. Ethnic identity undoubtedly adds texture to the characters in many of his films, but their dilemmas are not dependent on it. By contrast, as a rare exception to the rule, in *Shadows and Fog* (1992), Max Kleinman (Woody Allen) flees from the authorities and from roving gangs of thugs in an unnamed city in prewar central Europe. His plight, both frightening and comic, resonates with the terror experienced by Jews during this period, and the parallel to the Nazi terror is inescapable. Kleinman may well be victimized precisely because he his Jewish, and if he were not Jewish, there would be no story. In most of the other films, I would maintain, Allen mines the rich heritage of Jewish comedy and explores Jewish urban culture, but without the self-conscious, intergroup tensions that mark much of Lumet's work. For Woody Allen, Latinos, Italians, African Americans, or South Asians do not function as adversaries or rivals simply because in his universe they do not exist.

Sidney Lumet's childhood on the Lower East Side could be considered a bit exotic—a father acting in Yiddish theater and radio, the Professional Children's School, an early career on the stage—but Allen's was extraordinary in its ordinariness. The Konigsbergs struggled through the Depression, as did many working-class families. His mother worked as a bookkeeper, often leaving young Allan with relatives or with sitters of varied levels of competence. His parents argued, most often about money, but again, that would not be uncommon for a Depression-era family. Although his parents were outgoing and demonstrative, Allan was quiet and became a bit of a loner as a child. As family fortunes deteriorated and the Konigsbergs shared apartments with various relatives, Allan attended several different public schools and Hebrew schools. He attributes his solitary childhood to his constantly finding himself the new kid in school and having to make new friends as the outsider. To fill his lonely hours, he developed an interest in magic tricks and, of course, the movies, which he attended several times a week. His sister, Hetty Aronson, eight years his junior and trained in dealing with emotionally disturbed children, maintains that he was extraordinarily talented as a child and felt that he simply did not fit in. At the same time, he played organized baseball in the Police Athletic League, so he could not be called pathologically withdrawn.

Whether extraordinary or not, his talents did attract attention. Allan was selected to enroll in a program for gifted children at Hunter College, but his mother did not want to send him away to Manhattan, which seemed a great distance from home for a child. For a Brooklynite, it must be recalled, New York is another city. Instead, he attended PS 99 in the neighborhood and resented the blue-haired, mainly Irish, teachers who provided "the zenith of discipline and regimentation: a humorless, educationless experience provided by nasty and unpleasant teachers."[7] Later, he went to Midwood High School, again in the neighborhood, one of the very fine city high schools of the time. He recalls being an indifferent student with a flair for writing. He had few friends. In hindsight, he remembers it as a rather unhappy time in his life. "Don't talk to me about that place," he reportedly said to an old classmate. "I hated everything about that period."[8] During these years he sought escape from his mundane world by regular attendance at the several local movie houses near his home, seeing all the then current, now classic, films in breathtaking black and white.

Eric Lax, Allen's biographer, records a conversation in which Allen reflects on his childhood in terms of the Brooklyn-Manhattan antipathy. After returning to Manhattan from a nostalgia tour through the old neighborhood, Allen comments: "My biggest regret in retrospect is that my parents didn't live in Manhattan."[9] He continues the reflection: "It's such a regret of mine. They thought they were doing the right thing and probably thought they couldn't afford to move. In a certain sense, given who my parents were and how much money they had, it was fine to live in Brooklyn. But the truth is, if they were a little more enlightened, I would have grown up in Manhattan in the late thirties and forties. I would have loved that." His regret at having grown up on the wrong side of the East River mixes with an endemic sense of Brooklyn inferiority and reaches near resentment directed toward his parents for their lack of "enlightenment." Again, Norman Podhoretz gives voice to young Jewish artists' desire to rise above their background: "I was never aware . . . how inextricably my 'noblest' ambitions were tied to the vulgar desire to rise above the class into which I was born."[10] Allen has been rising above Brooklyn all his life.

Crossing the East River

If Woody Allen has negative recollections of Brooklyn, what was this Manhattan that the adult remembers from his childhood years? This much can be said with some confidence: It certainly stood several paces from reality. Lax calls Allan Konigsberg's imaginary re-creation of New York simply "the wonderland across the river." Allen recalls his first trip to Times Square with his father when he was six. He was captivated by the astounding concentration of movie houses showing first-run films, although in recounting the story as an adult, he attributes a highly unlikely level of precocity and movie sophistication to a first-grader. At any rate, this is how the adult filmmaker reconstructs his childhood, and for an artist, imagination and memory are far more significant that actuality. What's more, he recalls, he could see in real life the famous restaurants and buildings he had seen in the movies. He imagined them as teeming with gangsters and beautiful women from the stage. Even if the years have distorted his recollections, what he describes is the classic case of Baudrillard's tourist who becomes enchanted at the realization that real New York looked just like the movies. For the next fifty years, Allen has tried to re-create the Manhattan of his childhood imagination, which in turn was shaped by the movies. The mutual dependence continues to this day, much like the facing mirrors in the climactic scene of *Citizen Kane* (Welles, 1941) that reflect the image of Charles Foster Kane back upon itself in infinite regression so that the reality becomes lost in the succession of images. For the mature Woody Allen, the enchantment with the dream has never faded. In a lengthy interview with Richard Schickel, he recalls, "And the minute I saw [Times Square], you know, all that I ever wanted to do was live in Manhattan and work in Manhattan. I couldn't get enough of it."[11] He continues: "And to this day I feel the same way about it."

The sad fact is that the New York of Woody Allen's memories, as well as the New York of his movies, never existed, then or now. Very soon after leaving Brooklyn and after a short stay as a television writer in Los Angeles, he established himself in Manhattan as a very successful young man with the financial resources to live where and how he chose. He could afford the comfortable enclaves of the city while avoiding the rest. In effect, by this time he had the means to make his childhood dream city a reality. As a result, his New York has no crime in the streets, no poverty, no slums or crack houses, no racial tension or gang wars; people never go hungry, never have noisy children, barking dogs, or loud radios; they never use heroin, sleep on ventilation grates, or even ride crowded subways to boring jobs they hate. His New York is populated by affluent, refined, well-educated Jews and WASPs but has little room for other identifiable ethnic groups, for working people, or for the severely impoverished. Chinatown, Hell's Kitchen, Little Italy, and Spanish Harlem don't exist. If he deals with people who are not up to his standards, he locates them in New Jersey (*Broadway Danny Rose, Small Time Crooks, Purple Rose of Cairo*) or in Brooklyn (*Radio Days* or *Annie Hall* in his two nostalgic trips back to his childhood). The exceptions to this sanitized version of the City are rare. The Italian gangsters in *Bullets over Broadway,* the Chinese cameraman in *Hollywood Ending,* the Chinese herbalist in *Alice,* or even the prostitute and porn queen (Mira Sorvino) in *Mighty Aphrodite* are stock comic characters from other movies, not from New York life. They function as props and foils for the central figures, who are Allen-style Manhattanites.

For Woody Allen, a George Gershwin score plays in the background continually, as it does in the opening sequence of *Manhattan.* Witty people from publishing or academia or the arts spend more time in tastefully furnished apartments and chic restaurants than at their jobs, and they rarely worry about paying their bills at the end of the month. In Manhattan, no one grows old or gets sick or has to share a flat with impossible in-laws or failing grandparents, as they did in the Brooklyn of *Radio Days.* People may lose jobs for a while, but the effects on their lifestyle are minimal, nothing like the Depression. No one goes to a social club or a blue-collar tavern for a beer after work, or to church or temple, except for an occasional wedding or funeral. No one rides the subway; for Allen, living in Manhattan involves urban combat no more serious than competition for taxicabs, which in fact most native New Yorkers cannot afford. Most important, no one has a neighborhood. To live in Woody Allen's version of Manhattan is to be freed from the ordinary cares of human existence, like shopping for groceries or doing laundry. An Uptown address makes one cosmopolitan, self-sufficient, unrooted, and uncommitted to any cause or community. Relationships, even within marriage, tend to be transitory, and they end once they serve their purpose. In these impersonal apartment houses, one rarely has neighbors, either as friends or adversaries. (In *Manhattan Murder Mystery,* the friendly neighbors soon provide grist for the sleuthing couple next door.) In short, Manhattan is everything Brooklyn is not. Most important for Woody Allen, being in Manhattan means not being in Brooklyn. This is not New York; this is a fantasy fashioned by someone on a tourist visa from Flatbush.

Unfortunately, as Dorothy discovered after her visit to Oz, once the dream ends, there's still Kansas. Likewise, the six-year-old Allan Konigsberg learned that after he gaped at the bright lights of Times Square, he had to take the IRT back to Flatbush, where he belonged. As an adult, he has been able to reconstruct and inhabit the Oz of elegant restaurants, beautiful women, and courtside seats at Knicks games in the Garden, but even after his legendary success at turning himself into a New Yorker, if his films are any indication, he continues to live in this world as a resident alien. As the kid from Brooklyn, he feels as though he really doesn't belong by birthright. He projects that dislocation on his central characters. As artists and lovers they are strivers, constantly looking over their shoulders lest someone identify them as impostors, pretenders, or arrivistes. As a result, like Dorothy, his characters put up a brave front and wear the ruby slippers to create the illusion that they really fit in to this magical realm, but at heart they remain uncomfortable around the witches, Munchkins, and Emerald Palaces of Manhattan.

A Comedy of Displacement

Those two-way subway rides between Brooklyn and Manhattan of young Allan Konigsberg, tourist and movie fan, I would submit, provide yet one more nuance to a critical understanding of the mature Woody Allen, resident and filmmaker. Most of his critics have agreed for years that his central comic figure, recycled in many guises, is the insecure, neurotic outsider who feels misplaced, misunderstood, and misused in contemporary society. Because displacements of various kinds underlie almost all comedy, from sophisticated satire to clownish slapstick, it often helps to examine the modes and sources of the disjuncture between the comedian and his or her larger world. In Allen, the motifs set in the comedies, with the bungling outsider, will carry through even to his more serious films with notable consistency. Judah Rosenthal (Martin Landau), for example, in *Crimes and Misdemeanors,* is a prosperous Manhattan ophthalmologist who arranges to have his mistress murdered. Suffering a momentary pang of conscience, he returns to his childhood home in Brooklyn in search of some moral compass. He realizes that he has become no better than his brother Jack (Jerry Orbach), now a professional criminal. Throughout the film, Rosenthal struggles with this dual identity, a respected New York philanthropist and a Brooklyn thug.

Perhaps a comparison with Charlie Chaplin, another notorious comic misfit, could be useful at this point. Like Chaplin, Allen's characters generally embody a shopping list of fragilities, but Allen's style of fragility makes him quite different from Chaplin. The Tramp's ill-fitting costume visually suggests that he does not fit into urban society. He dons the tattered remnants of formal wear: derby, walking stick, cutaway coat, and striped pants, the attire of a pretender who would like to mingle with men who dress formally as they dine at the club. But clearly the shabbiness of the outfit marks him as a hobo, not a prosperous tycoon. He suffers humiliation for his "difference" and usually accepts his degradation with comic politeness, but on occasion, he erupts in bursts of aggressive behavior to assert his individuality and dignity. When he has been pushed beyond his limits of endurance, he kicks his tormentors in the seat of the pants, just as they have kicked him.

Allen's misfits deal with adversity with greater degrees of subtlety. His characters appear on the surface to fit in perfectly. They dress in regulation Manhattan L. L. Bean casuals; they hold good professional-level jobs, have witty friends, and dine at fashionable but not extravagant restaurants. Although Chaplin fights back against external adversaries, Allen's characters surrender without a struggle. They allow themselves to be crushed because more often than not, the imagined enemies remain polite but attack the depths of the psyche, which turns out to be their greatest weakness. For Allen's heroes, the vulnerability is internal. This leads to a key difference. Chaplin reacts to his exclusion from desired relationships with hostility directed outward. He wants desperately to belong and reacts violently when others reject him. The Charlie character may require restraints, but not psychoanalysis. Allen, however, directs his hostilities inward. He becomes his own antagonist.

The Allen character tries to cope with life and desperately wants to fulfill his dream of the good life by finding the perfect companion and the perfect job. Quite often he is successful in attaining these goals, at least for a time, but when he does, he finds that they inevitably fail to bring lasting happiness. He accepts defeat as one who really never deserves success, or, to put it more precisely, as one who does not deserve to live among the successful. He belongs back in Brooklyn and has to suffer for thinking he could make it in Manhattan. Chaplin lashes out at others for his defeat; Allen lashes out at himself.

The tragic element of their roles enters in at different times. As a clown in a clown's costume, Chaplin rarely meets with success, even on a temporary basis. No one, not even Charlie himself, really expects the clown to win the girl or become an accepted leader in society. The absurdity of the quest underlies the Tramp's comedy. In contrast, for Allen's characters, the goals stand maddeningly within reach. A bright, talented man holds achievement in his hands, but he can never savor the rewards of his accomplishment for long. He establishes a perfect relationship, but then the chemistry shifts; his loved one suddenly moves on, or he tires of her and moves on himself. The outcome of his labors never lives up to expectations. Chaplin's tragicomedy arises from his never catching a break; he is the outsider whose dreams of acceptance seem preposterous and doomed from the outset. Allen's characters are generally accepted for their talents, but then they sabotage their own standing and find themselves on the outside. Spiritually undefeated, Chaplin marches on with his bizarre life, ever striving and hoping for a better future; psychologically crushed, Allen acquiesces in the present. He is what he is, gets what he deserves, and nothing will change.

Although critics agree on the what (the comic outsider theme), they continue to offer various explanations of the why. Each theory holds a fragment of truth; none explains it totally. As a sampling of critical opinions, Nancy Pogol situates Woody Allen in the tradition of "the little man" set upon by modern society, and she stresses his continuity with the silent movie greats Charlie Chaplin and Buster Keaton.[12] Annette Wernblad adds a specifically Jewish note by placing Allen in the tradition of the stock comic figure, the schlemiel, a much put-upon loser, that resurfaces in various forms in the fiction of American Jewish authors.[13] In an earlier study, I even went beyond Jewish cultural roots to trace a relationship between Allen's view of the world and the stories of the Hebrew Bible, with God's continually warning the Israelites through the prophets that they were not living up to God's high expectations for them.[14] Peter J. Bailey approaches the theme by looking at Allen as an artist whose life has developed in a kind of symbiotic relationship to the films Allen saw as a youngster and the films he now makes as an adult.[15] Bailey characterizes Allen's heroes as "not fully at ease," and he explains that in the tradition of Jewish comedy, he reacts to this poor fit with society by his stream of one-liners.[16] All of these explanations add something for an appreciation of what is behind the filmmaker's angst. So, I maintain, does the commute from Brooklyn, which can be traced through a cross section of Allen's films.

Two Early Comedies

With *Bananas* (1971) and *Sleeper* (1973) Woody Allen began to establish himself as a major filmmaker. In these he turned to original material spun out of his own mind, while the earlier ventures were collaborative and derivative.[17] He was a writer for *What's New, Pussycat,* directed by Clive Donner in 1965. He wrote the script and directed the English version of *What's Up, Tiger Lily?* (1966), a film originally shot as a spy thriller in Japanese and dubbed with highly improbable Allenesque dialogue that seems to have very little relationship to the original.[18] *Don't Drink the Water* (1969) was originally written for the stage by Woody Allen but was rewritten for the screen by Harvey Bullock and R. S. Allen and directed by Howard Morris. With *Take the Money and Run* (1969), Allen made the breakthrough as a filmmaker in control of his work. He wrote, directed, and starred, but, disappointed with reactions from test audiences for Allen's original version, Palomar-ABC films called in veteran editor Ralph Rosenblum to recut the material into a form they could distribute. In quasi-documentary form, the film spoofs the classic gangster films in a style that might be a clever television parody, a genre that easily lends itself to mockery. In this film, the comic effect depends clearly on familiarity with earlier films and television documentaries.

In the process of making *Bananas* and *Sleeper* Allen finds his own voice. Although the earlier films seem like experiments, these later efforts have the look and feel of authentic Woody Allen films, and they set several of the themes that will preoccupy him for the next forty years. Both are comedies of displacement, with the central character, played by Allen, finding himself a helpless alien in a distant land, where his life is threatened. The comic tension arises from a conflict the character experiences. He desperately wants to succeed with some improbable but grandiose project in the foreign territory with its strange customs and so win the affection of his love interest. At the same time he longs to return to his more familiar and presumably safer native environment. Adventure, success, and glory present themselves in the alien land, but the character realizes that he doesn't belong there and seems destined to fail because of his ineptitude. If he is discovered as an impostor, the consequences could be dire. Going home assures safety, but it also represents defeat. Once home, he will have security but an impossibly dull life. These films then recycle the conflicted feelings of the Brooklyn boy trying to make it in New York.

The point need not be elevated to psychoanalytic status. Clearly, Woody Allen the artist *has* made it in New York and was a successful author for the *New Yorker,* stand-up comedian, and television writer by the time he made these early films. He had every reason to feel secure in his position among the famous and near-famous of show business. But he never really fit in, at least to the extent that he never bought the complete package of celebrity, a cultural phenomenon he examines in some detail in two later films, *Celebrity* and *Deconstructing Harry.* His need for privacy in a tabloid world soon developed into a reputation for being "eccentric" or a "loner." As one who had made the passage across the Brooklyn Bridge and established a successful beachhead in Manhattan, he was able to perceive and develop the comic potential of the displacement he experienced in his own life and was able to re-create in his characters.

Bananas features multiple levels of displacement. The hero, Fielding Mellish (Woody Allen), has a job as a products tester. In the opening sequence, he demonstrates the Execuciser, an executive desk rigged with exercise equipment, so that the busy corporate manager can maintain a fitness routine without leaving his work station. The machine goes berserk, much like Chaplin's feeding machine in *Modern Times,* and bombards Fielding with basketballs faster than he can toss them into the attached hoop. Fielding admits to coworkers that this is the wrong job for him because machines hate him. Spurned by a date, he tries the receptionist, who has a reputation for generous hospitality. She rejects his advances, explaining that she plans to spend the evening watching pornographic films with friends. Professionally and socially, Fielding clearly does not belong in this company.

Spurned in romance, Fielding stops to buy an adult magazine, but an older woman's accusing glance puts him ill at ease. He tries to be blasé, as though buying pornographic magazines were a commonplace event for urban sophisticates, but clearly, he is uncomfortable with his purchase, and when the cashier calls attention to his title, *Orgasm,* he becomes visibly flustered. Isolated in the office and humiliated at the newsstand, Fielding goes home by subway to an unspecified destination. He takes the IRT, which threads its way through all boroughs except Staten Island. His home could be Brooklyn, but in any event, he lives at some distance from the commercial district in which he works. At home he settles into a comfortable routine, like wrestling with a frozen TV dinner that repeatedly slips from his hands and slides across the kitchen floor. The trip from one universe to the other becomes itself a perilous journey when young thugs, including a very boyish-looking Sylvester Stallone, board the train and terrorize the passengers.

His dinner is interrupted when Nancy (Louise Lasser, the second Mrs. Allen) knocks on the door with a petition in support of the rebels in San Marcos. Because she is a philosophy major from City College, Fielding tries to impress her with pretentious but absolutely uninformed comments about Kierkegaard. They agree that he is Danish, but he contends that the Vatican has a branch office in Denmark, which justifies his assertion that he once visited Kierkegaard's homeland. Clearly, he appears out of place in both locations as well as in the conversation. He claims to have experience of City College from eating in the cafeteria once, where he caught trichinosis. The disease comes from eating undercooked pork, which would be a sign of further displacement for an identifiably Jewish character.

In pursuit of a romance of opportunity, Fielding joins her in various protest marches, but she recognizes his intellectual and emotional immaturity, and in a roundabout conversation in Riverside Park, she announces the end of their relationship. Fielding furthers his plans by traveling beyond the alien world of campus radicalism to San Marcos, where he can participate in the revolution himself. He tells his parents of his plans in an operating room as they perform surgery on a conscious patient. In street clothes, he is visibly a misfit in the hospital. Doting parents that they are, they still hope that he will one day follow them into a career in medicine, even though he never went to college. To keep his interest alive, they encourage him to complete the operation. He goes through the motions, but he doesn't belong there.

In San Marcos his dislocation reaches its outermost limit. Before he can make contact with the rebels, the president invites him to dine at the palace, where a series of stock dinner table gaffes shows that Fielding has little experience with formal dining. The president's advisers plan to have him killed by rebels so that they can get aid from the United States to help them put down a rebellion that threatens American citizens. The dictator's army proves incompetent, and Fielding falls prisoner to the rebels.

At the rebel camp, he proves equally incompetent in camouflage, weaponry, and calisthenics. He gags at an army meal of rice and lizard, but when sent to seize supplies, he talks to the counterman at a cantina as though he were ordering at a delicatessen on the West Side: sandwiches on whole wheat with mayo and with slaw on the side. His ardor for the beautiful Yolanda (Navidad Abascal) cools appreciably when he discovers that in the revolutionary manner, she does not remove her paratrooper boots during lovemaking.

His imposture reaches its climax when a revolution within the revolution replaces its apparently insane leader with Fielding, who plays the part of a revolutionary by wearing fatigues and an absurdly false red beard that suggests Fidel Castro. Traveling to New York to enlist aid for the new republic, he addresses a diplomatic dinner with outrageously inappropriate off-color jokes. Even as head of state, he does not fit in. The FBI uncovers the plot, and during his trial, J. Edgar Hoover, appearing as a large black woman, and the prosecution accuse him of being a New York, Jewish, intellectual crackpot. Miss America denounces him for having ideas that are too different from ours. Of course, he is convicted for daring to be different and moving beyond his allotted state in life. The judge suspends the fifteen-year sentence on the condition that Fielding never move into his neighborhood.

All is not lost, however. He meets Nancy in an elevator. Captivated by the idea of Latin American revolutionaries, she cannot see through the absurd disguise. Seduction offers little challenge, even to one of Fielding's social ineptitude. Nancy echoes Fielding, down to the red hair and stammering speech. Their presence together, in bed in New York, indicates that Fielding has come home. After the trial, they renew their relationship. In a mock interview, staged to suggest a postfight show on a sports show on television, Howard Cosell, the legendary sportscaster, asks the couple about their encounter as though they were prizefighters rather than lovers. Nancy confides that her opponent was all right, but nothing special. After his adventures, Fielding has returned to his routine, at home with someone much like himself. Yolanda and San Marcos will soon become fading memories. After a tour of fantasy to San Marcos (a Manhattan of the imagination), he finds himself back in Brooklyn.

Sleeper involves even more extensive travel, not only through space, but through time as well. It opens on pure yellow screen, and as the camera pulls back, it reveals a futuristic fantasy city, complete with silent electric cars and molded architecture. It is a child's comic-book version of a dreamworld, echoing, perhaps, the fantasies of a young boy from Brooklyn as he imagines an ideal, sophisticated utopia across the river. As Miles Monroe (Woody Allen) discovers, the beautiful, sleek buildings and high-tech modernism can be deceiving. As he gets to know it, this sanitized dreamworld somewhere in the Western Sector, in the year 2173, becomes a nightmare. Once more, as a visitor he finds himself not only displaced in an alien land but menaced by enemies who try to rearrange his mind, and failing that, will not hesitate to kill him.

Miles, part-time clarinet player and proprietor of the Happy Carrot health food store on Bleecker Street in Lower Manhattan, had gone into St. Vincent's Hospital in the Village for a routine operation for an ulcer. Something went wrong, and he did not survive. He was cryogenically frozen, and two hundred years later, he finds himself thawed by scientists in their laboratory in a police state even more repressive than San Marcos. Like Frankenstein's creation, he has to adjust to his new environment, and in the process, he discovers that despite its appearances of an advanced civilization, under the surface, his new world is scarcely a congenial environment. Before he even leaves the laboratory, he finds he cannot speak or walk without help. He does little better with a motorized wheelchair, with which he runs over the feet of the scientists and the police, who come to investigate rumors of an "alien." With his oily, disheveled hair, signature dark-rimmed glasses, and ill-fitting hospital pajamas, he is clearly an alien in a world of the impeccably groomed and tailored.

To escape the authorities, Miles impersonates a domestic robot and is delivered to the futuristic home of Luna (Diane Keaton). His nonhuman status allows him to observe close up the life in his new environment as a participant observer. He is in this world, but not of it. In fact, Miles must surrender his real identity in order to be admitted to their company. Luna prepares for her cocktail party wearing a green mud pack on her face that makes her look even more robotic than he, with his white metallic makeup. Guests arrive. They are the beautiful people, with perfectly sculptured bodies and chic clothes, but the level of inanity in their chitchat surpasses the most stultifying, pretentious conversation at any arty Manhattan soiree. The beautiful people lounge on cushions rubbing a metal orb that produces the effects of marijuana. Inane is bad; inane and stoned is insufferable. Occasionally couples absent themselves for a moment of recreational sex in the Orgasmatron, a cylindrical booth that provides satisfaction without the bother of personal relationship. Later, as romance blossoms between Miles and Luna, he realizes that he prefers a more natural, old-fashioned version of sex. Luna recites her poetry to impress a potential partner, but she has the sequence of caterpillar and butterfly backward. When he points out the mistake, she throws a tantrum. Luna and partygoers consider themselves fascinating; Miles the Robot knows otherwise. They are the robots; he is alive. They are the sleepers; he is awake.

Food provides a recurring motif of alienation, just as it did in *Bananas*. With his experience in the health food store, Miles has his own ideas about sensible nutrition. He doesn't even recognize the sticky blue paste the scientists offer him as a first meal after his resuscitation. In Luna's kitchen, as he tries to carry off his impersonation of a domestic robot, Miles prepares what he thinks is instant pudding, but the bloblike concoction swells to immense proportions like an enormous inflatable rubber life raft. When he and Luna escape into the woods, he finds a futuristic farm, with a "banana the size of a canoe," equally monstrous celery stalks, and a chicken that may be ten feet tall. Miles is captured and the authorities reprogram his brain, but when Luna (now converted into a rebel) and the guerrilla leader Erno (John Beck) try to restore him to his old self, they reenact a family dinner, complete with parents quarreling with heavy Yiddish accents. As a sign of Luna's conversion to the rebel camp, she chews on a piece of raw meat thrown on the ground as though she were an animal in a zoo. Miles stands between extremes, clearly uncomfortable with both the trendy space-age cuisine of the socialites and the feral trough of the self-proclaimed revolutionaries.

Scientific achievements in the new world prove to be anything but improvements. The cars run without noise or pollution, but when Miles needs one to escape, he uses a 200-year-old Volkswagen, which springs to life at the first touch of the ignition. The police use an electronic bazooka against him, but the contraption always misfires. When the authorities try to reprogram him with a series of electrodes bristling from a metal helmet, they miscalculate and he becomes Miss Montana in a Miss America pageant. Two robots with Yiddish accents use an electronic device to take Miles's measurements for a new suit, but the results are catastrophic, a disgrace to the memory of generations of Jewish tailors that built the garment industry in New York. Miles uses a one-man flying machine that looks like a knapsack helicopter, and although he eludes his pursuers, he winds up trapped in a tree, spinning slowly while the police search the forest floor. Later Luna persuades him to don a space suit so she can capture him for the police. When the captors arrive, they plan to arrest Luna as well because she has been contaminated by contact with the alien. The inflated space suit becomes a rubber raft that allows both of them to escape across the water, propelled by a puncture that allows air to escape and drive them along the surface like a rapidly deflating balloon.

Sleeper ends with a science-based comic caper sequence, in which Miles and Luna sneak into a huge medical complex on a mission to steal the nose of the Great Leader—the only part that remains after a terrible accident—before it can be cloned and the Leader restored to power. Again, Miles is an impostor who clearly does not fit into this setting. He and Luna dress as scientists and try to use a huge computer, laced with magnetic tape like an old thirty-five-millimeter film projector, to gain access to the operating theater, where they will pretend to be surgeons in charge of the cloning procedure. They bounce around the table like burlesque clowns before their cover is blown and they flee, with the nose. At the implausible ending, typical of screwball comedies of the 1930s, these mismatched and once hostile lovers discover each other and live happily ever after, separated both from the establishment of the Great Leader and from the rebels of the Western Sector. They have both awakened from a slumber and have found happiness in being themselves.

Underlying the comedy and apparent nihilism is a profoundly humanistic statement. Humanity can survive the fads of the 1960s and the phony sophistication of this emerging new world, where an authoritarian government provides enough comfort and science enough toys to lull the unsuspecting into a torpor of complacency. Real people don't belong in such an artificial world; they belong in Brooklyn.

Beachhead in Manhattan

Woody Allen's visual appearance as Alvy Singer in *Annie Hall* (1977) indicates a remarkable shift in his screen character and in his sensibility

of displacement. In the opening shot, he appears against a plain backdrop, speaking directly into the camera, dressed in a nicely tailored tweed
jacket and polo shirt buttoned to the top. His hair is stylishly long, for
the fashion of the day, but neatly combed. The clownish look, with the
wildly disheveled mane, oddball costumes, and dopey facial expressions
that he adopted in earlier films, has yielded to a more natural look. The
persona is still nervous, stammering, and a bit high strung, but no longer
visibly befuddled. Were it not for the signature eyeglasses, one could
pass him on any sidewalk in New York without noticing. Alvy, like his
creator, now fits in. If he is not comfortable with his environment, he
has at least made a truce with it. Alvy has steady work as a stand-up
comedian and writer, lives in a comfortable apartment, and belongs to a
health club where he regularly plays a competent game of squash or
tennis with his friends, who are equally successful young professionals.

External appearances may be a bit deceptive, however. In an early
scene, shot on a quiet Manhattan side street, Alvy and his friend Rob
(Tony Roberts), come in voice-over before they actually appear in frame.
Alvy explains his discomfort with a perceived anti-Semitic comment
from a colleague at lunch who asked: "Did you eat yet?" which he perceives as "Jew eat yet." Another colleague, named significantly Tom
Christie, conceivably a diminutive form of "Christ," answers: "No. Did
you?" which Alvy hears as "No. Jew."[19] He tells about a clerk in a record
store recommending Wagner, which again he takes as an indirect slur
because of the composer's supposed Nazi connections. During the entire conversation, Rob continually refers to him as "Max," as though his
entire identity comes under assault in this environment. Outside the
Jewish neighborhood in Brooklyn, one must constantly be on the alert
for attacks by Manhattanites, even those who are close friends.

Although Alvy feels challenged in Manhattan, he has the status and
financial security to fend off his adversaries and survive. His position
still has elements of insecurity, but at least he can protect himself as
long as he remains in the familiar surroundings of New York. Once he
leaves it, however, his usual defenses break down. His relationship to
the rest of the country remains one of antagonism. Even if Manhattan
represents the Brooklyn boy's springboard to the mainstream cultural
life of the nation, there is no guarantee that one will be able to use that
springboard to leap into the rest of the country. Like many New Yorkers, Alvy shrugs off the very idea of permanently moving beyond the

confines of the City with the implication, Who'd want to? Alvy ventures outside Manhattan twice, reluctantly and with disastrous results. His first is a trip to Chippewa Falls, Wisconsin, to visit Annie's family for a traditional ham dinner for Easter. Although he gamely eats the nonkosher food on this most Christian of holidays, he senses hostility, especially from Grammy Hall, who stares at him as though he were an alien. In his discomfort at her gaze, he imagines himself as fulfilling her fantasies by appearing on screen for an instant in the broad-brimmed hat and full beard of a Lubavitcher from Crown Heights, a section of Brooklyn not too far from Midwood. As the evening with the Halls comes to an end, Annie's brother Duane (Christopher Walken) drives Alvy to the airport, after confessing a fantasy about driving his car at top speed into oncoming traffic. Outside New York, his being is threatened by racists and madmen.

A journey to Los Angeles provides the second anxiety attack. Rob, who has relocated there to further his own television career, urges Alvy to follow. He certainly would not consider a permanent move. His instinctive revulsion is confirmed when he goes to Hollywood to emcee an awards show and he becomes so ill that he must cancel his appearance. It's Christmastime, another Christian holiday as alien to him as the Halls' Easter celebration. When he visits the studio where Rob is dubbing a laugh track onto a sitcom he produces, the artificiality of the technique violates his sensibility as an artist. As a performer, he is accustomed to facing a live audience. Alvy and Annie return to New York, but on the plane, they decide to end their relationship. To further her career as a singer, Annie (Diane Keaton) accepts an invitation from Tony Lacy (Paul Simon), a recording company producer, to return California to cut an album. (Annie's singing reinforces Allen's sense of the phoniness of California art. In New York, she sings complete songs before live audiences; in Hollywood, she presumably sings alone in Tony's studio, which is no doubt as filled with performance-enhancing gimmicks as Rob's television studio. We never see her working at a recording session.) While they are working on the album, she stays in Lacy's mansion and soon begins a relationship with him.

After a short stay back in New York alone, Alvy recognizes his loss and returns to California to pursue Annie, but he doesn't belong in her new world. In a health food restaurant, where he plans to meet Annie, he orders "alfalfa sprouts and, uh, a plate of mashed yeast," food which is as alien to him as the pastrami sandwich that Annie orders with mayonnaise on white bread, an abomination to any delicatessen worker in New York (97). He rents a car at the airport, but between his inexperience as a driver and his emotional state after Annie's rejection, he imitates a demolition derby in his attempt to leave the parking lot. His frantic but implausible explanation (incomprehensible to a Los Angeles police officer) lands him in jail. Strangely, Annie, the small-town girl from Chippewa Falls, makes a series of transitions in both her career and her location with much more ease than Alvy. He can make it across the East River, but not across the continent without landing in jail.

Even as a Manhattanite, Alvy remains haunted by Brooklyn. In an early scene he takes Annie and Rob to visit his old neighborhood, where his family lived under the Cyclone, the famous roller coaster at Coney Island. (Coney Island Avenue runs through Midwood, where Allen actually grew up, to the beach and amusement park at Coney Island, a considerable distance away.) In flashback, he goes back to a childhood episode when he went into a depression and stopped doing his homework. His mother explains to the doctor that he has discovered that the universe is expanding and all will come to nothing. Alvy, and perhaps his creator as well, finds it difficult to imagine their worlds expanding beyond the familiar. In his introductory monologue he recalls the other children in his class in public school, who are now doing "Brooklyn" things: "run a dress company," "make tallisis," "heroin addict," "into leather" (8). He seems to suggest that they have remained in the old neighborhood, while he has moved on to un-Brooklyn pursuits. In his fictional recollection, Alvy seems particularly harsh about both his teachers and his classmates, as does his creator, but this is the background he emerged from and has been trying to escape without too much success.

During Alvy's infamous Easter dinner with the Halls, Allen splits the screen, with half showing the refined—and if the truth be known, stultifying—conversation of the Halls, and the other the squabbling, bumptious table conversation of the Singers in Brooklyn. The screen technique summarizes the key idea of his film. At this stage in his life, Alvy is caught between two sharply contrasting worlds, with Manhattan between them, at the center of the tensions. The first consists of uncomfortable memories of his family in Coney Island, which he lampoons cruelly. At the same time, he finds Chippewa Falls stupefying in its dullness and Los Angeles repulsive in its superficiality. For Alvy,

Manhattan functions as an island of refuge between Brooklyn and the rest of America. At the bittersweet ending, when he and Annie meet at O'Neill's Balloon, across the street from Lincoln Center, and separate as friends, Alvy recognizes a sense of loss. He cannot, at least at this time, have the kind of permanent relationship that his parents enjoyed in Brooklyn, yet he has the memory of the many great moments he shared with Annie when he and the girl from Chippewa Falls first met in New York: "I realized what a terrific person she was and how much fun it was just knowing her" (105).

The Cultural Anthropologist

Manhattan provides another take on the struggles of displacement, but with a reverse-angle perspective. In *Annie Hall* Allen makes Alvy Singer the center of his attention. He looks at the displaced Brooklyn boy trying to find his way as he moves from the homeland toward wider horizons, first of New York and then beyond. Transitions do not come easily to him, and after several attempts at forming lasting relationships, he ends up alone with the memories of his failures—or more accurately, his transitory successes, with equal emphasis on the adjective and the noun. The film portrays the anguish of one trying to adjust to a new environment but with limited success. In *Manhattan* (1979, a mere two years after *Annie Hall*) he reverses direction and looks outward to investigate his adopted homeland with the eye of a critical participant-observer of the social mores of his adopted habitat. Although the narration centers on Isaac Davis, a character quite similar to Alvy, the eponymous hero of the film, its thematic core is Manhattan, not Isaac. Although *Annie Hall* unreels a complex but seamless pattern of flashbacks that fill out the personal recollections introduced in the opening monologue, *Manhattan* follows a more straightforward narrative design, more suited to scientific exposition of the landscape Isaac explores in his travels. Of course, told as it is from Isaac Davis's perspective, the story provides much more than social science.

The film opens with Isaac Davis (Woody Allen) doing a voice-over as he dictates the introduction to a novel he is writing about New York. His feelings about his subject matter are conflicted to such an extent that he seems stuck on the opening sentence of Chapter One. He revises, contradicts, and begins again. The overly romanticized image created by the little boy visiting Times Square for the first time remains for Isaac/Allen, but it is balanced with an adult's experience of actually living there. Isaac's fictional but clearly autobiographical first-person hero, so identified by the reference to "his black-rimmed glasses," confesses an infatuation with the charms of the City, with its "beautiful women and street-smart guys who knew all the angles."[20] It continually "pulsates to the great tunes of George Gershwin." Yet the adult vision overlays without negating the child's vision: "It was a metaphor for the decay of contemporary culture."

As the offscreen monologue continues, the letterbox screen is filled with a series of glorious black-and-white cityscapes by cinematographer Gordon Willis, showing off Manhattan, with its parks and avenues, its buildings and bridges, its teeming pedestrian and automobile traffic in all seasons and at all hours. The sequence builds to a climax with fireworks exploding over Central Park, synched in to the exuberant strains of "Rhapsody in Blue" as played, appropriately enough, by the New York Philharmonic (181). In a later scene, he observes a demolition project with some regret at the changing face of the City. Even as he tries to understand New York—and his life, for that matter—it changes before his gaze. His is an ephemeral world in constant transition. In *Manhattan* Isaac makes no reference to family or to roots in Brooklyn, elements of stability that created a counterpoint to Alvy's rootless life in Manhattan. In Isaac's Manhattan, families and stability simply do not exist.

As a satirical stand-up comedian on the university circuit, Alvy Singer stands apart from and slightly above his environment. Isaac wallows in it. During his trip to California, Alvy shows how much he despises Hollywood television for its artifice, but Isaac has grown wealthy as a writer for *Human Beings, Wow!* When he appears in the studio, he looks down on the stage from a control booth filled with as much electronic gimmickry as Rob's in Los Angeles. A web of lights and cables separates him from the human participants in the show, a visual indication of the dehumanized nature of the program. To his credit, he realizes that he has become part of the electronic lobotomy industry and storms out of the studio before the banality destroys him. Still, the work has been good to him. He lives in an elegant duplex apartment where he entertains Tracy (Mariel Hemingway), his seventeen-year-old girlfriend, who routinely stays over. He eats at Elaine's, a fashionable restaurant on upper Second Avenue, and belongs to a club, where he regularly plays racquetball. He frequents museums, movie theaters, and concert halls. In short, his life fulfills the Manhattan fantasies of the boy from Brooklyn.

Isaac, however, aspires to become a serious writer. His fiction is set in Manhattan, and because of this project, he must delve beneath the surfaces. He must gain perspective and insight, first into the shallowness of others around him and then eventually into the emptiness of his own life. In the opening scene, immediately after the Gershwin prelude, during dinner at Elaine's, he admits to his friends Yale (Michael Murphy) and his wife, Emily (Anne Byrne), that his relationship with a seventeen-year-old is unusual, but he is not inclined to examine it at any depth. This is striking because the two couples have engaged in a theoretical discussion about the ethical imperative of diving into icy water to save a drowning man, but they cannot direct ethical reflection toward their own lives. As far as Isaac is concerned, Tracy is beautiful, sexually sophisticated, and compliant—in short, a world-class trophy. Her welfare holds little interest for him, and his sophisticated friends accept them as a couple unquestioningly. Tracy's sexual appetites are voracious but oddly innocent. Her utter amorality springs from her youth. She goes to an expensive private school, does homework, and apparently has a home that she may or may not return to in the evenings, but anything like parental supervision or responsibility is never mentioned. At this stage in the story, Isaac, like Tracy, inhabits a self-centered teenage universe in which actions bear no consequences and have no effect on the lives of others. In the solipsistic world that Isaac has created for himself, there are no moral restraints from friends or family. In Manhattan, one simply does what brings gratification at the moment. Life is a story told exclusively in the present tense.

Near the end of the film, however, Isaac's moral vision has deepened appreciably, not because of personal reflection but rather because of circumstances forced upon him by others. After an on-again, off-again affair with Mary Wilke (Diane Keaton), Yale finally decides to leave his wife for her. Isaac and Mary had been living together, and Mary, like Tracy, sees no adult implications of her drifting casually back and forth between Yale and Isaac, other than an increase of stress that interferes with her work and increases her Valium consumption. At this point, Isaac believes he loves her and is stunned by her decision to rejoin Yale. Isaac confronts Yale in an anthropology seminar room at Columbia, next to the classroom where he is teaching literature. Surrounded by skeletal remains of various primates, Isaac finally grasps the lasting consequences of human action. Yale whines like a child about his needs, with no reference to Emily. Isaac refers to Mary as worthy of the Zelda Fitzgerald Emotional Maturity Award and asks Yale: "What're you—six years old?" (264) Yale fights back by declaring that he is "no saint," finally yelling, "I mean, we're just people, we're just human beings, you know. You think you're God." In response, Isaac points to the skeleton next to him and says: "This is what happens to us! You know, uh, it's very important to have—to have some kind of personal integrity."

Throughout the film, Isaac has discovered that personal integrity is a rare commodity in Manhattan. Isaac first meets Mary at the Guggenheim Museum, where she and Yale introduce Isaac and Tracy to their Academy of the Overrated, which includes Mahler, Dinesen, Jung, and Walt Whitman. Their conversation is laced with the inane clichés of cocktail party intellectuals. The last straw for Isaac is their arch dismissal of Ingmar Bergman, one of Isaac's (and Allen's) giants. She has graduated from Radcliffe, and he is a professor at Columbia; they feel they have the right to dismiss others as "overrated." Yet Mary writes personality pieces for artsy magazines and grinds out "novelized" versions of popular films. Yale plans to do the definitive biography of Eugene O'Neill, but he never quite gets to it. He has been saving money to start a quarterly, but decides to use the money for a Porsche instead. In a later scene, Yale and Mary arrange an afternoon's tryst in a hotel while shopping at the cosmetics counter in Bloomingdale's, a store that Allen frequently uses as a shorthand image of New York's decadent consumerism.

Isaac's ex-wife Jill (Meryl Streep) is bisexual and should receive some credit for authenticity for leaving Isaac to join her companion, Connie (Karen Ludwig). No so. Jill has turned their failed marriage into material for a book, *Marriage, Divorce and Selfhood.* The last word is key; Jill is just another Manhattan narcissist; she writes casually about the intimate details of their marriage and breakup with little concern for Isaac or their son Willie (Damion Sheller). She is negotiating film rights. Allen will later recycle this odious, destructive, self-centered writer in the person of Harry Bloch, in *Deconstructing Harry* (1997).

The characters occasionally leave their cocoon in Manhattan, but they never travel as far away as Chippewa Falls or Los Angeles. Emily wants to move to Connecticut to start a family, but Yale dismisses the prospect as impossible because of his career. Yale, Emily, Mary, and Isaac take the new Porsche across the Tappan Zee Bridge for a day trip to Nyack, but it is there, in a bookshop on Main Street, that they discover Jill's book, which they read aloud, humiliating Isaac and amusing themselves. Two other car trips are noted. Emily and Yale return from New Jersey, and Mary and Isaac take cab back from having dinner in Brooklyn. In both instances, the couples discuss their futures together, but the dialogue is voice-over, while the camera shows only the exterior of the vehicles making their way through the maze of the urban highway system. Coming to Manhattan seems to depersonalize their relationships. It's all talk.

Thus it is no accident that the most tender love scene in the film is set on a reconstruction of the lunar surface at the Hayden Planetarium. Mary and Isaac have been caught in a thunderstorm during a Sunday afternoon stroll in Central Park. Wet and disheveled, and therefore least artificial, they cross Central Park West and seek shelter from the storm and from life's tumult amid the lunar rocks and craters. It's a moment of genuine affection, shot in silhouette with soft backlighting, and one they will refer to later as their relationship deepens—at least for the moment. Ironically, the moon is about as far away from Manhattan as one can imagine, and as such, it is a place where love is possible.

Mary Wilke comes from Philadelphia, a fact she mentions twice as an indication that living in New York (in addition to Radcliffe, of course) has made her what she is. When Isaac finally challenges her Academy of the Overrated during their first meeting, she backs away from the challenge: "I don't even wanna have this conversation. I mean—really—I'm just from Philadelphia. You know, I mean, we believe in God" (195). Only in New York has she lost her moorings and become a pretentious snob. Later in the film, at the Museum of Modern Art, she and Isaac meet a filmmaker who tries to explain his current project, which deals with orgasms. Mary stammers: "No, I'm from Philadelphia. We never talk about things like that" (204). In New York, she seems quite comfortable with her new sophisticated persona, but at odd moments, she realizes she is a resident alien.

Mary is all surfaces. Even during one of her breakups with Yale, she reassures herself: "I'm a beautiful woman, I'm young, I'm highly intelligent, I got everything going for me" (232). After her first cordial meeting with Isaac, when the two walk her dachshund Waffles to Sutton Place with the Fifty-ninth Street Bridge framing them as they watch the sunrise, her beauty does indeed seem to reflect the beauty of the setting for Isaac. Only as time passes will he discover the destructive side of both Mary and the City.

Yet for all the rapidly mutating relationships in Manhattan, the characters appear distant on the screen, even as they engage in emotionally charged dialogue. Employing the full dimensions of the wide screen, Allen often alternately positions Isaac and Mary, or Isaac and Tracy, alone on opposite edges of the screen, rather than in the normal two-shot. They engage in simultaneous monologues. By contrast, in one of the final sequences, Isaac and Emily meet over lunch and share their experiences as two adult friends who have been hurt, but who are determined to move on with their lives. In this scene Allen uses the standard reverse angle shots, with the over-the-shoulder setup keeping both actors on camera throughout the conversation. It is one of the few instances in the film where two characters actually communicate without performing for the other. The images on the screen reveal the intimacy of friendship rather than sexuality. In this scene, Emily grows in stature as the most adult and most likable character in the film, and she is the one who wants to move away to Connecticut and start a family.

After his conversation with Emily, Isaac realizes, or thinks he realizes, how much he loved Tracy. He tries to reclaim her before it is too late. He races through the City, past the shops on upper Second Avenue and Gramercy Park, and finally meets her in the vestibule of her apartment as she is about to take a cab to Kennedy, where she will fly to London for a semester of study in a drama school. Dressed in a stylish skirted traveling suit rather than her customary high-schoolish jeans and T-shirts, Tracy has clearly become a woman. In fact, while they have been separated, she has celebrated her eighteenth birthday. For the first time, she mentions her parents, who are in London making arrangements for her. Outside New York, normal family relationships can be resumed. Isaac whines and pleads with her to change her plans, but when she refuses, he smiles on her, as though she finally can be saved from the City and establish a real life for herself.

Manhattan, like *Annie Hall,* ends in a separation, but with a difference. Alvy Singer looks backward at the good times he once enjoyed with Annie. Isaac Davis looks forward with disappointment for himself but with satisfaction at the prospects Tracy will face outside Manhattan. Alvy's thoughts are self-centered, perhaps a bit narcissistic, and in his role of stand-up comic, he relies on a lengthy joke to express his sense of loss. He tells the story about the man who goes to a psychiatrist because his brother thinks he's a chicken. When the doctor offers to see him, the man replies that he would, but they need the eggs. Moving from the joke to a reflection on relationships, Alvy concludes, "they're totally irrational and crazy and absurd and . . . but, uh, I guess we keep going through it because, uh, most of us need the eggs" (105). Isaac for once is reduced to silence. He can only look on as Tracy continues her life without him, and without Manhattan.

Isaac's smile embodies the ambiguity of his feelings about Tracy and about Manhattan. By his last-minute effort to keep her for himself, he shows no change in his willingness to use others for his own gratification, yet he seems almost pleased at her adult decision to leave Manhattan and him. He offers no sign that he is ready to seek a wider horizon himself; in fact his commitment to his book about Manhattan, which has received a favorable first reading from Viking, suggests that he is more entrenched than ever. Manhattan remains his life, but at least he can recognize that there may be something different, something better, in store for Tracy. The film ends as it began, with "Rhapsody in Blue" and the skyline shots of Manhattan. The City remains; it is the people who change. Or who don't. Or who can't.

You Can Go Home Again

Radio Days (1987) represents a return to Brooklyn, even though it is set in Rockaway Beach, which is technically part of Queens, as are all the islands on the south side of Jamaica Bay, including Breezy Point and Fort Tilden, which are east of the Flatbush Avenue Bridge and thus geographically off the coast of Brooklyn. Connected to the rest of the City by the bridge and the IND subway, it is a small town even more isolated than most neighborhoods in Brooklyn/Queens. In the film Uncle Abe (Josh Mostel) has connections on the mainland (of Long Island) because he routinely brings uncleaned fish back from Sheepshead Bay, an inlet for commercial and party fishing boats in Brooklyn. In the Rockaway of *Radio Days,* everyone has a Jewish name. The narrative begins in the period immediately before World War II, and it ends with the New Year celebration of 1944. In short, it represents the time and— with some elasticity—the place of Woody Allen's childhood.

From his Manhattan perspective as an adult, Allen's recollection of those days is tinted with a charming nostalgia. With few exceptions, the action takes place in winter when the day trippers visiting for a dose of sun and surf have vanished, and the local people reclaim their neighborhood. In voice-over, Allen reflects on the beauty of the place when the skies are overcast and rain sweeps across the streets. In these months, Rockaway Playland is boarded up for the season, and children play under the boardwalk and on the beach with little interference from outsiders. Boys wear plaid mackinaws with zippered hoods (always left open), knickers with knee socks, and, if they are really stylish, leather aviator helmets with goggles. Cinematographer Carlo Di Palma captures the misty past through the muted shadows cast by hesitant winter light; the interiors of the family house reconstructed by Santo Loquasto radiate warmth through the reds and browns that glow in a golden light from yellow and cream lampshades.

Through the prism of years, the old neighborhood has its beauty, but has its drawbacks. No one assimilated to life in Manhattan as an adult could ever revert to such a world. The living is tight. Three nuclear families share one modest-sized house. Joe (Seth Green), the red-haired eight-year-old, lives with his mother, Tess (Julie Kavner), and his father (Michael Tucker), and in the final sequences with a newly arrived baby sister. Uncle Abe and his wife, Ceil (Renee Lippin), have a teenage daughter, Cousin Ruthie (Joy Newman). Aunt Bea (Dianne Wiest) remains unmarried but ever hopeful, and two grandparents complete the family circle. They constantly bicker and insult one another with barbs worthy of a borscht-circuit comedian. Joe, who strongly resembles what Woody Allen might have looked like as a child, imagines his parents appearing on a radio show that provides on-the-air marriage counseling. When the host concludes that they deserve each other, Tess reacts with a quizzical denial: "I love him, but what did I do to deserve him?" That remark summarizes Allen's perspective on this bumptious extended family. He treats the characters with a mixture of affection and exasperation. Although autobiographical parallels may be overly stressed in discussions of many of his films, it's worth noting that Woody Allen has commented on his own experience of sharing apartments with relatives at various times during his childhood.

Even outside the family residence, privacy is unknown in the neighborhood. Ruthie amuses herself by eavesdropping on her neighbors' telephone conversations. Thanks to Ruthie, Mrs. Waldbaum's forthcoming surgery to remove her ovaries becomes public knowledge. (Party lines, with several households sharing the same phone lines, were still common in the late 1930s.) The Waldbaums' loud radio disrupts the Yom Kippur observance. They are known to be atheists and Communists. Uncle Abe confronts them for their blasphemous behavior, only to be converted to their passion for the masses over an emphatically nonkosher meal of pork chops and clams, which brings divine retribution in the form of indigestion. The Waldbaums' free-spirited daughter kisses the black man who brings her home from a folk music concert, but her indiscretion becomes a notorious scandal when the nosy Mrs. Silberman (Belle Berger) witnesses the event from her front porch and has a stroke on the spot. Joe and his friends scour the horizon for German planes from their observation post on a rooftop. Instead of Junkers and Messerschmitts, they spot a woman wrapped in a towel dancing in front of a mirror. The towel drops away. Later, the woman reappears as Miss Gordon (Sydney Blake), a substitute teacher for Joe's class, and Joe is delighted at having a teacher whom he has seen naked. At a show-and-tell session in school, one third-grader produces a condom he found in his parents' night table. When Mr. Zipsky (Joel Eidelsberg) has his breakdown, he runs through the street in his underwear menacing neighbors with a meat cleaver. The neighborhood seems like a family writ large.

On the other side of the East River, however, the rich and famous have luxurious apartments that provide all the space and privacy one could want, but paradoxically, they crave notoriety. The contrast forms a consistent theme throughout the film. In an early scene, while Tess works away in her cramped kitchen, she listens to *Irene and Roger,* a breakfast-time celebrity talk show like the actual shows *Dorothy and Dick* and *Tex and Jinx* that were popular in the 1940s. The scene shifts from Rockaway to their spacious Art Deco home in Midtown, where Irene (Julie Kurnitz) and Roger (David Warrilow) enjoy an elegant, served breakfast while chatting about the charming, witty people they met at the Stork Club the previous evening. The accents are affected, the talk precious. In Manhattan café society, it is important to see and be seen, and so they have access to the stars. So wide is the gulf that separates these worlds that when Ceil asks Abe to take her to the Stork Club some day, Abe responds simply that they don't let Jews in: "No Jews. No colored."

Young Joe ventures into Manhattan twice with Aunt Bea and her current boyfriends. Both trips represent journeys into a fantasy world. In the first, they visit Radio City Music Hall to see *Philadelphia Story* (Cukor, 1940). The cavernous lobby, with its lush carpets, massive staircases, and overpowering sculptures provides Joe with an alternate universe of wonder and delight. During the second, he shoots a machine gun at German planes in a penny arcade, eats lunch at the Automat, sees Aunt Bea win fifty silver dollars for identifying fish on a radio quiz show, gets a chemistry set with her winnings, and ends the evening watching Bea and Sy dance while he sits behind a bottle of Pepsi Cola. Allen in voice-over comments that this was one of the best days of his life. For him, Manhattan becomes inextricably connected with the world of entertainment.

Brooklyn, by contrast, is a workaday world, but in an oddly unspecific way. Joe goes to school, but no one else seems to go to work. Uncle Abe spends time among the fishing boats at Sheepshead Bay but gives no indication of working there. Joe's father even refuses to tell his son what he does; only by accident does Joe discover him driving a cab, and with that he drops the subject. Aunt Bea tells the radio quizmaster that she is a bookkeeper, but she always seems to be at home, always planning a date with another marriageable man. Tess berates her husband for not having business sense and for investing in various mail-order projects that never pan out. In Manhattan, relationships are fluid, but accomplishment, notoriety, and wealth are taken for granted. In Rockaway success is a rare commodity, but being a member of the family counts for everything.

One character spans both worlds. Sally White (Mia Farrow) sells cigarettes in a swank nightclub. She also cultivates a relationship with Roger, who has promised to further her career in show business. When Irene discovers them together, she has Sally fired, and later she, Roger, and her Latin bandleader-companion are said to take a vacation in Havana as a romantic threesome. Conventional morality, it seems, applies to Sally, but not to the chic set. Sally moves on to become a hat-check girl in a Mafia-connected restaurant, whose owner suffers an indisposition at closing time. Sally witnesses the murder, but Rocco the hit man (Danny Aiello) runs out of ammunition and is forced to take her home to Brooklyn, where he can obtain bullets from his mother (Gina De Angelis). Although mother and son discuss the best place to dump the body, Sally enjoys Mama's hospitality with a huge Italian meal. During the table conversation, they discover that Sally comes from their old neighborhood in Canarsie, Brooklyn; they know the same people and frequent the same shops. This makes her almost one of the family. Rather than kill her, they arrange for a muscularly influential cousin to have her hired for a radio program. Unfortunately, Sally loses her big break when the program is canceled because of the attack on Pearl Harbor.

Sally realizes that she must leave her Canarsie ways behind her to further her career. She takes speech lessons, drops her voice by a full octave, and becomes a radio star by hosting a popular program for celebrity gossip, *Sally White on the Great White Way.* As a working girl from Brooklyn, she was charming, vulnerable, and very funny. As a celebrity, she becomes as affected and obnoxious as the stars whose lives she reports on her program. On New Year's Eve, she ostentatiously gives the cigarette girl a generous tip, and just for an instant she lapses back into her old voice and accent, which shows that despite the ponderous airs she adopts, she is still Brooklyn.

Although Joe, the red-haired boy from Rockaway, provides the narrative and autobiographical center of the story, as is clear from Allen's providing the nostalgic voice-over commentary by the adult Joe, Sally embodies the thematic core as the Allen surrogate. Although the adult Joe reminisces about his childhood, Allen never reveals anything about Joe's adult life. He does, however, carefully describe the transformation in Sally's life. She did not hesitate to play the whore for Roger in the hope of furthering her career. Her breakthrough comes through the intervention of organized crime. Although her Brooklyn connections saved her life, she systematically purges her accent and childlike simplicity, and becomes as inane and affected as any Manhattanite. Through her, Allen shows the high price of moving from Brooklyn to Manhattan.

The title of the film introduces Allen's reflections on art with extraordinary precision. This was the brief period in American history, little more than twenty years, when radio was the dominant medium, and as such shaped the imagination then, and now the memories, of a generation. In the days of radio, Rockaway represents the consumer, Manhattan the producer. The themes of radio and neighborhood are introduced in the opening sequence when burglars pick up the phone as they are robbing the Needleman's house. *Guess That Tune* has selected the phone number at random and asks the burglars to identify three songs. They guess the tunes, and a few days later, a van delivers a cornucopia of lavish prizes to the Needlemans, who clearly made a profit on the robbery. In this present age of action-adventure mayhem, video games, and MTV, it's hard to imagine a time when a mixed-genre production of quiz show, band show, and phone participation could captivate a radio audience, but such shows did.

The entertainment industry, by its very nature, thrives on artifice and preys on the less sophisticated. In the radio studio scenes, staff men cue the audiences for applause, emcees tell horrible, condescending jokes, and the bands increase excitement with an insistent barrage of fanfares. In addition to listening to Irene and Roger while she washes the breakfast dishes, Tess enjoys a radio ventriloquist, but her husband points out the absurdity of the idea because no one can see whether his lips move. Uncle Abe likes Bill Kern's sports stories, far-fetched tales of sports figures who overcome overwhelming odds, like the pitcher who loses an arm and a leg and goes blind, but who continues playing baseball. Ruthie and her friends have a syrupy crooner, who sings of love, while the girls perch on stools at the soda fountain and the boys sit several feet away in booths, incapable of any expression of cordiality, let alone romance. Bea has her popular music, too, even though its perky, romantic songs seem far removed from her series of comically failed relationships, one of which ended when she was abandoned at Breezy Point by a suitor who panicked during Orson Welles's famous program about Martians invading New Jersey. Her other romances include a married man who delays leaving his wife and then changes his mind, and a delicate suitor who bursts into tears when he remembers his late fiancé, named Leonard. Joe has his boys' serial adventures, like *Biff Baxter and the Masked Avenger,* which are infinitely more interesting than public school and Hebrew lessons with Rabbi Baumel (Kenneth Mars).

Allen cannot be completely negative about the entertainment industry. Even while he exposes its artificiality, he recognizes the genuine pleasure it provides for its consumers in Rockaway. In fact, radio has its privileged moments. Amid the escapist entertainment, Allen includes a news bulletin that segues into a remote hookup to Stroudsburg, Pennsylvania, far from Manhattan. A little girl, Polly Phelps, scarcely a celebrity, has fallen into a well, and rescue teams are desperately trying to reach her. In a series of shots, Allen shows ordinary citizens in varied settings around the country, listening to the radio for news of the trapped child. They, and audiences today, experience a sinking feeling when they, and we, learn that Polly is dead.

Even entertainment programming can have its sublime moments, when artifice is stripped away and pure talent takes over. In a show from the USO center on Times Square, Sally White, who has not yet undergone her transformation, sings "I Don't Want to Walk Without You" to the accompaniment of three women musicians. Sailors sitting together over their beer listen, transfixed by her simple rendition, which is doubly poignant for those who remember the painful dislocations of World War II. In the final sequence, Diane Keaton appears as a band vocalist, singing a straightforward rendition of "Seems Like Old Times" as part of the New Year's celebration at a swank nightclub. In the audience sit the new Sally, Roger, and Irene, as well as the Masked Avenger (Wallace Shawn) and several other familiar personalities. Even in such artificial, Manhattanish surroundings, genuine art is possible.

As was the case in *Manhattan,* Allen provides an unflattering picture of life amid the glitterati of New York. Through Sally, with her ambition and personal compromise, he shows the dark side of the artifice that replaces reality west of the East River. Through Joe, the adult voice-over narrator, he expresses affection for an authentic world that has passed away and can never be recovered. Although expressed in terms of the polarity between Rockaway and Manhattan, the story essentially confronts the conundrum of Woody Allen aging as a person and maturing as an artist in a world that rejects permanence as a matter of principle.

No Business Like Show Business

In *Bullets over Broadway* (1994), one of the mature comedies, Allen explores at some depth the tension between his roles as successful Manhattan artist, which he feels makes him essentially an impostor, and the authentic person from Brooklyn who happens to have had a number of roles forced upon him. David Shayne (John Cusack), the main character, expresses this conflict when he continually asks the women in his life if they love him as an artist or as a man. Allen does not appear as an actor in the film, but David suffers through the standard Allen trauma of displacement. Once again, geography provides a handy metaphor for his analysis. Shayne has made the journey not across the East River, but across the Appalachian Mountains and the Hudson. He has arrived from

Pittsburgh with his fiancée Ellen (Mary-Louise Parker) in order to stake his claim to immortality as a playwright in New York. Shayne may be Jewish, but the script offers no reason to believe he is. Ethnic identity, so important for both the humor and the sense of displacement in many of Allen's films, holds no particular significance in this film. David rather embodies a New Yorker's version of Middle Western values. (Only in New York would Pittsburgh be considered the Midwest.) He is earnest, confident, hard-working, principled, and a trifle dull. He is also hopelessly naive, a very poor judge of his own talent and most unprepared to swim among the sharks of Broadway. More at home at the tranquil confluence of the Allegheny and Monongahela, he fails to appreciate the sinister fact that Manhattan is an island surrounded by Hell Gate on the East River Side and Spuyten Dyvil (the Devil's Whirlpool) on the Hudson, and that both of these eventually flow into Gravesend Bay in Brooklyn. As a writer, he should have been more alert to the symbolism.

After the brief prologue of a mob execution, the film opens with David engaging in a lively discussion with his agent, Julian Marx (Jack Warden). David has finished a play, but he insists on directing it himself, to prevent others from compromising his vision. As a veteran of Times Square, Julian knows that without compromise, the curtain will never rise on this play. David's artistic role model, up to a point, is the totally uncompromising and absolutely unproduced playwright Sheldon Flender (Rob Reiner), a political radical who holds forth in sidewalk cafés in Greenwich Village. With his bluster and his accent, Sheldon is a stereotypical New York bohemian, and with his anger and cynicism, he clearly understands the rules. He has rejected the establishment and takes pride in writing plays that he knows will never be performed. David admires Sheldon's integrity, but not his obscurity. He wants fame and fortune along with his integrity.

David receives word that his play will be produced, but he soon learns just how many artistic compromises he must make before the curtain rises. After the first deal with his angel, he wakes up screaming that he has made a pact with the devil. At first, as director, he indulges in artistic tantrums and on occasion storms out of the theater. As time passes, however, he learns to accept the advice from the experienced New Yorkers that surround him. With their help, he makes striking improvements, and the play opens to rave reviews in the New York press. The critics identify David as the second Eugene O'Neill. Touched by realism, David feels that the success belongs to others who brought the play to its final version. Incapable of sharing the rewards of this collaborative venture, he concludes that he has no talent and really doesn't belong in New York. He reaches the only honest conclusion when he decides to take Ellen back to Pittsburgh.

This reflection is doubly poignant for any artist working in film. Even an established director of legendary independence, like Woody Allen, must rely on the talents of others to make his films succeed. Allen knows cinematography and editing quite well, but he still hires the best cinematographers and editors in the business to work with him, presumably because of the artistic contributions they can make to the finished product. And despite his oft-repeated disdain for critics, reviewers, and box office, Allen, like every other filmmaker, still needs a modicum of success, at least on occasion, to secure funding for future projects. Collaboration and compromise form essential elements of the motion picture industry, even for Woody Allen.

The steps that lead David back to Pittsburgh are instructive. Each of them presents a reflection on the role of the artist, and each involves a stereotypical New Yorker who contributes to his education. David goes ahead with his project when Nick Valenti (Joe Viterelli), a mob boss, bankrolls the entire project. As a condition, he insists that his girlfriend, Olive (Jennifer Tilly), receive an important part. Olive, who has been growing unhappy with her role in the chorus of a speakeasy, conditions her continued affection on his taking steps to further her career. Unfortunately, she has neither acting experience nor talent, and her voice suggests fingernails sliding across a chalkboard, but no one refuses Nick. Casting her as a psychiatrist unhinges the entire play.

David's initial resistance to Nick's advice makes perfect sense because even an inexperienced director can spot disaster in the wings, but his decision to accept Olive brought with it several of the proverbial unintended consequences. Because of the ongoing mob war that was illustrated in the opening sequence, Nick decides that Olive needs a bodyguard to protect her from his business competitors. He assigns a reliable associate, Cheech (Chazz Palminteri), to protect her interests. He escorts her to and from the theater and waits in the orchestra during the rehearsals. When David suggests cutting lines that Olive continually flubs, Cheech assures David that her part will not be diminished.

During one insuperable conflict between actresses, Cheech suggests a new conclusion for the troublesome scene. The emendation takes the play in a new direction, but everyone agrees it is a brilliant adjustment. Gradually, Cheech begins rewriting the dialogue and referring to "my" play. David gradually comes to admire Cheech's natural gifts. David has been to school and read all the important books, but Cheech has the instinct, the raw talent, of a born playwright. Finding strong-arm work for the mob a more congenial way of life than education, he left school and marked his departure by burning down the building on Lincoln's birthday, a holiday, so no one would get hurt. Cheech dismisses David's schooling by telling him how much he hated the "blue-haired bitches" that were his teachers and struck him with a ruler. In this comment, he echoes Allen's own sentiments about his school days in Brooklyn.

Cheech realizes as well as anyone that Olive is ruining the play. In a scene of macabre black comedy, he takes Olive to the waterfront, and tells her, "Olive, I think you should know this. You're a terrible actress." The sound of four shots from his revolver is followed by a loud splash. Cheech is smart enough to know that his action will bring two inevitable consequences. As a playwright, he is confident that Olive's understudy (Jennifer Van Dyck) will bring the play to life and ensure its stunning success. As a hit man, he also knows that Nick will pursue the killer and in all likelihood will see through his contrived story about the rival mob's taking out Olive. During an informal interrogation, Cheech's explanation stumbles over its own contradictions. In the end, Cheech literally gives his life for the integrity of his art. And his dying words to David involve one final suggestion for the play. David, of course, cannot understand Cheech's assumption that art carries more value than human life. Cheech is an artist and a New Yorker; David is neither.

Although Olive's unwelcome presence threatens the survival of the play, Helen Sinclair (Dianne Wiest) ensures its success. Alcoholic and a bit beyond her prime, this flamboyant star schemes to put her stamp on both the play and its author. She uses flattery and seduction to induce him to enlarge her part. David becomes a willing accomplice because he wants desperately to fit in with her chic Broadway circle. She brandishes a long cigarette holder. He doesn't smoke, but after she gives him a silver cigarette case, once given to her by Noel Coward, he follows her example with an equally long holder. During her manipulative and ostensibly romantic dialogues, she continually puts her hand to his lips and tells him to be still. She is in fact silencing his artistic voice as well as his human responses.

Warner Purcell (Jim Broadbent) provides a living cautionary tale for David. He is an accomplished actor of the old-time rhetorical school. He also has a problem with his weight, but he has slimmed down for the play. When the cast gathers for a first read-through, he passes on the buffet table and asks for hot water with lemon. As he gets into the part, his waistline balloons with his ego. His appetite extends beyond the pastries to Olive, a morsel that could constitute a serious personal health risk for Warner, if Nick caught on. When Cheech offers a bit of friendly advice concerning Olive, Warner consoles himself in an elegant restaurant, where he systematically eats his way through the menu. He keeps his blossoming foreground in check with an immense corset, which Olive uncovers during one of their dressing-room trysts. Self-indulgence in the form of food, sex, or ego, Warner demonstrates, can destroy an artist, and if one cannot control it, as he apparently cannot, then one must take appropriate measures to disguise it.

Finally, Sheldon Flender gives David an insight into the lot of the pure artist. Sheldon is a coffeehouse revolutionary who loves to pontificate about his radical politics and self-centered philosophy. When David is trying to straighten out his complex relationships, it is Sheldon who advises him by uttering the famous Allen dictum: "The artist creates his own moral universe." Of course, because no one has ever seen any of his plays, it's difficult to judge whether he is an artist or a charlatan. While David engages in his dalliance with Helen, Sheldon begins a relationship with David's companion Ellen, a fact that David discovers during a session of mutual confession in their apartment. They break up.

At his Broadway opening, David has his startling epiphany. The audience clearly loves the play, but David is not happy with his life or his art. During the last act, the mob settles its disagreement with Cheech in the matter of Olive. When Cheech dies backstage, David finally understands the cost of becoming an artist and decides that life in New York demands a price he will not pay. Cheech will not only kill for art, he will die for it. David will not. He rushes to Sheldon's apartment in the Village, where as he expected, he finds Ellen. During their confrontation, Sheldon again mouths his slogans in support of his own radical amorality, but Ellen sees through the bluster. She decides to leave Sheldon, and his New York ways, and return to Pittsburgh with David.

The city of his dreams has become a city of nightmares, created largely by his feelings of inadequacy in an alien setting.

A Gray Line Bus Tour of Allentown

Over on Eighth Avenue, between Fifty-third and Fifty-fourth Streets, squats the nondescript terminal of Gray Line Bus Tours. For a hefty but not exorbitant fee, tourists can choose any one of several routes and board a double-decker bright red bus to visit some of the key landmarks in Manhattan and Brooklyn in a few hours. Visitors with limited time find the survey helpful in sampling the flavor of the City. Those on a more leisurely schedule can decide which sites would be worthy of a return visit. The choices allow them to stop at only the places that interest them and bypass others. It's a good model to follow in surveying the works of a prolific filmmaker like Woody Allen. One can't stop everywhere and see everything on one trip, but a quick overview gives a sense of the terrain.

After spending some time with several of Woody Allen's most popular films, a Gray Line tour through his some of his mature works might prove useful in gaining a more comprehensive view of his work as a Flatbush expatriate in Manhattan. This survey of several of the later Allen films reveals a consistent theme of displacement with an extraordinary range of variations on the theme. In comic and serious films alike, the Allen hero most commonly finds himself in territory where he feels he does not belong. Ever afraid of being unmasked as an impostor or interloper—or worse, of being recognized as a failure—he becomes a nervous mass of insecurities and defenses. He can tough it out, like Sally White in *Radio Days,* or he can go back to his hometown, like David Shayne in *Bullets over Broadway.* He can view his failure like Alvy Singer in *Annie Hall* and conclude that his struggle was worth the effort, or like Isaac Davis in *Manhattan,* can hope for a better future, if not for himself, then for someone he loves.

The theme of losing one's identity in an alien milieu appears most explicitly in *Zelig* (1983). Allen plays Leonard Zelig, the Chameleon Man of the Jazz Age, who mysteriously becomes transformed into whatever his context suggests. With Indians, African Americans, or Chinese, he adapts their ethnic characteristics. With athletes, he suits up and joins the team. With politicians, he becomes a statesman. His capacity for adaptation has its dark side as well because he absorbs not only harmless, external physical characteristics, but the moral ethos of the environment as well. Near the end of the film, Zelig appears on a balcony with Hitler, dressed in the uniform of a storm trooper. Women come forth to accuse him of exploitation during his days in show business. Eventually, the narrator tells us, "He is sued for bigamy, adultery, automobile accidents, plagiarism, household damages, negligence, property damages and performing unnecessary dental extractions."[21] This absence of an inner core becomes recognized as a psychiatric disorder, and authorities confine him for observation and treatment.

The outcome is not entirely negative, however. Zelig eventually marries his psychiatrist, Dr. Eudora Fletcher (Mia Farrow), who comes from a wealthy family in Philadelphia, like Mary Wilke in *Manhattan.* In her dealings with Zelig she reveals that despite her renown as a scientist and aviatrix, she leads a lonely personal life, even with her prestigious practice on the East Side of Manhattan. The voice-over narrator says: "For her, fame and recognition are empty rewards and do not live up to the adolescent fantasies that prompted her ambition."[22] The two mismatched lovers heal each other of their emptiness, overcome several crises in their marriage, and apparently live happily ever after. After Eudora rescues Zelig from the clutches of the Nazis and the two escape in a stolen plane despite pursuit by Nazi fighter planes, the two receive a ticker-tape parade in New York, where they receive the Medal of Valor at City Hall. In a rare happy ending, both Zelig and Eudora successfully adjust to their new environment in Manhattan, and in fact triumph there. The autobiographical strain in Allen's films appears in *Zelig,* as it does in all of Allen's work. The hero must adjust to many identities and leave much of his past behind as he gradually assimilates to life in Manhattan.

"Oedipus Wrecks" is Allen's contribution to *New York Stories* (1989), the trilogy of short films that he made with Francis Coppola and Martin Scorsese. Sheldon Mills's (Woody Allen) sense of displacement comes from his being Jewish in a predominantly gentile world. As a successful partner in a New York law firm, he has changed his name from Millstein and is planning marriage to Lisa (Mia Farrow), a blonde, divorced mother of three who comes from Vermont. As the film opens, Sheldon is telling his psychiatrist about his mother's constant intrusions into his life. Sadie Millstein (Mae Questel) clearly disapproves of Sheldon's fiancée. In a dreadful dinner meeting, she reminds Lisa of Sheldon's changed name and even refers to her apartment as seeming "too Jewish" in his eyes. Sadie clings to Sheldon's past, displaying his baby pictures and telling Lisa of his security blanket and bed-wetting. Because of his plan to marry a blonde woman with three children, she tells Sheldon he must think he's an astronaut.

Sheldon's subconscious wish to be free of his mother comes true when she inexplicably disappears during a magic act. With her out of the way, he can walk away from his past. But Sadie just as mysteriously reappears as a huge head in the sky, haunting him with recollections of his past. Distraught by the notoriety, Lisa ends their engagement and returns to Vermont. Unable to rid himself of his mother's apparition, Sheldon consults a psychic, Treva (Julie Kavner), whose Jewish name, nasal voice, New York accent, and boiled chicken dinner make her a younger version of Sadie. Despite himself, Sheldon falls in love with her. Satisfied with his choice, Sadie returns to earth and proudly displays Sheldon's baby pictures to her future daughter-in-law. In this instance, Allen has allowed his hero to bring his past to Manhattan with him. His quest for romance has ended happily with Treva, but thematically, Allen suggests that he has no choice. Sheldon cannot shed the past and his Jewishness, even in midtown Manhattan, and because Treva is a younger version of Sadie, it seems fairly certain that before long, Sheldon Mills will be back in his psychiatrist's office, trying once more to resolve his ambivalence about his roots.

Despite its quasi-comic characters who appear in the intertwined web of subplots, *Crimes and Misdemeanors* (1989) must be listed among Allen's most serious films. Dr. Judah Rosenthal (Martin Landau) has become one of the leading ophthalmologists in the City. He comes from Brooklyn, and when he suffers from moral vertigo because of his crimes, he drives back to the family home and imagines himself back among his quarreling relatives during a seder. The discussion centers around questions of belief in God and morality, with Judah's father (David S. Howard) upholding traditional values and Aunt May (Anna Berger) taking a decidedly existentialist and atheistic position: the human person simply creates his or her own values. Because Hitler got away with murdering six million Jews, Aunt May reasons, there is no morality.

As Judah has become established in Manhattan as a "man of science," as he describes himself, he has good reason to look back to a time of simpler morality. He has achieved professional recognition and has an adoring wife and daughter, yet he risks everything by having a long, adulterous relationship with Dolores (Anjelica Huston). When she demands marriage, he simply arranges to have her murdered. In one of their final arguments, she tells him she knows about his embezzlement of hospital funds. During this downward spiral, he falsifies records and lies to his wife and the police. In the concluding conversation in the film, Judah recounts his story to Cliff (Woody Allen), a documentary filmmaker, as though it were an outline of a film script. Judah argues that the most frightening part of the story is that the characters' crimes make no difference. He goes on to live a happy and rewarding life. Back in Brooklyn, God and morality provided material for serious debate. Once he has become a successful physician in Manhattan, such questions have become irrelevant to his life. In the end, he has sided with Aunt May: There is no morality.

Manhattan Murder Mystery (1993) involves another murder of an inconvenient woman, but without the moral explorations of *Crimes and Misdemeanors*. It's a frothy genre film that follows the pattern of the comic detective capers most associated with the Thin Man series of the 1930s. Larry and Carol Lipton (Woody Allen and Diane Keaton) fit comfortably into their Manhattan apartment. He is a successful book editor, and she has enough money to be scouting out locations for her new restaurant. To show just how much they have entered the scene, they have a subway sign from Canal Street (with Chinese characters to indicate Chinatown) hanging over their bed.

Larry and Carol may be the most engaging Manhattan couple Allen has ever created. They are a bit high-strung, but they lack that abrasive edge of neurosis that marks most of his characters. They remain devoted to each other, even though both receive uninvited, but not unwelcome, attention from their friends, she from Ted (Alan Alda) and he from Marcia (Anjelica Huston). Their comfortable lives suffer a bit of a jolt when they become suspicious that a neighbor has murdered his wife. They function exceptionally well in a world of fashionable lounges and high-powered offices, but they become figures of Allen's comic displacement when they turn their attention to crime. As sleuths, they enter alien territory. After a clever ploy to gather evidence in a suspect's apartment, she leaves her reading glasses behind. A stakeout at a past-its-prime residential hotel leads to their being trapped in an elevator

Davis (Henry Fonda) stands alone in a superior moral position as he confronts Juror 3 (Lee J. Cobb) and the others while protecting the rights of a minority defendant on trial for murder in *Twelve Angry Men*.

In *The Verdict* Frank Galvin (Paul Newman) finds himself hemmed in by the medical establishment, the Catholic Archdiocese of Boston, and the courts as he tries to find a just settlement for the claim of his working-class client.

Sol Nazerman (Rod Steiger), in *The Pawnbroker*, writhes in pain in his shop as he gradually comes to understand the many cages he has constructed to separate himself from the outside world.

Above, Sonny Wortzik (Al Pacino), the gay bank robber in *Dog Day Afternoon,* uses a shotgun to separate himself from the female clerks and the bank manager. *Below,* As an undercover cop turned informer, Danny Ciello (Treat Williams) in *Prince of the City,* argues with his handler, a federal prosecutor whose name, Brooks Paige (Paul Roebling), and clothing identify him as a member of the privileged establishment.

Above, In *Q & A*, Lt. Mike Brennan (Nick Nolte) dominates the center of a cross section of the New York Police Department as he entertains them with a comic narrative about abusing a suspect after his arrest. *Below,* Miles Monroe (Woody Allen) exchanges his human identity for a robot's in order to survive in the futuristic world of *Sleeper.*

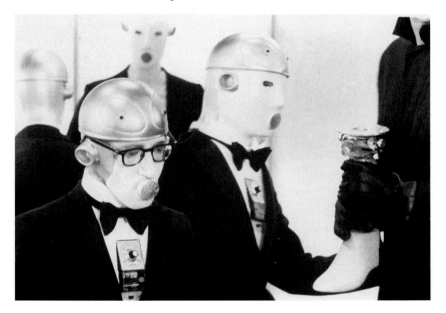

Above, In his fantasy in *Annie Hall,* Alvy Singer (Woody Allen) reverts to his childhood in Brooklyn where he fits in with the other children. *Below,* In the "Oedipus Wrecks" segment of *New York Stories,* Sheldon Mills (Woody Allen) brings Lisa (Mia Farrow) to meet his mother (Mae Questel) and finds the clash of cultures difficult to manage.

The Museum of Modern Art provides a dreamlike setting for a romantic exchange between Isaac Davis (Woody Allen) and Mary Wilke (Diane Keaton) in *Manhattan*.

The Woody Allen surrogate, David Shayne (John Cusack), an aspiring play-wright from Pittsburgh, feels inadequate in the company of the ultra-sophis-ticated star Helen Sinclair (Dianne Wiest) in *Bullets over Broadway*.

Above, Johnny Boy (Robert DeNiro) and Charlie (Harvey Keitel) engage in financial negotiations in the closed world of *Mean Streets. Below,* From his steel and glass cocoon, Travis Bickel (Robert DeNiro) observes the larger world of midtown Manhattan with a combination of fascination and disgust in *Taxi Driver.*

By the side of the municipal pool in their neighborhood in the Bronx, Jake and Vickie La Motta (Robert DeNiro and Cathy Moriarty) enjoy an intimate moment before Jake breaks into the big time in *Raging Bull*.

Above, A diner near Kennedy Airport provides the setting for a business conference between Jimmy Conway (Robert DeNiro) and Henry Hill (Ray Liotta) in *GoodFellas. Below,* In *Age of Innocence,* Countess Olenska (Michelle Pfeiffer) turns away from New York society in order to respond to the greeting of Newland Archer (Daniel Day-Lewis).

Mars Blackman (Spike Lee) romances Nola Darling (Tracy Camilla Johns) on the Brooklyn side of the East River, with their backs turned toward Manhattan in *She's Gotta Have It*.

The Carmichaels provide the portrait of an idealized family on the stoop of their brownstone home in *Crooklyn*.

In *Jungle Fever*, Gator (Samuel L. Jackson) terrorizes his mother, Lucinda (Ruby Dee), for drug money. His addiction spurs the disintegration of the family and touches the lives of everyone connected with him.

Vinny (John Leguizamo), in *Summer of Sam*, stands in the center of his friends, who support him and yet form a suffocating presence in his life.

Malcolm (Denzel Washington) taps his own spiritual resources when he separates himself from group pressures and becomes his own man in *Malcolm X.*

Pierre Delacroix (Damon Wayans) and Sloane Hopkins (Jada Pinkett Smith) are educated, successful, and stylish, yet they still wrestle with their African American roots in the barbed satire *Bamboozled*.

with a corpse and their trying to escape through an ink-black cellar. They cross the George Washington Bridge to a foundry in New Jersey, where they suspect the victim's body has been vaporized and where they clearly do not belong. Escaping incineration in New Jersey, they find themselves caught in a backstage shootout in a downtown theater. They muddle through, but barely. Their ineptitude in dealing with murder provides many comic moments, but Allen also suggests, perhaps unwittingly, that dangerous police work, which involves dealing with places and people far different from their experience, should be left to cops from New Jersey or Brooklyn.

In *Mighty Aphrodite* (1995) Allen deals with displacement on several levels at once. The film itself returns to familiar comic territory, but it features a classic Greek chorus commenting on the action as though it were high tragedy. Lenny Winerib (Woody Allen) covers sports for a New York newspaper, and his wife, Amanda (Helena Bonham Carter), runs a gallery in SoHo. He is a likable character, a clone of Larry Lipton, but Amanda has a bit of an edge to her. She gives herself completely to her profession and cannot interrupt her work with pregnancy, but she urges Lenny to adopt a child. Lenny has some initial reservations about the idea, but he quickly fits into the role of doting father and becomes fascinated by the boy's manifest talents. In time, he becomes curious about the child's birth parents, whom he assumes must be truly gifted. He uses his reporter's skills to conduct a private investigation, and he discovers that the boy's mother has several names, comes from Philadelphia, has starred in porn films, and now supports herself at a fashionable address by entertaining gentlemen callers. Lenny eventually overcomes his disbelief and determines to help the mother of his son form a new life for herself. Linda Ash (Mira Sorvino), as she now calls herself, provides her professional services to express her gratitude to Lenny, but he remains committed to Amanda. Amanda for her part finds the attentions of fellow gallery owner Jerry Bender (Peter Weller) a real option for her future and concludes that he could provide a welcome change for her. Lenny struggles to understand Linda's world; Amanda functions quite comfortably in her own chic Manhattan ambiance without much thought for anyone else.

As part of his rehabilitation plan, Lenny tries to arrange a match for Linda with Kevin (Michael Rapaport), an onion farmer turned boxer from Wampsville, New York, midway between Utica and Syracuse. Kevin is scarcely a refugee from a Mensa recruiting committee and suspects nothing about Linda. His friends, however, bring a pornographic video to the bachelor party, and he sees the bride-to-be in action. Kevin cannot deal with her past any more than he can deal with New York City ways, and he returns to Wampsville without her. Linda, however, meets a helicopter pilot, who literally drops from the sky like a deus ex machina, and takes her home to Connecticut. Amanda finally decides to stay with Lenny. According to this Hollywood happy ending, everyone finds happiness by being where they belong: Kevin and Linda by moving out of Manhattan, and Amanda and Lenny by remaining there.

Deconstructing Harry (1997) and *Celebrity* (1998) reveal a nasty side to Allen's take on life in Manhattan—or, more accurately, the films demonstrate what Manhattan does to people, who for the sake of art become accomplices in their own spiritual assassinations. *Deconstructing Harry* is by far the more bitter. Borrowing heavily from Ingmar Bergman's *Wild Strawberries* (1957), Allen has the odious, self-centered, and self-destructive author Harry Block (Woody Allen) travel to his alma mater in upstate New York to receive an honorary degree. No one will travel with him. Rather than go alone, he takes Cookie (Hazel Goodman), a prostitute he has hired for the day, his son, whom he has kidnapped, and his best friend Richard (Bob Balaban) who dies in the back seat. It seems that Harry brings death and debauchery with him wherever he goes. The film begins with his sister-in-law Lucy (Judy Davis) threatening to kill him, and as his journey continues, he realizes that she was mild in her expression of rage in comparison to others whose personal tragedies he has recycled for his thinly disguised fiction. Harry has become a great success as a literary figure in Manhattan, but at the cost of alienating everyone around him and surrendering everything human about himself.

Celebrity features Kenneth Branagh playing Lee Simon, the Allen surrogate with all the mannerisms of the original. Lee writes personality sketches and travel pieces for coffee-table magazines, but he harbors ambitions about becoming a serious novelist. He drives a vintage Aston-Martin to keep up appearances, but he wrecks it during a flirtation with a lingerie model (Charlize Theron), an event that suggests the self-destructive pattern of his life as he pursues his infatuation of the moment. Of course, the model disappears from his life immediately. Because he feels he needs room to grow as an artist, he leaves his wife, Robin (Judy

Davis), and bounces from one sexual pursuit to another. He even invites his editor Bonnie (Famke Janssen) to share his apartment, but even as the movers bring in her belongings, he tells her that he loves someone else. Like Harry Block, he cares little about anyone else in his life. In retaliation, Bonnie scatters the only copy of his manuscript, page by page, from the deck of a Hoboken ferry. Once again, he has destroyed his life with self-centered relationships. With his literary ambitions washed away, Lee returns to his life as a Manhattan celebrity chaser.

After their separation, Robin's life takes a dramatic turn. She describes herself as "a schoolteacher," and indeed the camera of Sven Nyquist scarcely flatters her in the opening scenes. She reverts to her Catholic roots by trying to put her life together at a retreat house, but she is too tightly wound for a prolonged period of reflection with guitar-playing nuns, television priests, and a barrackslike refectory with wooden picnic tables and overcooked food. She next tries to build a new self through plastic surgery, but a few minutes with the manic physician dissuades her from that solution. In his office, however, she meets a television producer, Tony Gardella (Joe Mantegna). He is filming a documentary on the doctor as miracle worker, but after seeing Robin, he is instantly smitten with her just the way she is. He takes her on as an administrative assistant at the station. Eventually, he arranges for her to host a celebrity talk show, and with her new hair color and a svelte business suit, she becomes a glamorous celebrity in her own right. But she also loses her vulnerability and becomes as inane and pretentious as the rich and famous she tracks down for her interviews.

Small Time Crooks (2000) is a welcome throwback to Allen's earlier comedies. Ray Winkler (Woody Allen) has more in common with the bumbling heroes of the early films than with the neurotic professionals of Allen's mainstream works. An ex-convict, Ray masterminds a bank heist that requires renting an adjacent store as a front and tunneling through the basement walls to the vault. His gang botches the job at every step. Ray's wife, Frenchy (Tracy Ullman), a retired stripper, takes charge of the storefront, using her secret recipe for chocolate chip cookies. In no time, her neighborhood bakery is so popular that the shop soon blossoms into a huge factory and the Winklers enjoy more wealth than they could have with a dozen successful bank robberies.

As their bank accounts grow, so do Frenchy's pretensions. She tries to furnish her apartment with works of art, but her efforts result in an urban version of *Beverly Hillbillies,* a popular sitcom of the 1960s about a rustic family who struck oil on their farm and moved to California, where they simply did not fit in. With her new money and social ambition, Frenchy becomes an attractive target for David (Hugh Grant), a would-be gold digger who offers to educate her tastes while picking her pocket. Although Frenchy tries the Park Avenue style, Ray stays home with television and fast food. Frenchy's comedy arises from her frantic efforts to become a Manhattanite; Ray's from his discomfort with the whole idea. He wants to preserve his Brooklyn identity. Both suffer from the indignities of displacement and reach in opposite directions for a solution.

In *Hollywood Ending* (2002) Val Waxman (Woody Allen) suffers from multiple displacements. A once-successful film director, he cannot fit in with the Hollywood studio heads. Everyone knows that he is impossible to work with, and even as an independent filmmaker in New York, he has an unbroken string of losers to his credit. As the film opens, Val calls Lori Fox (Debra Messing), his live-in girlfriend and a would-be actress, from northern Canada to tell her he has just been fired from his deodorant commercial. With his temperament, he has become a misfit in the industry.

When his ex-wife Ellie (Téa Leoni), a studio executive, persuades Galaxy Pictures to give him a chance to shoot his kind of New York film, Val overcomes his hostility and accepts the job. His need for work and money overcomes his pride. He enters into the preproduction work energetically, but just as the cast assembles for the first day of shooting, Val loses his vision. Doctors assure him the problem has psychological rather than physical origins, but that offers little consolation. He has become a blind movie director. He hopes the condition will soon pass, and with Ellie's collusion, he bluffs it, working with a crazed set designer (Isaac Mizrahi) who insists on rebuilding Times Square for a more authentic look, and a Chinese camera operator (Yu Lu) who can communicate only through a Chinese business major from NYU (Barney Cheng). With these obstacles, he goes through the motions as a filmmaker, but he knows that he is a fraud. He doesn't know what he is doing, and naturally he is terrified that others will discover his charade and send him back where he belongs, wherever that is. Nonetheless, he's stuck, and he has no alternative but to see the project through to completion. At the end of the shooting, he recovers his sight and sees just how terrible the film really is. His work is not only fraudulent, it is bad, and the critics are savage. In sum, Val's experience shows that working in Manhattan involves both personal fraud and artistic failure. Of course, the improbable Hollywood ending of the title compounds the fraud. Everything turns out well, as it must in movies, but real life is another matter, especially in Manhattan.

These examples most readily support the sense of displacement that runs as a consistent thread through Woody Allen's films. The list does not include all the films, to be sure, but these show how the theme has been reworked in an amazing set of variations. Woody Allen has indeed emerged as a modern-day chronicler of life in New York, as even his most severe critics must concede. He loves his City, but as his art has matured, his affection has grown beyond the starry-eyed infatuation of the boy from Brooklyn seeing Times Square for the first time. Through the years in his adopted homeland, he has experienced its negative side as well. As one who remains to some extent an outsider and observer, while living as an archetypical Manhattanite, he has kept a remarkable sense of perspective about the City and its citizens. As he sees it, New York provides a stimulating environment for its artists, yet it shelters charlatans as well. It enables some to grow to full maturity, yet it fosters infantile narcissism. If asked about his relationship to New York, Woody Allen might well paraphrase Tess's summary of her marriage in *Radio Days:* "I love it, but what did I do to deserve it?"

Martin Scorsese

Filmography

Aviator, The (2004)

Gangs of New York (2002)

Bringing Out the Dead (1999)

Kundun (1997)

Casino (1995)

Age of Innocence, The (1993)

Cape Fear (1991)

GoodFellas (1990)

New York Stories (1989) (segment "Life Lessons")

Last Temptation of Christ, The (1988)

Color of Money, The (1986)

After Hours (1985)

King of Comedy, The (1983)

Raging Bull (1980)

Last Waltz, The (1978)

New York, New York (1977)

Taxi Driver (1976)

Alice Doesn't Live Here Anymore (1974)

Italianamerican (1974)

Mean Streets (1973)

Boxcar Bertha (1972)

Big Shave, The (1967)

Who's That Knocking at My Door? (1967)

It's Not Just You, Murray! (1964)

What's a Nice Girl Like You Doing in a Place Like This? (1963)

Vesuvius VI (1959)

Little Italy
Martin Scorsese

Martin Scorsese is far more Italian than he has any right to be. He was born in New York, as were both his parents, but as we have seen, culturally, "New York" means nothing and the neighborhood means everything. In the case of the Scorsese family, home was the Sicilian community that settled around Elizabeth Street on the Lower East Side of Manhattan, only a few blocks away from the Jewish section where Sidney Lumet grew up. Culturally, it was another country, and it ensured the Scorseses' Italianness through a third generation. In an interview with James Lipton on the television series *Inside the Actors' Studio,* Scorsese describes gathering with his extended family in front of a sixteen-inch black-and-white television to watch one of the Italian neorealist movies shown on a local New York station on Friday nights for the Italian American community. He comments that the people in the movie and the people in the room were speaking the same language, and as a child, he wasn't sure whether he was in Italy or America.

Although the nation he was in may have been a matter of some confusion for the young Scorsese, the neighborhood was not. In fact, so precise were the boundaries of this world that in his documentary film *Italianamerican* (1974), his father, Charles Scorsese, makes a clear distinction between their street and the Neapolitan settlement two blocks over on Mulberry Street. Although outsiders might speak of New York and New Yorkers of Little Italy, as though those labels explain anything, the residents view their area as a federation of even smaller enclaves, each with its own personality. One didn't hang out with people from other streets, Scorsese comments. In such an area, assimilation into the mainstream comes slowly, and when it comes, it has its own distinct tint. At the risk of a bit of overstatement, Martin Scorsese grew up in a Sicilian village that happened to be located on Elizabeth Street in Manhattan.

The Sicilian Factor

The local culture reinforced his genetic heritage. His grandfather, Francesco Scorsese, came from Polizzi Generosa, in the region around Palermo, the major metropolis of the island.[1] After his mother's death, Francesco hired on as a live-in farmhand, and at the age of nineteen he fulfilled his dream by migrating to America. He settled on Elizabeth Street with his wife, Teresa, also from Polizzi Generosa. He supported his family as a laborer in the shipyards during World War I and later as a pipe fitter and then manager for the New York Steam Company, which was to become incorporated into Consolidated Edison, the major power company in the New York City region. By his son's account, he rose to a significant managerial position, despite his lack of formal education. Francesco's son Luciano, or Charles, Martin's father, was born in 1912.

On the other side of Elizabeth Street lived the Cappa family from Cimmina, a village south of Palermo in the center of the island. Orphaned at an early age, Martin Cappa left his stepparents and joined the cavalry. In *Italianamerican* Catherine Scorsese tells a lovely, if romanticized, version of her parents' meeting and their love at first sight. As Martin rode through town in his dashing blue uniform, her mother, Domenica, spotted him from her second-floor balcony, and an exchange of glances and a touch of fingertips started them down the path to marriage. Reluctantly leaving his new bride behind, he came to New York to seek his fortune. He eventually sent for her, and they settled on Elizabeth Street, where he supported his wife and nine children as a scaffold rigger. For a time the family tried the rustic life in Staten Island, but eventually they moved back to Elizabeth Street, where they supplemented their income by taking in three boarders who shared quarters with the eleven Cappas. In the closed atmosphere of the block, probability edged into inevitability that Catherine Cappa and Charles Scorsese would get to know each other and eventually marry.

Assimilation into American life came slowly for both sides of the family. In the film, Catherine tells about her father's taking an interpreter with him to his naturalization hearing because after thirty years in America, he still had little confidence in his English. The immigration officer expressed some dismay at his failure to learn the language of his adopted country after so many years. Martin the patriarch may not have been proficient, but he did know enough to realize that he had been insulted, and he was able to reply in the idiomatic English he had learned on the construction sites. For him, at any rate, in the closed world of Elizabeth Street and the even more closed world of his own apartment, the English language was superfluous.

Money was tight during the Depression, even for those who had regular work. Young Charles Scorsese gave up on his plans to continue his education and went to work in the garment industry, first making vests and eventually working as a presser of very expensive formal wear. Catherine Cappa, her mother, and her sisters did piecework at home to supplement their father's income and rent from the boarders. After their marriage, Charles and Catherine moved across the East River to Sunnyside in the borough of Queens, where Frank was born, and then Corona, Queens, where Martin was born (the names of their two grandfathers). When Martin was six, the family gave up the house with a lawn and trees and moved back to Elizabeth Street. Until they found their own place, they stayed with his grandparents, Francesco and Teresa Scorsese, for four months. Martin Scorsese claims that he never understood the reason for their move. One explanation he offers is that his father ran into "business problems," but this scarcely clarifies the case because he continued to work as a wage earner and never went into business on his own. More likely is an alternate explanation that they had trouble with the landlord.[2] In any event, after a bucolic infancy, Martin Scorsese grew up in the very same street where his grandparents first struck roots in New York.

As a youngster Martin suffered from asthma, and as a result he had to stay close to the apartment and the neighborhood. Unable to participate in sports or the rough-and-tumble social life on the streets, "Marty Pills" (as he was known to his friends) took refuge in the movies and television. To compensate for his lack of ordinary play with boys his age, his father, and to a lesser degree his older brother, Frank, regularly took him to the movies. The family also invested in one of the first television sets in the neighborhood, surely as a means of providing Marty with a form of recreation that did not place a strain on his precarious health. For amusement, he drew sketches to illustrate stories just like the comic books, but the hobby soon matured into a form of storyboarding for film setups. His assimilation into the American mainstream, and more to the point his early understanding of the America beyond Elizabeth Street, came from the media—comics, television, and the movies—rather than from personal contact with the outside world.

Neighboring Villages

During Martin Scorsese's childhood, Elizabeth Street marked the eastern extremity of Italian Manhattan. Despite clear delineations of Lower East Side neighborhoods on tourist maps, the ethnic mix was always fluid. The shifting boundaries brought a kind of neighborhood xenophobia. The next street over was the Bowery, known to outsiders for its infamous skid row, but where the remnants of the most recent arrivals of the Irish community settled as Little Italy expanded in the earlier decades of the twentieth century. This "frontier" region provided a particular flavor to the New York experience for people of Martin Scorsese's background. The Irish and Italians were united in a common religion and shared Old St. Patrick's Cathedral on Mulberry Street, with its parochial school, but of course each had its own traditions and values. The teaching sisters were Irish Sisters of Mercy, but the priests were Italian. Of course, as Catholics, both the Irish and the Italians saw themselves as quite different from the Jews beyond the Bowery to the east or the residents of Chinatown to the south.

The relationship between the groups was ambivalent, and this ambivalence will be a key in unraveling Scorsese's films. Defining outsiders and insiders would become a project that has preoccupied Martin Scorsese for over thirty years, as his characters become trapped as individuals amid shifting tribal alliances and find themselves struggling for personal integrity at best, and survival at the least. In Scorsese's films one can find some traces of interethnic suspicion, rivalry, and even hostility, similar to those portrayed so powerfully in the films of Sidney Lumet. At the same time, there are moments of mutual respect and altruism that stretch beyond the tribe. Through it all, Scorsese manages extraordinary tolerance for diverse groups and their own individual ethos. He rarely holds groups to account for their corporate or criminal practices. The problems arise when individuals get greedy, violate accepted mores, and strike out on their own, like the Irish, who had moved on into Citywide politics or the police force. Much of this tolerance stems from the ethos of the old neighborhood.

The relationship between Italians and Irish seems particularly important in Scorsese's perceptual universe. These two groups shared not only religion and parish, but a keen tradition of seeing themselves as white, just like other Americans, yet at the same time feeling the resentments and insecurities of newcomers and outsiders to the American city, even though the Irish were a step ahead in the process.[3] In several interviews, Martin Scorsese speaks with affection of the Irish nuns who taught him at St. Patrick's and encouraged his interest in drawing. He describes himself as coming from an Irish neighborhood that had become Italian. In *Italianamerican,* Charles describes the old days when the Irish were still strongly represented on the block, as attested to by the number of bars along the street. Catherine seems a bit embarrassed by the remark, perhaps feeling that it might be offensive, and when she goes to the kitchen to stir her sauce, she strikes a conciliatory tone by explaining that the Irish were entitled to feel some resentment. It was their neighborhood before the Italians moved in.

In an interview Scorsese echoes his mother's sense of tolerance. "The way we felt about the Puerto Ricans, they [the Irish] felt about us. We felt the same way about the Irish, of course. And yet, there was an incredible amount of respect on the part of the third generation of Italians."[4] He cites the appreciation of the films of John Ford, with all their Irishness, as a sign of their respect. He continues: "We felt a great deal of fascination, even obsession, with Irish history because of the Catholicism and because of the family structure. . . . I find Irish and Italians to be so similar that maybe that's why they can't get along. *So* similar." Clearly, this Manhattan is different from Woody Allen's where ethnic identity, let alone conflict, rarely exists.

In addition to religion and family, Scorsese found great similarity between the two groups in crime: "With organized crime, first you had the Irish gangs in New York, and then the Italians came over and showed them *really* how to do it." Oddly, or perhaps obviously in light of his films, he doesn't question the morality of criminal gangs. Crime is just what immigrant groups do to gain a foothold on the first rung on the ladder to assimilation. In *Casino* and *Gangs of New York,* he even mourns the passing of the age of organized gangs. In both films, trouble arises when one individual puts personal interests ahead of the organization.

The animosity toward the Irish rises appreciably when he sees them as forgetting their immigrant roots as they moved into the mainstream. Regardless of nation of origin, any civic authority would have had an uphill fight in this environment. Scorsese himself offers a comment worthy of a sociologist. He describes the culture as a transplanted feudal culture with neighborhood capos filling the role of the dukes in Sicily. Because Sicily was a penal colony for over two thousand years, he explained that Sicilians could never trust the authorities. He concludes, "There was no such thing as law. It was a feudal system. And they did the same in New York. Village to village."[5] Of course, Ireland had been under military occupation for four hundred years, so its emigrants also placed little trust in the authorities. Both groups had a tendency to take care of business themselves, and this provides a ready formula for occasional friction on the streets. Because the Irish were a generation ahead of the Italians, they moved into politics and the police, where they could cover their criminal activities with a flimsy veil of respectability. Because the Italians of Scorsese's generation connected the Irish and police so closely, the resentment had deep cultural roots that went beyond the usual turf wars one finds in neighborhoods in transition. In an interview in 1973 he recalls, "We hated the Irish, too, [in addition to the Jews] because of the Fifth Precinct. It was unknown for any of us to call a cop, unless it was to give him some graft. Cops were always Irish, always drinking, and always had their hands out. We used to bribe them to play stickball in the street. It's still that way—believe me, *Serpico* only skimmed the surface."[6]

At the same time, although he speaks of the capos as resolving "altercations" among the neighbors, he never mentions extortion and intimidation, which may have enhanced the effectiveness of their mediation. The Sicilian bosses worked within the established customs of the village. The Irish police represented an alien form of intimidation and corruption disguised as law enforcement, and in such a capacity, they could be lumped together with the other, earlier arrivals as part of the establishment.

Despite the best efforts of cops and capos to establish order, Scorsese remembers his move to Manhattan as an entry into a world as of extraordinary danger and degradation. "I was old enough to realize that there were some tough guys around," he recalls. "You might be playing in a sandbox and something would fall behind you—not a bag of garbage as you might expect, but a little baby that had fallen off a roof."[7] The next street to the east of Elizabeth Street is the Bowery, a name that has come to symbolize urban blight and the last stop for many of the homeless, alcoholic, addicted, depraved, and deranged. One can only imagine the impression this environment made on an artistically sensitive and sickly nine-year-old, newly arrived from the relatively suburban security of Corona. In interviews he describes seeing derelicts fighting with broken bottles and his walking around blood on the streets on his way to school. He recalls seeing men engaged in oral sex: "I was about thirteen then, but I will never forget the images. Never forget them."[8] Yet he contends that his was not a particularly disturbing childhood: "This was just the environment I was in. It was like the Wild West, the frontier. . . . coming back late at night you found derelicts in the halls or people robbing each other in the halls." Yet he recalls hearing of Dorothy Day's Catholic Worker shelter on Chrystie Street and wondering why anyone would care for such people. This sense of admiration for those who care for "hopeless cases" would provide the spiritual foundation for *Mean Streets.*

This apparently contradictory combination of his recollection of images of graphic violence coupled with his seeming nonchalance about his experience helps explain the terrifying but dispassionate violence of the films. He presents the dark side of life and death as they are, without need for special-effects enhancement that many contemporary filmmakers use for shock value. The bloody aftermath of the shootout in *Taxi Driver* is terrifying, and the fight scenes in *Raging Bull* provide high-contrast black-and-white and slow-motion images to communicate the brutal nature of professional boxing. Both scenes are terrifying in their violence, but neither provokes sadistic pleasure in pain common to many action-adventure films in the age of computer-generated graphics. In *Bringing Out the Dead* he reveals the horrors of the addicts and derelicts picked up on the street and brought by ambulance to an emergency room. For the drivers and medical personnel, they are just part of the nightly routine. Scorsese finds little need to enhance their misery. He aims for reality as he experienced it, rather than shock as audiences might expect.

The Village Church

As a rather frail youngster whose health limited his activities, young Martin Scorsese found the parochial school and Old St. Patrick's Cathedral an improbably congenial environment after two years of public school in Queens. Neither of his parents were particularly religious. Their sending their son to the Catholic school did not reveal any particular act of devotion on their part, but it was rather the standard practice for even nominally Catholic families in New York at the time. The Archdiocese of New York and the Diocese of Brooklyn across the river both supported enormous school systems, which in many locales equaled or surpassed public school enrollment. With the number of teaching sisters volunteering their services during this period, most parishes were able to provide free elementary education for their parishioners. His going to St. Patrick's rather than to public school should not be conceived of in contemporary terms as a family's financial sacrifice to send their son to a private school.

In Martin Scorsese's case, the choice of St. Patrick's over public school was in fact particularly fortuitous. Catholic schools and churches of the time bristled with religious images representing incidents in the life of Jesus, the Virgin Mary, and the saints. Each image told a story in a way that carried a desired emotional impact. The art may not have been very good, but to a child, the connection between picture and story stamps the imagination forever. As an altar boy, who dressed in ecclesiastical robes and assisted at church services, Martin Scorsese witnessed up close the splendid rituals reenacting the events of the liturgical year: Christmas, Lent, Easter, and the celebrations of the feasts of the Blessed Virgin, Joseph, and the other saints. Each of the rites brought its own delight of senses: the vestments, candles, shimmering altar vessels, incense, and music. In catechism class, he would have learned about the hierarchical structure of the Church, with its leaders and followers, the importance of unquestioning loyalty to group mores, and the dread of excommunication, all of which eerily colors his portrayal of criminal gangs, or in the case of *The Age of Innocence,* the equally closed upper reaches of Edith Wharton's New York society in the nineteenth century. Involved as he was with church activities, Martin became close to a young parish priest, Father Frank Principe, who encouraged his interests in music and art, especially the movies. This relationship stirred in this sensitive youngster the desire to become a priest himself.

Scorsese's decision to enter Cathedral Prep, the minor seminary of the Archdiocese, at the age of fourteen was perfectly consistent with his parochial school background. These early priestly ambitions took him away from the sanctuary of Elizabeth Street all the way uptown to West Eighty-sixth Street. As a genuine New Yorker, he took the subway, under the heart of midtown, with its legitimate theater and movie cathedrals, right to the door of the school. Although Woody Allen recalls feeling a childhood awe at the sight of the midtown movie cathedrals like the Radio City Music Hall, and although Sidney Lumet began his artistic career on the stage, both of these elements form little part of Martin Scorsese's artistic biography. For him, going to a swank uptown theater meant the Academy of Music on Fourteenth Street, an area that even by the 1950s was well past its prime. The commercial life of the area was dominated by the huge cut-rate department store, S. Klein's, on Union Square, a minipark noted for its radical left-wing political speakers. Or so we thought in the 1950s.

After little more than a year at Cathedral Prep, Scorsese had second thoughts about his priestly vocation, prompted in part by poor academic performance, and withdrew from the prep seminary. He continued his studies at Cardinal Hayes High School in the Bronx, which involved an even longer ride on the subway underneath the length of Manhattan. The schools changed, but the grades did not. Finishing in the bottom quarter of his graduating class, he failed to gain admission to Fordham University, also in the Bronx. Thus ended his ten-year involvement with Catholic schools. It would be misleading to conclude that this early education was parochial in the pejorative sense of the word, and therefore an obstacle to his development as a mature artist. Clearly, his later productivity demonstrates that he was scarcely hobbled by his early education. The schooling, coupled with his quasi-confinement to his immediate geographical surroundings, provides a point of entry for understanding Scorsese's sense of commitment to immediate circles of friends and families that marks the internal struggles of many of his individualistic and even narcissistic characters.

Especially around the time of the release of *The Last Temptation of Christ* and its surrounding controversies, Scorsese provided several quotable protestations of his lingering belief in Catholicism, including, most famously, " I wanted to be a priest, My whole life has been movies and religion. That's it. Nothing else."[9] At the same time, he explains his alienation from the Church beginning in 1965, after hearing a priest in Union City, New Jersey, preach about the Vietnam War as a holy enterprise. After several divorces and failure to "make his Easter duty" for years, Scorsese considers himself "excommunicated," even though, as he explains, "I haven't gotten a letter yet."[10] Yet his Catholic awareness of good and evil, of redemption and forgiveness, of community and loyalty, remain at the heart of his filmmaking.[11]

The Wider Horizon

Even after the disappointment of being refused admission to Fordham, and with several questions about Church teaching beginning to arise in his life, Martin Scorsese did not totally abandon his idea of becoming a priest, but it was becoming less likely. He was starting to move out of the restricted family environment of his childhood and Catholic schooling toward new territories of young adulthood.

A significant first step was his growing alienation from the Catholic Church. In various interviews, he specifies his difficulties with the Church, and they seem to cover a fairly standard repertoire for young men of his background in the 1950s. He experienced the predictable clash between parochial-school scrupulosity and puberty. In addition, after ten years of catechism, he found Church dogma and discipline overly concerned with peripheral matters, and he mentions being puzzled that after teaching for a thousand years that eating meat on Friday was enough to consign one to eternal damnation, the Church suddenly changed the rules and said that it was all right after all. Because of his passion for movies, Scorsese experienced a rather unusual "crisis of faith" in that he found the ratings provided by Catholic Legion of Decency more than a bit troubling. According to the popular understanding of its rules at the time, a Catholic would commit a mortal sin by seeing a film the Legion placed on its condemned list. Yet his friend, Father Principe, assured him that he could disregard this strict interpretation because of his artistic interest in films. Such advice seems merely sensible today, but in the Catholic world of the 1950s, it must have seemed quite daring to the former altar boy and seminarian.

As Scorsese recalls, his sense of the Church's apparent intolerance, especially toward Jews, became especially troubling. This perception remains a source of discomfort for many Catholics even today, and it provides a basis of harsh criticism from many non-Catholics. The controversies over the history of Jewish-Catholic relations are complex and still unresolved, but to be fair, Scorsese's assessment of the Church's intolerance may be shaped as much by the ethnic boundaries he experienced growing up in his homogeneous working-class environment as by Church teaching and practice. Scorsese graduated from high school in 1960, only two years after the death of Pope Pius XII. At that time, the questions raised about his policies during World War II may have been a source of concern for scholars, but they scarcely would have reached the consciousness of a teenager in a Catholic high school. Ecumenism and interfaith dialogue, to say nothing of openly hostile criticism of Vatican officials, would come only years later, most markedly after the presentation of Rolf Hochhuth's play about Pius XII, *The Deputy*, in 1963. In the popular perception of the day—erroneous as it was—there lingered the suspicion that those outside the Church might not make it unless God took special and mysterious steps to intervene. Intolerance lies a short step away from such distorted beliefs, but one has to wonder if non-Christians too, like the Chinese in Chinatown or the Jews on Hester Street, might not have harbored their own forms of Lower East Side antagonism toward other ethnic groups.

Scorsese recalls a painful event that gives some indication of feelings that were not uncommon in ethnic enclaves. When he was five and his brother twelve and they were still living in Queens, they came upon a man unconscious and bleeding on the street. Martin was upset, but his brother Frank assured him that it was "only a Jew."[12] "It was one of my earliest memories," Scorsese explains, and the event surely remains a shameful childhood memory for him to this day. Yet when he tried to create an authentic portrait of life in Little Italy in *Mean Streets*, the young hoods and hustlers on the streets do not shy from equally brutal references to Jews and African Americans. Such bigotry sadly existed in far more overt forms then than it does today, but how the Catholic Church contributed to such attitudes by complicity or silence is a question that resists simple explanations. Denial, whitewash, and collective amnesia will not do; but neither will blanket denunciations.

Whatever his feelings about the Church, Scorsese remained a church-goer, but by 1960 he had begun a transition in his life. His graduation from Cardinal Hayes and his rejection by Fordham put an end to his involvement with Catholic education and marked his entry into the more diverse collection of cultures and ideas at New York University. At the same time, his decision to attend a college located on Washington Square in Greenwich Village essentially brought him back to the neigh-borhood to continue his schooling. The school was a short walk from Elizabeth Street, so he was able to remain at home while attending classes. Still the Village, long known as a haven for writers, artists, radical po-litical activists, and nonconformists, was a different cultural universe from Little Italy. Scorsese claims to have visited the Village only a few times before enrolling at NYU. This is quite plausible. The subway lines run north and south, and Washington Square lies to the west of Eliza-beth Street. As noted in the case of Woody Allen's roots in Flatbush, most native New Yorkers are hopelessly bound to their immediate neigh-borhood. They take the subway to work, or in Scorsese's case to Cardi-nal Hayes High School in the Bronx, with very little awareness of other sections of the City, even one as close as the Village was to Little Italy.

Life at NYU opened new horizons for Scorsese to a far greater ex-tent than college life does for most undergraduates. He enrolled in the film program with an English minor, with the vague idea of becoming a teacher, possibly a priest-teacher, like Father Principe or those he had experienced in high school. Film studies, however, soon subverted his backup plan for a safe, traditional career path. He entered the film pro-gram under the direction of the legendary teacher Haig Manoogian and found himself captivated by images, much as he had been with his child-hood sketches. The program began with upward of two hundred stu-dents each year, and after two semesters of history and criticism, the class was reduced to thirty-six. These surviving few were allowed to touch a sixteen-millimeter camera and make a film. Scorsese recalls: "Most of the kids took the class because they thought they wouldn't have to do anything much except watch films and get two credits for it. But Haig was brutal."[13] As a bonus to classroom work, the immediate vicinity of the campus included the best art houses in the City: the Art and the Eighth Street Playhouse and of course the Bleecker Street Cinema. Before the days of videotape libraries, access to foreign films in the neighborhood movie theaters made NYU a film student's paradise.

The paradox cannot be overemphasized. Scorsese grew as an artist and reached out to world cinema while he himself was physically confined to a very small region of New York City, below Fourteenth Street in Manhattan. This has enormous implications for his filmmaking. To a far greater extent than either Sidney Lumet or Woody Allen, Scorsese has not confined his films to New Yorkers in New York settings, although arguably his strongest films, like *Mean Streets, Taxi Driver,* and *Raging Bull,* do in fact emerge from the New York streets. Still, despite his confined physical surroundings, his imagination reaches out to embrace a universe of human experience. Whether the films are set on the Carolina coast (*Cape Fear*), Las Vegas (*Casino*), Tibet (*Kundun*), ancient Israel (*The Last Temptation of Christ*), or the Arizona desert (*Alice Doesn't Live Here Any More*), they remain marked by their origins in Lower Manhattan. His characters reflect the neighborhood's mistrust of outsiders in general and authorities in particular, a compulsion to take care of business according to the rules of the group without judging its methods, and an often destructive conflict between personal integrity and tribal loyalties. The conflicts often lead to violence, not as an excuse for cinematic voyeurism, but as a simple acknowledgment that human conflict frequently leads to terrifying violence. It's the way life is. At least it's life as Martin Scorsese experienced it around Little Italy.

Close to Home

During his five years at NYU, Martin Scorsese made his first student film and never stopped making them in the eight years between graduation and his breakthrough film, *Mean Streets,* in 1973. On seeing them now, a critic might rightly conclude that his early efforts were technically competent efforts by a talented student filmmaker working with extremely limited resources, but otherwise of little interest. But more than technique can be detected in these early films. Haig Manoogian, his mentor at NYU, advised him to stick close to his experience of the Lower East Side, and Scorsese followed this suggestion explicitly in his early years, and later, as he moved out into other settings, he took a large part of the old neighborhood with him.[14] These early student films form a bridge between Little Italy and the outside world. They set the pattern for his treatment of the tensions he feels between group loyalty and personal integrity. Much of this struggle is framed through a Catholic sensibility formed in school, church, and Elizabeth Street culture. When explaining his belief that Scorsese's individual characters are at root moralists dealing with conflict, critic Michael Bliss convincingly explains this tension as an "attempt to resolve the opposition between the behests of Catholicism as derived from the Bible and the rigorous demands of living in the world."[15]

That understanding of Scorsese's conflicted characters is crucial, but the analysis can be taken a step further. What is more to the point at present is that these struggling individuals are self-consciously members of a group, which precisely as a definable group also strives to reconcile its own integrity to "the rigorous demands of living in a world" amid other competing groups with their own characteristic value systems. The small-time gangster struggles to make it in Elizabeth Street society, while Elizabeth Street and the mob try to find their place in the larger cluster of communities that surround it. One can then imagine a typical Scorsese conflict as a set of concentric circles. At the core is the individual striving for identity within a tight organization or community, and then the community struggling for its own collective survival within the mainstream, and presumably hostile, majority society. The individual may be tempted to jump over the immediate circle and reach for the outer rim, but he does so at the risk of losing personal identity. Several films illustrate this dual conflict, starting with his earliest efforts as a fledgling artist at NYU.

An early student film, *What's a Nice Girl Like You Doing in a Place Like This?* (1963), is a nine-minute sixteen-millimeter narrative film about a character with writer's block. He has two names, Algernon and Harry, as though he is searching for his true identity before he enters the world of art. The Harry/Algernon conundrum mirrors Scorsese's own awareness of his ethnic roots and desire to enter the larger, mainstream world of art and artists. The character seems to resolve his problem by marrying an ideal woman and leading an ordinary family life, just like that of his own parents, but his striving for artistic success creates a new set of tensions for him. At the end of the film, the young writer becomes trapped in a photograph he contemplates, torn between "reality" and art, his marriage and his work. In turn, the world of art stands in contrast to the larger world, of ordinary people who work to preserve ordinary values, like marriage. Can an artist like Scorsese have both?

In scarcely fifteen minutes and again in sixteen millimeter, *It's Not Just You, Murray* (1964) presents the story of a small-time hood from the neighborhood who boasts of his friendship and indebtedness to his friend Joe. Murray measures success in material possessions and his position in the neighborhood. He eventually discovers that Joe has betrayed his business interests, had been instrumental in sending him to prison, and, as the final indignity, has been involved with Murray's wife. These factors would normally end a friendship, but Joe manages to reestablish the relationship by offering Murray a car. According to the logic prevalent in this world of petty gangsters, the payoff is a perfectly legitimate way to right past wrongs. Murray accepts the gift and forgets the betrayal by his friend. In Sicilian culture, male friendship and loyalty despite injuries received is a paramount value. When the injuries become too great, the vendetta replaces loyalty, and an enemy must pay dearly for betrayal. Scorsese's characters frequently wrestle with the decision to cross the boundary and seek revenge from a former friend. By turning his back on the wrongs he has suffered from Joe, Murray has preserved the laws and mores of his group, maintained unity, and seen his position enhanced by the acquisition of a new car. Joe, for his part, has redeemed himself on the cheap. Outsiders might find his reactions grotesque, but insiders know that this is the ordinary way of doing business. Murray acquiesces to the values of the small band of petty criminals, yet these warped values place them outside the comprehension of the outside world, and Scorsese knows it, even if Murray does not.

The Big Shave (1967), originally titled *Viet '67*, is an ugly six-minute sixteen-millimeter film that Scorsese completed two years after graduation from NYU. From this point in time, the metaphor seems contrived, but in the 1960s, everything artistic seemed to have a symbolic connection to the hated Vietnam War. A nameless man enters a gleaming white bathroom and begins to shave. As his strokes become more vigorous, he repeatedly cuts himself until the blood runs down his face and into the sink, in a shot reminiscent of the final shot in Hitchcock's famous shower scene in *Psycho* (1960). The action could suggest America's cutting its own throat through the war, or it could call attention to the gratuitous violence inflicted on the Vietnamese people, both themes commonplace during the 1960s. The film merits a mention here simply because it provides an extreme example of Scorsese's using an extraordinarily confined space (the bathroom) to explore an issue of worldwide significance. The shaver is in conflict with America, and America is in conflict with the world.

Throughout his career, Scorsese will use readily identifiable and somewhat quirky subcultures to explore wider philosophic, theological, and moral issues. In his most important films, he will universalize his experience of Little Italy by using Elizabeth Street as a lens through which he will explore the world of his conflicted characters. His gangsters, for example, gradually branch out from petty loan-sharking in *Mean Streets* to cocaine trafficking and a multimillion-dollar Lufthansa robbery at Kennedy Airport in *GoodFellas* to the incredible wealth flowing across the gaming tables every day in *Casino*. The enormity of the crimes changes, but the series of conflicts remains essentially the same.

Scorsese makes his transition into commercial filmmaking with *Who's That Knocking at My Door?* (1969). Also released at various times under the titles *Bring on the Dancing Girls, I Call First,* and *JR,* this film was originally conceived as the middle chapter in a trilogy. Scorsese wrote an extensive treatment of the first, *Jerusalem, Jerusalem,* while he was still at NYU, but he never was able to shoot it. The story recalls the experiences of several Catholic high-school seniors who have gone away on a retreat, which consists mostly of ominous admonitions about the dangers of sex. Several episodes of the Gospels were to be relived on the streets of Little Italy as the boys reflect on their lives. This of course looks forward to the opening of *Mean Streets,* the projected third part of the trilogy, where Charlie (Harvey Keitel) comments that one does not find salvation in church, but in the streets.

With *Jerusalem, Jerusalem* on the shelf—permanently, as it turned out—Scorsese began work on *Who's That Knocking on My Door?* Fresh out of college when the work began in 1965, he had clearly begun to question both the Church and the ethos of Little Italy. His first marriage ended during this period as well. The film clearly grows out of these changes going on in his own life. The hero of the film, JR (Harvey Keitel, in his first role), is another of Scorsese's local toughs. He has a few rackets, a few friends, and little future. He drinks, gambles, and pursues women as his personal prey. JR's Catholic conflict about sex intrudes upon his life when, despite his apparent promiscuity, he decides that he will not sleep with his fiancée, who is not given a name and who is referred to simply as the Girl (Zina Bethune) until after their marriage. When he discovers that she had been raped by a previous boyfriend, he calls off the marriage, blaming her for her loss of virginity. After consoling himself by partying with his friends, he decides to "forgive" her and go ahead with the wedding. He sees his gesture as magnanimous, but she sees it as a sign of JR's ignorance and warped values. She throws him out, and he is left walking down a street with his old friend Joey.

JR's odious conduct exists within the culture of the street, where most women are regarded as sources of entertainment but where a select few are expected to remain virginal until marriage. JR's situation is compounded by his sense of guilt that comes from his Catholicism for his own failure to live up to the demands of self-control, even though his ill treatment of the Girl seems beyond his comprehension or remorse. Religious imagery abounds throughout the film. JR emerges not only as a despicable cad, but also as the victim of his own claustrophobic world, the male-centered Sicilian Catholic ghetto. As Scorsese sees it, his behavior is shaped more by ignorance and immaturity than by malice. His own biography up to this point in his life suggests that there may be more than a bit of the young Martin Scorsese in JR: seeing himself as remaining a pious Catholic despite his growing estrangement from the Church while admiring the carefree life at school and on the streets with his friends. Clearly, too, like JR, he had not yet resolved the conflicts between his Catholic upbringing and desire for a family on one side and the sexual revolution that was reaching its peak in campus life throughout the country in general and in Greenwich Village in particular. Like many artists from small towns or ethnic enclaves, it was as hard to leave home as it was to stay.

Mean Streets of Home

After what he considered the artistic disaster of *Boxcar Bertha* (1972), the story of union organizers in Arkansas during the Depression, Martin Scorsese was ready to come home. The film served its purpose, however. For producer Roger Corman, it contained the requisite number of nude scenes and episodes of gratuitous violence, and despite what the reviewers said about it, it made a modest profit for Allied International Pictures. According to these criteria, it was a success. For Scorsese, it opened doors to the Hollywood studios, got him admitted into the Screen Directors Guild, and proved that he could work quickly, follow the directives of a producer, and function with a tight budget and an impossible shooting schedule. The film marks his progression from the status as clever student filmmaker from New York to that of a recognizable name within the industry. He could attend parties, meet people, and make himself known to Hollywood insiders. Scorsese himself disliked the film intensely and was stung when his idol John Cassavetes accused him of wasting his time with such a potboiler. He knew that his future did not lie with period pieces set in Arkansas and with nude scenes every fifteen minutes to keep the audience's attention at the drive-ins. He was ready to negotiate a return to the world that Manoogian had strenuously recommended to him years earlier.

Mean Streets (1973), which drips with New York flavor, was actually shot in Los Angeles, with the exception of several exteriors Scorsese was able to shoot during an eight-day period in New York. This convincing re-creation of village life in an artificial setting indicates how thoroughly he had absorbed the atmosphere of his home territory and how well he could transfer it to other locations. Scorsese believes that *Mean Streets* is "really an anthropological or a sociological tract."[16] He explains: "[It] was an attempt to put myself and my old friends on the screen, to show how we lived, what life was like in Little Italy." He introduces the notion that his film is a record of his friends by running eight-millimeter home movies of the principals with the titles. The diverse scenes within the film construct a mosaic of locations within an extremely small geographic area, yet each one reveals a facet of the constricted, claustrophobic world of the main character, Charlie (Harvey Keitel). The action takes place in Charlie's small apartment, the roof, and the adjacent stairwell; in Tony's bar; in a social club and in a pool hall; in the interior of Old St. Patrick's Cathedral and in its cemetery; in Oscar's upscale restaurant; in a movie theater; and of course in the streets connecting them.

All these settings are within easy walking distance of one another. The characters have little opportunity to escape from the neighborhood. Charlie can walk from one setting to another, but he rarely leaves his home turf. When he stands on the beach with his girlfriend Teresa (Amy Robinson), he admits to feeling uncomfortable because of the open-air surroundings rather than because of the awkward conversation about their future together. Teresa, for her part, talks about taking an apartment uptown, but her chances of following her dream appear slim. Cars offer little promise of escape to a world beyond Little Italy. For Charlie cars are associated with death. He enters one the first time when he and his friends run from the police after a shooting in Tony's bar. At the climax of the film, he travels by car to Brooklyn with Johnny Boy and Teresa to get away from Michael and his shooters, and the three of them are gunned down by a hit man played by Scorsese himself. For Michael cars represent frustration, as we will see; they provide the settings to show that he is a only a small-time hood who will never leave the street.

Charlie's world consists of people much like himself, and this provides both comfort and limitations. In several scenes he expresses interest in Diane (Jeanie Bell), the African American go-go dancer at Tony's bar. Charlie jumps on the stage to dance with her. He speaks to her about getting together—not as a date, surely—but to offer her a job as hostess when he takes over a restaurant. As he drives through the street late at night, he seems distressed to discover her standing on the street corner, apparently working as a prostitute. He would like to draw closer to her, but the racial barrier is insuperable. In a raucous conversation in the bar, one customer reveals that a mutual friend was seen kissing a black woman under the bridge in New Jersey. Such a thing could never happen in their neighborhood, and the revelation provokes expressions of disgust—and more, it suggests the unspoken threat that the men in the bar will have to make their friend regret his aberration. Black men, of course, never venture into this territory unless on business. A black police officer breaks up a fight in the pool hall, in the company of an Irish-looking colleague, and then shakes the owner down for "carfare" back to New Jersey in exchange for forgetting about the incident. The exchange provides another perspective on the resentment of the Italian Americans in the neighborhood toward other outsiders who forget their origins and become corrupt insiders.

Jews fare little better than African Americans. Johnny Boy (Robert DeNiro) brings two Jewish girls into the bar and negotiates the pairings with Charlie, presuming the amoral compliance of the women, who, according to the belief of the streets, are not burdened with Catholic inhibitions. In a later scene, Johnny Boy sees a woman at Tony's bar, identifies her as Jewish, and makes a lame joke about seeing her playing volleyball at the convent. He seems deliberately offensive. When her escort, who may or not be Jewish himself, returns, Johnny Boy insults both of them, and persuades the woman to dump her boyfriend. He leaves, but Johnny Boy becomes furious when the woman will not stay with him. Again, he seems to work on the premise that Jewish women are available. Jewish men do not appear in the film at all.

The all-male Italian American world includes a wide spectrum of characters, but few of Charlie's friends seem to hold full-time jobs within the limits of the law. On the outer limits of respectability is Charlie's friend Johnny Boy, who is clearly at best immature, or at worst sociopathic. He first appears on the screen putting an explosive device in a mailbox for no apparent reason beyond his own personal amusement. Later, he fires his pistol from a tenement rooftop, explaining to Charlie that he is trying to shoot out the lights of the Empire State Building, a good two miles to the north. Before Charlie interrupts his shooting spree, he fires one shot through the window of a woman he can't stand. As they leave together, he tosses a huge firecracker from the roof with the idea of waking up the neighborhood. Johnny Boy is clearly a child in a man's body, charming in his brash way but ultimately dangerous to himself as well as to others. When he accompanies Charlie to a pool hall to collect a debt, he deliberately provokes the owner, and a free-for-all breaks out. The huge pool-hall operator wants to make peace and offers his visitors a drink, but Johnny Boy insults him again, and the fight resumes until it is broken up by the two police officers on the take.

Johnny Boy's irresponsibility propels the plot. He cannot repay a rapidly escalating debt to Michael, the loan shark, and even though he knows the consequences of failing to meet his obligations, he never quite treats his predicament seriously. He struts through life with bravado, convinced that in the end he can talk his way out of any situation and that his friend Charlie will use his influence with his uncle Giovanni, a mob capo, to delay the reckoning, which he seems to believe will never happen. Having missed several installments on his promised payment, he brings the two Jewish women into Tony's bar and tries to throw money around by buying drinks to impress them, knowing that the story of his generous behavior will soon make its way back to his shylocks. To impress his dates with his wit, he takes his pants off and tries to get the coat-check attendant to take them. The women giggle at his prank without realizing how much this witless joke reveals an adolescent vulnerability that borders on the suicidal.

Michael (Richard Romanus), the loan shark, is a suave street thug with limited prospects for moving up in the mob. He first appears during a hijacking under the old West Side Highway. He and his henchmen transfer goods from one truck to another, and in the following scene, when he tries to fence his stolen goods, which he believes are valuable German lenses, he discovers that they are worthless Japanese knockoffs. The buyer refuses to take them. At his best, he is able to con two teenagers from Riverdale into giving him money for illegal fireworks that he has no intention of delivering.[17] Rather than enjoy his moment of triumph, he discovers that the two boys have given him only a fraction of what they pretended to give him. Michael ends up with only enough profit for a movie. Despite numerous attempts, he proves no more successful in getting his money from Johnny Boy. He threatens Johnny Boy personally, tells Charlie to "straighten him out," sets up meetings that Johnny Boy skips, and at Charlie's request, even cuts the debt by a third, but Johnny Boy earns little money and what he has soon dribbles through his fingers before it reaches Michael. When he finally corners Johnny Boy in Tony's bar, Johnny Boy mocks him for being the only one on the block stupid enough to lend him money. When he and his henchmen threaten physical harm, Johnny pulls a gun and escapes again. After this show of disrespect, breaking his legs, the earlier threat, is no longer sufficient. Michael's only option, according to his code, is to have Johnny Boy killed, a course of action that will save face, even though it will not get him his money. The attempted assassination in a Brooklyn driveway ultimately fails, however, leaving Johnny Boy, Charlie, and his girlfriend Teresa seriously wounded but presumably still able to testify one day against Michael and his backseat hit man, played by Martin Scorsese himself.

Giovanni (Cesare Danova), Charlie's uncle, runs the neighborhood from his table in the social club. Despite his recognized power over life and death on the street, he is cool and deliberate in his business dealings. In one such business relationship, Oscar (Murray Moston), who owns a respectable, almost elegant, restaurant, owes money, but unlike Michael, Giovanni is content to wait for a time before he acts. He knows that eventually he will get either Oscar's money or the restaurant, and because of his confidence in his status, he feels no need to bluster and threaten violence. The threat is there without his having to call attention to it. Another instance of his understated authority occurs when a young gun for the mob kills a drunk at Tony's bar. The shooter believes that avenging a perceived insult to another member of the family will increase his own reputation and standing. Giovanni will have no part in the next round of vengeance, either as enforcer or protector. He tells the killer's father to have his son leave town for a while until everyone forgets about the event. His quiet moral authority bears more weight than the strong-arm tactics of his lieutenants.

In contrast to the street hoods, Oscar with his restaurant and Tony with his bar run real businesses. Oscar works hard, but to keep his place open, he borrows heavily from Giovanni. He realizes that he cannot repay the debt and knows without anyone having to tell him that he will have to forfeit his restaurant. Giovanni dispatches his nephew to remind Oscar of his debt, but Charlie is ambivalent about his errand. Charlie likes Oscar and sympathizes with his plight, but he also knows that if Oscar defaults, Giovanni will almost certainly make him manager of the restaurant. The pressure on Oscar rises when his partner, Groppi, commits suicide rather than face the mob, but Oscar will survive, albeit without his restaurant. Oscar holds no grudges against Giovanni because he realizes that Giovanni is simply conducting business according to time-tested rules that both men understand quite well.

Tony (David Proval) owns the bar that functions as the central locale of the film. He welcomes everyone as a friend as well as a customer. By way of exception, in an opening scene, he discovers an addict shooting up in the men's room and throws him out onto the street. For his customers' entertainment, he has hired Diane, an African American, surely a sign of open-mindedness in that neighborhood at that time. During a welcome-home party for a returning Vietnam veteran, Tony allows his friends to get a bit out of control with their roughhousing and stops the party only when the guest of honor grabs at a woman guest, who is also quite drunk, but who rejects his crude advances. Tony puts up with Johnny Boy's antics and with a staggering drunk climbing up on the bar for a nap before he is murdered by the young hit man. After the murder of the drunk, Tony drives Charlie, Johnny Boy, and two nameless gays away from the crime scene before they have to face questioning by the police as eyewitnesses. As the film marches toward its tragic climax in an alley in Brooklyn, Tony lends his car to Charlie and Johnny Boy so that they can avoid Michael after Johnny Boy pulled the gun on him in the bar. Tony is truly dedicated to his bar, but he will sacrifice everything for loyalty to his friends.

As the central character, Charlie holds the narrative together, and as he interacts with the others, he reveals himself as the most complex of the lot. He has maintained strong religious convictions, even though he discovered that the priest who conducted his high-school retreat had made up the story about the couple struck by a truck as they engaged in "sinful behavior" in the back seat of a car. Yet while he feels deceived by churchmen, he clings to his belief in sin and redemption. In an early scene set in a church, Charlie has come from making his confession and yet states that "you don't make up for your sins in church, but on the street." Still in church, he holds his finger over a votive candle to remind himself of the pains of hell, a technique he learned during his high-school retreat. Later, as he inspects the kitchen at the restaurant, while Oscar and Giovanni discuss business in the dining room, he again holds his hand over a flame, this time of the gas range, as though he feels some guilt at his probable gain once Oscar goes down. He will run the restaurant for Giovanni. He feels some need for atonement, but it will not stop him from accepting his new role.

No doubt Scorsese's own progressive alienation from the Catholic Church, as Charlie's recollections of deceit indicate, was balanced by his continuing admiration of Dorothy Day's Catholic Worker House on Chrystie Street, a few blocks from his childhood home, and by his continuing personal friendship with Father Principe. At this time, he may well be distancing himself from the institutional side of Catholicism, but he remains wedded to the culture. He situates the action of *Mean Streets,* with its violence and ruthless business codes, within the context of Little Italy's annual San Gennaro festival, which features a week of religious processions and bands, lights, fireworks, and food stalls and a Mass in commemoration of the feast.[18] In keeping with the story of the martyr San Gennaro, Charlie is destined to suffer through many ordeals before he finds redemption. In addition, the inclusion of the film's narrative within this context offers a comment that the folk religion in the area really exercises very little influence on the mores of its inhabitants.

Charlie's ethical instincts run much deeper than recollections of a high-school retreat or the folkways of the neighborhood. Throughout the film, he struggles to find his own personal integrity not only within this morally and religiously ambiguous atmosphere, but despite it. Although others see Johnny Boy as a flake or plainly insane, as does his cousin Teresa, Charlie regards him as a kind of divine fool, in the model of Dostoevsky's *The Idiot.* He takes upon himself the special mission of protecting him from harm, particularly from Michael because of the loan, and even from himself when he goes on his shooting spree on the rooftops. Close association with Johnny Boy jeopardizes his standing with Giovanni because a man with flawed judgment about his friends could scarcely be entrusted with the restaurant.

Charlie's relationships with women are quite instructive. He treats Diane with respect and affection, even though he knows that race precludes any romantic involvement. When the Vietnam veteran assaults the intoxicated woman at his welcome-home dinner, Charlie steps in and rescues the woman, who then passes out in his arms. He takes her to the back room, gently places her on a cot, and covers her with a blanket, apparently without any thought of taking advantage of her. Although Johnny Boy makes a practice of being obnoxious with women in the bar, Charlie keeps his distance; he is friendly but respectful and clearly annoyed at Johnny Boy's behavior.

Charlie's ability to reach out to wounded souls extends to his girl-friend, Teresa (Amy Robinson), who is also Johnny Boy's cousin. She suffers from epileptic seizures, but according to the wisdom of the neighborhood, she is simply "crazy." Giovanni tells him directly to dump Teresa, and it is at that point that Charlie goes into the kitchen of the restaurant and tests his moral resolve by holding his hand over a burner of the gas range. Ironically, it was Teresa who was most strenuous in urging Charlie to stay away from Johnny Boy. Following his conscience and better instincts, he remains faithful to both of them, and the three of them are together in the car when they are gunned down in Brooklyn. In a sacramental touch, the car swerves into a fire hydrant and the resulting gush of water, suggesting the redemptive waters of baptism, washes over them.

After *Mean Streets* and *Italianamerican,* made the next year, Scorsese moved his settings from Little Italy—or to put it more accurately, he reconstructed the spiritual milieu of Little Italy in distant and varied locations. Like the Sicilians from Elizabeth Street, his later characters struggle for personal identity within an enclosed subculture that is constrained, not necessarily by geography or ethnicity, as was the case in *Mean Streets,* but by other threats from outside forces. *Mean Streets* set the pattern. Subsequent films would situate that pattern within different contexts.

Mean Streets of Brooklyn and Queens

Over the years since *Mean Streets,* Scorsese developed a reputation for his unflinching, or as he would call it, his "anthropological," look at the rougher side of New York City life in films like *Taxi Driver* (1975), *New York, New York* (1977), *Raging Bull* (1980), *The King of Comedy* (1982), *After Hours* (1985), and "Life Lessons," a segment in the trilogy *New York Stories* (1988), yet he never really returned to the mob until *GoodFellas* (1990), which is set mainly in Brooklyn and Queens. Five years later, in *Casino* (1995), he will follow the mob to its headquarters in Kansas City and its operations in distant Las Vegas. No matter how far he removed his gangsters from Little Italy, the scents of Elizabeth Street still clung to their polyester suits.

Based on Nicholas Pileggi's *Wiseguy,* a best seller in 1985, *GoodFellas* provides an antidote to the romanticized image of the Mafia that had become popularized in director Francis Coppola's and writer Mario Puzo's enormously successful first two *Godfather* films of 1972 and 1974. Although Coppola and Puzo created a genteel veneer of Old World aristocracy, with ritual language and rigid codes of loyalty, Scorsese showed lower-level organized crime figures as street hustlers and opportunists on the make. Henry's wife, Karen, dispels the myth of Mafia gentility when she offers the voice-over comment: "Our husbands weren't brain surgeons. They were blue-collar guys. The only way they could make extra money, real extra money, was to go out and cut a few corners."[19] Scorsese's Mafiosi are indeed working men out on the streets trying to earn a living, and their occupation frequently involves violence and intimidation rather than polite, ritualized executions. Although the money might be abundant, job security was always in question, and they had to work hard to maintain their positions. They worried about security, like other working men. The bosses in turn worry about keeping discipline to ensure their share of the take; respect and hand-kissing ranks very low in their order of priorities when compared to regular payoffs from underlings.

GoodFellas allows Scorsese to move his mob beyond the streets of Little Italy and petty street crime like loan-sharking, extortion, and swindling teenagers with the promise of illegal fireworks. Even more significantly, the society he portrays is no longer a transplanted Sicilian village, as it was in *Mean Streets.* After a full generation in its new homeland, the Mafia has eased its membership requirements to a certain extent, and in a sense has compromised its traditions. It is a passing of the old ways that Scorsese notes with some regret. He seems to look back on the past with nostalgia, when the Mafia's elegant Sicilian customs still regulated the behavior of the mobsters, as it does in Coppola's romanticized version of the criminal underworld.

In *GoodFellas* the central character, Henry Hill (Ray Liotta), has a Sicilian mother but an Irish father, and Jimmy Conway (Robert DeNiro) is presumably Irish as well. Although they are well established in the aristocracy of the crime family, as non-Sicilians, they face a ceiling in their advancement through the hierarchy. They can never become "made men," a class of untouchables, something like an officer corps in the organization. In contrast, the highly volatile Tommy DeVito (Joe Pesci) poses a threat to the others because of his temper and poor judgment, but simply because he is Sicilian, he can be admitted to the inner circle. Or so he thinks. He behaves as though he considers himself untouchable. In the opening scene he brutally murders Billy Batts (Frank Vincent), who is tied up in the trunk of a car. As it turns out, Billy is a "made man" himself, and the murder violates the code. For a time, the episode remains curiously detached from the rest of the narrative, as the main story line turns to the beginning of Henry Hill's life as a gangster. At the midpoint of the film, however, the script fills in the murder's background. Tommy, it explains, had gotten into a silly argument with Billy in a bar, and their exchange led to name-calling and shoving. Murdering Billy was merely Tommy's way of clearing his reputation and restoring his honor. Henry sees Tommy's behavior as perfectly reasonable and even helps him dispose of the body, after stopping off on the way for a late-night dinner prepared by Tommy's mother (Catherine Scorsese). The bosses take a different view of the matter. They lure Tommy into a trap by promising to induct him into the ranks of "made men," then execute him for his violation of the code for murdering one of their own.

Even as an outsider who can never become a true insider, Henry never shows resentment for his exclusion. He not only accepts this as the proper order of things, but he also has great admiration for the Old World ways of the Sicilians. In this respect, Henry reflects Scorsese's own sense of appreciation for the tribal ways that are now passing from the scene. As a twelve-year-old, he begins running errands for the local boss Paulie Cicero (Paul Sorvino). In voice-over, he explains: "As far back as I can remember, I always wanted to be a gangster" (4). Being a member of the mob meant having respect in the neighborhood, which is the East New York section of Brooklyn, a heterogeneous working-class area that is largely Italian but lacks the history and character of Little Italy. Paulie wears loud Hawaiian shirts and conducts business from a dingy cab stand. He represents a generational and cultural antitype to Coppola's courtly Old World Vito Corleone, or even the younger, suave, and Americanized Michael Corleone.

Appearances of modernity may be deceiving, however. The gang may have changed its dress code and opened its doors to non-Italians, but in many ways, the old ways still prevail as a means of self-preservation that keeps the mob from disappearing altogether into mainstream society. Paulie adopts Henry and allows him and Jimmy Conway to work their way up in the chain of command despite their Irish backgrounds. Trouble arises for Henry, as it did for Tommy, when he violates the rules and operates from self-interest, which runs counter to the tribal ethic of the mob. His first questionable act is marrying Karen (Lorraine Bracco), who is Jewish. Instead of moving closer to the clan by marrying a Sicilian, he moves further away by marrying a woman who is not even a Catholic.

The religious/ethnic conflict in Henry remains. He compromises his identity when Karen tells him to tuck his gold cross under his shirt when he first meets her mother. Although the wedding was a Jewish ceremony, the mother-in-law is never reconciled to her gentile son-in-law. When Henry stays out all night—with Janice Rossi, his mistress, as it turns out—she tells her daughter: "He's not Jewish. Did you know how these people live?" (44). When he returns from his tryst, it is the mother-in-law who assails him despite Karen's pleas for her mother to stay out of their family business. Henry simply turns around and walks out of the house.

Karen wants to stay with Henry, but she cannot resign herself to Janice (Gina Mastrogiacomo). She tries to break in on them in the garish apartment Henry has set up for Janice, and which he uses to flirt with Janice's girlfriends—and more than flirt. One night in their bedroom, Karen awakens Henry while pointing an automatic at his head. He disarms her and storms out. Their relationship remains troubled, but they remain together. In the godfather tradition, Paulie tells Henry to go back to his wife and he will take care of Janice: "Please, there's no other way. You're not gonna get a divorce. We're not *animali*" (75). In time, Karen accepts the notion that a man in Henry's position keeps a mistress. It's clear that she cannot leave him. She has become addicted to the power and danger that goes with life in the crime family. And of course, she likes the money. The mob applies Sicilian rules to Henry and Karen even though they are not the typical Sicilian couple, but the Hills comply with the rules as though they were.

Karen makes an effort to fit in with her new social set, but she never quite acclimates to it. In fact, she considers herself superior to the crude-talking Italian wives whom she socializes with. The families form a tight-knit clan, attending one another's weddings and christenings, playing cards, and going on vacations together. The forced camaraderie grates on Karen. When the wives gather for their own party, Karen comments in voice-over: "They had bad skin and wore too much make-up. . . . They looked beat-up. And the stuff they wore was thrown together and cheap. A lot of pant suits and double knits. . . . And they talked about how rotten their kids were and about beating them with broom handles and leather belts." The gulf separating her from the Italian wives becomes striking when one of the women comments about growing up in Miami: "It's like you died and woke up in Jew heaven" (46, 45). By this time, Karen doesn't even notice the remark—or if she does, she says nothing.

Henry's growing separation from the culture of the gang reaches its critical phase during his stay in prison. He does a strong-arm job for Paulie in Tampa, but then discovers that the victim has a sister who works for the FBI, which is less accustomed to accommodating Paulie's methods than the New York police. Henry joins several of his former associates in the federal prison at Lewisburg, Pennsylvania. The Sicilians bribe the guards to provide liquor, wine, lobsters, and steaks for their regular Italian feasts. One slices garlic with a razor blade so that it liquefies in the pan. Henry, however, uses his time to set up a heroin distribution network for the prisoners, even though narcotics dealing in or out of prison is strictly forbidden by the mob. Drugs attract federal agents, who are less likely than the police to take a gift and look the other way. Karen brings in the heroin during her regular visits with the children. Henry also arranges for Janice Rossi to visit him, possibly with conjugal privileges. Karen discovers her name on the visitors' list and rages at Henry, but she continues to supply the drugs for his business.

His four years in prison have enabled Henry to form a good business relationship with a supplier in Pittsburgh, and after his parole, he has a ready-made operation to expand to the outside world as an independent businessman. He bypasses Paulie and keeps all the profits for himself. When Paulie hears of Henry's extracurricular activities, he tells Henry to give up the drug business, not for any lofty moral purpose but simply because federal officials come down hard on an entire organization when they find any member engaged in drug trafficking: "Gribbs [another boss] got twenty years just for saying hello to some fuck who was sneakin' behind his back selling junk. I don't need that" (85). Henry promises to comply, but he shatters what remains of their relationship by continuing his highly profitable business. When self-interest outweighs tribal loyalty, only disaster can follow.

Federal narcotics agents close in and arrest Henry in his driveway with his runner in the car. Before they break into the house, Karen flushes the drugs, worth about $60,000, down the toilet. Henry realizes he no longer has the protection of the mob, and even worse, Paulie could arrange for him to be killed in jail. He knows that he is on his own. Karen's mother supplies bail money to get him out of jail before the trial, but when Henry discovers what happened to the drugs that he planned to sell to raise money for his escape, he realizes that he has no choice but to surrender his identity altogether and go into the witness protection program. His choice of self-interest over communal values leads to his tragic lament in the final scene when, dressed in a bathrobe, he picks up a newspaper in front of a modest tract house: "I'm an average nobody. I get to live the rest of my life like a schnook" (131). A title card reveals that Karen left him after a few years in the program, apparently no more capable than he of living an ordinary life without the danger, the power, and the money.

Henry's plight is regrettable but not tragic: he violated the basic principles of the code by defying Paulie's orders and going into the drug business on his own. It was neither tragic destiny nor bad luck that ended his career. It was simple greed, coupled with duplicity and bad judgment. He simply gets caught and pays for his crimes. At the same time, because *GoodFellas* unfolds from Henry's point of view, his capture provides little sense of the triumph of good over evil that one might expect in a crime drama. The police earn little sympathy or respect.

The narcotics agent who offers him a tough deal, with little sympathy is Edward McDonald (playing himself), an outsider and a variation on the Irish cops whom Scorsese remembers for demanding money in exchange for letting the neighborhood boys play stickball on the streets of Little Italy. In one earlier scene, the police arrive at Henry's house and ask Karen to sign a search warrant. In voice-over, she comments, "Mostly they were just looking for a hand-out, a few bucks to keep things quiet, no matter what they found. I always asked them if they wanted coffee" (48). During the final chase scene, before Henry's arrest, the array of helicopters, radios, wiretaps, and police cars make one wonder why they weren't able to break up Henry's drug-dealing business earlier. The police as well as the criminals were simply doing their respective jobs. Henry's downfall stirs few feelings of regret and his arrest little satisfaction.

A major subplot reinforces the theme of tribal loyalty in the form of a cautionary tale. Jimmy Conway, who is Irish, masterminds a multimillion-dollar robbery at the Lufthansa freight terminal at Idlewild Air Terminal, now JFK. In assembling his team, he makes the tragic mistake of recruiting a team outside the regular channels of the Mafia. Because they lack the necessary tribal spirit that is presumed among the Mafiosi, these outsiders will act in their own self-interest and make mistakes after the robbery that will force Jimmy to eliminate them. Stacks Edwards (Samuel L. Jackson), an African American, got high on drugs and was careless with the getaway truck. He had to be eliminated before the police could trace it. Morrie Kessler (Chuck Low), a manufacturer of hairpieces, is clearly Jewish. After the robbery, he becomes insistent about getting his money immediately, with vague suggestions that he might talk to the police if he didn't get his cut soon. Afraid that Morrie might have already told his wife about the job, Jimmy gives the order to have them dispatched. The Italians, for their part, are little better in putting their personal greed before the interests of the group. Johnny Roastbeef (John Williams) and Frankie Carbone (Frank Silvero) both defy Jimmy's orders to keep a low profile. They buy extravagant Christmas presents for their wives, which Jimmy fears may make the police suspicious. As a result, both have to be eliminated. In the coda at the end of the film, Scorsese uses title cards to explain that although the Lufthansa robbery has never been solved, Jimmy is serving a long sentence for murder. It does not mention which murder, but as a matter of speculation, the victim may well have been one of his former accomplices. It's a bittersweet ending. Justice has been served, yet a way of life has come to an end, and the world is no better off with Paulie's crime family out of the way.

Still Mean in Las Vegas

Casino (1995) starts with a bang, literally. The third of Scorsese's Mafia trilogy begins with an explosion that, like the gruesome murder of Billy Batts that opens *GoodFellas,* is not explained until near the end of the story. As we will discover, the booby-trapped car belongs to Ace Rothstein (Robert DeNiro), an elegant manager of the Tangiers, one of the most successful casinos in Las Vegas, and the story backs up to tell the story of his rise and fall in the family. In this respect, the plot structure is similar to that of *GoodFellas.* Likewise, it chronicles the disintegration of the old-time Mafia, whose demise Scorsese again views with some regret.

Despite these obvious structural and thematic similarities, in several respects *Casino* represents a departure from the earlier mob films. In this film Scorsese and the Mafia have completed their migration from Sicilian roots. Charlie in *Mean Streets* belonged to the Sicilian clan and was destined to inherit his position as proprietor of a mob-run restaurant as a birthright. Henry Hill of *GoodFellas* had a Sicilian mother, whose parents came from the same village as Paulie Cicero's, but he also had an Irish father and a Jewish wife. Ace Rothstein is Jewish; his relationship to the Mafia is based not on bloodlines, but purely on his professional competence. He is an employee whose position is secure as long as he turns a profit, and in turn, he is well rewarded for his services. In three steps, the trilogy has traced the development of organized crime from Sicilian village life relocated in Little Italy to a quintessential multiethnic American business enterprise in an artificially concocted city of neon and glitz in the Nevada desert. With a few very important exceptions, as we will see, everyone seems to have come from someplace else to make a fortune in Las Vegas.

Thus the geography changes along with the ethnic roots. As the American Mafia expanded to assimilate non-Sicilians, Scorsese has moved its operations from a social club on Elizabeth Street in *Mean Streets,* to East New York in Brooklyn in *GoodFellas,* and in *Casino* to Kansas City and Las Vegas. As the script explains, because of prior convictions for illegal gambling in the East, the old-time bosses were excluded from the burgeoning gambling industries in Las Vegas. Physical presence made little difference to them, however. They float a loan from the teamsters' pension fund, set up a syndicate, and open the Tangiers, one of the most lavish casinos on the Strip. From the back room of an Italian food store in Kansas City, the old dons talk and drink grappa, like feudal lords in the manor house, while their trusted lieutenants in the field operate the casinos and their runners bring back tribute, in the form of suitcases full of cash. Still touched with nostalgia for the old ways, Scorsese presents them as benevolent grandfather types from his home neighborhood. He even casts his mother, Catherine Scorsese, as the proprietor of the food market and has her complain about the coarse language one of the soldiers uses making his report. The man apologizes, but does not change his vocabulary. These are benevolent chieftains; they know that some of their underlings are skimming profits, but as long as the money flows in, they prefer to allow their agents on the scene see that the leakage is kept within acceptable limits. In an opening scene, Scorsese's camera shows the high-tech counting rooms, with machines for sorting and stacking the bills. The Tangiers is a factory for making money, and the bosses would be foolish to let greed slow down the assembly line by disrupting the chain of command to stop some relatively insignificant skimming.

As veterans of the illegal gambling business of the East Coast and not quite accustomed to the multibillion-dollar legal entertainment industry in Las Vegas, the bosses of Kansas City dispatch one of their own, Nicky Santoro (Joe Pesci), to provide enforcement, if any is necessary. Ace has learned how to work within the new rules. He sees Nicky's presence as a potential problem, and of course he is right. The character reprises the volatile Tommy DeVito in *GoodFellas*. Nicky has risen through the ranks, but he still functions like a strong-arm man from the neighborhood. A criminal anachronism, he soon becomes first an embarrassment, then a liability. In Las Vegas, Nicky is mesmerized by the immense fortunes passing across the gaming tables and becomes restless to get a bigger cut for himself. When he is banned from the casinos because of his criminal record, he reverts to more traditional activities, like robbery, fencing, and extortion. Even more oblivious to the new ways than his bosses in Kansas City, Tommy fails to understand that gambling is legal in Las Vegas, and the rules have changed from the old days of numbers running in bars and barber shops. His violent tactics draw too much attention to the operations, and the bosses warn him to pull back. In a rage, he even shoots up the house of a police officer who had arrested one of his men. Ace tries to reason with him, but Nicky continues to put self-interest above the interests of the organization. Inevitably, he must pay for his crimes against the clan. After being beaten senseless with baseball bats, he is buried alive in a cornfield. The old-time Mafia style that he lived by caught up with him in death.

Ace represents the new style of Mafia leadership. As a technician of crime and near-crime, he operates on the edges of the law, but he rarely soils his hands with traditional tactics. He manages a business that is legitimate in Nevada, even though his record with illegal gambling should disqualify him from the job. He remains within the law as long as his application for a gambling license is pending. When the gaming commission is set to review his case, he switches his official title and applies for a new license and again his papers go to the bottom of the bureaucratic stack. Even though he is careful to work the loopholes within legal boundaries, Ace is not above allowing his staff to smash the dealing hand of a crooked gambler with a hammer, but this is an extraordinary situation, and the dirty work is left to underlings. Ace is a technocrat who has built a reputation as the best handicapper in the business. As an odds maker, at the start of his career, he left nothing to chance. As manager of the Tangiers, he counts the number of berries in the muffins and personally supervises the weigh-ins of the showgirls. Oddly enough, his meticulous management style leads to his downfall. He reprimands a floor manager for placing the slot machines in a poor location. Later, when the same machines yield an improbably huge payout, Ace concludes that the floor manager was either in on the fix or too stupid to realize the winners had rigged the machines. Ace fires him on the spot. Unfortunately, the man comes from an old Las Vegas family, and these old WASP families still control the legal establishment in town.

The tribal solidarity of the old Las Vegans hardens against this Jewish newcomer and his outside organization. At his license hearing, the commissioners refuse to review his petition and simply deny his application. During the heated exchange, Ace reveals that the commissioners stayed at the Tangiers as nonpaying guests and had requested receipts to put on their expense accounts. They are corrupt, but they have the power, just like the Irish policemen shaking down the Italian boys to allow them to play stickball on the streets of Little Italy.

Another respectable member of the Las Vegas social establishment acted as a silent partner to enable the mob to set up a front corporation to open the Tangiers. As the money flows east to Kansas City, she becomes greedy and demands a bigger cut, and she even threatens that if she doesn't get it, she will tell the police about the various arrangements between the teamsters, the mob, the corporation, and the Tangiers. Nicky murders her, and of course the police must respond to the murder of a prominent citizen by a vigorous investigation of all her business dealings, including the casino. Obviously, the police would have little trouble tracing the connections from Nicky, who was rash enough to shoot up the home of a fellow officer, through the Tangiers, back to Kansas City.

Ace is clearly caught in the middle, fighting for survival. On one side, he has the authorities, whom he feels he can finesse by payoffs and keeping within the law while operating a legitimate business for the syndicate. On the other side, he has the old-time Mafia, with its penchant for wanton violence, as embodied in Nicky Santoro. Ace, as a non-Sicilian, tries to use his Jewish gift for accommodation to help the mob acclimate to the new rules, yet he remains loyal to the bosses in Kansas City and respects their ways of doing business. The tension he feels is a third-generation immigrant's experience: the need for assimilation to new circumstances balanced against the inevitable loss of identity that comes with abandoning the old ways. In a sense, the dramatic conflict of the film has grown out of Scorsese's experience of the tensions of cultural life in Little Italy during the 1950s and 1960s. Driven to desperation, Ace tries to relieve the pressure by telling the bosses that he feels Nicky's tactics have become a liability to their operations. If the bosses themselves rein in Nicky, Ace feels he can still deal with the WASPs. Nicky sees this as a personal betrayal and plans to eliminate Ace by planting the bomb that explodes in Ace's car in the first scene.

The relationship between Nicky and Ace had already grown strained because of the tangled relationships centered around Ginger McKenna (Sharon Stone), whose Irishness provokes several comments. Ginger, possibly an expensive call girl, now separated from her boyfriend and manager Lester Diamond (James Woods), is playing the tables when she attracts Ace's attention. Ace pursues her, they have a child, and then, at Ace's urging, decide to marry. Eager to settle into a traditional relationship at this phase of his life, he offers her an extremely generous prenuptial contract that gives her access to much of his assets. Ginger becomes progressively more unstable, clearly becoming dependent on alcohol, pills, and cocaine. She can't be trusted with their daughter Amy (Darla House). When Lester reappears, her old dependency on him reasserts itself, and he persuades her to raid the joint bank accounts Ace has set up. Public drunkenness and abuse of their daughter has poisoned their marriage, and the final betrayal with Lester is too much. Ace throws her out. She goes to Nicky for protection and enters into a sexual relationship with him to assure his loyalty. Nicky, married with children in a Catholic elementary school, falls into her trap and sees Ace as a rival. Ace's complaints about Nicky's tactics to the bosses in Kansas City merely put the final seal on the death certificate that Nicky had written for himself some time earlier.

This clash of cultures leads to a violent end. Ginger returns to Los Angeles with Lester and seems to have resumed her former profession. She last appears staggering down the hallway of a dingy motel and falls to the floor in a coma. We learn that she died of a "hot dose" of uncut heroin after all the money she took from Ace is gone. Nicky had to pay the ultimate price for defying the instructions of the bosses and setting his own rules. Ace survived the blast, but with all the investigations and publicity, he could not remain at the Tangiers. He returns to his old line of work, setting odds for the bookmakers, and he is still one of the best.

Scorsese seems dispassionate about the fate of his three principal figures. For him, Las Vegas is a tough world, and losers always outnumber winners. Ace, Ginger, and Nicky each drew bad cards, but they knew the rules of the game before they started. The only sense of loss Scorsese voices at the end of his 172-minute film is for Las Vegas itself. The mob is gone and impersonal multinational corporations have taken over, with their well-manicured boards of directors in New York, Toronto, or Tokyo directing operations, just like the old dons in the food shop in Kansas City. The machines for sorting and counting money that Scorsese has shown in great detail have made Las Vegas a robotic assembly line for profits, only now the money flows into international holding companies rather than into a back room. The bosses sipping coffee in the back room and giving orders gave the industry a human face, but in the end, they are squeezed out by impersonal MBAs and their accountants. The glitter and glamour are gone, and as far as Scorsese sees it, Las Vegas has become a theme park for wealthy retirees wearing polyester. For him, the film ends with a sense of loss for a passing generation.

Back to Manhattan

With *Gangs of New York* (2002) Scorsese returns to his geographic roots in Lower Manhattan, but at more than a century's distance from his own personal experience. His gangs are not Sicilians facing the dilemma of assimilation or annihilation, but the Irish who are trying to fight their way into mainstream America. The apparent adversary in this case is not the police and federal agents but the culture of Nativist Americans, the descendants of veterans of the Wars of Independence fought by their ancestors in 1776 and 1812, who believe that this land is theirs by birthright.[20] More recent arrivals from Ireland provide cheap labor for the blossoming economy, but they also threaten Nativist hegemony. Both groups feel they must fight for survival. The Nativists believe that their ancestors earned the right to control local politics, jobs, and crime, and no ragtag band of newcomers can take it from them. The stakes are even higher for the Irish. If they are to gain a toehold in their new homeland, they will have to adopt the violent ways of their oppressors, and by so doing shed their own tribal and rural way of life. Much like the second-generation Mafia in the Scorsese's gangster trilogy set a century later, the Irish must adjust to new urban and democratic realities in a multiethnic, cosmopolitan city.

This story of Irish immigration, then, is the summation and restatement of the characteristic Scorsese theme: cities, and by extension the nation, must be conceived as evolving organisms. The evolution necessarily involves violent conflict. When a neighborhood faces change, the conflict takes place on two levels at once. First, the groups as a whole compete against one another, and second, individuals within the group struggle to define themselves in opposition to the collectivity. In *Gangs of New York,* Scorsese has returned to his familiar Manhattan setting, but the historical distance has provided a wider perspective for his consistent theme. Richard Corliss perceptively observed in his review in *Time,* "*Gangs* is the prototype of all of Scorsese's films; it just happens to come after them."[21]

William "Bill the Butcher" Cutting (Daniel Day-Lewis), with his glass eye embossed with the American eagle, his grotesque accent, and his brutal ways, stands as a salutary reminder that not all WASPs came over on the *Mayflower* and settled into a life of the genteel aristocracy on Beacon Hill in Boston or on the plantations of Virginia. Many were indentured servants and laborers who remained at the bottom of the urban ladder for generations because the Anglo American, Protestant aristocracy that owned the land and controlled the capital found it politically and economically expedient to keep them there. If the Irish could provide the same services at an even cheaper rate, then expediency trumped tribal loyalties, and the poor Nativist Americans would be sacrificed on the barons' altar of profit. In America, urban conflict wears an ethnic mask, but the underlying issue is invariably economic. Scorsese's Mafia may be self-consciously Sicilian, but greed for their cut of the action is the cement that holds the brotherhood together.

The Butcher leads the thugs who have fought their way into control of the notorious Five Points area of Lower Manhattan. Supremacy brings with it not only jobs and respect, but also the income from robbery, extortion, and prostitution, much like the situation of the Mafia of a later generation. The gangs run their business with little interference from the authorities, such as they are in mid-nineteenth-century New York, because they can deliver the votes to Boss Tweed (Jim Broadbent) and his Tammany Hall machine. The newcomers threaten this arrangement. The Irish have the language and the numbers, and they are gradually getting the vote, a reality that Tweed and his associates understand quite well. The Butcher's Americans find themselves challenged as never before, and they feel they have no alternative but to fight back to preserve their ascendancy.

His counterpart, Priest Vallon (Liam Neeson), leads a confederation of Irish gangs, whose numbers have grown into a potent force in the streets but who have not yet dislodged the Nativists from their position of political power. The opening sequence shows preparations for a bloody battle between these competing groups that sets the theme of ethnic conflict for the entire film, a theme found in most of Scorsese's earlier films.

The first scenes are set in a cavernous atrium, apparently at least partially underground and soaring five or six stories high, with rickety porches teetering over an indoor courtyard, a visual image of the social unrest boiling beneath the surface of the City. The Irish seethe in this smoky inferno, but they are prepared to burst out of the underground into the light of day. As though in solemn ritual, Priest and his men vest for battle with all manner of protective armor, and a bearded priest administers the Eucharist to each of the warriors as they assemble to join battle for their cause. Catholicism helps define the newcomers, who form ranks behind the Celtic cross. Priest leads his warrior acolytes in a prayer for protection and victory to St. Michael the Archangel, the most warlike of the angels, who, according to Revelation 12:7–9, defeats Satan and his army of fallen angels and casts them into hell on the last day of the cosmic battle between the forces of good and evil. Priest recites a prayer long used in the Catholic Church: "Saint Michael the Archangel, defend us in battle; be our protection against the malice and snares of the devil. May God rebuke him, we humbly pray: and do thou, O Prince of the heavenly host, by the power of God, thrust into hell Satan and all the evil spirits who prowl about the world seeking the ruin of souls."[22] Despite its anachronism, the prayer, composed in the later nineteenth century to assist the Church in its confrontation with cosmic forces of evil, has no less importance for those about to join battle on the streets of lower Manhattan. The legions of Butcher Bill threaten their very existence. In fact, the prayer is well placed but ultimately unsuccessful because the Butcher and his minions triumph, and Priest is killed in combat with his adversary.

Oddly, while the Butcher advertises his contempt of the Irish as a group, he holds Priest in great respect as a worthy opponent. They meet in hand-to-hand combat, and the Butcher is victorious, but killing Priest does not resolve a personal vendetta; the Butcher sees it merely as a necessary step needed to preserve the natural order of the world of Five Points. It is his duty to kill a man he respects. As Priest surrenders his soul, his young son Amsterdam (Cian McCormick) looks on, and realizing that he is now alone, he runs for his life.

The story lurches forward seventeen years to 1863, when Amsterdam, now a young man (Leonardo DiCaprio), is released from Hell Gate School, a combination of reformatory and orphanage. "Hell Gate" is actually the name given to the treacherous tidewaters where the East River meets Long Island Sound between northern Manhattan and the Bronx on one side and Queens on the other. For the purposes of the film, the name fortuitously recalls the cosmic struggle between angelic forces. True to his Catholic tradition, but clearly without any accompanying faith, morals, or religiosity, he tosses into the river the Bible he received from the Protestant superintendent as a kind of graduation present. Amsterdam has two competing goals in mind, survival and revenge, and he soon discovers that these objectives may be incompatible. He will join the Butcher and become one of his key lieutenants, and with him he achieves respect and a certain level of prosperity. He may be tempted to switch sides, but revenge can only be delayed; it cannot be denied. To keep his position secure, he must at least appear to turn away from his Irish roots even while he endures degrading slurs from the Nativists in the Butcher's gang.

The relationship between the Butcher and Amsterdam falls apart over a woman, a conflict that symbolically signifies the right to form a family, settle in, and take possession of the future. Jenny Everdeane (Cameron Diaz) supports herself as a pickpocket and skilled burglar who at times disguises herself as a maid, enters the mansions of the wealthy, and plunders their valuables. She makes little of her own ethnic roots and seems content to attach herself to any man who can offer her protection or money. Ever representing the future, she plans to leave for California when the ongoing gang wars jeopardize her possibilities with Amsterdam in Five Points. She realizes, perhaps more clearly than Amsterdam does himself, that after an informer uncovers his identity as the son of Priest Vallon, the wheel will begin turning toward an inevitable, deadly confrontation.

Scorsese places the conflict between rival gangs in a larger context of the established institutions of civil society. In fact, the real conflict puts both gangs on the same side in their violent confrontation with progress. They represent the old way of life that will have no place in the City that is gradually evolving around them. The struggle is only beginning to take shape, and Scorsese, who shows little respect for civil authorities in his gangster trilogy, shows the forces of "civilization" as little better than the gangs. The police, of course, take bribes to allow the Butcher and his hoodlums to continue their lucrative trade in stolen merchandise, gambling, and prostitution. Rival fire departments fight for the rights to loot a burning building, and to keep peace, they simply torch an adjacent property to provide enough for both companies to steal. On a higher level, Boss Tweed, initially a close ally of the Butcher, can count votes, and he will provide favors for the newly enfranchised Irish as long as they can keep his party in office. With Tweed's cynical switch in allegiance, the Butcher and his tribe risk becoming just another minority, just like the Irish, struggling for power in a multiethnic city, a prospect that only raises tensions.

Although the fortunes of the Irish rise through Tweed's corrupt political power, they, no less than the Nativists, begin to lose their identity through assimilation.[23] The real conflict, as Scorsese comments in the coda of the film, is not between the Butcher and Amsterdam, or even between the Irish and Nativists, but rather between all the strivers, newcomers and Nativists alike, against the assimilated, prosperous, and impersonal American nation that is inevitably rising in the future. Irish men are enlisted into the Union army right on the docks as they disembark from their immigrant ships. They have no allegiance to their new country and no understanding of the conflict. Still, joining the army means food, clothes, lodging, a job, and a fast track to citizenship. (Two new recruits wonder about the location of Tennessee, their supposed destination.) In a stunning crane shot, as the Irish regiment boards a military transport, the camera tilts down to reveal rows of the coffins of those fallen in battle after being removed from the same ship. The image suggests the equation between assimilation and death for the Irish. Scorsese repeats the theme in the final sequence when the Nativists and Irish join in battle against each other and against the establishment that has enacted the draft, with its pernicious clause exempting those who could pay a $300 fee, a preposterous sum for poor Irish and Nativists alike. As the two groups meet in sectarian violence and the City burns in chaos, the impersonal naval guns in the harbor and the equally impersonal military units fresh from Gettysburg both open up on the mobs. In the end, according to Scorsese, it is power of the distant abstraction of America that crushes the quarreling factions, indiscriminately killing Irish and Nativists alike to establish order.

But the conclusion is scarcely a neo-Marxist condemnation of corporate America and the institutions that support it. As was the case in the earlier films, Scorsese remains strikingly ambivalent about progress. In a time-lapse coda to the main action of the film, the Butcher and Amsterdam lie buried side by side in a cemetery in Brooklyn, overlooking the East River. Slowly the Brooklyn Bridge appears over the river, and gradually the skyline of Lower Manhattan rises to its present stature in the distance. The old way of life—tribal, violent, and profoundly human—must pass away to make way for the cold, impersonal metropolis that has assumed its place among the premier cities of the modern world.

This is the conclusion that Scorsese has been exploring throughout his career. The final scene in *Gangs of New York* is the clearest statement yet of the tension between Scorsese's nostalgia for the old ways and his realistic, if reluctant, acceptance of modernity. *Mean Streets* ends in bloodshed, again in Brooklyn, as a grudging acknowledgment that the ways of the street, with its casual internecine warfare, have become anachronisms in contemporary New York. If Charlie survives his wounds, he may well become the manager of a restaurant rather than a gangster. Henry Hill in *GoodFellas* learns that his way of life, a boyhood fantasy become reality, has yielded to the realities of law enforcement imposed by the larger society. His days as a gangster have passed, and he is condemned to live the rest of his days as a "schnook" in a tract house far from Manhattan under an assumed name in the FBI's witness-protection program. *Casino* also ends far from New York. The old-time mob, already displaced from New York to the Middle West, again finds its strong-arm tactics, represented by Nicky, out of place in contemporary Nevada. Through the efforts of the courts and local politicians, as corrupt as they are, the Mafia finds itself replaced by international business conglomerates. The new Las Vegas, according to Scorsese, has become more American, but in the process quite dull. Nativists, Irish, Italians, or Jews, it makes no difference—all have had their day before becoming steamrollered into modern America. They made the nation what it is, but in the process, they lost their own identity.

By way of comparison, this ambivalence about modernity echoes the standard message of the Westerns, especially those by John Ford, and thus the idea is commonplace in American popular culture. The Westerns, like *Gangs of New York,* shamelessly mix myth and history in their presentation of the foundations of America. The myth idealizes the past, while history recognizes that it is past. In his study of the evolution of the Western genre, film historian Scott Simmon notes, "There is a final paradox in the ways that the Western represents the past. On the one hand the west is the region where the past is most treasured. On the other, it is the place where men are allowed to have no past."[24] As the camera looks across the East River in the final scene, it presents the paradox in an Eastern, but nonetheless frontier, setting. Like Western heroes, the Butcher and Amsterdam have become treasured as myths for making the City possible. Yet in actuality, they were both ruthless, violent criminals who killed for self-interest and the interests of their respective tribes.

Time passes, of course. The Western hero uses his guns to subdue outlaws, Mexicans, greedy ranchers, or hostile Indians to establish American civilization on the frontier. Once the task is done and the towns are safe, the gun-toting hero finds himself replaced by shopkeepers, lawyers, and schoolteachers. The man of violence clearly has no place in the new order and must ride off into the sunset, further west to new frontiers. In his films, Scorsese, like John Ford in his Westerns, tries to express the ambiguity of the American experience, looking back with nostalgia to a romanticized past that was for them far more interesting than the present, yet realizing that the colorful figures of the past had to vanish before a new nation could be born. This is in fact the same ambivalent nostalgia that colors his portrayal of the Mafia.

Other Mean Streets in Manhattan

In addition to his films dealing with criminal gangs in New York, Scorsese has revisited his themes of group rivalry and personal integrity in a changing environment in many of his works, both those set in New York and those set elsewhere. With the pattern set in the gangster films, a brief mention of several of the other films should be sufficient to suggest the consistency of his thematic concerns within a wide spectrum of narrative structures.

Taxi Driver (1972) shows Travis Bickle (Robert DeNiro) in total isolation within his sordid environment. He refers to himself in his journal as "God's lonely man," and as he sinks further into his delusions, he casts himself in the role of a messiah, commissioned to clean the City streets of "whores, skunk pussies, buggers, queens, fairies, dopers, junkies, sick, venal. Someday a real rain will come and wash all this scum off the streets."[25] Despite his best efforts to set himself apart from this world he detests, as a taxi driver, he is part of it. This is the typical Scorsese tension between the individual and the social setting. Travis appears isolated from the outside world as he rides in the steel-and-glass cocoon of the cab and in off hours as he sits alone in his tiny, cluttered apartment. Even when he is with other cabbies at the Belmore Cafeteria, he stands silently apart from their banter.

Yet his insulation from the outside world is not total. He picks up prostitutes and their customers and talks about cleaning the back seat of his cab after their encounters. He knows how to contact a gun dealer when he decides to take action himself, and he knows how to stalk a presidential candidate, possibly with the intent to assassinate him, and how to track down Iris (Jodie Foster), the child prostitute. He seems unperturbed when he picks up a nameless fare (Martin Scorsese) who seems intent on murdering his unfaithful wife. This passivity in the face of an imminent crime would undoubtedly make Travis a criminal accomplice. As he shops in a convenience store, an armed robber threatens the cashier, but without trying to disarm the holdup man, Travis calmly shoots him in the head. Finally, in the bloody climax of the film, he takes his illegal weapons and engages his enemies within this dark underworld in an explosion of violence worthy of Armageddon.

Although Travis tries to survive in the streets, he becomes aware of another, more genteel world represented by Betsy (Cybill Shepherd), a blonde, impeccably tailored young woman working on the presidential campaign staff of Charles Palantine (Leonard Harris). When he enters the headquarters to meet her, his awkwardness reveals that he clearly doesn't belong in this world of respectability. Improbably, Betsy agrees to meet him, and even more improbably, she agrees to go into a pornographic movie theater with him. Predictably, she is revolted at the spectacle and storms out. Her world of propriety and refinement produces presidential candidates who exercise real power; his world produces gunmen and drug pushers. Clearly he cannot make the leap into hers, and he decides that he must resort to bloodshed to purify his own by undertaking a suicide mission to rescue Iris and kill Sport (Harvey Keitel), her pimp.

In *Taxi Driver* the cultural conflict lies not in the struggle between the mob, comprised mainly of Italian Americans from Little Italy and law enforcement agents, who are mainly WASP or Irish, but between social classes. On one side of Broadway lies the underclass caught in its criminal ghetto. On the other side lies the America of privilege, law, and respectability. Again, Scorsese shows his ambivalence about the underworld. For all his edginess, Travis elicits sympathy and even admiration in his mad adventures. Palantine, by contrast, is a pompous, hypocritical phony who feigns interest in Travis's inane opinions when riding in his cab. The letter from Iris's father describing his daughter's return to the life of a normal, working-class schoolgirl has a bittersweet note about it. Her spark has been quashed. When Betsy steps out of Travis's cab in the final scene, she leaves the world of real people and vanishes into her dull world of wealth and comfort, no doubt impoverished by her failure to understand his universe. The future clearly lies with Palantine and Betsy, and that is sad because it will lose the color and excitement of an avenging angel like Travis Bickle, much as contemporary New York now lacks the energy of its founders, Amsterdam and the Butcher.

In *Raging Bull* (1980) Scorsese revisits the displaced loner in New York. Jake LaMotta (Robert DeNiro) first appears dancing around an empty ring, dressed in his hooded silk robe with a leopard-skin pattern. He continues to appear alone in confined spaces, like telephone booths, small apartments, and a jail cell. He sees himself as the tough guy who stands alone and takes everything the world can throw at him. He invites opponents and his brother Joey (Joe Pesci) to hit him as hard as they can. As others try to draw close, he repels them with outbursts of abuse that erupt into physical violence. He threatens and assaults his two wives, his children, his brother, and even those who act civilly toward his wife. In the ring, he did not fight with the idea of besting his opponents in an athletic contest; he fought to destroy them. Like Travis, Jake is the loner who arms himself behind a personal fortress of privacy and steps beyond its walls only to work violence on the outside world.

But again like Travis, Jake is also part of a distinct subculture. Scorsese fills in details of the closed Italian American community around Arthur Avenue in the Bronx in the 1940s. Much of the early action takes place around the neighborhood swimming pool, in the social clubs where neighborhood Mafia bosses conduct business, and on a tenement roof ("tar beach," in New York parlance) during a wedding reception, in the parish hall of the local Catholic church, and in cramped apartments where the neighbors shout insults and threats to one another across the open courtyard, which is little more than an air shaft. Success in the ring allows Jake to move his family to a relatively prosperous area along Pelham Parkway, in the Bronx, but his life still bears the marks of the tenement. Financially prosperous as a major contender, he walks around his living room dressed in his underwear eating a hero sandwich. Even in a luxury hotel room, as he waits out a rain-delayed fight and in the Copacabana, he remains the street thug and surrounds himself with people from the old neighborhood. Civil conversation is beyond him.

When Jake's fighting days end and his body balloons by a full sixty pounds, he moves to Florida to start a new life, but he cannot fit in with larger society. He takes the tenements with him, and even with his relative prosperity, he fails to develop social skills. He insults the state assistant attorney general in front of his wife, tells unfunny jokes as a stand-up comedian, and finally faces prosecution for pandering when he serves liquor to underage girls and introduces them to men, an act which in the eyes of the authorities amounts to soliciting. After putting up a frightening struggle with guards, he is confined to a tiny jail cell, where he pounds his head against the stone wall. He has merely moved his world of criminality and self-destructive violence to a new location. Even though he once tried to separate himself from the mob after they forced him to throw a fight, he remains the mobster at heart and has no place in wider society.

After his divorce and conviction in Florida, he returns to New York to try to earn a living on his past reputation.[26] His crude comedy routine in a run-down bar becomes an embarrassment as the audience becomes restless and then shouts insults at him. In the final scene, he waits—again alone—in a tiny dressing room before he tries his routine once again, this time in a somewhat better club. He rehearses Marlon Brando's "coulda been a contender" speech from *On the Waterfront* (Elia Kazan, 1954) while looking at himself in the dressing table mirror. Although Brando's character, Terry Malloy, blames his brother Charlie for his downfall, Jake knows that he is the architect of his own tragedy. He goes out shadow boxing, ready to take on anything life, or the nightclub audience, will throw at him, ever aware that the outcome is not assured. He remains a creature of the violent world in which he found his moment of success, but that moment is long past for him. Once a champion, he may never make it through the gates of his social and cultural prison into a world of respectability.

Comic Turns

The patterns of isolation within a group appear consistently, even as Scorsese varies the texture of his films. In his two often overlooked New York comedies, Scorsese shows his protagonists as loners, yet members of a larger community trying to break through the boundaries to another psychological neighborhood and ultimately failing. In *The King of Comedy* (1982) and *After Hours* (1985) he explores the comic dimensions of a protagonist's trying to become something other than the creature of his own background. In both cases, however, the character's attempt to cross over into another world backfires, with disastrous and very funny unintended consequences.

In *The King of Comedy* Rupert Pupkin (Robert DeNiro) lives on the west bank of the Hudson in one of the working-class communities of New Jersey. He can look down to the end of his street and see the towers of Manhattan standing a short ride away on the PATH (Port Authority Trans-Hudson) train, but yet in another galaxy. A man of little more ostensible comedic talent than Jake LaMotta, he practices his stand-up comedy routines alone in front of a cardboard-cutout audience in the basement of his mother's house. His isolation even within his own family home reaches comic dimensions when his mother (Catherine Scorsese) summons him to dinner as a disembodied voice coming through the stairwell. She never appears on camera. Even while working as a messenger in Manhattan, he wears the styled hair, white shoes, and flashy polyester jackets of a professional comedian. Taking time off from his delivery route, he haunts the offices of Jerry Langford (Jerry Lewis) in the hope of landing a guest appearance of Langford's popular late-night variety show. Failing to gain an audition with the star in his office after many increasingly insistent attempts, Rupert and his girlfriend Rita (Diahnne Abbott) attempt to crash into his suburban home as weekend guests, with Rupert pretending—or possibly deluding himself into believing—that he has been invited. He is hurt and angry when Jerry threatens to call the police; Rita is profoundly embarrassed.

Failing to push his way into the world of big-time entertainment, Rupert and another girlfriend, Masha (Sandra Bernhard), take more desperate measures. Equally fixated, Masha is infatuated with Jerry Langford and wants desperately to have sex with him. The two kidnap the star and hold him at Masha's home until the network agrees to give Rupert his guest appearance. Left alone with Jerry during Rupert's debut on network television, Masha does her best, but her comic seduction leads nowhere. Rupert gets his guest shot, but he is apprehended immediately. Ironically, his mad stunt brings Rupert the notoriety he has craved. With his million-dollar advance, he uses his prison time to write his autobiography, which becomes a best seller, and of course after his release, he gets his own late-night television show. His crude tactics may be reprehensible, but they succeed. In the end, he has made it across the Hudson and into the mainstream, but of course his odyssey is a joke that says more about show business, the cult of personalities, the fifteen-minutes-of-fame rule, and show business (television, or in Scorsese's autobiographical estimation, film) than it does about Rupert and his crazed drive for recognition. Rupert may have a network television show, but he is still the crude, no-talent comic from the Jersey side of the river.

In *After Hours* Paul Hackett tries to make the voyage in the opposite direction. He finds himself imprisoned in a ghetto of modest financial security, respectability, and routine. He works behind a computer terminal in the back office of a bank on Twenty-third Street and lives alone in an apartment on the Upper East Side, passing his lonely evenings with cable television. Desperate for some form of human companionship, he goes out for coffee and strikes up a conversation at the counter with Marcy (Rosanna Arquette), who tells him about her artistic roommate, Kiki (Linda Fiorentino), who makes plaster paperweights in the form of oversized bagels and cream cheese. Later in the evening, Paul calls Marcy with a far-fetched story about having to buy a paperweight that very night. Kiki takes the call and invites him to their loft in SoHo, less than three miles away geographically, but culturally, several light-years distant from the Upper East Side. (In distinguishing Manhattan neighborhoods, spatial distance is irrelevant.) On the way, his last $20 bill flies out the window of the cab, and thus, without carfare, his return route is cut off. Bravely, he plunges into a caldron of artists, dominatrixes, punk rockers, neighborhood vigilantes, users, and suicides. The night is filled with adventure, more than he ever dreamed possible. The dream, once realized, becomes a nightmare. But like Homer's Odysseus, he longs to end his ordeals and just go home, even if home means a lonely apartment and his dull job.

By being in the wrong place at the wrong time, Paul finds himself pursued by a menacing Mr. Softee ice-cream truck and an angry mob that blames him for the wave of burglaries in the neighborhood. He escapes through the ministrations of June (Verna Bloom), also a sculptor, who covers him in plaster and disguises him as a statue. At this point, his immersion in the art world is total. Before June can free him from his full-body cast, two real burglars mistake him for a piece of art and load him into the back of their van. As they make their getaway, the statue falls out of the van and shatters right in front of Paul's bank just as the gates are opening for another day's work. Covered with plaster dust, Paul passes through the prisonlike bars of the front door and returns to his office. For the last shot, one of Scorsese's characteristic long traveling shots, the camera weaves slowly through the labyrinth of desks and alcoves, showing that despite his nocturnal wanderings, Paul remains trapped in the daytime maze of his own life.

Once again, Scorsese has demonstrated the impermeable boundaries that separate classes in Manhattan. Paul entered SoHo on a tourist visa and clearly did not belong there. He could never establish residency and gain citizenship in this alien land. In Paul's case, establishment and authority figures, like capitalists or police or politicians, have no need to close ranks to destroy or exclude a potential interloper. Through his night of misadventures, Paul reaches the inevitable conclusion himself: he belongs in the respectable corporate world; he cannot survive outside its boundaries. As a loner, he realizes that he needs a community, but for him it cannot be the Bohemian world downtown; his mob will consist of dull bank tellers, secretaries, and computer programmers.

In *The Age of Innocence* (1993) Scorsese moves Paul's conundrum from the bittersweet conclusion of black comedy to a the realm of romantic tragedy. Adapted from Edith Wharton's 1920 novel, the film explores the hermetically sealed culture developed by the extremely wealthy nineteenth-century New Yorkers who have clustered around the fringes of newly developed Central Park and built their mansions on the east side of Fifth Avenue. As both Wharton and Scorsese point out, their code of conduct and their web of Byzantine loyalties and vendettas may in fact be even more rigid and more destructive than that of the Mafia. Like Paul Hackett, Newland Archer (Daniel Day-Lewis) realizes that he cannot escape. At the end, he discovers that his allegiance to his class has in fact destroyed him spiritually.

The film opens at the Metropolitan Opera House, which had recently opened uptown in October 1883 at Broadway and Thirty-ninth Street, much closer to its nearly suburban clientele uptown than to the homes of the working classes of Lower Manhattan. Because this is a formal occasion, the men are dressed in identical white ties and tails. The theme of conformity will be repeated later in the film during a street scene in which an all-male band of pedestrians marches against the wind wearing identical derbies. The Countess Ellen Olenska (Michelle Pfeiffer), who has just returned to New York after a failed marriage in Europe, enters a box, attracting gasps not so much for her stunning beauty as for the brazenness of appearing in public so soon after her scandalous escapade. Leaving one's husband is simply not done. She sits with her cousin May Welland (Winona Ryder), the teenage daughter of a leading family and the fiancée of Newland Archer.

Newland's courteous interest in the new arrival soon blossoms into romance, but of course violating his own engagement to woo a divorced woman—even if the count would consent to a divorce, and he hasn't to this point—would bring social ostracism and probably financial ruin. Although Newland and Ellen make their feelings known to each other, Newland delays his decision, even after a furtive but frustrated meeting on a country estate in the Hudson Valley and another failed tryst at Newport, where Newland declines to address Ellen unless she turns before a sailboat passes a lighthouse. She does not turn, and he returns to the summerhouse alone. Newland marries May, according to the plan scripted by their families. In marriage, May's youthful vivaciousness mellows into matronly snobbishness, a change that Newland surely notices. May senses Newland's restiveness and takes devious steps to protect their marriage, which in effect means trapping Newland. She tells Ellen of her pregnancy, even before she receives confirmation from the doctors and before she tells Newland, knowing very well that Ellen will leave the scene. Her strategy works perfectly. Ellen returns to Europe, and Newland, of course, takes the honorable way forward. He becomes a family man and an investment lawyer whose work seems as drab as Paul Hackett's.

The final sequence reveals Scorsese's characteristic nostalgia for a way of life passing from this scene. The old, insulated world of the New York aristocracy has already begun to crumble in the turbulence of the new century, and of course, Newland Archer is no longer a young man. The action leaps forward in time through the voice-over narration by Joanne Woodward reading the words of Edith Wharton, underscored visually through the changes in furniture in the room that had been central to the many passages in Newland's life: christenings, marriages, and death. The voice reveals that "He was a dutiful loving father and a faithful husband. When May had died of infectious pneumonia after nursing Bill [their younger son] through, he [Newland] had honestly mourned her. The world of her youth had fallen into pieces and had rebuilt itself without her ever noticing."[27] Time and death change nothing for Newland. Through a telephone conversation (servants no longer deliver handwritten notes on silver trays), Newland agrees to accompany his elder son Theodore (Robert Sean Leonard) on a business trip to Paris. There they will have the opportunity to visit May's cousin, Ellen Olenska, but when the time comes, Newland can only sit on a bench while his son goes in to pay his respects to his aging cousin. Although he is no longer bound to May, Newland remains imprisoned by tribal custom and fear of reproach; he denies his past feelings and walks away from the only true romance in his life. His adherence to the code of his caste has destroyed his human sensibilities. Quite simply, he is no longer capable of love—devotion and fidelity, yes, but not love. Even in his memories, propriety trumps passion.

Still Other Avenues

Tensions between competing groups and between the individual and the group have appeared in a seemingly endless variety through many, if not all, of Scorsese's films. In *New York, New York* (1977) he places his romantic couple in incompatible artistic worlds. Francine Evans (Liza Minnelli) is a successful band vocalist who rises to fame as a movie star. Jimmy Doyle (Robert DeNiro) is a jazz saxophonist whose improvisational style and volatile temperament clash with Francine's more mainline talent. When bop develops its own audience in the 1950s, Jimmy finds his audience in small jazz clubs, but by this time Francine has become well established as a star in her own right. Among jazz enthusiasts, he has acquired a modest reputation, but she has become a genuine celebrity for the masses. Strengthened by his success, he asks her to return to him, but after some hesitation, she declines. Jimmy's style undoubtedly represents the progressive edge of music, and Scorsese allows him to revel in his vindication as a musician ahead of his time. The director clearly respects artists who break new ground. But at the same time, in Francine's lavish production number, he pays loving homage to the great Busby Berkeley routines at Warner Bros. in the 1930s or the Arthur Freed musicals at MGM in the in 1940s and 1950s. Through the enthusiasm of the singers and dancers on the screen, Scorsese once again betrays his nostalgia for the past while he shows respect for progress.

Bringing Out the Dead (1999) in many ways signals Scorsese's return to his early fascination with New York street life and represents a reprise of several earlier themes and characters. Little wonder, because it is another collaboration with Paul Schrader, who also scripted *Taxi Driver* and *Raging Bull* with Scorsese. Like their earlier works, *Bringing Out the Dead* takes a poetic, almost voyeuristic look at the darkest side of New York life. Frank Pierce (Nicolas Cage) drives through midtown as an emergency medical technician. Like Travis in his cab, Frank looks out at the street life through the windows of his ambulance, but with an important difference. Travis at first struggles to remain passive and tolerant despite his contempt for what he sees as the low life around him, until he casts himself in the role of an avenging angel and resolves to clean up the dirt himself though his bloody, suicidal rampage. Frank, by contrast, wants to help the derelicts, addicts, and wounded criminals he ferries over to Our Lady of Perpetual Mercy Hospital (in reality St. Clare's on Fifty-first Street) in Hell's Kitchen (now renamed Clinton) on the West Side of mid-Manhattan.

His immediate community consists of health care professionals, especially his partners in the ambulance. For Larry (John Goodman), the work is only a job that will give him the credentials to set up his own ambulance service out on Long Island. For the flamboyant Marcus (Ving Rhames), the night shift provides a ringside seat to the world's greatest freak show. He enjoys being part of the excitement. Walls (Tom Sizemore) can only be described as a sadist who enjoys adding to the misery of his patients. Because he is trapped in the unsavory world within an even more unsavory world, Frank drinks heavily and pops pills, even during his shift. Again like Travis, he lives alone in an apartment, where his daily routine consists in drinking himself to sleep and then sobering up enough to go to work. His career options stand slightly below zero, and as an emergency medic, he can do almost nothing to relieve the pain he encounters every night. At the end of this story, he finds some form of redemption in his love for Mary Burke (Patricia Arquette), a former drug addict trying to keep clean and care for her dying father. They have a great deal in common. Both have remained in Hell's Kitchen, once a notorious Irish ghetto, long after the more successful Irish moved on to more desirable neighborhoods in Brooklyn and the Bronx.

Because of their addictions, Frank and Mary will probably never be able to leave Hell's Kitchen, but at least they have found each other, and that fact alone introduces a note of optimism that Scorsese and Schrader refused to permit in *Taxi Driver* and *Raging Bull,* where at the end both Travis and Jake remained absolutely isolated. In the last shot, the light that washes out the image of Frank and Mary, holding each other, provides a moment of hope in an otherwise bleak film. It also reveals Scorsese's nostalgia for the kind of tough friendship and mutual support that one can often find in the poorest, most crime-ridden environments. As Hell's Kitchen morphs into Clinton through the relentless march of gentrification, and wealthy young professionals invest in condos where the old Irish tenements once stood, Scorsese may be pardoned for a note of regret for the loss of the kind of people who were able to help one another survive in a trying environment. Like Jake LaMotta, they may not be able to overcome their surroundings, but like him, they will keep fighting. There is a difference. Frank and Mary have each other, while Jake foolishly insisted on going it alone.

On the Other Side of the World

Finally, two films set far from New York provide some indication of the extent to which Scorsese brings Little Italy with him, no matter where he locates his stories. In *The Last Temptation of Christ* (1988), another collaboration with Paul Schrader, Scorsese develops the novel of Nikos Kazantzakis along characteristic lines. Jesus (Willem Dafoe) feels himself called to a mission greater than that of a carpenter in a tight-knit Jewish community under Roman occupation. Through his prayer in the desert and his association with criminals and outcasts, he discovers a mission to something better, both for himself and for his community. Although he gathers a band of devoted followers, local society rejects his teaching and executes him. His last temptation involves the terrifying possibility that all his work and suffering was futile in the first place and that he could have accomplished just as much by conforming to the ordinary expectations of family and business. Of course, he rejects the final temptation to despair and dies with a sense of tranquility, if not accomplishment. Dying as an executed criminal, with few prospects of changing his society, the Jesus figure fits into the pattern of Scorsese's trapped and self-destructive heroes. Yet his fidelity to his own personal integrity within the group has enabled him to triumph over his environment. The Jewish community struggles to keep its own identity under Roman rule, much as Jesus struggles as a Jew within the besieged group. Scorsese admires the toughness of both the man and the community.

Kundun (1997) sets an identical struggle for integrity in twentieth-century Tibet. The young Dalai Lama (Tenzin Thuthob Tsarong) assumes office just as the Communist regime of Mao Tse Tung begins its annexation of Tibet. The all-male counsel of advisers, much like the Mafia, has its own infighting and factions as different leaders jockey for position under their new, inexperienced leader. The country, isolated as it is, has maintained the old religious traditions and social structures. In fact, it is far more enclosed and self-contained than Little Italy. The invasion of the Chinese army, representing a ruthlessly atheistic regime, will necessarily set off a cultural earthquake in traditionalist Tibet.

Faced with radical change in his country, the Dalai Lama is clearly torn as an individual. He sees the need for industrialization, for reform in his government, and for social restructuring for his people, yet he finds himself struggling to preserve the old Tibetan theocracy from being swallowed up by the modern world, as represented by Red China. As a man of the modern world, he is intrigued by automobiles, radios, photomagazines, telescopes, and an old motion picture projector. Yet as Scorsese shows in lavish scenes of court ritual, he acknowledges his role as the cultural curator of his people. With their overpowering military might, the Chinese consolidate their power and begin the process of annexation by moving in Chinese settlers. The Dalai Lama faces a dilemma: if he stays and opposes the Chinese, he will probably become a martyr for his country, but it is unlikely that he will be able to change the flow of history. If he leaves Tibet, he may be able to rally support among other nations, but he will be seen as having deserted his people when they most need his leadership. The alternatives are equally undesirable. At the end, he bows to the inevitable and chooses exile, hoping that he can help his nation more by presenting its plight to the outside world.

Although Scorsese presents the Dalai Lama as a saint in a distant land, thematically, *Kundun* takes its place in the line of his New York gangster films. The elements are all there: a way of life threatened by a larger, impersonal establishment that controls all the power; a closed, traditionalist society that takes care of its own despite its corruption; an individual wrestling with his conscience, chafing under the stifling demands of the backward-looking group, yet committed to its preservation. Without doubt, Scorsese himself looks upon the old ways with respect and affection. He regrets the passing of Tibetan civilization even as he acknowledges its inevitability. Men like Kazantzakis's Jesus, Frank

Pierce, and the Dalai Lama stand out as moral giants, not because they transform their societies or successfully move on to better worlds, but because they are able to transcend the limitations of their time and place. They achieve greatness by maintaining tribal identity in themselves and then trying to help their community survive by marshaling its own best resources.

For Scorsese, New York tribalism takes many forms beyond the fundamental pattern of the Sicilian Mafia protecting itself against the encroachments of the majority culture. Through the years, Scorsese the artist has expanded his horizons beyond Little Italy and has been able to see personal and social tensions in a much wider context. His heroes grow restless under the restraints of their social caste, but they cannot move into another caste. Their own tribe will not let them go and the alternate tribe will not accept them, or most tragically, as in the case of Newland Archer, they simply lack the inner strength to make the transition. Some few succeed, not by moving to another tribe, but by finding what is best in their own.

Spike Lee

Filmography

She Hate Me (2004)
25th Hour (2002)
Ten Minutes Older: The Trumpet (2002)
   (segment "We Wuz Robbed")
Jim Brown All American (2002)
Come Rain or Come Shine (2001)
Bamboozled (2000)
Original Kings of Comedy, The (2000)
Summer of Sam (1999)
He Got Game (1998)
4 Little Girls (1997)
Get on the Bus (1996)
Girl 6 (1996)
Lumière et compagnie (1995)
Clockers (1995)
Crooklyn (1994)
Malcolm X (1992)
Jungle Fever (1991)
Mo' Better Blues (1990)
Do the Right Thing (1989)
School Daze (1988)
She's Gotta Have It (1986)
Joe's Bed-Stuy Barbershop: We Cut Heads
   (1983)
Sarah (1981)
Answer, The (1980)
Last Hustle in Brooklyn (1977)

Fort Greene
Spike Lee

Shelton Jackson Lee took his own sweet time to get to the Fort Greene section of Brooklyn, left it for both high school and college, and eventually moved over to the Upper East Side of Manhattan, but his childhood neighborhood has left its mark on the artist and the films. In the summer of 2004, he still maintains his production company, 40 Acres and a Mule, on DeKalb Avenue and has been active in trying to turn a vacant lot into a Little League baseball field in the neighborhood, despite the desires of the present gentrified residents to create a quiet green space.[1]

Despite his streetwise films and rough-edge language in both his films and his interviews, Spike Lee was not a tough kid from the Brooklyn projects.[2] The Lees are an old middle-class Atlanta family, as middle-class as it was possible for a black family to be in the segregated South. His father and grandfather attended the historically black Morehouse College in Atlanta, and thus it was inevitable that "Spike," as his mother would jokingly refer to her active baby, would follow the family tradition. His mother and grandmother attended Spelman College, the women's college across the street from Morehouse. His great-grandfather, William James Lee, graduated from Tuskegee Institute in Tuskegee, Alabama, and, a disciple of Booker T. Washington, became a notable author and educator in his own right. Bill Lee, Spike's father, developed a successful career as a jazz bassist, composer, and arranger, and he has provided the scores for several of his son's films. His mother, Jacquelyn Shelton Lee, taught art and English at St. Anne's High School in Brooklyn Heights. She died of liver cancer in 1977, when Spike was in college.

Shelton Lee himself arrived in this world on March 20, 1957, the oldest child of a family of five. With this family background, Lee's respect for education, obsession with self-esteem in his characters, take-charge attitude, impatience with gross stereotypes, and attraction to the arts were all but preordained. Fort Greene, a predominantly black neighborhood in a state of transition, added the final ingredient to the mix. It provided a normal setting for a teenager. Like his fellow Brooklynite Woody Allen, to whom he is frequently compared, Spike Lee played baseball as a young man and holds season tickets to the New York Knicks basketball team. Also like Allen, he is somewhat below average stature and plays on his size in several of the on-screen roles he has taken in his films. (He dislikes the comparison.) Fort Greene provided a normal setting for a youngster, but it also provided a rich background for the young artist to draw upon.

The family left Atlanta when Spike was a baby. After a short stay in Chicago, a hub of contemporary jazz, in 1961, Bill Lee brought his family to Brooklyn, and after a few months on Union Street in the Crown Heights section, they settled in the now quite fashionable area of Cobble Hill, also in Brooklyn, with its spectacular view of the East River, the Brooklyn Bridge, and Lower Manhattan. With adjacent Boerum Hill and Brooklyn Heights, this area has been at the center of the gentrification that brought a renaissance to downtown Brooklyn. The Lees were the only African American family on the block, but as Spike Lee recalls those childhood years, he found few racial problems beyond an occasional episode of name-calling among the local children. There were no gangs, only the usual school-yard bullies who took lunch money from the smaller children. He surmises that as the only black family, they were not seen as a threat. He attended the neighborhood public school. Most of the neighbors were Italian, with many Jewish families, which he found, if not welcoming, at least more tolerant than many other ethnic groups he encountered in his early days in Brooklyn. His best friend was Louis Tucci, and he played stickball with the other children in the neighborhood, but he was not allowed to join the Cub Scouts. The scout pack was all white, and because it was sponsored by the Catholic Church, he was told the program was open only to Catholics.[3]

The Other Side of Downtown

It wasn't until 1969 that the Lees moved eastward from the New York side of the Fulton Street commercial area, known simply as Downtown, to its western boundary. The family purchased a brownstone house in Fort Greene, a old multiethnic enclave with a long history of both tolerance and artistic activity. Hidden securely behind the Brooklyn Navy Yard, in its early days, Fort Greene provided housing for both free blacks and immigrants who came to work at the New York Naval Shipyard on Wallabout Bay, which opened in 1801.[4] The area was named for General Nathaniel Greene, the Revolutionary War hero, who originally commanded the fort in the area as part of the doomed defense of Brooklyn during the battle of Long Island in August 1776. Walt Whitman lived in the neighborhood when he edited the *Brooklyn Eagle* (1846–1848), and Colored School No. 1 opened there in 1847. The Presbyterian Church on Lafayette Avenue became a center of abolitionist activity in 1857 and brought Frederick Douglass and Harriet Tubman in for speaking engagements. Populated by working people with steady incomes, the area remained middle class throughout most of its existence.

Located near the thriving downtown hub of Brooklyn, Fort Greene became an artistic center for an independent city ever eager to define itself in opposition to that other city across the river with its own well-known enclaves of artists around Greenwich Village. Fort Greene Park, designed in 1867 by Fredrick Law Olmstead before he built Central Park in Manhattan, features a striking memorial to the "Prison Ships Martyrs," who died in the floating dungeons in Wallabout Bay maintained by the British during the Revolutionary War. The Brooklyn Academy of Music opened in the downtown area in 1861, but after a fire, it was rebuilt and reopened on Lafayette Avenue in Fort Greene in 1906, the same year that the Martyrs monument was dedicated. Enrico Caruso sang at the grand opening. Pratt Institute of Art opened in 1887, expanded its operations to New York, but kept its main campus in Brooklyn throughout several transitions in the neighborhood. To this day it remains one of the leading art schools in the country. By 1926 Long Island University opened its doors nearby. St. James Pro-cathedral, recently renamed St. James Basilica, the spiritual and administrative center of the Catholic diocese of Brooklyn, which at the time included all of Long Island, was opened in 1823 and was rebuilt in 1902 on Tillary Street, just north of Fort Greene Park. After Brooklyn's amalgamation into Greater New York in 1898 and the building of the bridges to Manhattan, artists fleeing the increasingly high rents over in New York found a congenial setting in the artistic community around Fort Greene.

World War II brought change to Fort Greene, much of it unwelcome. During the 1940s, the New York Naval Shipyard, known simply as the Brooklyn Navy Yard, dramatically expanded to meet the needs of the war effort. Workers poured into the area, and many landlords found a bonanza by converting their stately old brownstones into rooming houses. In addition, the government slapped together additional housing to accommodate the influx of shipyard workers. After the war, activities at the shipyard slowed, the workforce shrank, the housing market collapsed, and urban blight spread into the region. The wartime buildings morphed into the Fort Greene projects, a public housing complex of 3,500 units, known officially as the Walt Whitman and Raymond V. Ingersoll houses. Unofficially, one area was simply called "the Jungle." The proud Brooklyn Academy of Music used its performance spaces for martial arts programs. In the years after the war, the area became predominantly black, although the political and social institutions remained in the control of white people, even after the white flight to Long Island, New Jersey, and, with the opening of the Verrazano Bridge in 1964, Staten Island. The Navy Yard was officially decommissioned in 1966. The area began to resemble its blighted neighbor, Bedford-Stuyvesant, known to both residents and apprehensive outsiders simply as Bed-Stuy, a name that has become a shorthand for urban decay.

Even as the situation appeared to grow hopeless, new life stirred in Fort Greene. The collapse did not last very long. The low real estate prices seem to have attracted many middle-class families like the Lees to make a move into home ownership in 1969. Under new leadership, the Brooklyn Academy of Music reinvented itself as BAM, a sponsor of avant-garde drama and music for the past thirty years. As costs for both business and residential properties soared in Manhattan, Fort Greene became an attractive alternative once again for artists and the young urban professionals, black as well as white. A twenty-minute subway ride brought the new homesteaders to their offices around Wall Street in Lower Manhattan. The cultural institutions that remained were able to anchor a gradual but determined rejuvenation of the neighborhood. With the closing of the Navy Yard, the region no longer depended on transient workers. After confronting its postwar problems, Fort Greene began to revert to its more genteel tradition. The Lees arrived as the process of rejuvenation was just beginning. Bill Lee's shrewd investment could be perceived as a gift of prophecy.[5]

Shortly after relocating to Fort Greene, Spike began high school, which involved a long daily commute from the northern reaches of Brooklyn on the East River to the southern extremity on the Atlantic Ocean by taking the Brighton Line of the BMT to John Dewey High School on Avenue X, near Coney Island. The school was known for its flexible scheduling and progressive methods, in keeping with its name, and it served a mixed population. It had its problems, like all urban high schools, but it was scarcely a blackboard jungle, as some urban high schools are frequently described. As Lee looks back on his high-school career, he sees himself as a leader among his peers but an indifferent student. He recalls some name-calling as he and other black students made their way back to the subway in the afternoon, but the problem was much less serious than his friends described at other Brooklyn high schools.[6] Like any teenager, he enjoyed going to the movies, but it was just an afternoon's entertainment. He rejects the notion of an epiphany that occurred when he suddenly decided to become a filmmaker on the basis of some childhood experience at the movies. He remains dubious about other filmmakers who claim to be cradle auteurs.

Moving On

Despite his mediocre grades in high school, Spike Lee was admitted to Morehouse College in Atlanta. If his academic performance in high school was less than stellar, he was, after all, a third-generation legacy, and he had no trouble gaining admission. During his mother's illness, the family experienced some financial stress, and his grandmother, Zimmie Jackson Shelton, helped out with tuition. In 1978, the year after his mother's death, Bill Lee married Susan Kaplan. Despite their growing apart as his father's interests shifted to his new family, Spike never lost his admiration for Bill Lee's ability and had him provide the scores for several of his films. His father's marriage to a Jewish woman also helped make Spike Lee aware of the tensions that often arise because of interracial relationships, a topic he has treated with astonishing frankness in several of his films.

As a mass media and communications major, he supplemented his program at Morehouse by taking film courses at Clark College, now Clark Atlanta University, also a historically African American institution. Only at this time did his interest in filmmaking begin to solidify. Between his third and fourth year, he bought an eight-millimeter camera and made shorts entitled *Black College: The Talented Tenth* and *Last Hustle in Brooklyn,* subject matter he would revisit as a professional filmmaker. After graduation in 1979, he landed a summer internship at Columbia Pictures in Los Angeles, and at the end of the summer he began a three-year MFA program at the Tisch School of the Arts at NYU, a short subway ride from the room he rented in the old neighborhood in Fort Greene. Tuition, fees, and funding for film projects totaled over $100,000 in those days, and once again, his grandmother was able to see him through. His first student project, which was rejected for production (and, he believes, nearly finished his career at NYU), was *The Answer,* a ten-minute story of a black scriptwriter doing a remake of *The Birth of a Nation,* D. W. Griffith's racist epic of 1915. His thesis film for his graduation in 1982 was a forty-five-minute narrative entitled *Joe's Bed-Stuy Barbershop: We Cut Heads,* which was screened at Lincoln Center and received an Academy Award as the best student film of the year.

After graduation, Spike Lee hired an agent, but like many other film-school alumni, he found the industry a tough nut to crack. While sending out grant applications, he took a job as messenger and film cleaner at First Run Features, which for a film student had the advantage of being located in the same building as the legendary Bleecker Street Cinema, a few blocks from Tisch in Greenwich Village. The American Film Institute gave him money to work on *The Messenger,* but when the project failed to receive additional backing, the grant was rescinded and Lee had to scrap the idea.[7] Undeterred, he put together another package of grant money and investments from backers, including once more his grandmother, and went to work on *She's Gotta Have It* (1986), a comic account of a black woman named Nora Darling who tries to balance three relationships at the same time. The film was both a critical and financial success, and it opened the way for his next film *School Daze*

(1988), a satiric look at student life at Mission College, a transparent surrogate for Morehouse College. Although the first commercial film had a title and heroine's name that would suggest a porn flick, the second was more like a black version of *National Lampoon's Animal House* (John Landis, 1978), with its sharp, very funny critique of snobbery in campus life. As a film student, Spike Lee began his career with a clear grasp of film genres, which he exploited and recycled into his own unique artistic vision. He also had the business sense to realize that sex and college comedies draw distributors and consequently sell tickets. Through these two early ventures, Spike Lee established himself as a commercially viable filmmaker with strong support among African American audiences and with the potential to attract the white audiences as well. He would establish his crossover potential in his third commercial film, *Do the Right Thing* (1989).

Traces of Fort Greene

Fort Greene clearly left its mark on these early films, to be sure, but it remains a cultural lens for the later films as well. Living in a largely white neighborhood as a child gave Lee the sense of being an outsider on the basis of race alone. His family was, after all, just as solidly middle-class and respectable as any of his Jewish and Italian neighbors in Cobble Hill, but even as a child, he could not escape the fact that because he was black, he was somehow different—at least different enough to be excluded from the Cub Scouts. In Fort Greene, however, he became immersed in a black community, but paradoxically, because of his previous experience in a diverse community, he was able to view the struggling world of Fort Greene as both an observer looking in on a distinct culture and as an African American very much at home in his new surroundings. During his years at Morehouse, as his early films demonstrate, he solidified his identification with the black community while remaining a shrewd observer of both its innate strengths and weaknesses.

In many ways Fort Greene provided a rare laboratory for the observation of a black neighborhood at a crossroads. As an adolescent college student and young filmmaker, he saw up close the struggles of a community fighting urban blight but with enormous cultural resources at its disposal. Fort Greene seemed to be making it, and as a result, it became a kind of metaphor for the trials experienced by many of the characters in his films. His portrayal of many black people is unblinking. They have problems, some of their own creation. "Making it" comes at a cost that some are not able or willing to pay. Some have given up their dignity and match the worst stereotypes that burden hard-working, upwardly mobile families like the Lees. That is their tragedy. Others possess great depths of dignity and courage that allow them to succeed in the most difficult of circumstances. Some fail, of course, but despite the odds against them, some manage to triumph, and that is what is really important.

Like most New Yorkers, young Spike Lee kept close to his own neighborhood, traveling by subway through other areas back and forth to high school in Coney Island, and then after his return from Atlanta, to NYU in Lower Manhattan. Also, like many New Yorkers, he developed a series of mythologies about other areas, and these later provided the basis of his re-creation of multicultural New York in his films. The point is worth repeating that native New Yorkers are extremely territorial animals, and although they regularly travel to Manhattan for work, shopping, or entertainment, they seldom visit other residential areas in the City. For people living in Bensonhurst, for example, Bedford-Stuyvesant might as well be Calcutta, and their only familiarity with it would come from tabloids and local television newscasts reporting the latest shooting or drug raid. These reports create an image that becomes an unshakable certainty. Conversely, Lee mentions Bensonhurst as an area a black person would not visit, even on business; therefore, his creation of Italian enclaves comes from research and imagination, not from the experience of Italians he had in multicultural Cobble Hill as a child.

Spike Lee proved no exception to this rule of insularity, even in his re-creation of African American communities. He had little contact with Harlem, yet through his reading, he saw the Harlem Renaissance as a golden age of African American achievement in the 1920s and 1930s. Harlem was in fact at that time a neighborhood that served as a showcase and nurturer for the talents of a group of gifted artists who mined their own distinct culture for their work. By the 1970s and 1980s, however, Harlem had changed, but the legend lived on in Spike Lee's imagination. With its splendid residential architecture, Strivers Row, West One Hundred Thirty-eighth and One Hundred Thirty-ninth Streets in Harlem, remained a fashionable address for wealthy African Americans even as others areas deteriorated, and for Lee, it remained emblematic of Harlem as a whole. In *Jungle Fever* it becomes the ultimate symbol for affluence for a black architect who has made it. On the other extreme, Bedford-Stuyvesant, a few blocks to the south and east of Fort Greene, represents the horrifying negative image of black-on-black crime, gangs, and drugs. For Spike Lee, Fort Greene functions like the observation tower, as though one could stand atop the column of the Martyrs Monument and look out on other areas of Brooklyn and the rest of New York. Sometimes what he sees and reports can make others, especially black audiences, quite uncomfortable.

The Others

Looking out from a his own vantage point, Spike Lee sees the other groups in the City with keen artistic insight that can at times cross the boundaries into caricature. The working-class Italian Americans who appear in *Do the Right Thing, Jungle Fever,* and *Summer of Sam* seethe with rage and bigotry. They stand one step away from mindless mob violence, especially when "moolies" are involved. Mo and Josh Flatbush, the obviously Jewish owners of the jazz club in *Mo' Better Blues,* embody stereotypical miserliness, which becomes ever more marked when set in contrast to the ineffectiveness of the inept business manager, Giant, played by Spike Lee himself. In the arena of interethnic competition, the Jews embody nasty shrewdness, the blacks bumbling incompetence. It's not a flattering image of either group. In *25th Hour,* the convicted Irish American drug dealer (Edward Norton) preparing to go to prison comes from Bay Ridge, Brooklyn, a predominantly Irish section on the western edge of Brooklyn, overlooking the Harbor and Staten Island on the other side of the bay. His father, a recovering alcoholic who has retired from the fire department, had, years earlier, joined the white flight across the Verrazano Bridge to Staten Island and opened a bar that caters to firemen on Bay Street. A boyhood friend assures him that when he gets out of prison, as two Irish kids from Bay Ridge, they can always open a bar. For Spike Lee, Jews suggest money, Italians violence, and Irish alcohol.

Like most New Yorkers who spend their formative years in an ethnic neighborhood, Spike Lee could not avoid the awareness of race and nationality that, as if by osmosis, seeps into the consciousness and in moments of conflict can break through the surface and erupt into hatred. In both *Do the Right Thing* and *25th Hour*, he interrupts the narrative to let characters voice in the crudest terms their inner contempt for other definable ethnic groups: white, black, Korean shopkeepers, Irish cops, Pakistani cab drivers. Although the racial tension is always present in the films, it only rarely breaks out into interracial violence. His powerful documentary about the bombing of a Baptist church in Atlanta in 1963, *4 Little Girls* (1997), provides a moving reconstruction of an act of unspeakable violence, but if anything, it is both a condemnation of what one reporter calls "pathological racism" and a testimony to the dignity of the survivors. Neither Lee nor the families he interviews call for racially motivated revenge. In *Do the Right Thing*, the death of a black teenager at the hands of overly aggressive white police officers leads to a mindless destruction of property as an expression of frustration, but as Lee quite properly insists, the violence was directed toward property, not persons. In *Malcolm X* the threat of organized interracial violence simmers under the surface, but the entire point is that Malcolm X chooses not to use it, and in fact falls victim himself to the violence of a rival faction within the Nation of Islam. Under scrutiny, then, the films provide an anthropological study of the dynamics of racial thinking so common in New York neighborhoods, and to reach that end, Lee selects, exaggerates, and at times caricatures negative ethnic traits. Race and ethnicity flavor all Lee's films.

In this regard, Spike Lee stands apart from the older generation of New York filmmakers, who take a more oblique approach to ethnicity. For Woody Allen, it rarely arises as an issue at all. Several of his characters are self-consciously Jewish, but their background provides material for tensions within themselves rather than overt conflict with members of other groups. For Sidney Lumet and Martin Scorsese, ethnic identity often shapes the struggle that the characters encounter with other groups within their larger society. Group differences lurk in the background, add color to the setting, and add tension to dramatic situations. Their struggling heroes are aware of their ethnic status, refer to it, and generally work around it as an inevitable part of their New York environment, but neither director puts ethnicity at the core of the narrative. For Spike Lee, race and class often function as the basis of the conflicts in his films. If his characters were not black or Italian, poor or uneducated, they would not face the problems they do.

Lee's preoccupation with ethnic cultures has led some critics to identify a strand of racism in his own thinking. When confronted with the observation, his response is complex and takes a bit of effort to digest. In an interview with David Breskin, he defends his statement that black people cannot be racist, but he continues immediately, "Black people can be prejudiced. But to me, racism is the *institution*."[8] The distinction helps to clarify a great deal in his films. According to Spike Lee, every group, including African Americans, can be guilty of prejudice and racial hatred, even when they maintain that they are not. Racism, however, is the residue of social bias that remains in American culture after centuries of slavery and decades of segregation. Lee's films deal with both issues simultaneously. The black characters have problems rooted in racist society. Lee feels that they often have one more hurdle to overcome than white people and does not shrink from pointing out what he calls the double standard applied to blacks and whites in America. Still, any of the characters, black or white, can be guilty of racial stereotyping, like the waitress at Sylvia's restaurant in Harlem in *Jungle Fever*, who refuses service and then insults an interracial couple. Lee has little patience with black characters who blame white society for all their problems. With characteristic verve, he writes in the Introduction to *Spike Lee's Gotta Have It:* "We're tired of that alibi, 'White man this, white man that.' YO! Fuck dat! So let's all do the work that needs to be done by us all."[9]

An Odd Kind of Conservative

Lee's consistent message of self-reliance may strike one as surprisingly conservative. Lee believes that with hard work and self-respect, African Americans can succeed, and in fact, many do. The determining factor comes from the community. Family support and reliable friends provide the key to success, but one seldom, if ever, sees a social worker or a welfare check solving someone's personal problems in a Spike Lee film.

Success, however, poses additional problems for many of Spike Lee's black characters because it shifts their core conflict from race to class. Prejudice thus takes on an added complexity for his black characters because of class distinctions. Lee's family, his time at Morehouse, and his life in Fort Greene showed him that many African Americans are resolutely middle class; they are well educated, prosperous, articulate, and quite comfortable with themselves and in dealing with the wider culture. They have seized life's opportunities and made the most of them. Others trapped in their own despair adopt self-defeating strategies for coping with life—self-pity and surrender, with the inevitable result of poverty, crime, and drugs. In Lee's films, successful black characters find that speaking well and succeeding in a profession create as many problems as they solve. The relationship between social classes within the black community and the friction generated by different ways of being black lie at the crux of the dramatic conflict as often as do interracial issues. He doesn't dismiss the inequities of racial bias in American society, but he doesn't allow his characters to excuse their failures because of it. He places much of the blame on the educational system for high failure rates among African Americans, but he describes as "sick" the belief among many young African Americans that speaking good English and doing well in school is "white" and a betrayal of black cultural values.[10]

For Spike Lee success means earning the right of self-determination, and he sees that his independence as an artist is inevitably tied to financial security. Whoever controls the purse strings controls the product. He laments the fact that so few African Americans have reached the stature in Hollywood to be able to dictate which pictures get made.[11] As a struggling student filmmaker, he started his own production company, 40 Acres and a Mule Filmworks, and located it in Fort Greene rather than work as a contract director for one of the studios in Hollywood. At this early stage in his career, he became convinced that he could make the pictures he wanted only if he raised the money and paid the salaries of the people who worked with him. For this reason he views filmmaking as a business as well as an art form. He told David Breskin, "Am I a capitalist? We all are over here. And I'm just trying to get the power to do what I have to do. To get that power you have to accumulate some kind of bank. And that's what I've done. I've always tried to be in an entrepreneurial mode of thinking."[12] In addition to his production company, he has launched a recording studio, 40 Acres and a Mule Musicworks, and a retail outlet, Spike's Joint, for merchandise connected with his movies.

Spike Lee has not been shy about publishing ventures that open additional profit windows for his films. On the basis of his very first commercial success, he published *Spike Lee's "Gotta Have It": Inside*

Guerrilla Filmmaking (1987) and continued the practice of book tie-ins with *Uplift the Race: The Construction of "School Daze"* (1989), *"Do the Right Thing": A Spike Lee Joint* (1990) and *Mo' Better Blues* (1991), all with photographs by his brother David Lee. *The Films of Spike Lee: Five for Five* (1991), a coffee-table-style retrospective of the five early films, includes frame enlargements and stills from the sets prepared by his brother David Lee and essays on each film by prominent black scholars and authors.[13] He also published *By Any Means Necessary: The Trials and Tribulations of Making "Malcolm X"* (1993), coauthored with Ralph Wiley. More recently, with the editorial assistance of Cynthia Fuchs, he released *Spike Lee Interviews* (2002), a collection of twenty-one interviews he has given during his career.

A Capitalism of Social Responsibility

Spike Lee's dedication to capitalism and individual self-reliance comes with a strong sense of social responsibility. As one who controls the purse strings, he used his influence to open doors for other African Americans trying to break into the film industry. Like Francis Coppola, he has not shied away from including his family in his film projects. His father, Bill, has done several musical scores, and his sister Joie appears regularly on screen. Through his photography, David Lee, Spike's younger brother, has collaborated on the published companion pieces to the films.

Ever aware that white people control the decision-making power within the industry, continue to hire people like themselves, and thus indirectly exclude African American technicians, Lee has used his clout to reverse the practice of informal but institutionalized racial bias. For example, he used Ernest Dickerson, a Howard graduate and the only other black student in Lee's class at Tisch to have made a place for himself in the film business, as his regular cinematographer from the earliest student films through *Malcolm X* in 1991. At that time, well established as a cinematographer, Dickerson went off on his own to begin a busy career as a director in both film and television. Several actors landed choice parts with Lee while roles for black actors were scarce, and they went on to become major stars in mainstream Hollywood, among them Samuel L. Jackson, Larry Fishburne, Halle Berry, Wesley Snipes, and Denzel Washington.

Spike Lee's willingness to use his financial power to further the interests of the African American community extends beyond the film industry. He maintains that the success of several black entertainers and athletes have created the illusion of progress, but the black underclass is bigger than ever. While filming in New York and thus providing a great deal of work for the teamsters' union, he openly criticized them for failing to open their membership to minorities.[14] Although he actively supports issues of interest to African Americans, he refuses to see himself as somehow obliged to use his wealth for philanthropic purposes. In his interview with David Breskin, he became indignant when the interviewer reiterated a question posed by an earlier television interviewer about what he would do with the profits from his retail store. He pointed out that white entertainers had a right to make money and nobody asks anything about it. When a black man makes money it becomes a "racist question."[15] He wants to make money and doesn't feel the need to give it away for charitable purposes. At the same time, when *Malcolm X* was running over budget and faced termination by Warner Bros., he contacted several black entertainers and sports stars for the additional financing he needed to finish the project.[16] The whole purpose of amassing money is to enable one to take on important projects, and networking based on cultural loyalties is a perfectly legitimate way of doing business in America.

Spike Lee, like Fort Greene itself, remains a bundle of contradictions, as do his films. He stands at the confluence of many social currents. This central location provides a vantage point that allows him to be the perfect participant-observer. He is proud of his tradition, aware of its weaknesses as well as its strengths, and strives to be a catalyst for change. He recognizes the debilitating side of racism and poverty and does not shy away from portraying it honestly in his films. At the same time, he keeps alive the dream that with hard work, life can get better. He remains firmly rooted in the black community but does not hesitate to collaborate with the majority community as an equal partner. Although only marginally religious at best, he follows the Protestant ethic of self-reliance and personal responsibility with a conviction that borders on devotional. In the midst of grim realities, he finds room for comedy. After his considerable successes as an artist and entrepreneur, he remains a professional committed to family and communitarian values; he wants to use his wealth and position to help his family and the

African American community at large, but he would prefer to be seen as a businessman rather than a philanthropist. For present purposes, both titles may be put into the background. Foremost of all, Spike Lee is a filmmaker, and that role is of primary interest in the pages that follow.

Gotta Have Bank

Spike Lee soon discovered that his success as a student filmmaker with *Joe's Bed-Stuy Barbershop: We Cut Heads* (1983) would not translate into immediate recognition as a professional filmmaker. One could quibble about the term "student film." Even though he had technically completed the program at Tisch and fulfilled the requirements for his MFA by 1983, the school wisely allowed him to stay on and use its equipment to complete *Barbershop,* and this technicality allowed it to be entered in the "student film" category for the Academy Awards, which it received as a joint production of NYU and 40 Acres and a Mule Filmworks, with his grandmother Zimmie Shelton listed as coproducer with Lee himself. The one-hour film is set in a neighborhood barbershop used as a numbers drop, and when the owner is murdered in a dispute with the syndicate operative, Zack (Monty Ross), his successor, has to decide whether to keep going without the supplementary income from gambling, reopen for business giving traditional haircuts, or just leave town. He opts to keep his business open in the neighborhood. The decision reveals Lee's early interest in the question of black entrepreneurship and its relationship to the community.

With the collapse of the *Messenger* project, a story about one of those kamikaze bicycle messengers who terrorized Manhattan streets before fax and e-mail became the preferred methods of interoffice communication, Spike Lee understood that if he were to realize his dream of becoming a truly independent filmmaker through his 40 Acres and a Mule Filmworks, he would need a commercial success. Knowing that sex sells, he picked the suggestive title *She's Gotta Have It,* and by giving his central character the name of Nola Darling (Tracy Camilla Johns), he left little doubt about what "it" was. The film deals with the issue of serial sex and contains several explicit scenes that would have been unthinkable twenty years earlier. Several critics, including Abiola Sinclair of the *Amsterdam News,* labeled the film pornographic.[17] Despite the controversy, it got a favorable reception at the festivals, went into theatrical distribution, and sold enough tickets to give Spike Lee a beach-head in the industry.

She's Gotta Have It treats sexuality with frankness, but it is quite a bit more than a porn flick with jokes. It may have profited from the curiosity value of being a sexy romantic comedy with a black director and an all-black cast, but it demonstrated respectable appeal beyond the African American community. Nola Darling tries to juggle three lovers at the same time, each of whom has his own sex scene with her. The concept then involves a gender-role reversal of the stereotype of the promiscuous black male, a factor that upset some critics for perpetuating a negative image. Commenting on the popular image, and at times the reality, of promiscuity among black men, Lee tells interviewer Marlaine Glicksman, "So I decided, let's make a film about a woman who is actually living her life like a man."[18] At one point, she experiences an attempted lesbian seduction by Opal (Raye Dowell), and although she admits curiosity about a different form of sexual expression, she asks Opal to leave after the first kiss. Left alone after her lovers have abandoned her, she masturbates. Frustrated by Nola's need for multiple partners, one of her lovers tells her she is a sex addict and needs therapy. She follows his advice, and after a few sessions with Dr. Jamison (Epatha Merkerson), she ends the therapy with her doctor's concurrence that she does not have an addiction, but merely a healthy sex drive. With her endless good humor and electric smile, Nola remains a sympathetic character even as she seems absolutely unconcerned about her self-centered disregard for the others in her life. Their feelings and needs rarely enter her erotic calculus. Lee's script offers no criticism of her promiscuous behavior, however. She merely plays her natural role in a sexually charged atmosphere.

The unflattering stereotypes arise from Nola's lovers, each of whom is aware of his two rivals for her attention. Jamie Overstreet (Tommy Redmond Hicks) is respectable, reliable, and considerate, but he is also a trifle dull. He does have a romantic side, however. When Nola is in bed with a cold, he brings groceries to her and offers to stay with her. He finds Opal in the apartment, insists on her leaving, and then questions Nola about the nature of her friendship with Opal. In a musical interlude in color inserted into the black-and-white narrative portion of the film, he celebrates Nola's birthday by bringing her to Fort Greene Park, where two dancers perform a romantic ballet at the base of the

Prison Martyrs Monument while the two lovers enjoy a lavish picnic that he has prepared. As time drags on, Jamie grows tired of Nola's reluctance to separate herself from the other two men. He finds another lover, actually the dancer from the birthday party, and while they are in bed together, Nola calls and asks him to come over because of an emergency. In fact, she needs him only because she is lonely. Jamie goes to her but becomes increasing angry when he realizes that Nola simply wants to make love, and as a clear instance of gender-role reversal, he feels he is merely being used as the most convenient partner. He initially refuses, but when she tries to seduce him, he says he will provide sex, not love. Jamie treats her roughly and seems intent on degrading her. He continues his brutal assault (describing his activity as rape would not be an exaggeration) even when she whimpers that he is hurting her. As he leaves, he tells her that he felt good about what he did to her.

Mars Blackman (Spike Lee) is Nola's most improbable lover. He never grew up. He is twenty-six but looks sixteen. He meets Nola under the Williamsburg Bridge as he pushes his ten-speed bicycle along the promenade. Looking as though he were competing in the Tour de France, he wears a biker cap and tight spandex pants and jacket, which he sets off with a huge gold medallion spelling out "Mars" on his chest. His short haircut features an arrow shaved into the back of his head. He has not had a job in two years, yet in addition to his biking paraphernalia, he wears expensive Cazals eyeglasses, a high-fashion item among city teenagers at the time, and Air Jordan sneakers, which he even wears while making love to Nola. Despite his obvious immaturity, Nola finds him a congenial companion. Reality rarely infiltrates his high spirits and comic sensibility. Nola enjoys his sense of humor even when it is a bit childish. He has a maddening habit of repeating himself, like DeNiro improvising for Scorsese, but Nola doesn't mind. She seems happy to help him cope; she infuriates Jamie by canceling a date because she has to help Mars find an apartment.

The third lover is Greer Childs (John Canada Terrell), a successful model who finds himself imprisoned by his own good looks. He introduces himself by driving his red Jaguar convertible into a gated garden, describes himself in self-aggrandizing terms, and before the action moves on, he rearranges his carefully treated hair. He offers the opinion that he was the best thing that ever happened to Nola because he saved her from "common street trash."[19] The action moves to Nola's apartment. Nola recognizes his vanity and tells him, "I've never met anyone who loved to look at themselves as much as you do" (302). He responds by telling her that he will leave her as soon as she gets fat. Some days later, as they exercise together, he announces that he has gotten a cover shoot for *GQ* (*Gentlemen's Quarterly*). As though offering a reward for his professional success, she moves over to the "loving bed" and starts to remove her clothes. He follows, but he takes so much time carefully folding his T-shirt and shorts that Nola seems to lose interest. When they dine at a fine restaurant, Nola wears her hair treated with pomade and slicked back against her scalp, just like Greer's. It is the only time in the film that she abandons her natural look. He wants to take her away from Brooklyn, which he finds uncivilized, and her other lovers, whom he calls "ignorant ghetto Negroes" (329). At a disastrous Thanksgiving dinner that Nola hosts for her three lovers, Greer asks for white meat, much to the amusement of the other two (326). Mars claims that Greer has had a "nose job" (319).

In the final portion of the film, Nola decides to change her life and meets with each of her three lovers in turn. She simply tells Greer and Mars that they are no longer part of her life. The meeting with Jamie, however, is far more ambiguous. Even after their ugly sexual encounter, she decides that she wants him and tells him so, but with the added note that she intends to be celibate for a while (360). When Jamie asks what he should do while she's a nun, Nola tells him to go back to his other woman until she's ready again. He rejects her offer and she leaves. He pursues her and says he will take her back. As they walk up the Hundred Steps toward the Prison Martyrs Monument, they step back from each other. He has suggested marriage, and she concludes, "I'm not a one-man woman. Bottom line" (361). The final shot shows Nola alone in her "loving bed," perhaps waiting for new lovers, perhaps regretting that she has lost the lovers she once had.

From the point of view of Lee's background, several observations are pertinent. Despite his awareness of the sexually irresponsible behavior of all the characters and the fact that their quests for companionship ultimately fail, Lee presents them as essentially sympathetic people. It must be noted that the film was made before the public fully appreciated the horror of the AIDS epidemic. By way of exception, Lee makes Greer reprehensible—not because of his overpowering narcissism, but because he has tried to deny his identity as a black man. Coming over from Manhattan to Fort Greene to woo Nola, he insults her other lovers as "hoodlums" and "ignorant ghetto Negroes." He treats his hair with gel and has Nola do the same. His greatest enticement to Nola is the promise to take her out of Brooklyn, which is for her (and Spike Lee) irrevocably intertwined with black identity. He has money, a convertible, and a nice apartment, but he considers himself above the African American community. When Nola finally cuts him loose, his parting remark is that he can get a white woman to replace her. As an obviously successful man who despises his rivals, he introduces class distinctions within the black community.

Lee portrays Mars as irresponsible. In truth, he never appeared a serious contender for Nola's affection—not to her, to himself, or to the audience. He fits into the category of the "dogs" in an opening sequence, when fifteen men in turn give their blustery but transparently dumb pick-up lines. They are brash and hollow at the same time. They're funny, and one has to admire their spunk, but they don't stand a chance. In contrast, Lee portrays Jamie as serious but domineering. From the moment he spotted Nola and followed her through the crowds on the Fulton Street Mall, he knows that he loves her, but on his own terms, which for Nola seem old-fashioned and repressive. In his references to Opal, he reveals a strong homophobic streak. Although Nola and the audience can admire his serious side, especially in contrast to Greer and Mars, he has a deep and traditional sense of the proper role for a woman. He would suffocate someone like Nola. Both men are admirable in their way: Mars is amusing and Jamie dependable, but neither can meet Nola's expectation for a long-term relationship, if she would ever be interested in having one.

At the center of the film, of course, is Nola, who despite her unconventional view of human relationships remains a strong character precisely because of her independence. She lives her life according to her own rules. Nola took music lessons to please her musician father, but when she moved out on her own, she stopped practicing. She works as a graphic designer and no longer needs a man to support her. Aside from the dinner date with Greer, she doesn't go out. Nola meets her men in public areas, like parks and promenades under the East River Bridges, and invites partners to her apartment for sex. She maintains that she will never make love in anyone else's bed. She asks Opal about lesbian sex as a matter of curiosity but definitively rejects her advances. In a word, she is her own woman.

Nola Darling provides an offbeat but illuminating paradigm of Spike Lee's Fort Greene experience. She never rejects her culture or demeans the stereotypical characters she finds in it. Nola is no fool; she sees the flaws in her suitors, but she also respects them, and that makes her decision all the more difficult. She won't compromise her racial identity like Greer. Nor will she opt out of the adult world like Mars. Nor, finally, will she accept a fully traditional female role as defined by Jamie. She has the inner resources to succeed on her own terms. As a perfectly autonomous individual, she knows what she wants and will pursue it, no matter how society judges her conduct. In a dream sequence, the three girlfriends of her three lovers appear and berate her for poaching their men, and then the bed bursts into flames. Nola knows that her lifestyle is judged harshly by others, but ultimately, she cannot compromise her own integrity to meet others' expectations of her. She never sinks into a paralysis of self-pity. For Spike Lee, her personal integrity outweighs her confused actions. As novelist Terry McMillan put it, "She's going to continue doing things her way."[20] And in Lee's eyes that makes her, and by extension the Fort Greene community, admirable indeed.

Back to Atlanta

Spike Lee's scrutiny of the black community takes an autobiographical twist when he re-creates his experience at Morehouse College for his next film, *School Daze* (1988). It is not surprising to speculate that his sharp observations of student life may be influenced by his self-image as a sophisticated New Yorker on a campus in the South and among students from other parts of the country, some of which are undeniably rural. In the film one of his characters asserts his authority over another by boasting, "I'm from Detroit, the home of Motown," but for a competitive undergraduate like a teenage Spike Lee, what is Detroit compared to New York, or Motown compared to the Harlem Renaissance? On the basis of the success of *She's Gotta Have It,* Columbia Pictures provided the money for Lee to take his project to his alma mater, but as the school authorities became more aware of the content of the film, they asked him to leave, and he had to complete filming at Atlanta College. Combining the popular genres of the gross-out college-life satire and the musical comedy, Lee uses the fictional Mission College, founded in 1883 with its motto "Uplift the Race," as a microcosm of the efforts of today's young African Americans to improve their conditions. The students are on the way up, like Fort Greene, but Lee asks them to stop, join him, and, as though standing on the vantage point of the Prison Martyrs Monument, take a hard look at their world. He sees a population divided by class and color—yes, by color—and by economic background, self-image, and ideology. The men are misogynistic, and many of the women foolishly go along with them by playing the roles assigned to them by the male students. The situation provides fertile ground for biting satire.

Because *School Daze* deals with intrinsically sensitive social issues in the context of a raucous comedy, as a result, it met with a mixed reaction. It is a Rorschach test for critics, as satire frequently is. For whites with little sympathy for African Americans and for self-hating black people, it confirms negative images already in place. Feminists regret that its degrading treatment of women is made to seem normal or even acceptable among the black population.[21] Some black critics credit Lee for having the honesty to point out issues that divide them but fault him for airing dirty linen before the public, when such problems should be handled within the family. Spike Lee explains his own motivation: "I wanted to look at some of the issues that keep African Americans from being a more unified people, these issues really being superficial stuff."[22] The comparison to *All in the Family*, the popular television sitcom of the 1970s, is helpful. The program was created by Norman Lear to lampoon the prejudices of Archie Bunker (Carroll O'Connor), a working-class white man living in Queens. Undoubtedly, some Bunkeresque viewers enjoyed hearing him express sentiments they agreed with but were no longer permitted to utter in polite society. As a result, some viewers found the show offensively racist and sexist, while others, including its creators, saw it as unabashedly liberal in its making Archie a fool for his benighted attitudes.

Clearly, these are sensitive issues for any critic—especially a European American like myself—to try to resolve. On the whole, I'm willing to offer a modest defense for Spike Lee. Working within the context of broad comedy, he presents a cast of stereotypical characters and points out their self-defeating foibles and foolishness, not so much to degrade them but to hold them up as examples of what not to do and how not to act. To extrapolate a bit from the text of *School Daze* (and perhaps I am influenced here by my viewing of his *Get On the Bus* [1996], made some eight years later by a more mature artist), Lee strikes me as saying that African Americans have enormous resources, but they risk being sidetracked by misguided people, misplaced values, and phony issues. From my admittedly limited perspective as an outsider, it seems that once one works through the crude satire, one can find a positive message at the core of *School Daze*: people have to get together to accomplish their objectives; they can't waste their energies on pointless infighting. Although he seems intent on creating an incisive social commentary for African Americans to consider, he has perhaps inadvertently pointed out serious issues that touch every group within American society. The pun in the title implies an admonition. In his opinion, the students at Mission College are indeed in a daze, and by extension, so are many black people and, by further extension, many white Americans. Although Spike Lee offers little by way of suggestion for positive action, the final scene is a wake-up call for all of us.

Like *She's Gotta Have It*, *School Daze* deals with dynamics within the African American community. With the exception of one very important scene in a fast-food restaurant in town, it takes place in the insulated world of Mission College on homecoming weekend. It has no white characters whatsoever, and in fact the only reference to white people occurs obliquely in the president's office, when the chairman of the board complains that alumni have failed to support the school, the way Catholics support Notre Dame, Jews Yeshiva, and Mormons Brigham Young. The college would go under if it weren't for government subsidies and philanthropists like the Snodgrass family, whose white faces in portraits loom paternalistically over the conversation. Where Spike Lee used individuals to represent different traits he observed within the group in the earlier film, in this one, he uses competing groups or factions. His critique has more of a bite. Although the individuals within the group may have admirable traits, the cliques have little to commend them. In the pursuit of the common good, they are divisive and sap the energies of the individuals who participate in them and the collective that contains them.

Lee opens the film with a montage of stills illustrating the shared heritage of black people in America. It begins with a print showing the outline of slave ships with their human cargo stacked in the hold, through

Frederic Douglass, Booker T. Washington, and the training shops of the Tuskegee Institute, and then to students at academic black colleges, to black soldiers fighting in World War I, to Martin Luther King Jr., Malcolm X, Jesse Jackson, and familiar shots from civil rights demonstrations, to icons of popular culture like Joe Louis, Willie Mays, and Bessie Smith.

After the opening titles, the action moves to a campus demonstration gathered on the steps of the administration building to protest the college's investments in companies that do business in South Africa. It is led by Dap (Larry Fishburne), the resident political activist and informal leader of Da Fellas, a loose association of male students whose main relationship comes from friendship in the residence halls rather than the frat houses. Although Dap denounces the administration for coming late to the divestment issue, long after the prestigious and white Ivy League institutions, the rally is interrupted by the entry of a band of Gamma pledges, dressed in comic silver and black costumes and marching under the command of Julian (Giancarlo Esposito), the manic president of the fraternity. Naturally, Julian takes the establishment position and orders Dap to stop his disruptive activity. The argument is heating up when Virgil (Gregg Burge), the president of the student council, persuades them to stop. Dap proves to be a half-hearted revolutionary. He backs down almost immediately, as he will later in the film when he is ordered to remove his political banner from the parade leading into the stadium for the homecoming game. Dap also seems singularly unsuccessful in marshaling support. Once they realize that their protest involves the possibility of disciplinary action, Dap's followers opt out rather than jeopardize their standing in school and their future careers. One of his inner circle explains that his parents "slaved" to send him to college, and he is the first in his family to have this opportunity. He cannot mess up. Under Dap's leadership, they are willing to fight for their cause, but not at the risk of their personal security.

Immediately after their disagreement, Dap's friends decide to patch up their friendship by taking him to nearby a Kentucky Fried Chicken restaurant. During the ride, they boast about their extraordinary sexual exploits, which almost certainly arise more from their imaginations than from reality. While they are enjoying their meal, they get into a shouting match with four locals, led by Leed (Samuel L. Jackson), an outspoken young townie with a cap. They resent what they call "the Missionaries" for coming to town and looking down on them. They maintain that they can't find jobs because of the college boys, but the connection between absence of jobs and presence of the college is never clear and sounds more like an excuse for their inactivity. Leed demands to know if Dap is black after all his education. The townies refer to themselves as "niggers," and Dap assures them that they are not. In the car on the way back to campus, Dap and his friends chew over the allegations and wonder whether their adversaries might have a point. Maybe they have grown away from African Americans who have not had the same opportunities for education that they have. When Grady (Bill Nunn) observes that life is simple—you work and get ahead—the commonsense rejoinder is equally simple: What if you work and fail?

Julian has no such problems of conscience and social justice. He struts like a drill sergeant and heaps abuse on his Gamma pledges as though they were recruits in Marine boot camp. He wears his hair gelled and parted in the middle, with the result that he looks like Flattop in the old Dick Tracy comic strips. He intimidates his lieutenants with his bluster. He insists on being addressed by his fraternity title, "Dean Big Brother Almighty." As a symbol of his authority, he carries a ceremonial scepter made from a sawed-off baseball bat. He conducts sadistic, humiliating initiation rituals to weed out the pledges who are unfit to become Gamma men. He focuses his frenzy on Half Pint (Spike Lee), publicly accusing him of being a virgin. Half Pint endures it silently because he desperately needs the affirmation of his self-worth that membership will give him. Lee is harsh with both of them. Julian has status, hollow though it is outside the closed world of the campus, but he abuses it. Half Pint degrades himself and finally allows himself to be corrupted in order to be accepted into a worthless organization.

Lee uses the men on campus to exemplify class and power. The women, on the other hand, demonstrate the lunacy of status based on physical appearance and its result, sexual attractiveness. The sorority sisters, the Gamma Rays, have light skin and treated hair. Jane (Tisha Campbell), their apparent leader, wears a huge crown of straightened orange "big" hair and blue contact lenses. They dress in revealing clothes and primp to please the men of Gamma Phi Gamma; they clean the fraternity house and use their own money from a bake sale to provide refreshments for a forthcoming social with the Gammas. They also take for granted that they are sexually available for the Gammas, and in fact take pride in the status they receive from being attached to the Big Men on Campus. They, and other women, are regarded as "pussy," and several sophomoric puns and references to this vulgarism appear in the dialogue. Rather than resent this demeaning anatomical reference, they adopt as their sorority password "Meow," which they recite in purring unison as a statement of sisterhood.

Serving the whims of the Gammas turns brutal in a concluding sequence. Julian has announced to his council that he has grown tired of Jane, and he is ready to pass her along to anyone who wants her. She may be the homecoming queen, but Julian finds her "too young" for his level of sophistication. In a sex scene, she does seem to be experienced, but he still feels it's time to move on. In a cruel hoax that cuts in several degrading directions at once, Julian tells Half Pint that he cannot accept a virgin into the fraternity. As part of the initiation, Half Pint will have to bring a "freak"—that is, a compliant woman—into the "Bone Room" in the fraternity house. Half Pint's pathetic search among strangers for a willing sex partner fails, understandably. Once Half Pint is pledged, however, Julian "gives" him Jane. Julian tells her that if she really loves him and the Gammas, she will provide this service for them. When he sees Jane's distraught appearance, Half Pint retains a touch of human decency and at first rejects the arranged liaison. Jane is teary and Half Pint is hesitant, but group pressure prevails. When Jane emerges and tells Julian she did what he asked, he tells her that he didn't mean it. He accuses her of betraying him by her infidelity, and he wants nothing more to do with her. Despite her artificial beauty and the triumph of her homecoming coronation, Jane, rumpled and disheveled, sits on a radiator and sobs. Half Pint, for his part, runs across the campus and gets Dap out of bed to boast of his achievement. He has become a full Gamma man, and a complete fool.

Although all the women on campus find themselves commodities traded and discarded by the men, they cannot unite to form a united front against abuse. Even worse, they remain seriously divided among themselves. The divisions erupt in an energetic musical number in Madame Re-Re's beauty parlor, where all the women converge before the crowning of the homecoming queen and the coronation ball. A testy exchange in a hallway between the sorority sisters and some other women involves racial name-calling, and this incident segues into a spirited challenge song-and-dance number between the light-skinned "Wannabes" and the darker "Jigaboos." The first group insults the second for their "nappy" hair and dark complexions. The second retaliates by pointing out the artificiality and pretense of the first, who really "wannabe" white. They join in the chorus: "Good or bad hair/whether you're dark or you're fair." Class, gender, and now physical appearance set the artificial hierarchies that divide the student body at Mission College.

Prejudice, however, moves in both directions. As the song in the beauty salon clearly indicates, the dark girls regard the light girls as airheads. As a pan-African nationalist, Dap boasts that he has pure Negro blood, but his girlfriend, Rachael (Kyme), doesn't believe him. She does, however, believe, accurately enough, that Dap finds her attractive simply because she is one of the darkest girls on campus. They make love in a dorm room under a poster of Nelson Mandela. Dap becomes outraged when Rachael confesses that she intends to pledge to Delta sorority in her final semester at Mission. She later admits that she postponed her decision because she knew Dap would not approve. She was right, as it turns out. They argue, and he tells her to leave. As part of his great awakening, he goes to her residence hall and subjects himself to the abuse of the other women, one of whom throws a bucket of water at him. Rachel sees his devotion, forgives him, and takes him back to his room. His awakening takes a further step when Half Pint pounds on the door to tell him about his escapade with Jane. Dap is disgusted with sex that lacks the kind of devotion that has grown between him and Rachel. He simply sends Half Pint away.

The experience of the evening gives Dap an insight into what is happening to them on campus. He rises from Rachel's side and runs from building to building, shouting "wake up." He rings the ceremonial bell in front of the administration building. Students and president, light women and dark women, Gammas and Fellas emerge from their beds and come together as Dap continues his call to wake up, a call he never explains. The visuals carry the image. The camera moves into an extreme close-up of Dap as he repeats his call. The sudden, urgent gathering with everyone in robes, pajamas, rumpled hair, curlers, and no makeup becomes a great leveler. People who have just been summoned from bed have few pretenses about them. The film ends with Dap and Julian in frame together, as though they have finally resolved their differences and discovered their commonality. At last this sleep-rumpled band gathers together as a community.

School Daze has a didactic strand running through it. In a pregame locker-room speech, Coach Odom (Ossie Davis) urges his team to fight as one. "There is no 'I' in 'team,'" he tells them. The team loses badly, but Spike Lee shows nothing of the activity on the field. Instead, he turns his attention to the stands. Different factions shout their own cheers and play their own music, and in the end, Dap gets into a fight with the frat boys. The lesson is clear: Mission can't win while it is divided. During the coronation festivities, frats and fellas compete in a dance number, but they soon turn to insulting one another, much like the women in Madame Re-Re's beauty salon. The insults become sharper, and the contest ends with a fistfight. Dap's wake-up call in the final scene recalls the absurdity of the issues that have divided the student body in the earlier, comic scenes of the film. If Mission is to live up to its stated mission, "Uplift the Race," then it will have to reject its self-destructive attitudes about gender, social class, self-interest, and physical appearance. Spike Lee addresses his message to the African American community, but its implications surely touch all Americans.

Bed-Stuy: The Town Next Door

Walking east from Fort Greene Park along DeKalb Avenue some twenty-two short blocks and eight long ones, past the main campus of Pratt Institute, to Stuyvesant Avenue, and then five blocks south to Quincy Street brings one to Bedford-Stuyvesant, the setting of *Do The Right Thing* (1989), Spike Lee's most widely acclaimed film. The two locations are scarcely two miles distant, but they represent different universes. Fort Greene boasts a strong artistic community, cultural life, and growing prosperity. The Bedford-Stuyvesant area has become a nationally recognized symbol for urban blight, crime, drugs, and hopelessness. In contrast to nearby Fort Greene, Bed-Stuy provides the perfect metaphor for frustration for African Americans, yet Lee uses it as a metaphor for unity by stressing neighborhood bonds rather than the problems that tear it apart. Despite its mythic reputation, Bed-Stuy is a place where ordinary people try to get along with their lives.

Spike Lee expands his horizons markedly in *Do the Right Thing*. In his earlier films he dealt with issues within the black community. His unexpressed contention was that many of these internal conflicts were created or exacerbated for a group living within a larger, white-dominated society, but explicitly interracial conflicts never appeared on the screen. In his previous films, white people were largely irrelevant. In *Do the Right Thing,* Lee takes a hard look at friction among the three races living and working side by side in Brooklyn. If Bed-Stuy functions as an image of the destructive effects of inequality, then the opening sequence with Rosie Perez doing an energetic dance to the accompaniment of Public Enemy's "Fight the Power" announces the theme of fighting back. As she dances, her costume changes from stylish minidress to a boxing trunks and gloves. The questions Lee poses in the film are who to fight against, and by what means. He is particularly incisive in his observations of the varied reactions African Americans have to their life in Bed-Stuy.

As the action begins after the titles, Lee provides a few quick strokes to establish the setting. Mr. Señor Love Daddy (Samuel L. Jackson), the smooth-talking disc jockey for the neighborhood radio station WLOV, echoes the theme from the end of *School Daze* when he encourages his audience to "wake up" and face the new day, a Saturday, which will be the hottest day of the year. Da Mayor (Ossie Davis) emerges from his rumpled bed, eager to face the day and find his first bottle of Miller High Life beer.

Smiley (Roger Guenveur Smith), a deaf-mute, stands outside a Baptist Church selling pictures of Martin Luther King Jr. and Malcolm X together, and through his pained stammer, he tries to enunciate the message of the two leaders. Malcolm X was murdered in 1965 and Dr. King in 1968, and since the film takes place in the present (1989), both were dead around the time Smiley was born. In *School Daze,* Dap dismisses the advice of the college president because he is part of what he calls the "civil rights generation" that marched with King. Dap feels the president has nothing to say to the present generation. Lee himself, born in 1957, was a child during those traumatic events. Lee makes Smiley an image of the disabled community trying to recapture the words and thoughts of the two fallen leaders, now a generation past and in danger of becoming irrelevant.

The scene shifts to Mookie (Spike Lee) sitting on his bed, counting his money. He climbs into bed on top of Jade (Joie Lee) and awakens her by nuzzling her neck. His actions seem erotic, and it comes as a surprise to learn that they are brother and sister. Their contact reflects a childlike innocence, which in turn reflects Mookie's immaturity. The character is reminiscent of Mars in *She's Gotta Have It.* Jade complains that Saturday is the only day she can sleep in, which indicates that she has a job. Like a mother dealing with a teenager, she tells him to brush his teeth because his breath stinks. Later, she will complain that she has grown tired of supporting a grown man who earns "peanuts" as a pizza delivery man. With the exception of Mookie and Jade, no other black person in the film seems to have any employment whatsoever, which is Lee's comment on both limited opportunities and the reluctance of many people to seek out the opportunities that are available. Mookie has fathered a child with Tina (Rosie Perez), and although he keeps in touch with her, she complains that he never comes around to spend time with them. She has to have him deliver a pizza from Sal's to get him into the apartment. When he arrives, they engage in lovemaking, even though he's on the job. He shows up for work, but late, and takes time off to go home to take a shower without telling Sal. At least he is trying, although not very hard. He ingratiates himself to Sal to keep his job, but the neighborhood people also like him, and this allows him to function as a mediator. One character admonishes him to "stay black."

Mookie is a complex character who balances the various tensions in his life without ever really resolving them. He will survive, but he will never triumph. As a child-man, he evokes affection and exasperation in equal proportion. From his Fort Greene perspective, where upward mobility is a real option, Lee invests Mookie with a set of Bed-Stuy contradictions that embody Lee's perception of the conflicted role of the black man at the bottom of the economic ladder. Mookie is victimized twice: once by society, and once by himself.

Lee's Bed-Stuy, cleaned of litter and painted in warm primary colors, is a land of Oz, a children's paradise, where people sit on the stoops, play street games, open a fire hydrant as a makeshift water park, drink beer, and eat pizza. Lee never intended to present the neighborhood with documentary accuracy. His Bed-Stuy is more mythic than realistic, and he peoples the street with characters that represent types rather than fully drawn persons.

Da Mayor and Mother Sister (Ruby Dee) function as a pair. They are the oldest characters in the film; both have accents from the South and share a common homespun wisdom. Da Mayor, an aging alcoholic, struggles to keep his dignity even as he accepts his status as a failure who attributes his sorry condition to the fact that at one time he could not even earn enough to feed his hungry children. A young man listens to his self-revelation and then taunts him as a useless drunk; he

boasts that if he had been in Da Mayor's situation, he would have gotten a job to protect his family. His cruel tirade is tainted with the tragic
myopia of youth. He apparently has no job himself, nor is he aware that
at times jobs are hard to come by. Da Mayor's comic antagonist is Mother
Sister, a seer who observes the block from her front window and misses
nothing. She sets herself up as a paragon of respectability bordering on
self-righteousness, and with seemingly unwarranted harshness, she shows
contempt for Da Mayor for having allowed himself to succumb to drink.
She icily rejects all his offers of friendship, including a bouquet of flow-
ers that he could ill afford. But after he saves a child at the risk of his
own life, she recognizes his worth and thanks him. In the final sequence,
it is Da Mayor's composure that rescues Mother Sister, who goes into
hysterics during the climactic outbreak of violence. At one point he
promises that someday they will speak kindly to each other, if only from
the grave. In their reconciliation in the closing sequence, Lee returns to
his theme of unity: the righteous have no right to condemn the broken
members of the community. If the struggle is to succeed, they must join
together.

A second pairing involves Buggin' Out and Radio Raheem, two
contemporaries and longtime friends of Mookie. Buggin' Out (Giancarlo
Esposito) vibrates with unbridled nervous energy, much like Julian in
School Daze. He even thinks at the top of his lungs. He appears ready to
start a fight when Clifford (John Savage), a young white man wearing a
Larry Byrd Boston Celtics shirt, inadvertently steps on his new Air Jordan sneakers. An apology fails to satisfy him. After a testy exchange
with Sal about the price for extra cheese on his pizza, he protests with
equal vehemence the absence of any African Americans among the Italian Americans on the Wall of Fame, on which Sal has hung photos of
important Italians and Italian Americans. (Prominent among them is
Pope Paul VI, an Italian pope. Pope John Paul II, who was Polish, became pope in 1978, eleven years before the action in the film, but does
not appear on the wall.) Buggin' Out tries to organize a boycott to force
Sal to add some black celebrities to his wall, but he meets with little
success among his friends, who seem to regard him as a classic loudmouth. For them, it is a meaningless issue. Besides, they like the pizza.
In contrast, Radio Raheem (Bill Nunn) speaks softly and rarely. He
carries a huge boom box that he plays at top volume. Physically imposing, he wears huge brass knuckles, with "Love" and "Hate" spelled out

across their width. In a quasi-musical number, Radio Raheem raps out a parable about love and hate, which he narrates in terms of a violent boxing match. Love is on the ropes but fights back and knocks out Hate, he chants, while punching the air with his armored fists.

Buggin' Out might be viewed as a dangerous troublemaker by white people, but the neighborhood doesn't really take him seriously. White people might also regard Radio Raheem as a sullen menace, but the neighborhood people take for granted that noise is intrinsic to his sense of self-worth.[23] He challenges a group of Latinos to a ghetto-blaster war: their salsa against his rap. The name-calling and aggressive gestures may strike some outsiders as a prelude to physical violence, but for them it is merely a question of staking out acoustical space. Radio Raheem's box overpowers theirs, and he walks away satisfied while the Latinos continue to shout after him. Both have salvaged their pride. But with his boom box blaring "Fight the Power" at top volume, he is intimidating for white people. For them, the noise is a direct provocation and a warning that violence lies very close to the surface; any unpredictable incident could bring the eruption. Like Buggin' Out, Radio Raheem also challenges Sal about the price of extra cheese, but his rejoinders come quietly through clenched teeth. Similarly, when he goes into the Korean grocery store to buy a new supply of batteries, he becomes gratuitously belligerent, and the shopkeepers wisely follow his instructions to recount the number of batteries and recheck their expiration dates. Taken together, the two men represent two forms of the standard white fear of the black man in an urban environment.

Three mythic presences function like a Greek chorus commenting on the action. Sweet Dick Willlie (Robin Harris), ML (Paul Benjamin), and Coconut Sid (Frankie Faison) sit under a battered umbrella in front of a bright red wall and pass the time drinking beer and commenting on events on the street. Unemployment has not quashed their spirits. They are shrewd and resilient. They tell Buggin' Out that if he wants to boycott someone, he should boycott the barber that "messed up" his head with an oddly sculpted hairstyle. They tell Radio Raheem to turn down his radio. Most tellingly of all, they reflect on the Korean grocery store owner with a mixture of admiration and regret. One year after they got off the boat, they observe, the Koreans took over an abandoned building, opened a business, and began taking money out of the black community. They lament that African Americans lack the initiative for business. The Koreans' presence is indeed an irritant. Even Da Mayor, despite his courtly manners, berates the shop owners for failing to stock Miller High Life beer. When the white-owned businesses left, it was the Koreans, not black people, who filled the void. The local people smart under this perceived failure of their own community to run businesses that serve their needs. It's all talk about what they're going to do, but as Sweet Dick Willie points out, they'll "never do a goddam thing." Lee uses the chorus and the Koreans to restate his theme of the importance of entrepreneurship rather than talk.

Sal (Danny Aiello) is the entrepreneur who has made it. He arrives in front of his pizzeria in a white Cadillac as though he were arriving from a different planet. The only other white visitors to the street also arrive (and leave) by car. The first instance provides a touch of comedy. After neighborhood children open a fire hydrant, Charlie (Frank Vincent) tries to pass through the makeshift swimming hole in his convertible. The boys wave him through, then hose him down with a full-force stream they direct through a tin can. He sputters in rage and tries to get the police to arrest the pranksters, but the best description he can give is the obvious fact that the perpetrators are black. The police wisely advise him to drive off before his car is stripped to the chassis. In a far more sinister visitation, the police travel slowly through the street in their prowl car, with a light-haired officer staring out over the sidewalks with a mixture of loathing and challenge, as though daring anyone to make trouble while he is on the job.

Unlike these transient white people, Sal actually belongs. He opened his business on Stuyvesant Avenue twenty-five years earlier, before the neighborhood changed from Italian to African American. During the period of white flight, he moved his home and family to Bensonhurst, but he remains committed to his old business location, and as the only visible white presence in the area, he seems to be accepted as a local institution. The pizzeria does quite well, in fact. His older son Pino (John Turturro) hates the place, the neighborhood, and its current residents. He urges his father to relocate among their own kind. His slow-witted younger brother, Vito (Richard Edson), is more muted in his reactions. He feels intimidated by his brother, but he seems almost embarrassed by Pino's virulent racism, and what is worse in Pino's eyes, he considers Mookie a friend. When they arrive at the shop, Sal tells Pino to sweep the sidewalk before the customers arrive. Pino pushes the job off on Vito. Vito tells Mookie to do it. Finally, the work gets done when Da Mayor comes in looking for an odd job to help him earn enough to get his first beer of the day. The owner has the money and the power, and the unpleasant tasks work down the chain of command to the most desperate members of society.

Sal exercises the rights of owner in an oddly ambivalent way, almost like the lord of the manor. He shows remarkable tolerance toward Mookie when he comes in late and takes time off during the day. He treats Da Mayor with kindness and respect, and gives him money in advance. One wonders if he makes allowances for them while berating Pino and Vito, simply because of what they are, rather than who they are. If so, Lee raises the question that deep down, Sal may be a racist—a benevolent racist, but a racist nonetheless. When Jade comes in for lunch, Sal's attention borders on flirtation. Pino and Vito look on with revulsion at their father's behavior, and Mookie takes his sister outside to tell her to stay away, because to him Sal's intentions are transparent. Jade denies it, but the argument takes place under a huge graffito, "Tawana told the truth," a reference to Tawana Brawley, the young African American girl who claimed she was abducted and assaulted by six white police officers.[24] Mookie, Da Mayor, and Jade are black, but they represent no threat or challenge to Sal's authority. He can afford to be kind to them. This is not the case with Buggin' Out and Radio Raheem, who pose a challenge by refusing to acquiesce to his way of doing business. Their argument about the extra cheese sets the stage. Later, when Buggin' Out starts yelling about Sal's not having any brothers on the wall, Sal throws him out and tells him to get his own place, then he can decorate it as he pleases. He forces Radio Raheem to turn down his box the first time because the noise is interfering with his space and his business. When Radio Raheem comes back a second time with Buggin' Out and refuses to turn down the volume, Sal smashes the radio with a baseball bat after screaming racial epithets. The two young men had broken the rules for his place of business, and for Sal, the provocation was intolerable.

For Radio Raheem, the destruction of the radio is a personal attack, and he retaliates with all the rage that had been simmering under the surface. He grabs Sal by the throat and pulls him across the counter. The fight spills out onto the street, where a crowd gathers. The police arrive, and the light-haired officer, who seemed edgy as he rode silently in his prowl car, continues choking Radio Raheem with his nightstick even as the other officers tell him to stop. Buggin' Out, screaming as ever, is bundled into the back of a police car, where an officer tries to silence him by poking him repeatedly in the chest with his stick. Both the police and the crowd realize that Radio Raheem is dead, and the police dump him into another car and take off under a barrage of missiles hurled by the crowd. The sullen face-off between Sal and the crowd erupts into a full riot when Mookie hurls a garbage can through the window. His action provides the cue for the mob to erupt into a frenzy of destruction. Smiley lights the match that completes the devastation. Mother Sister becomes hysterical, supported only by Da Mayor. Sal and his sons watch helplessly from a nearby stoop, realizing that any attempt at intervention would be futile.

The crowd then turns its attention to the Korean shop across the street, but the owner defends himself with a broom long enough for the mob to cool down a bit, and the crowd decides to limit its action to Sal's shop. When the fire trucks arrive, the crowd tries to stop them, chanting "Howard Beach! Howard Beach!," the scene of an ugly racial incident in Queens in 1986.[25] In a scene reminiscent of Birmingham twenty-five years earlier, the firefighters turn the hoses on the rioters, knocking people into the sidewalks, against walls, and over the hoods of parked cars. After the worst has past, Smiley enters the smoldering ruins and pins one of his photographs of Dr. King and Malcolm X to the charred remains of the Wall of Fame. The symbolic gesture underscores the futility of mob action. They have achieved Buggin' Out's objective, but it brings little satisfaction to take possession of a ruin. Buggin' Out is in jail, Radio Raheem is dead, and Sal's pizzeria is lost to owner and neighborhood alike. Everyone loses, but has anyone learned anything from the experience?

The final scene suggests that they have not. The value systems and symbolic worlds of the two groups still lie far apart. Early on Sunday morning, Mookie gets out of bed and goes to the site of the ruined pizzeria to demand his week's salary. His timing suggests that he has little appreciation of Sal's loss and few regrets about his role in the riot. The conversation begins in a civil fashion, but their anger rapidly escalates. Sal maintains that he built the business with his own hands, and Mookie responds that insurance will pay for it. For his part, Sal shows little remorse in the fact that his angry outburst led to the loss of human life. In negative terms, Mookie places little value on property, even when it is so closely associated with a man's identity. Sal for his part seems to place little significance on the loss of a black man's life. Sal tries to use his wealth to humiliate Mookie by rolling up five $100 bills, twice what he owes Mookie, and throwing them one at a time in Mookie's face. Mookie only wants what he has earned and throws two of the bills back at Sal, but Sal refuses to pick them up. They glare at each other. At the end, Mookie takes the extra bills and walks away. Despite his brave words of defiance, because he is willing to take Sal's money, he loses. Sal has cheapened himself by thinking he can buy Mookie off with his money; he loses as well.

As the screen goes black, quotations from both Martin Luther King Jr. and Malcolm X appear on the screen. Dr. King warns about the destructive effects of violence; Malcolm X argues that in a situation of self-defense, the use of violence should simply be considered intelligence. The pairing of apparently contradictory quotations, along with the repeated image of what is believed to be the only photograph the two men ever had taken together, recalls the pairing of Dap and Julian at the end of *School Daze*. Neither side holds a monopoly of "doing the right thing." Neither Dap with his activism nor Julian with his ambition offer a sure path to the future; nor Dr. King with his nonviolence, or Malcolm X with his apparent militancy. Lee does not want to force his viewers to make a decision between them. Nearly a generation has passed since the high hopes of the civil rights movement and the words of the principal leaders of the period.

Seconds before the crowd trashes the pizzeria, Sal mutters, "Do what you gotta do," and that's precisely what Mookie and the crowd do. That, in the last analysis, is "the right thing." Ideology from the past provides few prescriptions and little motivation for the present. By ending both films with ambiguous tension, Spike Lee points out that the optimistic expectations of the 1960s have fizzled for many African Americans. According to his perspective as one who has already begun to build not only a career but a corporation, and as a contributor to a community making slow but consistent progress in the Fort Greene area, Spike Lee holds out hope that one day Sal and Mookie may be able to live and work together, but they both have a long way to go. Neither is a hero. Both are burdened with the legacy of their ethnicity. Martin and Malcolm made their contributions to the effort, but now the challenge has passed to a new generation of ordinary people like Mookie and Sal.

Back to Fort Greene

Scarcely a year after the commercial and critical success of *Do the Right Thing*, Spike Lee returned to familiar territory with *Mo' Better Blues* (1990). After opening his lens to embrace the tangled moral and inter-racial issues that enveloped Sal and Mookie, in his next film, Lee nar-rowed his focus to the world of a small group of African American artists trying to make their way through the jazz clubs of downtown Brooklyn to the big time. Lee admits to trying to create an accurate picture of struggling black musicians to balance what he felt were distortions put forward by white directors like Clint Eastwood in *Bird* (1988), the story of Charlie Parker, and Bertrand Tavernier in the fictional *'Round Midnight* (1986). The task took on some urgency when he heard rumors that Woody Allen, an amateur jazz clarinetist, was planning his own jazz film, which, as it turned out, never materialized.[26] Some years later, Lee denied that an urge to rebut the other jazz films motivated him to any great extent. Having grown up surrounded by music because of his father's profession, Spike Lee felt confident he could tell the story of jazz men from an authentic African American perspective more accu-rately than the earlier works.[27]

Lee uses the story as a moral parable that underlines several of his characteristic themes. The film opens with the title setting the scene as Brooklyn in 1969 in a neighborhood that resembles Fort Greene but is not identified as such. Four youngsters with their baseball gear swagger purposefully down a street lined with elegant old brownstones and thickly leaved shade trees. They call for young Bleek Gilliam (Zakee Howze) to come and join them, but his mother (Abby Lincoln) insists on his stay-ing in to complete his trumpet practice. He whines that he hates his trumpet and wants to play baseball with his friends. His father is watch-ing a Dodgers-Pirates game on television and wants to let the boy go, especially when he hears that the other boys are calling him "sissy," but his mother prevails. As it turns out, Mother knows best. Hard work pays off for him because the shot dissolves from a close-up of the boy playing scales to the adult Bleek Gilliam (Denzel Washington) playing an elaborate bop trumpet with his own combo in a crowded jazz club. Obviously, if one want to be a success in life, dedication to the task and rejection of peer pressure must be part of the strategy.

Once again, Lee structures his propositions in terms of pairs. The

"Mo' Better" of the title is a noun that means simply "sex." Bleek is torn between art, which for him is essentially solitary, and sex, which will ripen from "a dick thing," as he calls it initially, into love and a desire for lasting human relationship. The transition will take time and will come at an enormous cost to Bleek. The conflict becomes apparent in an early scene when Bleek is immersed in his practice session in his apartment, and Clarke Betancourt (Cynda Williams) interrupts by calling on the intercom and insisting on coming up. At first he is annoyed at the intrusion, but eventually they fall into a passionate embrace. For him, it's just sex, an important imperative in his life, but a potential distraction from his dedication to his music. For the rest of the film, Lee will explore the balance for Bleek, and for African Americans, between individual work and accomplishment on one side, and loyalty, commitment, and love on the other.

For her part, Clarke forms a pair with Indigo Downes (Joie Lee), another of Bleek's current girlfriends. Although Clarke longs to break into the glamorous life of show business, Indigo claims she likes the music well enough, but simply doesn't enjoy the atmosphere of the club. She is, in fact, an accountant. In an indirect restatement of the theme of *School Daze*, Clarke is fair and has her hair carefully treated into a Louise Brooks bob; Indigo (the very name suggests a deep color) is darker and wears her hair in natural styles. When Indigo finally appears at the club, named Beneath the Underdog, to hear Bleek, she arrives on the same night as Clarke, and even worse, both women are wearing the identical red dresses Bleek brought them from Paris. Bleek has to tap his deepest resources of charm—and duplicity—to work his way out of the predicament. In the end, he makes it clear that he really doesn't care what they think. He tells Shadow Henderson (Wesley Snipes), his sax player, that Clarke doesn't have his name written on her, so if he wants to make a move himself, he has no objections. In one comic scene, as he makes love to Clarke, she suddenly morphs into Indigo, and then back again. He confuses the names. The women are not fools. They see through Bleek's game and drop him. Once again, Lee portrays Bleek as totally alone with his art.

The conflict between art and sex is restated with racial overtones in an second disruptive romance. The pianist, Left Hand Lacey (Giancarlo Esposito), has a French girlfriend, Jeanne (Linda Hawkins). Race already sets her apart from the combo, but she become a wedge when she distracts Left Hand and makes him consistently late for rehearsals. She breaks a taboo by coming into the dressing room before they go on. Her presence sets up a conflict that threatens the survival of the band.

Bleek's solitary concept of art is illustrated through his own pairing with Shadow, who plays saxophone in Bleek's quintet and becomes his rival for Clarke. Bleek is a purist who insists on playing his music his way, and Shadow's crowd-pleasing solos become a source of friction between them. Bleek plays for himself, but Shadow is the entertainer who plays what the audiences want; he will succeed in the music business, while Bleek's self-centered style jeopardizes the success of the group. He faces a threat from another direction as well. Clarke wants to sing with the group. She has a stunning presence and would undoubtedly be popular with the patrons, but Bleek tells her she is not ready and refuses to let her go on. When Shadow takes over, Clarke will be a headliner, and the combo will pack the best jazz clubs in Brooklyn. By this time, Lee's theme of unity and cooperation as the key to success and self-interest as the formula for failure have become standard messages in his films.

Bleek also forms a pair with Giant (Spike Lee), a spectacularly incompetent agent who cannot arrange an adjustment in the band's contract after they have become a sensation and play to capacity audiences every night. He is certainly no match for Josh and Moe Flatbush (John and Nicholas Turturro), the miserly club owners who not only refuse to renegotiate the contract, but threaten to sue the band if they try to back out of the their original agreement.[28] Bleek is above mundane details, like contracts and percentages, and lets Giant handle the matter, even though the other members of the band want to fire him. In a way, Giant is too much concerned with money. He is a compulsive gambler, but no more skilled in handling bets than contracts. His losses eventually take Bleek down with him. Petey (Ruben Bladés) holds Giant's markers and has advanced several loans to him. Finally, he loses patience with Giant and looses his strong-arm men on him. They break his fingers to send a message, and when he still fails to pay his debts, they return and administer a terrible beating in the alley behind the club. Bleek tries to stop them. In the scuffle, Madlock (Samuel L. Jackson) grabs his trumpet and smashes it across Bleek's face. The blow pulverizes Bleek's lip so badly that he will never play again.

Without his music, Bleek collapses into himself. He lies on the floor of his cluttered apartment listening to records. As time passes, he tries a comeback with Shadow's combo, composed of his old group and Clarke, but the lip is gone and his playing is an embarrassment to Shadow, to Clarke, and especially to himself. On the way out, he gives his trumpet to Giant, who has taken a job as doorman at the club. With his self-assurance gone, he returns to Indigo, who eventually takes him back, and in an unconvincing final sequence, they marry and have a family. At last he admitted his need of other people. His long loneliness comes to an end, but he has lost his art. Bleek, Indigo, and their children appear to live comfortably, even though no mention is made of their source of income. The final scene repeats the opening. Bleek's son Miles (Zakee Howze, who also played Bleek as a child) is at his trumpet lesson. When the neighborhood boys come to play football, Bleek tells him to go out. Solidarity with others is just as important as his art, and being a successful person is far more important than being a successful musician.

After the success of *Do The Right Thing*, Spike Lee asserted that he wanted to do something apolitical. He succeeded, but only to a degree. *Mo' Better Blues* came as a letdown after the success of the previous year. It was received as a run-of-the mill romance with a fine jazz score and a Disneyesque happy ending with overtones of a moral fable. Even as the pedestrian narrative unfolds, Lee's political agenda stalks around the edges. Through Bleek and Shadow, Lee demonstrates the possibility of success, despite obstacles from white society like Jeanne and the Flatbush brothers. He lampoons Giant's incompetence and his self-destructive get-rich-quick fantasies based on gambling rather than planning and hard work. This self-delusion will leave him a broken man walking with a cane and working nights as a doorman. Lee shows little sympathy for Bleek's treatment of women and points out that a true partnership with Indigo will be the key to his happiness. In the final scene, a repetition with variation of the opening scene, he shows that although history does repeat itself, Bleek is capable of learning from his mistakes in the past.

From Strivers Row to Bensonhurst

Spike Lee's departure from his political agenda was short-lived. His next film, *Jungle Fever* (1991), is arguably the most political of all his films.

He returns to the conflict between African Americans and Italian Americans as two hostile communities and makes the mixture even more volatile by adding the ingredient of interracial sex, a theme he merely hinted at in Sal's quasi-flirtation with Jade in *Do the Right Thing*. He dedicates the film to the memory of sixteen-year-old Yusuf Hawkins, a young black man who was murdered in Bensonhurst by young Italians in August 1989. The neighborhood vigilantes thought that he and his friends were trying to attend a party, when they were actually in the area to respond to an ad for a used car.[29] As Lee worked on the film, the issue was still very much a point of friction in both communities.

As was the case in *School Daze,* in *Jungle Fever,* race becomes entangled in issues of class. Lee complicates the matter by reversing the stereotypical race/class distinctions. From his Fort Greene perspective, he set his action in two areas that represent cultural countertypes bordering on parody: Harlem represents the best and worst of the African American community, while Bensonhurst represents the white working classes, especially Italian Americans, at their benighted worst. A resident of contemporary Harlem, Flipper Purify (Wesley Snipes), holds a key position in an architectural firm, and his wife Drew (Lonette McKee) is a buyer for Bloomingdale's, an East Side fashion mecca on Third Avenue and Fifty-ninth Street in Midtown Manhattan.[30] They live in a beautiful brownstone on Strivers Row, and as a sign of their sophistication, they have the *New York Times* delivered to the door. As the film opens, they are making passionate love, much to the amusement of their ten-year-old daughter, Ming (Veronica Timbers), who listens intently to the noises coming from the next room. The Spelman College T-shirt she wears as a nightgown indicates that her parents are trying to keep her in touch with her roots. The Purifys seem to have everything in abundance, and their future prospects are even better. Flipper fully expects that his success with a Japanese client will lead to an invitation to become a partner in the firm any day.

Flipper's new secretary is Angela Tucci (Annabella Sciorra), whose name recalls Louis Tucci, Spike Lee's boyhood pal from Cobble Hill. Her sweatshirt identifies her as a graduate of Bishop Kearney, a girls' high school run by the Sisters of St. Joseph on Sixtieth Street and Twentieth Avenue in Bensonhurst, just a few blocks from the Regina Pacis shrine on Sixty-fifth Street, the center of Italian Catholic culture in Brooklyn. When she comes home from work laden with groceries, her father and brothers complain that they have been waiting for their dinner. While she serves the meal, one brother comments that her cooking does not match their dead mother's. She takes for granted that a woman's role involves a full day's work in an office, followed by shopping, cooking, serving, and cleaning up. Angie's only escape from this culturally mandated drudgery will be marriage, and even then, she will only start the domestic cycle over again with her own family. Her sometime boyfriend is Paulie Carbone (John Turturro), a mild-mannered guy who likes chess, reads, and intends to start night school someday. In the meantime, he lives with his father over their candy store, where he tends the fountain. The owner, Lou Carbone (Anthony Quinn), rejects the suggestion that he stock copies of the *New York Times* because he believes there is little call for it in this neighborhood. (The *Times,* it must be noted, serves as a quintessential symbol of New York only to outsiders. Within the City, it is a recognizable marker of class distinction.) Paulie is a loser, and since he is Angie's obvious route of escape from her loutish father and brothers, he is also a clear indication of her dead-end life.

Flipper's racial consciousness goes beyond T-shirts for his daughter and a home in Harlem. He resents the company's hiring Angie when he explicitly asked for an African American assistant. In his testy exchange with the partners, Leslie and Jerry (Brad Dourif and Tim Robbins), he provides an example of Lee's belief in the responsibility of well-positioned African Americans to bring other black people on board. He loses the argument, and the bosses imply that his request is merely racist. In a later scene, he issues a demand that he be made a partner immediately, and when his ultimatum is rejected, he is convinced that race is the sole reason. Actually, both sides have a case. Flipper is prickly and arrogant; still, in white people these traits are often perceived as drive. His frustration seems rooted in equal measure in his bosses' unconscious racism and his own political naïveté. He might well have backed himself into a corner by threatening to quit on the spot if his demands were not met. He allows no room for compromise on the issue, and as a result, he signs his letter of resignation with a theatrical flourish, packs his briefcase, and walks out. He will explain to his friend Cyrus (Spike Lee) that he intends to start his own business, and Cyrus repeats Lee's theme that this is precisely what black people should be doing.

Flipper's temper tantrum could readily be explained by the turmoil in his private life. He has gotten over his objections to hiring Angie, and they learn to work quite well together. Predictably, working late one evening leads to a Chinese take-out dinner, and through a series of subsequent late nights, to self-revealing conversations, and finally to an impulsive sexual encounter on a drafting table. Angie takes advantage of the occasion to rebel against her suffocating home and neighborhood by breaking the ultimate taboo. Flipper's motivation is more complex. It may be simply a unpremeditated impulsive act. He may also simply be curious about white women, as he will explain to Cyrus. He may also feel that their relationship confirms his status as one who has arrived and can prove it to himself by defying the racial limitations Leslie and Jerry want to impose on him. Finally, he may just enjoy the position of power that he, as an executive, has in this situation. His reasons are not clear to Spike Lee, simply because they are not altogether clear to Flipper. At any rate, the relationship quickly progresses from a moment of passion to prolonged affair.

Both lovers realize they have wandered into perilous territory, for although Spike Lee believes racism is a white phenomenon, he readily admits that prejudice can infect anyone, as both Flipper and Angie discover. The race-tinged conversations at the candy store reinforce the stereotypical perception of Bensonhurst Italians. Angie knows her ethos quite well, and she knows that she is walking down a dangerous path. She might have been taken by surprise, however, to discover that prejudice works both ways. When Flipper takes her out to dinner at Sylvia's, a famous soul food restaurant on Lenox Avenue at One Hundred Twenty-sixth Street in Harlem, the waitress at first refuses to take their order, and when Flipper becomes insistent, she says exactly what she thinks of interracial couples in terms offensive to both of them. Flipper wants to see the manager; Angie just wants to leave. It was obvious to both of them that they could not go to Bensonhurst together, but they might have been surprised to discover that his attempt to introduce her to his Harlem, a Harlem beyond her caricature, was in many ways just as difficult. Spike Lee was only a child when the lunch counter sit-ins were going on across the South, but for audiences of a certain age, the irony of their being denied service in a Harlem restaurant is unmistakable.

Despite the extreme delicacy of their situation, which they both understand, Angie and Flipper inexplicably decide to confide in their friends, a decision that is not only foolhardy but nearly suicidal, as they should have known. Flipper talks to his old classmate Cyrus (Spike Lee), a bespectacled schoolteacher. When Flipper tells him she is Italian, he remarks: "H-Bomb." "From Bensonhurst," Flipper adds. Cyrus responds, "Nuclear megaton bomb." Cyrus concludes that it is just sex, the "jungle fever," and is slow to realize the emotional investment of the lovers. For her part, Angie can't resist telling her gum-snapping girlfriends, who are awestruck at the daring adventure, even though one finds it "personally disgusting." Angie swears them to secrecy, but she might just as well have had the story printed on the front page of the *Bay Ridge Spectator*. The girlfriends find the tidbit too good not to share with the rest of the neighborhood, but they are not the only gossips in New York. Cyrus tells his wife, who feels obliged to tell Drew, who throws Flipper's belongings out onto the street and refuses to let him back into their house. Angie's father, Mike Tucci (Frank Vincent), meets her at the door of their house, slaps her full in the face several times, throws her to the floor, and begins to slash at her with his belt until his sons restrain him.

Flipper follows Drew to Bloomingdale's and tries a reconciliation, but Drew refuses to yield. Because both Angie and Flipper have been forced out of their homes, they take an apartment together, but they never completely furnish it. It is a work in progress, just like their relationship. As each confided the secret to friends, the background consisted of a chain-link fence, a suggestion that both were caged in their respective neighborhoods and cultures and could never make it into new territory. Their relationship was doomed from the beginning. As they lie together on a mattress on the living room floor, Flipper admits that he could not bear the thought of having biracial children. He feels they have no future together, and when he awakens, she is gone. At the end of the film, she returns to her family's house in Bensonhurst, and as Mike closes the door behind her and seals the slatted jalousie on the storm door, it is clear that she will spend the rest of her life imprisoned in her neighborhood and in her class. But her status has changed; now, not even Paulie will have her.

Race and class are not the only issues keeping Flipper and Angie apart; they discover a moral issue as well. Flipper's father, the Good Reverend Doctor Purify (Ossie Davis), remains an unbending, righteous man, even though he has lost his pulpit for reasons that remain unspecified. When Flipper tells his parents that he and Drew are going through a difficult period and he wants to stay with them for a while,

Reverend Purify tells him that he has committed adultery and should return to his wife, not quite comprehending that she will not have him. Foolishly hoping that once they meet Angie, they will understand his situation, Flipper brings her over to dinner, and the Good Reverend Doctor refuses to eat with adulterers. Like Flipper's wife, Drew, he finds the infidelity exponentially worse because of racial disparity. Repeating the incident in Sylvia's Restaurant, they are forced to leave the table hungry, angry, and humiliated.

To underline the force of parental disapproval as a cultural problem rather than an individual quirk, Paulie Carbone has grown friendly with Orin Goode (Tyra Ferrell), a professional black woman who stops at the store each morning to pick up the *Daily News* for her parents and *Newsday* for herself. (She suggests once again that they carry the *Times,* but her attempt is once again futile.) A teacher and counselor, she brings Paulie application forms for Brooklyn College and encourages his reading. After his breakup with Angie, he feels free enough to suggest a casual date with Orin. When he finds out about his son's plans, Lou Carbone accuses him of betraying his mother's memory, disowns him, and threatens to throw him out of the house. Paulie's friends from the candy store intercept him on the way to meet Orin, taunt him verbally and then teach him a more physical lesson. Bruised, cut, and rumpled, he arrives at Orin's house, but both realize this is the last meeting they will have. As she lets him in, Orin looks nervously up and down the street because his presence in her home puts her in jeopardy as well.

In Spike Lee's perception, Flipper represents the ideal, successful black professional who undergoes a personal crisis. To sharpen his image, Lee pairs him with his older brother Gator (Samuel L. Jackson), a crack addict who has been banished from the Purify home but who continues to visit family members when he grows desperate for drug money. Without the Reverend's knowledge, Mrs. Purify, Lucinda (Ruby Dee) continues to help him out with housekeeping money. Gator finds Flipper and Angie's apartment and asks for money, and on another occasion warns him that he will turn to robbery if he doesn't get what he needs. At one point Lucinda grows frantic and asks Flipper to find Gator before he does something foolish. In one of the most powerful scenes in the film, Flipper follows clues from street people and traces him to the Taj Mahal, a huge crack house on One Hundred Forty-fifth Street. He passes prostitutes plying their trade in doorways to earn enough money for another hit. The contrast is shocking. Flipper, perfectly groomed and tailored, enters the squalid inferno filled with human wreckage, where he gags on the rancid fumes from the drugs. He finds Gator leaning against a soiled mattress, sucking the pipe with his girlfriend Vivian (Halle Berry). Both are filthy. He pleads with Gator to leave, but he refuses; the scene grows ugly, and only with difficulty does Flipper manage to escape alone.

In his final appearance in the film, Gator waits until the Good Reverend Doctor leaves the apartment to walk his dog and breaks in on his mother, who is alone. His pleading for drug money escalates into intimidation and threats, and he ransacks the kitchen searching for hidden money, empties her purse on the kitchen table, and even grabs at her simple necklace. When his father unexpectedly comes in and tells Gator to leave, Gator does an in-your-face jive dance to defy the patriarch, who quietly takes out a pistol and shoots Gator dead. The Good Reverend Doctor places the pistol on the open pages of his Bible, a suggestion that his unbending and religiously motivated righteousness might have been as much a cause of Gator's death as the gun. Although not particularly hostile to religion, Lee has little interest in church going himself, and attended only when he visited his grandparents in the South.[31] This image probably reflects the destructive quality of the Reverend's own rigid religiosity rather than an indictment of religion as an institution.

Spike Lee had been criticized for omitting any mention of drugs in his earlier films. In *Jungle Fever* he plunges into the issue in a subplot so powerful that it threatens to overwhelm the story of Flipper and Angie. The twin strands of the narrative underline the thematic development of the film. Flipper represents a world of possibilities open for African American men; Gator and Vivian demonstrate the fact that drugs destroy all hope.

The final sequence provides a reprise of the opening shot. Although Lee offers no reconciliation scene and no explanation of how or why the couple have become reunited, he shows Flipper and Drew making love in their bed, while Ming once again listens in the next bedroom. Drew is quietly crying. Despite the marital intimacy, they are not yet completely reconciled, and Flipper has to tell Ming he is not yet coming back to live with them, but will someday. She asks him to walk her to school, as he had in the past, but he leaves Drew's home alone, without Ming. As he walks along the sidewalk in the bright light of morning, a young girl appears from a side street and propositions Flipper for $2. Stunned, he pulls her face to his chest as though trying to protect her and screams in a long wailing note of one syllable, "No." Not only is he horrified by the girl's crude suggestion, but with the experience of Gator and Vivian still fresh in his mind, he knows that this may one day happen to his daughter because of drugs.

Throughout the film, Lee uses comic touches to soften his commentary about the two communities he is comparing. The crew that gathers in Carbone's candy story includes a silent older man, whose menacing presence indicates that he must be the local capo. The conversation approaches the moronic, especially when race is involved. The film was made during the hotly contested and racially charged mayoral campaign of David Dinkins and Rudolph Giuliani, and political conversation is lively over egg creams at Carbone's. They confuse Dinkins with Marion Berry, the mayor of Washington who had been accused of using drugs in office. They conclude that it makes no difference who did what because "they" are all the same.

Paired with the men in Carbone's candy store are the women who gather to console Drew after her breakup with Flipper. Cyrus refers to the meeting as a "war council" and warns Flipper not to "go in there." The scene was rehearsed, but the dialogue was largely improvised over a two-day period of shooting and edited into its present shape. Lee admits that he could never have written dialogue as painful as the raw emotions that these women ventilate in this scene.[32] In language both funny and bitter in turn, the women recapitulate several of Lee's key themes. Drew's breakup strikes them as tragic because there are so few available black men around. Too many are irresponsible, gay, in jail, or, worst of all, have gone chasing after white women. One demurs to a certain extent by bringing up the notion that black women are partially to blame because of their class consciousness. There are plenty of good working men, she claims, but professional women—meticulously coifed and expensively dressed as these are—would not look at them. Rich black men like actors and sports figures, they lament, are no longer content with light-skinned black women like Drew and Cyrus's wife, Vera (Veronica Webb); they want to parade a white woman on their arm to enhance their own prestige. One woman movingly describes her frustration and resentment at being considered ugly all her life because of her hair and dark complexion. White "bitches," in turn, prey upon black men for the adventure and because of the legendary sexual prowess of the black male. Again, they blame themselves for buying all these racial myths about beauty and desirability, just like black men.

At the end of the cathartic conversation, Drew concludes that it really makes little difference. Flipper is gone for good, a conclusion that the final sequence leaves very much in doubt. As they lie in bed together in the final sequence, one wonders what Drew's tears represent. Is she happy to have her husband back, or does she feel degraded by his presence in her home? Does she weep at the humiliation she will undergo in taking him back, or at the realization that their relationship can never be fully restored? One wonders, too, what the women in the war council would think and what they would encourage her to do.

The Journey of Malcolm X

Spike Lee was interested in Malcolm X from the time he read the *Autobiography of Malcolm X* while he was still at John Dewey High School. He was not alone. Various studios and producers had toyed with the idea of making a film out of the book almost from the time it was first published by Grove Press in 1965. Sidney Lumet, the legendary "Lion of the Left," had worked on a version written by David Mamet, and Norman Jewison, whose credentials for this type of project had been established by *In the Heat of the Night* (1967), came onto the scene around 1990 and had worked over a script originally written by Arnold Perl, who died in 1971, and revised by James Baldwin.[33] Other scripts that surfaced at different periods included two attempts by Charles Fuller and one each by Calder Willingham and David Bradley. Because racial tensions remained high through the 1970s and Malcolm X had a reputation, deserved or not, for condoning violent solutions to racial injustice, the mainstream studios remained cautious about seeming to endorse what many people believed could be construed as a call to action. No one wanted to be responsible for adding fuel to the racial fires that broke out in rioting in Newark, Detroit, Watts, and other cities during the terrible summers of the 1960s.

By the 1990s the climate had changed. The cities had quieted, and Malcolm X had been off the scene for a quarter of a century. Despite the ongoing interest in the concept, no one pulled it together until

Spike Lee, who by this time had established his credentials as a consistently bankable director. He argued that this was a film that had to be made by an African American director, with the obvious suggestion that as the most prominent black director in the business, he should get the job. Norman Jewison, still assigned to the film, agreed and gracefully withdrew from the project; Warner Bros. agreed to put up $28 million. Opting for the Perl/Baldwin script—because Baldwin had known Malcolm personally and knew Harlem firsthand during the 1950s and 1960s—Spike Lee was ready to move, and he did his own rewrite of the script.[34] He felt that nothing short of an epic in the manner of David Lean would be suitable and planned a three-hour film.[35] Warner Bros. failed to share Lee's grand aspirations and refused to extend additional backing when the film began to go over their initial budget allocation. Undeterred, he secured private financing from Bill Cosby, Prince, Michael Jordan, and Oprah Winfrey, and continued to make the film he had always envisioned.

Spike Lee's interest in the life of Malcolm X would come as no surprise to anyone who had seen his earlier films. In fact, were it not for the fact that Malcolm was a real person who was murdered in 1965 and whose autobiography was published when Lee was eight years old, the book would appear to be a scenario prepared for a Spike Lee film. From the wealth of material surrounding the man and the several scripts and treatments available to him, Lee selected episodes for the final script and shaped the film into a recapitulation and restatement of his earlier themes.

The Malcolm of the film is a work in progress, like Fort Greene and the African American community at large. He was taking giant steps forward, but the final outcome was not yet determined. In the film, the character goes through phases in his struggle to discover and possess his proper role. At crucial junctures, he has to rethink his position and reinvent himself. His tragedy stems from the fact that his life ended before the work was completed. No one knows what the final product would have been, but Lee suggests that his final years gave every reason to believe that his anger was cooling, and that he had begun to move away from his uncompromising exclusionism and the fiery rhetoric that still shades his reputation, making Malcolm X still remembered by many as a dangerous fanatic. In congruence with conflicts in all his earlier films, Lee situates the tragedy of Malcolm's death in the context of both racism in the white community and divisions within the black. Although Lee ends the film on a note of hope, which may strike some as artificial, the sad reality is that Malcolm X is no longer present to join in the optimistic chorus of children that closes the film.

As evidence that Lee had a wider agenda than a respectful biography of a historical figure, he begins his film with a crisp, motionless American flag filling the screen and the incendiary language of Malcolm X (Denzel Washington) on the sound track indicting all white people for their crimes against humanity. The motionless flag dissolves on several occasions into the famous videotape images of the Los Angeles police beating Rodney King, an event that took place in March 1991, the year before the release of the film. Slowly, the flag smolders and bursts into flame, and as fragments of charred cloth fall away, the remnants of the stars and stripes form a perfect block letter X. The flames and the fiery words recall the fact that on April 29, 1992, when a jury in conservative Simi County, California (with no African Americans impaneled), acquitted the police officers indicted in the King beating, the black community in Los Angeles erupted into riots to protest the injustice it perceived. Because the film debuted on November 18, 1992, the reference to the Rodney King case placed the film in a contemporary rather than a historical context, and the words of Malcolm X serve as both prophecy and warning for the future.

After the credits, the film moves to Boston during the World War II years, when a teenage Malcolm Little (Denzel Washington) and his friend Shorty (Spike Lee) strut the scene in their zoot suits and wide-brimmed hats, each trimmed with long bobbing feather. To complete his fashion statement, Malcolm has his hair "conked," or straightened, in a painful ordeal that involves a mixture of sliced potatoes and Red Devil lye. In his earlier films, Lee raised the issue of black people's preference for light complexions and straight hair, but always as a women's issue. In *Malcolm X,* hair straightening functions as a sign of male attempts to approximate white physical characteristics, which both Malcolm X and Spike Lee reject as an insidious form of self-hatred. At a dance, he ditches his date Laura (Theresa Randall), an innocent young woman he calls a "church-girl," who is much smitten by the dashing zoot suiter, when Sophia (Kate Vernon), a white woman, offers a blatant proposition. As the "war council" in *Jungle Fever* explained so well, Sophia craves the excitement provided by the legendary sexual prowess of the black man, and Malcolm finds any white woman superior to the loveliest of black women. He takes advantage of Sophia's infatuation by making her kiss his feet and feed him as though he were a baby. For him, humiliating a white woman is better for him than merely living with one. Some months later, he sees Laura in a bar, and a waitress tells him that she has joined up with a drug addict who will soon have to put her out on the streets to support him. The lesson is clear. Malcolm's infatuation with a white woman has destroyed a black woman.

In one of his trips to Harlem he links up with West Indian Archie (Delroy Lindo), a gangster who gives Malcolm full-time employment as a numbers runner and introduces him and Sophia to cocaine. Malcolm appears ready to move up in the mob, but he argues with Archie about a bet and escapes through a men's room window when Archie sends his lieutenants to kill him for challenging his integrity. He has to leave Harlem, but he has had a taste of gang life and finds it far preferable to his earlier job of selling sandwiches in Pullman cars.

Back in Boston, Malcolm and Shorty form a household with Sophia and her white girlfriend Peg (Debi Mazar), and they assemble their own team to rob houses. Malcolm shows the force of his personality by settling the matter of leadership through a game of Russian roulette with a upstart rival. He offers to go first. He palmed the bullet before pulling the trigger, but no matter. When Malcolm gives him the revolver, the rival backs down, and from that point on, the question of leadership is settled. Sophia is excited by his daring. Through these early scenes, Lee has sketched in the steps that led Malcolm Little to the bottom: vanity, unrealistic plans for getting rich quickly, gambling and crime, alcohol, drugs, degradation of black women and infatuation with white women. Lee has singled out all these self-destructive elements in other African American characters in earlier films, but in the earlier these constitute only half the story. Here they simmer at the core of Malcolm Little's downfall.

Racism in American society must share the blame for Malcolm's descent into crime. In a series of flashbacks, Lee fills in his background. Living in Omaha, Malcolm's father, Earl Little (Tommy Hollis), preached Marcus Garvey's doctrine of the separation of races. Known as a black nationalist, he became a target for the Ku Klux Klan in the 1920s, and while he was on a speaking engagement in Milwaukee, the Klansmen firebombed the family home, terrorizing his mother and siblings. The next time they returned, Mr. Little fired a pistol over their heads to frighten them off. He paid the ultimate price for his defiance: he was beaten with a hammer and stretched out in the path of an oncoming trolley. The insurance company claimed his death was suicide and refused to provide compensation. Unable to support her family, Louise Little (Lonette McKee) had to yield to the demands of a white social worker and place her children in foster care with white families, where they attended white schools. This violated her deepest sensitivities about white people. She attributed her own light complexion and delicate features to her mother's being raped by a white man, and she married Earl because he was dark. Young Malcolm Little excelled in school and expressed interest in law, but his teachers told him that was a foolish dream for a black child, or, as his counselor put it "for a nigger." He should have realistic ambitions, like carpentry. Frustrated in his legitimate aspiration to become a lawyer, he became a train porter, a drug addict, and a criminal.

Malcolm Little's conviction for robbery begins the second phase of his life. His pointless defiance of guards and their petty regulations lands him in solitary confinement for a prolonged period. The solitude gives him time to reconsider the trajectory of his life. His meaningless rebellion against prison rules had obviously accomplished nothing. At this point, Baines (Albert Hall), a Muslim proselytizer, begins working on him. He introduces Malcolm to the Nation of Islam and its teaching about the systematic destruction of dark peoples by light peoples. Gradually, Malcolm submits to Allah, and after great hesitation, begins to pray. He has the prison barber cut off his conked hair, and he has the courage to confront the prison chaplain (Christopher Plummer) on the hypocrisy of white Christianity. For Lee, the important step in Malcolm's conversion is more than religious and more than a rejection of his destructive criminal past; the key is his developing pride in his racial identity.[36]

After his release from prison, Malcolm Little, now known as Malcolm X, joins the Nation of Islam and quickly rises through the ranks from street preacher to financial officer. His success stirs jealousy, and some accuse him of ambition. Baines, his prison mentor, warns Elijah Muhammad (Al Freeman Jr.), the head of the Nation, that Malcolm is becoming too powerful. It's partially true. As a speaker, he is electrifying, and as the public face of the organization, he becomes more widely known to the outside world than Elijah Muhammad himself. When the police in Harlem beat an African American senseless, put him in jail without medical attention, and refuse to let anyone see him, it is Malcolm X who leads the demonstration that forces the police to bring him to a hospital. When they receive word that the man is out of danger, Malcolm smiles at the police captain and disperses the crowd with a single small gesture, leading Captain Green (Peter Boyle) to comment, "No one should have that much power." Malcolm X clearly enjoys his power, and he especially enjoys exercising it in the face of Captain Green. Still, Malcolm remains the faithful lieutenant within the organization. When Elijah Muhammad silences him after his imprudent remarks after the assassination of President Kennedy that brought harsh criticism upon the movement, Malcolm submits to his wishes.

Although Malcolm X acknowledges the leadership of Elijah Muhammad, he still has flashes of his old arrogance. During a campus speaking engagement, a well-intentioned white student asks what she can do to help the cause. His response is a curt "nothing," and he walks past her as though she does not exist. Not only is the young woman crushed, but in his absolutism, he has alienated the very type of white liberal that could prove a helpful ally in achieving his goals. Lee's presentation of Malcolm's rejection of the student's support adds a nuance to Lee's thinking. In previous films, white people are largely irrelevant to the progress that he sees as mainly an internal challenge for black people helping themselves. Here, Lee sees Malcolm X's crude rejection of allies as at least questionable.

Similarly, in another episode, after being impressed with Malcolm's actions in the encounter with Captain Green outside the hospital, a young black man follows him into a diner and asks to join the movement. Malcolm rejects him, saying icily, "You don't know enough." In this rejection, Lee portrays Malcolm's uncompromising idealism as a form of arrogance that can only divide the black community, especially alienating those segments of the community that have been slower to see the issues in his terms. Later, in a joint television interview with a moderate black leader, Malcolm makes the offensive reference to "house niggers," in an obvious affront to the other man's opinions and accomplishments. Lee sees Malcolm's certainty about his own tactics and disregard for others as a flaw. This character assessment is consistent with the earlier films, in which Lee continually places a high priority on inclusiveness and solidarity among African Americans, regardless of social class, education, or physical appearance.

Lee's portrait of Malcolm at this stage in his life maintains its critical balance. The other side of arrogance is personal integrity, which is an admirable trait in anyone. Malcolm follows the Muslim ethic, marries Betty Shabazz (Angela Bassett), and begins his family. The Islamic prescriptions on the role of women are harsh, but Betty and Malcolm seem to accept them without question. As a faithful husband and dedicated father, Malcolm is disturbed to learn that Elijah Muhammad has fathered children with two of his secretaries, and he is even more disturbed to hear both Muhammad's rationalization that it was his duty to plant the seed and the women's understanding that this was expected of them. Knowing their role within the Nation of Islam, they waive their rights and want nothing more than support for themselves and their children. Malcolm is upset, but nevertheless, he tells Betty that the good outweighs the bad, and he will stay with the organization.

But the relationship shows signs of strain. With his continued insinuations that Malcolm has ambitions within the Nation of Islam, Baines has become Iago to Elijah Muhammad's Othello. The fallout from the Kennedy statements has made the situation even more tense. Thinking that money will keep Malcolm in line, the hierarchy meets and offers him a bigger percentage of the income. Finally disillusioned, Malcolm X withdraws from the Nation and announces that he will form coalitions with other like-minded groups, many of which he had criticized earlier in his career. He makes the pilgrimage to Mecca and writes to Betty that he has shared meals with believers of all races. Although he has softened the racial edge to his message, he maintains his belief in black separatism and announces that he plans to go to the United Nations to denounce the United States for genocide.

For Spike Lee, the tragedy consists in the fact that this final redirection in the life of Malcolm X never had time to mature. In a moment of speculation prompted by an interviewer, Lee sees Malcolm X continuing his growth in tolerance and bridge building: "He wanted to include as many people as possible."[37] This never happened. In little more than a year after his return from Mecca, Malcolm X was dead.

Largely as a result of the demonstrations that had clustered around the Vietnam War and the civil rights movement, and after Robert Kennedy and Martin Luther King Jr. were murdered in 1968, the 1960s were a nervous time in American political life. It would get worse as the war dragged on. Because of Malcolm's incendiary rhetoric about racial violence and his statements at the time of the Kennedy assassination, the FBI had been keeping a close watch on him for years, and the CIA had filmed him through each step of his pilgrimage to Mecca. The agents bugged his home, filmed his activities on his speaking tours, and wire-tapped his phones, as they had with Martin Luther King Jr. The Nation of Islam continued to view him as a threat to its organization. Both groups would be happy to see Malcolm X eliminated. Lee has no doubt that thugs within the Nation of Islam planned and executed the assassination at the Audubon Ballroom at One Hundred Sixty-fifth Street and Broadway on February 21, 1965, and he also has few doubts that J. Edgar Hoover's FBI may have expedited the killing and surely did nothing to prevent it.[38]

The film ends with an assessment of the legacy, and again, the theme is solidarity. Martin Luther King Jr. offers the first response. His presence holds special significance for Spike Lee because of his pairing with Malcolm X in the coda of *Do the Right Thing*, when the two men appear to offer contradictory strategies for doing "the right thing." The film seems to reinforce the common perception that King advocated non-violence, whereas Malcolm X's pursuit of justice "by any means necessary" left open the possibility of violent confrontation. Lee felt that was a misreading, and he was really trying to present a synthesis of the two schools of thought. King's appearance at the end of *Malcolm X* provides the opportunity to restate his belief in a fusion of ideologies. Looking into the camera, King calls the assassination an "unfortunate tragedy." He laments the fact that "still numerous people in our nation have degenerated to the point of expressing dissent through murder. We haven't learned to disagree without being violently disagreeable." Implicit in his statement, one could reasonably argue, is the admission that he and Malcolm X had their disagreements, but that he regretted the loss of another powerful voice in the black community.

From Dr. King, Lee cuts to black-and-white footage of the funeral and burial, while Ossie Davis reads a eulogy that includes the argument that Malcolm X's memory is poorly served by those who remember him as an advocate of violence. He was in fact a gentle man who never took part in any act of violence in his pursuit of justice. He should be recalled as a spokesman of black manhood who loved his people and left them with a sense of personal dignity. A teacher tells her class that they are celebrating the birthday of Malcolm X on May 19, and several children rise up to proclaim "I am Malcolm X," in a vivid expression of Lee's key theme of solidarity. It will be up to them to reincarnate the spirit of the murdered hero and carry his struggle forward. The film ends with Nelson Mandela, also addressing a class, proclaiming his faith in the worth of all people and the dignity that it is their right to claim—and his exhortation is interrupted with a momentary excerpt from speech by Malcolm X consisting of his tag line, "by any means necessary," a variant of the sentiment included in the quotation at the end of *Do the Right Thing:* "We may have to preserve the right to do what is necessary."

Spike Lee's tribute to Malcolm X adds a note of urgency to his call for unity in building the future that he has made in his earlier films. Urgency in the pursuit of equality is not anger, but the two emotions do overlap and can easily be confused, especially by outsiders. A call to action frequently can be mistaken for a call to violence, and indeed often one does shade off into the other. Mookie, at the end of *Do the Right Thing,* had to do something, and his throwing a garbage can through the window sparked the riot that led to the trashing and burning of Sal's pizzeria. The story of Malcolm X, then, is not so much a film biography as a restatement of Spike Lee's ongoing reflections on the response of African Americans having to "wake up" and "do something" to end the racial disparities that linger in America. Lee admires Malcolm Little for growing through his self-destructive behavior patterns without apology, and despite conflicts and disagreements, for learning to work with others for a common goal. That is enough to raise him to heroic stature in Lee's eyes, and that is the Malcolm X who appears on the screen.

Back in Time to Brooklyn

Several of Spike Lee's later films reiterate his social and political commentary of his early films, but none with a softer touch than *Crooklyn* (1994). In this film, he returns to the Brooklyn of his childhood, recreated with the rosy glow of nostalgia through the warm earth tones of Ernest Dickerson's cinematography. The heroine is ten-year-old Troy Carmichael (Zelda Harris), a spunky little girl growing up with both parents and four brothers in a lovely brownstone on Arlington Place in

Bedford-Stuyvesant before drugs and gangs made the area a nightmare. They affectionately call their crooked little street between Fulton Street and Halsey Street "Crooklyn." In those days children were not afraid to leave the house and play on the streets. The neighbors know one another by name and take responsibility for one another's children. They squabble, of course, but without gunfire. The children insult one another, but because gangs do not yet rule the neighborhood, the name-calling rarely escalates into violence. From what we know of the next twenty years, the childish crimes that Lee includes in the film evoke sadness at the realization of what they will lead to. Two boys (one played by Spike Lee) inhale airplane glue in a brown paper bag and force Troy to join them for her first drug-induced high. A few years later, of course, the dealers will be pushing crack in the school yards in their efforts to hook a new generation of customers. Another girl instructs Troy in the art of shoplifting, but Troy bungles her first job and will not try that again for a while.

Lee creates an Ozzie-and-Harriet world, but with an African American twist, and the resemblance to his own childhood is striking. The matriarch Carolyn (Alfre Woodard) keeps the family together by working full-time as a schoolteacher. She sets the rules for homework, mealtimes, and television for her four sons and daughter, and as sole wage earner, she manages the finances. Her husband, Woody (Delroy Lindo), is a jazz musician. He loves his family dearly, but he finds it difficult to deal with practical details in the real world. As a musician, he grew tired of playing other composers' music and insists on performing only his own, and this has led to a long stretch of unemployment. Although Carolyn insists on a healthy diet, Woody treats the children to ice cream and laces their food and drink with sugar poured liberally from a five-pound bag. Oblivious to the value of money, he writes bad checks on their joint account, and as a result, Carolyn feels obliged to open her own account. Of course, he is humiliated and offended by her action; they quarrel, exchange blows, and separate for a short time. Because the story is told from Troy's perspective, Carolyn appears harsh and unreasonable at times. An older person would realize that she is being stretched to her emotional and physical limit.

As a family, they face humiliation together. Con Ed shuts off the electricity because they have failed to pay their bills, and they have to explain to the family renting the upper floor that they will be without power until they "straighten it out." They receive food stamps, but Troy is too embarrassed to use them, and in her childish mind, it seems more honorable to steal the groceries that her mother asks her to pick up. When she concocts a story about another girl named Peanut stealing both the stamps and the groceries, Carolyn berates her for not fighting back. And she scolds Troy for tormenting another child by telling him that his mother uses food stamps and his brothers and sisters all have different fathers. Through the harsh circumstances of their lives, the Carmichaels maintain their own dignity and insist on respecting the dignity of others. Self-respect and mutual respect among African Americans are by this time constant themes in Lee's films.

This gift for tolerance extends beyond Crooklyn. In midsummer, the family loads up the car and travels to Virginia to visit Aunt Song (Frances Foster), Uncle Clem (Norman Matlock), and Cousin Viola (Patriece Nelson). Country life calls for many adjustments, but once she gets over her initial homesickness, Troy grows in affection for the old ways down South. Aunt Song takes her pajamas and gives her one of Viola's nightgowns, and in a further rejection of Brooklyn ways, undoes her tight braids with a hot comb and sets it into double "Afro puffs" on either side of the top of her head, a style commonly worn by little girls. They kneel and pray at the side of the bed each night and watch evangelists on television. Viola and Troy become fast friends. The trip serves an unintended purpose of helping Troy to see a way of being African American outside her Brooklyn neighborhood, and thus she becomes ever more comfortable with her roots and her own identity.

The real purpose of the trip becomes clear only at the end of the summer, when Troy returns to LaGuardia Airport and is met by her Aunt Maxine (Joie Lee). Carolyn is in the hospital, and as it turns out, she is dying, a factor that explains her earlier impatience with Woody and the children. With Carolyn in the hospital, Troy becomes the woman of the house. She takes charge of her younger brothers and stakes out the kitchen as her own territory. One morning Troy and her brothers walk meditatively up the hundred steps of the Prison Martyrs Monument in Fort Greene Park as they try to absorb the brutal fact that their mother is dead. (Lee's own mother died when he was in college.) Troy initially refuses to attend the funeral and states her independence by rejecting the dress Maxine bought her for the occasion: "My mother hates polyester," Troy says. "She would never let me wear anything like that." Eventually, she yields to Maxine and her father and expresses solidarity with her living family and her dead mother by joining in the rituals of death. During the reception held after the funeral, a younger brother cries that Snuffy (Spike Lee), one of the dope sniffers, has taken his money. With the ferocity of a mother defending her young and scarcely intimidated by the older and bigger boy, she finds Snuffy sniffing glue on a stoop and pops him on the head with a stickball bat hard enough to draw blood. In the final scene, she appears outside her house wearing a big Afro, just like the one she had seen on a model in an Afro-Sheen commercial on *Soul Train*. Her hair becomes an expression of herself as a modern woman—well, almost a woman—who has outgrown both her mother's braids and Aunt Song's "puffs."

In the child-woman Troy, Lee has created a wonderful tribute to the resiliency of the black family and of the inner strength of the African American community. Although Lee places Troy—and the strength of the black matriarch—at the thematic center of the film, he also makes Woody grow in stature during the family's ordeal. To the end, he gives no indication of getting a paying job or of growing more responsible with money, but he does keep his family together. Assuming a maternal role, he holds all the children in his arms when he tells them that their mother is sicker than they thought. He explains the shared sorrow of death to Troy, persuades her to dress for the funeral, and cleans her face after she gets sick. At the end, the family is still together and still living in their brownstone house on Arlington Place, and that is quite an accomplishment for any father.

Another View of Brooklyn

In his next film *Clockers* (1995), Spike Lee presents the same sanitized image of Brooklyn neighborhoods, but with a startlingly different impact. In *She's Gotta Have It, Do the Right Thing,* and *Crooklyn,* the neat streets and orderly homes of residential areas focus his attention on the tender side of city life. It is Brooklyn life as Lee would like to have it and would like to have outsiders see it. His characters have their problems, but they survive their difficulties because they have supportive families, friends, and neighborhoods. It is Brooklyn through the nostalgia-tinted lens of Fort Greene. In *Clockers,* the sun-drenched lawns and parks in the center of the Nelson Mandela Houses in the Gowanus section of

Brooklyn heighten the contrast to the shadowy, chaotic lives of the young men, the "clockers," who sit on benches and sell drugs to visiting users.

In *Jungle Fever* Lee showed the devastating effect of drugs on Gator Purify and his family; in *Clockers* he widens focus and argues that drugs destroy entire communities. During the opening titles, Lee shows gory police photos of crime scenes, with close-ups of gaping wounds in murder victims, all attributable to the drug traffic. All the victims are young black men. One of the signs shown during this sequence is an advertisement for guns. Lee has often expressed his horror at black people killing one another, and never has he used such powerful images to illustrate the horrendous nature of violent crime. As the narrative begins, the police have entered a crime scene, and during their preliminary investigation, the white detectives exchange jokes at the expense of the victim. One young man in the background wears a T-shirt with a gun on it, and Spike Lee joins the crowd of onlookers wearing a white hard hat. He stands behind the crime-scene ribbon as a spectator to horrible violence.

Spike Lee next moves the story backward in time to fill in the background of the crime. The police raid the benches where the clockers await customers, and right on the spot, they conduct a strip search for weapons, drugs, and cash. Ronnie Dunham, known on the street as Strike (Mekhi Phifer), one of the young dealers, constantly drinks Moo chocolate drink to ease a severe ulcer, which is a sign of his moral sickness. After the police raid, actually little more than harassment, the organizer of the drug ring, Rodney Little (Delroy Lindo), takes Strike aside and tells him that if he wants to move up in the drug ring, he will have to murder Darryl Adams (Steve White), who deals at Ahab's Restaurant but holds out on Rodney's profits. In one brief scene, Lee demonstrates how easily a young man can go from petty dealing to murder, and how difficult it is to back away. In a later scene, when Rodney reminisces about his own first murder, he explains that it is important to kill for the boss, so that if the underling ever thinks of cooperating with the police, the top man will be able to charge his accuser with murder. The system ensures absolute loyalty.

Lee pairs Strike with his older brother Victor (Isaiah Washington), who has kept away from the gangs, and who as an adult supports his wife and two children by holding down two jobs, one as an assistant manager of a fast-food restaurant, Hambones, and the other as a security guard in an antique shop. Both employers consider him a conscientious employee. Victor is tired and frustrated with his life, and perhaps drinks a bit too much to ease the pain. He rarely sees Strike since Strike moved out on his own. Against all likelihood, Victor tells the police that he murdered Darryl, but his story seems highly improbable to Detective Rocco Klein (Harvey Keitel), who as half Italian and half Jewish, represents a composite white man. He assumes that Victor is covering for his brother Strike, whom Rocco knows as a street punk. He also understands the practice of contract killing to assure silence, and he thinks Rodney may be behind the murder.

Tyrone Jeeter (Peewee Love), a ten-year-old in the projects, could follow in the footsteps of either Victor or Strike. He admires Strike and the other clockers and accepts presents, including a stylish close haircut that makes him look like the bigger boys. Pulling him in another direction is a churchgoing firebrand of a mother, Iris Jeeter (Regina Taylor), who doesn't hesitate to take on Strike and his friends after the haircut incident. She accuses them of "selling their own people death." Her strongest ally is Andre the Giant (Keith David), a formidable and dedicated housing authority police officer who has organized a youth club to provide some alternative to the streets for the younger boys. Iris reminds the clockers that anyone who leads Tyrone into trouble can expect to deal with both of them, and lose. Iris has made it absolutely clear to both Tyrone and Strike that they will have nothing to do with each other.

Tyrone faces too many decisions for a child of his age. He retreats into the fantasy world of "Gangsta," a violent video game that he plays wearing goggles that provide virtual reality for his aggression. Sadly, he cannot adequately distinguish between the gangstas and the shooting in his game and those in the real world, and he murders Errol Barnes (Tom Byrd), a neighborhood drug dealer dying of AIDS, with the gun he took from Strike's apartment. Klein handles the investigation, and when Andre learns where Tyrone got the murder weapon, he goes after Strike.

Andre forms only a part of Strike's problem. Through an elaborate plan, Klein has allowed Rodney and the other clockers to believe that Strike has been cooperating with the police in gathering evidence against their drug business. Klein believes this pressure will force Strike to confess to the murder and try to make a deal with the authorities rather than face reprisals from Rodney. Strike finds himself caught between Andre and the police on one side and Rodney and the clockers on the other. When Mrs. Dunham (Frances Foster), the matriarch, finally comes forward with the evidence proving that her favorite son Victor is the killer after all, Klein tells Strike to leave the City and never return. Apparently, on the night of the killing, Strike had lost his nerve at the last minute and left without pulling the trigger on Darryl. Victor's unlikely story proves true.

Strike remains the central character in the narrative, and Lee presents his life as a tragic waste. In the early scenes, he is a smug, street-smart thug, destined to spend most of his life in jail if he is not killed first. As the complex plot unwinds, however, he earns a perverse kind of sympathy. He is trapped by his past, and any decision he makes will only tighten the noose around his throat. Life, even life in the Mandela Projects, presents alternatives, however, and men must take responsibility for their lives and live with the consequences. Victor, for example, seems at first to have made wise choices before his tragic blunder. Strike freely chose the path of easy money, but once he became involved in the drug trade, he could do nothing to escape his self-constructed ghetto.

The closing scenes of *Clockers* are unconvincing dramatically, but they do serve as a restatement of Spike Lee's usual themes. Solidarity and mutual support provide the key to success of the black community. Victor emerges from the Brooklyn Correctional Facility and into the arms of his mother, wife, and children. The children have not grown, so in Lee's world, a good family man can be acquitted or will serve a brief sentence, even after pumping four shots at close range into another black man because he was depressed. Rodney has smashed Strike's car with a baseball bat, apparently in a police station parking lot, and yet he remains at large, free to pursue Strike, despite the drug charges amassed against him. Tyrone and his mother, Iris, have gone along with the falsified statement Rocco has concocted for them, and Tyrone has been returned to the streets without any psychiatric counseling, even after he has killed a real man who happened to become part of his video game. In helping Tyrone explain his state of mind at the time of the killing, Klein has him agree that he felt peer pressure because he earned good grades in school, and as a result his friends accused him of trying to be white, a notion that Lee feels deeply.[39] Tyrone has inherited Strike's elaborate set of Lionel trains, and it remains to be seen how the journey of his life will continue. Strike himself has simply gotten on a train and headed west, across the vast deserts of the Southwest, in what seems an echo of the Western's ritual of the hero's riding into the sunset for a new but unspecified future on a new frontier further west. Strike's future, like Tyrone's and that of the African American community, remains ever open to new possibilities, even though Lee finds few guarantees in the future.

The final sequence includes a crime scene reminiscent of the opening sequence. The police and medical examiners have once again gathered around a bullet-torn body of a young black man. Lee once again condemns black-on-black crime, as he has throughout the film, but he also underlines the indifference of white police officers. After the usual macabre jokes at the expense of the deceased, one officer refers to the high rate of drug-related homicides as a "self-cleaning oven." When Klein drives Strike to Penn Station, Strike asks him why he cared about Victor. Pointedly, Klein refuses to acknowledge the question. Throughout the film, he has pursued the evidence as a matter of professional pride. A sense of racial justice supplies little motivation. Like the other detectives, Klein uses racial slurs with other white officers with such frequency that his African American lieutenant finally steps in to ask them to stop. He's a good cop, and in many ways a decent man who treats everyone fairly, but he can't answer the question because in Lee's opinion, he probably doesn't know.

Keeping Up the Beat

In an astonishing variety of genres in his more recent films, Spike Lee has kept on message. The packaging changes, but the content remains consistent, as a selection of his later films indicates. *Get On the Bus* (1996) is a fictional reenactment of the Million Man March, a mass demonstration organized by Louis Farrakhan and the Nation of Islam. The film follows the progression of a disparate group of African American men who make the journey by chartered bus from South Central Los Angeles to Washington, D.C., to participate in the rally that took place on October 16, 1995. Lee managed to produce the film in less than a year, in time to release it for the first anniversary of the event. Virtually all the action takes place on the bus, where the men talk about their differences, only to reassert what they have in common as black men. The framing story is of course the journey, and this provides the overarching narrative that the community, with all its diversity, is headed to some destination precisely as a community. It's trying to reinvent itself, just like Fort Greene.

One member is a Los Angeles police officer who is biracial, and his complexion and ancestry become an issue. Some don't welcome his presence because in their thinking, he is not really black. A young social worker reveals that while he was in the gangs, he killed other young black men, and the officer tells him that he will arrest him at the end of the journey. A father brings his reluctant teenage son. They are literally chained together by court order, and the young man despises the idea of the rally. He wants to be back home with his friends, who, he is forced to admit, prey on other black people. A gay couple has had a lovers' quarrel, and they provoke conversation about the role of gay black men. Outside Memphis they pick up a loudmouth who owns a Lexus dealership, and as they ride on toward Washington, he continually expresses contempt for other black men who have not succeeded as he has. His relentless use of the word *nigger* to refer to his less prosperous colleagues wears thin and soon becomes simply obnoxious. Because he has broken the bonds of solidarity, they unceremoniously put him off the bus.

After the first bus breaks down, a Jewish driver brings the replacement, and the passengers object to having a white driver. The driver is a civil-rights liberal who defends his liberal credentials but under constant needling, the black-Jewish antagonism breaks through the veneer of commonality. He can't take the constant harassment, and at a rest stop he announces that he is quitting. As far as he cares, they can drive their own bus, if that's what they want. On two occasions, black women object to their exclusion from the march, and the men discuss the leadership role women have traditionally assumed in the community. This, they conclude, is something the men have to do themselves. A narcissistic young actor frets more about the results of an audition than the march itself. A film student joins the group with his video camera in order to make a documentary for his thesis at USC. He is the Spike Lee surrogate, filming the dynamics within the black community during its journey into the future.

The internal tensions rise to the surface against a backdrop of white racism, according to the pattern of Lee's other films. Jeremiah (Ossie Davis), the godfather of the group, tells the story of his being passed over for promotion within his company, then being laid off, and finally, after being rehired at a lower salary and without benefits, of having his job simply eliminated. He turned to drink and lost both his family and his self-respect. Nearing the end of his life, his health is precarious, as he shows by removing a hospital bracelet before he boards the bus. The Tennessee state police arbitrarily stop them and bring on a drug-sniffing dog. The police officer on the bus shows his badge, but in a more insulting way than is necessary, and the state police remind him that this is not Los Angeles. Satisfied that the bus is clean, they wish "you boys" a nice trip out of the state. At a diner, two white men display their ignorance by not knowing there were many black riders in the old-time rodeos.

The strain of journey and discussion becomes too much for Jeremiah. He dies in a Washington hospital without ever having made it to the rally. The doctor, who reviews his medical history, reveals that he must have known that the trip would kill him. She was right. Jeremiah explained that since he missed the Poor People's March in 1963, he was determined not to miss this march, regardless of the personal cost. By way of eulogy, the informal leader of the group reminds the saddened passengers that the object of their journey was to be better men at the end than they were at the beginning. In this they seem to have been successful. They did not make it to the National Mall for the speeches, their ostensible destination, but the journey itself forced them to listen to one another and to maintain a vigil of solidarity for one of their own in the hospital waiting room. Their differences remain, but they have gained mutual respect and have formed the kind of community that Spike Lee repeatedly urges in his films. The title of the film is addressed to the African American community in the imperative mode, just like his earlier exhortation to "do the right thing" or his exhortation "wake up" at the end of *School Daze*. He urges people to "get on the bus" and listen to one another with respect, and as a result they will become better men by the end of the journey.

4 Little Girls (1996) is a classic documentary whose story emerges from editing rather than script. It includes a compilation of film clips in the standard television format: talking head interviews, newsreel footage, home movies, still photographs, slow pans over memorabilia, and exterior shots of various locales as they appear today with voice-over commentaries. Lee takes his audience, black and white alike, back to Birmingham, Alabama, on September 15, 1963. On that steamy Sunday morning, Robert (Dynamite Bob) Chambliss, described as a "pathological racist" and a member of the Ku Klux Klan, set off a bomb in the basement of the Baptist church that killed four girls, three fourteen years old and a fourth only eleven as they awaited the start of morning services.

Lee carefully provides the context for the atrocity. In this present age, we have grown accustomed to random violence, but familiarity does not soften the horror. Spike Lee provides a thorough reconstruction of the historical context because he realizes that a younger generation needs to understand the systematic repression that existed in the South—and in subtler forms in the North as well—during the last decades of the nineteenth century and the first of the twentieth. His subjects point out that steady work in the steel mills might have created a relatively prosperous black working class in Birmingham, but if a man could not buy his daughter lunch when he takes her shopping, his weekly salary has little value. Segregation was not a benign institution, and dismantling it would exact a terrible price that America has not yet paid in full. From miniature portraits of family life, Lee broadens the canvas to include once-familiar shots of police dogs and fire hoses turned on freedom marchers, stills of "white only" signs on drinking fountains and restrooms, institutionalized and unprosecuted lynchings—sad events that may have been crowded from contemporary consciousness by newer forms of ideological barbarism. The bombing of the church was clearly intended as a reprisal for recent lunch-counter demonstrations and an act of intimidation to prevent further challenges to the divinely ordained order of life in Birmingham. Chambliss's defense attorney, now a federal judge, describes Birmingham as a "fine place to live." The prosecuting attorney explained that the rapid growth of the steel industry created a volatile mixture of traditions: union violence that grew out of the struggles to organize, and rabid racism of rural areas as impoverished sharecroppers, both white and black, came in from tired farms to compete for work in the mills.

Chambliss failed in his efforts to perpetuate a segregated nation, as did Bull Connor, the chief of police, and Governor George Wallace, who personally stood in the door to prevent black students from entering the University of Alabama. The film demonstrates that they failed on two levels at once. They intimidated no one, and in fact black leaders from across the country converged on Birmingham to attend the funerals and lead the processions of solidarity. Walter Cronkite, the iconic

CBS news anchor, called the tragedy "the awakening," and within two years, President Lyndon Johnson would sign civil rights legislation guaranteeing the vote to all citizens. On a deeper level, the bombing failed to break the moral spirit of the community. In repeated interviews with surviving friends and family, Lee shows their sense of loss and invites us to mourn for what the children might have become. At the same time, he elicits from them a sense of courage and dignity. These men and women acknowledge their grief, but without anger or resentment. They do not seek revenge. They look to the future without buckling under the weight of the past. Most strikingly of all, Chambliss failed to make them hate.

Bamboozled (2000) is the stylistic countertype to *4 Little Girls*. It incorporates broad comedy, musical numbers, and social satire, but even so, the Spike Lee themes of progress, dignity, and solidarity among African Americans still provide the framework of the film. He uses the television industry as a laboratory to explore class distinctions and the exploitation of black culture by black and white people alike. He spares no one, and just to make sure audiences realize that his moral parable is a comedy, he has the main character, Pierre De La Croix (Damon Wayans), recite voice-over the dictionary definition of *satire* as he begins his day in his own nicely appointed apartment.

Dela, as he is known to his friends, has a Harvard education, speaks with absurdly affected diction, dresses impeccably, and holds an executive position as a writer-producer in a foundering television network, CNS. His success in the entertainment industry contrasts with two street performers, who dance for spare change in the plaza of his office building. Class clearly distinguishes them, but when Dela arrives late to a board meeting upstairs, he is still the black man who is chewed out for running his appointment schedule on CP Time—that is, colored people's time. The network is in trouble and Dela, as the token African American, has to come up with an idea to bring in black audiences. This is the proverbial last straw. He has grown uncomfortable in his role and wants to get out of his contract, but he cannot.

His solution to his legal problem dovetails with his mandate to create black-oriented programming. He designs a show that incorporates every conceivable offensive image of African Americans. Spike Lee has taken the grotesque television world of Sidney Lumet's *Network* (1976) and recast it with the absurdity of Mel Brooks's *The Producers,* in which the eponymous heroes must produce a flop in order to succeed. Dela calls his program *Mantan: The New Millennium Minstrel Show,* and of course in the tradition of minstrel shows, all the dancers and comics will appear in blackface. He hires the street dancers he has passed outside his office. They realize the material is insulting, but they have just been rousted from the apartment they occupied as squatters and simply need the money. Dela changes their names from Manray (Savion Glover) and Womach (Tommy Davidson) to Mantan and Sleep 'n' Eat. The band is called the Alabama Porch Monkeys, and most of the action takes place in a watermelon patch right next to a cotton field.

Much to Dela's horror, at first, the program becomes a huge hit. As the show builds its audience, Dela enjoys the power and prestige he has achieved within the corporation. Black performers exploit their blackness, while white audiences not only urge them on, but also adopt the styles themselves by wearing blackface to the program and proclaiming that they too are "niggers." This is Lee's commentary on white performers and audiences who seize upon the externals of black artists. White artists do rap, for example, and white teenagers in the suburbs adopt hip-hop styles.

Dela's administrative assistant, his onetime lover Sloane Hopkins (Jada Pinkett Smith), is outraged, but she plays along at first to preserve her job and eventually because she finds the show funny. She is paired with her brother, who calls himself Big Blak Africa—he rejects the conventional spelling of black—(Mos Def/Dante Beze), and leads a group of radical militants, which includes one white man who continually proclaims himself black. He finds the show degrading and promises violent action unless it is taken off the air. He tries to enlist his sister in the cause and visits her house on Strivers Row. Class conflict is inevitable. Sloane graduated from NYU's media department, dresses in boardroom chic, speaks with the precision of an NPR anchorwoman, wears fragile rimless glasses that enhance her professional image, and has pulled her hair back into a tight bun. Big Blak Africa dresses in hip-hop and struggles with the language. Sloane tries to tell him that his mishmash of inarticulate radical slogans and uninformed theories is counterproductive to the goals his group espouses. She calls them "stupid." They get into a shouting match about "house niggers" and "field niggers," a class antagonism that Lee insists prevents black people from cooperating to achieve common goals.

Dunwitty (Michael Rapaport), the white network president, tells Dela that his wife is black and he has two biracial children, and therefore he knows black audiences better than Dela. He wants the program to go ahead his way, despite the critics. Myrna Goldfarb (Dina Perlman), the network's public relations consultant with a PhD in Black Studies from Yale, agrees with Dunwitty. The show features commercials for expensive fashions by Timmi Hillnigger, who is white, and Da Bomb, an alcohol-enhanced beer that guarantees sexual conquest, as indicated by the suggestive dances performed by models in minimal costumes. In his vicious satire, Lee shows corporate (white) America offering consumer (black) America what it wants: mindless entertainment that humiliates while it amuses, expensive "signature" clothes it can ill afford, and alcohol consumption that leads to further degradation. Lee spreads the blame around equally. Shame on the white corporations. Shame on audiences, black and white, for wallowing in this crass entertainment. Shame on the muddled leadership like Big Blak Africa for not having the ability to deal with the problem more effectively. Shame on the performers like Mantan and Sleep 'n' Eat who allow their talents to be exploited for a price. And shame especially on Dela and Sloane, who know better, but place their own careers ahead of principle.

This is a serious indictment. In the final sequences, Spike Lee moves from absurdist comedy to tragedy. Sloane falls in love with Mantan, and her indiscretion leads Dela to fire her, saying he made a mistake in the beginning by fraternizing with "the help." Big Blak Africa makes good on his threat to kidnap and execute Mantan on television, and after some negotiations, the networks secure the rights and clearances to broadcast the murder live. The video link, however, allows the police to locate the origin of the signal. They arrive too late to rescue Mantan, but they do kill Big Blak Africa and all the gang members except the one white man, whom they cuff and bundle into a police car. Sloane takes the gun that her brother had given her and kills Dela. In the murder scene, she appears with her hair loosened from its customary tight bun, standing up in a natural look. At the end of the comedy, Spike Lee returns to his outrage at black people killing each other, spiritually as well as physically, rather than working together. This was a theme most directly stated in *Malcolm X* and *Clockers*.

Lee does more than restate his revulsion with a culture of violence. He aims directly at the entertainment industries, which he feels continue a process of spiritual genocide. *Bamboozled* ends with a montage of African American entertainers in demeaning roles and white entertainers from Al Jolson to Mickey Rooney putting on blackface for comic effect. The final shot shows Dela bleeding to death, surrounded by curios made to resemble stereotypical and comic images of black people. For Spike Lee the tragedy is compounded: Dela had the opportunity to use his position in the media for constructive purposes. Instead, he collaborated in a process of self-inflicted degradation. He could have looked to the future; instead, he turned to the past.

Summer of Sam (1999) marks a departure from Lee's earlier work in that its principal characters are all Italian Americans in the Throgs Neck area of the Bronx, a neighborhood wedged between the Bruckner Expressway and Eastchester Bay, where the East River meets the Long Island Sound. By natural geography and the access roads to the Whitestone and Throgs Neck Bridges to Long Island, it is every bit as isolated as Howard Beach in Queens. Protected as it seems to be from outside intruders, the residents form a community that is torn apart by its own inner dynamics. In this they are quite different from the Italians of Bensonhurst in *Jungle Fever* who fear encroachment on their cultural as well as geographic territory. As in *Do the Right Thing*, the action is set in the midst of a blistering heat wave, this one in the summer of 1977. The heat strains the electric grid, which leads to a power blackout, which in turn leads to widespread rioting and looting in black areas, and there is fear the lawlessness might spread. The East Bronx is particularly edgy because a serial killer, known as the Son of Sam or the .44 Caliber Killer (eventually identified as David Berkowitz), is on the loose in the area. They fear he may be one of their own.

Lee does not present a flattering picture of the Italian community. Its citizens have all the moral limitations of the Tuccis in *Jungle Fever* or Pino in *Do the Right Thing*. Spike Lee points out one key difference. In *Jungle Fever* the Bensonhurst culture, for all its limitations, has strong institutions that keep it together, for good or ill. The East Bronx in contrast is spinning through a social vortex. Vinny (John Leguizamo) is a compulsive womanizer, despite his marriage to Dionna (Mira Sorvino), who eventually reaches the breaking point in acquiescing to her husband's desires and infidelities. He turns to drugs. Ritchie (Adrien Brody) wants to be a rock star. He affects a Cockney accent and wears leather and spiked hair. To support himself until his big break, he performs in a gay strip show in Manhattan and between acts turns tricks for the customers. Like the people of Bed-Stuy in *Do the Right Thing,* most of the young men seem to spend their days hanging out together, boasting of their imaginary sexual conquests, and planning terrible reprisals when they capture the Son of Sam. The women flaunt their big hair and dangly earrings, understand their roles as objects for the enjoyment of men, and take pride in their conquests. Ritchie's ample mother (Patti LuPone) entertains her current boyfriend in her living room in midafternoon without locking the door. Gloria (Bebe Neuwirth) runs a beauty salon and uses the barber chair for her encounters with Vinny, her assistant. Ruby (Jennifer Esposito) has a reputation for her vast experience, and when Dionna asks for advice on pleasing Vinny, Ruby tells her, "You can't be married to him." Its isolation has enabled the neighborhood to maintain its identity without realizing how corrupt it has become.

As the residents become progressively paranoid about the Son of Sam, the police call on the Mafia for assistance. Gangs of young vigilantes prowl the streets with baseball bats and stop cars on the overpasses. They focus attention in turn on a bearded taxi driver, whom they assume is unbalanced after his war experience in Vietnam, and the parish priest, whom they believe must be a caldron of repressed sexual energy. A young man who was one of the neighborhood boys has come out of the closet as an effeminate gay, and he becomes a target, as does Ritchie, who has also become different in his own way. The institutions that might hold a neighborhood together—the police, the church, family, and old friendships—lose all meaning in the face of the crisis. This has become a community at war with itself. Its inhabitants have lost their moral compass. Once the ethnic solidarity goes, the neighborhood spirals into anarchy and faces far more danger from within than it does from the Son of Sam.

In *Summer of Sam,* Spike Lee has moved beyond his normal setting in varied African American communities, yet his didactic message remains consistent. He places paramount value on different groups coming together within the community in order to achieve common goals. Once they allow divisions, whether between competing classes or individuals, and once they lose their tolerance for diversity or for the occasional oddball, they suffer as a group. In the case of the East Bronx in *Summer of Sam,* the divisions appear terminal.

Spike Lee has studied many different types of communities during his pilgrimage from Cobble Hill to Fort Greene, with side trips to Morehouse in Atlanta and NYU in Manhattan before heading back to Fort Greene. He found African Americans functioning well in the middle class as a minority in Cobble Hill and striving for success as a homogeneous group at Morehouse. Fort Greene offered a unique experience, however. Here was a neighborhood that had great cultural resources and went through an extremely difficult time. It was predominantly black, but not exclusively so. It had poor people, but as time went on, many relatively comfortable families moved in. Artists and uneducated lived side by side, and somehow all these people managed to function as a community to improve the lives of everyone.

Spike Lee, like Bill Cosby, has been vilified by some as a harsh critic of African Americans. In a self-referential scene in *Summer of Sam,* he plays the part of John Jeffries, a local television news reporter covering the looting in Harlem. As he does his stand-up report, a African American woman accuses him of not liking black people very much. Such a criticism misses the point of Spike Lee's work. He has seen how the community can work in Fort Greene, and he becomes frustrated when any community, especially the black community, lets class divisions, ignorance, self-interest, drugs, guns, promiscuity, pessimism, defeatism, and loss of self-respect stand in its way. His films are in fact not only didactic, they are homiletic, and like any good revivalist, he preaches hellfire as a prelude to redemption.

Epilogue

For a native New Yorker, returning to the homeland after a lengthy absence provokes many conflicting responses. Much depends on the point of entry. A driver coming across the George Washington Bridge from Fort Lee, New Jersey, to connect to the West Side Highway or the Cross-Bronx Expressway can look out the right window of the car, and depending on weather conditions, can see the skyline of Manhattan to the south. The last time I made this trip, the Twin Towers of the World Trade Center were still clearly visible in the distance, and surely I'd notice the sickening void today. (No wonder Spike Lee made the memorial Towers of Light that pierced the night sky on the anniversary of the attacks, and the gaping scar where they once stood symbols of Monty Brogan's [Edward Norton] ruined life in *25th Hour.*) Yes, this is New York, the commercial and artistic capital of the country, if not the world. It's probably an illusion, but the pulse seems to race a bit more quickly, and the energy level rises as well. My driving certainly becomes more proactive. This is the New York of song and fable, a land where all rainbows end and on every street corner pots of gold await the talented, the aggressive, or the lucky. Welcome to Broadway, the "great white way," the "boulevard of broken dreams"; Times Square, the "crossroads of the world," Wall Street, Madison Square Garden, the Metropolitan Opera, Trump Tower. As Liza Minnelli and Frank Sinatra have promised, if you can make it there, you'll make it anywhere.

One can also take the southbound New Jersey Turnpike a bit further, cut through Elizabeth, New Jersey, and Staten Island and cross into Brooklyn by the Verrazano Bridge. On this bridge a driver can look through the right window to see Gravesend Bay, the enormous gray hulk of the Veterans Medical Center, some remaining green space within Fort Hamilton, and the forlorn skeleton of the parachute jump at Coney Island in the distance. To the left, Fort Hamilton High School exerts a dominant presence among the elegant private homes on Shore Road, and just before the exit ramp drops down to ground level, one can see the tiny War Memorial and cannon at the end of Fourth Avenue. The connecting road makes a loop from Irish Bay Ridge, past the edges of Italian Bensonhurst, skirts Scandinavian Sunset Park (now largely Latino) and the ivy-covered New York State Arsenal, and rises again to enter the elevated Gowanus Expressway. The road slides past the monstrous white fossils of the Bush Terminal industrial complex and the remnants of a working waterfront, finally plunging into the Brooklyn-Battery Tunnel to Lower Manhattan. This ride creates a time warp. It slows me down and brings me back in time to familiar people and houses, to schools and shops and churches, many of them lost long ago in the endless cycle of decay, renewal, and gentrification. It's my hometown.

Other people, even famous filmmakers, also have hometowns that provoke memories and a sense of belonging "here" before they made it "there" in midtown Manhattan. These are the parts of New York that stamp an impression on the imagination that lasts a lifetime. Over these past several chapters, I've tried to take four very well-known filmmakers out of the category of generic "New Yorker" and recover some sense of their real "hometown" in the hope that such a consideration might provide still one more avenue of access into their films. At the end of the project, I'm more convinced than ever of the importance of the origins of the directors as a valuable critical tool for understanding their work. At the same time, I'm much chastened in looking at the results of my endeavors. Let's examine both propositions.

To the first point: now that the project is finished, I remain confident of the validity of its thesis. Neighborhoods do indeed provide a key element for appreciating the development of an artist's view of the world. This assertion is simply a variation on mainstream auteur criticism. Since the mid-1960s, when Andrew Sarris introduced the auteur movement to American film viewers in his groundbreaking monograph in *Film Culture,* and through the 1980s, critics have routinely concentrated their attention on key directors.[1] During the years when the auteur method exercised dominance, film scholars were tireless in amassing information about the biographies and opinions of the artists they studied. The interview became one of the dominant genres in critical writing in the professional journals.

In the last few years, critics and film historians have moved away from their narrow focus on directors. Those who still deal with directors as the principal creators of a film, as I have in this book, have widened their perspectives to include their interaction with producers, studios, and business interests; writers and cinematographers; and even marquee movie stars. Auteur criticism is still practiced, but in a way that the early Andrew Sarris and writers of the *Cahiers de cinema* would scarcely recognize. It is now important to consider a director as part of a team, a business, an industry, or, in this instance, an ethos. This shift to a wider context has led to a far more sophisticated and nuanced appreciation of films and filmmakers as key contributors in a very complex artistic process.

As a result, a great deal of work remains for us classical auteur critics as we try to locate our subjects within an intricate network of relationships. Even during the period when the biographical auteurists ruled the journals and academic film departments, before the theorists came on the scene, and even after the auteurists expanded the scope of their study to include the artistic contexts of the directors, it is striking that much of the auteurist inquiry was limited in its scope. We fastened our inquiries to very few formative elements in the lives of the directors we studied and ignored several others.

In hindsight, this was not surprising. Through the 1960s to the 1980s, and to a certain extent even today, much of the academic world's perception of the universe was colored through the twin lenses of Marxism and gender studies, which in turn were developed out of its earlier preoccupations with Darwin and Freud. Of course film scholars were no exception to the general trend, and in fact, as practitioners of a relatively new discipline, we were eager to gain legitimacy by adapting the agenda of the more traditional fields of study. Plot and character development could be analyzed in terms of conflicts in power and stereotypical gender roles. The business end of the industry was characterized as "Fordism" and films as the product of economic determinism. As is often the case with academic research, inquiry into the artist's thinking often reflected the intellectual preoccupations of the scholar. The journals published studies whose purpose was to uncover the biographical elements that explain the political philosophy and perceptions of gender that influence his or her work. Who was on the blacklist, who supported the ACLU, who was gay, who marched at Selma, who protested Vietnam were seen as important questions. And they were, but they should not have been the only types of questions.

My discovery of a growing sense of the incomplete nature of auteur criticism arose from my own intellectual preoccupations, which were somewhat different from those of other film students. Because I studied theology before concentrating on film studies, I was acutely aware that in the intellectual climate of the time, religion was a topic that rarely appeared in serious critical analyses of directors and their films. When theological issues did appear in commentaries, they were often addressed on a primitive level and by scholars whose interest in film was secondary. Theologians could look for religious symbols in certain key films of Ingmar Bergman or Federico Fellini, for example. Pastors would explicate themes that were likely to be useful in raising topics for discussion. Much of the work was valuable for what the authors intended to achieve, but much of it remained oddly extrinsic to the films and filmmakers. Scripture scholars use the term *eisegesis* for reading a desired meaning into a text, and the word describes a lot of what was going on. If it is true that the Judeo-Christian imagination permeates American thought and artistic expression, then a film critic should rather engage in *exegesis*, and try to extract latent theological content out of the films, even—and this is important—in instances where no religious message is included, suggested, or intended.

With some rashness, I tried to do a theological analysis of the films of Woody Allen, a most secular American filmmaker.[2] The study had its roots in auteur theory, to be sure. Its premise was that because Woody Allen attended Hebrew school and synagogue as a child and absorbed the stories of the Bible, these early experiences exercised an influence on his imagination and view of the world, and these in turn influenced the purely secular films he put on the screen. He does not use religious symbols consciously, nor does he raise issues of belief, but his films are unmistakably colored by Judaism. As I reread my work some months after publication, I realized that the idea should go one step further by distinguishing between cultural Judaism and theological Judaism. Although Jews in Eastern Europe and Jews on the East Side of Manhattan share a theological heritage, and one could legitimately discuss it in the films, as I did, still, the criticism really needed further refinement. For all Jews, the writings of the prophets might have sharpened the sense of sin, guilt, or vulnerability before the inexplicable forces of the universe, or the historical books might have provided the self-image of cultural alienation, understood as something like a journey through a desert in search of a promised land. This assertion is defensible, I believe, but these biblical themes have been modified through centuries of Jewish experience and have taken a particular shape from life in Jerusalem, or Warsaw, or New York. Even at this point a further refinement would be useful. Certainly the New York Jewish experience for intellectuals and artists living in University Heights around Columbia on the Upper West Side of Manhattan would differ dramatically from that of the struggling working classes in Borough Park or recent immigrants in Brighton Beach in Brooklyn. Clearly, the idea of a Jewish religious imagination needed further precision through cultural and geographic distinctions.

Some years later, I tried to make some distinctions within the Catholic tradition by treating several Catholic filmmakers with very different experiences of being Catholic: Ford, Scorsese, Coppola, Hitchcock, Capra, and, on the farthest fringes, De Palma.[3] This grouping provided the opportunity to look at the Catholic religious experience as it was modulated by different ethnic identities, geographies, and age brackets. The Irish Catholicism of Ford and Hitchcock, for example, was quite different from its Italian counterpart in Capra and Scorsese. And even within the two ethnic groups, there still remained vast differences. Ford grew up in a heavily Irish Catholic town on the coast of Maine, and Hitchcock felt the occasional sting of prejudice as a scorned minority in working-class London. Although they both share a common Sicilian heritage, Capra grew up in agricultural Southern California and Scorsese amid the sweatshops in Manhattan. As this project drew to its conclusion, it seemed clear that although they shared a common Catholic imagination, the ethnic differences demanded more attention than I was able to give them. To speak of a shared sacramental sense, or their valuation of community over the individual, or a redemption paradigms, or the sense of sin, guilt, forgiveness, and regeneration again made a valid point, but surely other cultural factors entered in and modified the shared Catholic sensitivities these directors brought to their films.

It was clear, even to me, that it was time to move beyond my initial interest in religious identity and to look into another area that has attracted little attention in most works of auteur criticism. Identifying and investigating the ethnic neighborhoods of these four directors has been rewarding for me, as I hope it has been for readers. The study has helped me look at the films with a richer sense of why these men picked certain projects, became preoccupied with some themes and not others, regularly dealt with certain types of characters and settings, and became associated with certain styles and genres and stayed away from others.

This present study represents a definite step beyond my earlier auteurist studies in that it omits religious influences almost entirely and focuses on ethnic neighborhoods as a key influence on the imaginations of these four New York directors. Although those of us who stay with auteur criticism have embraced the notion that film is a collaborative art form and other artists as well as business considerations contribute to the finished product, still we maintain our belief that a strong director leaves readily identifiable fingerprints on the work. The film remains an artifact touched and shaped by the director's imagination, as that imagination in turn has been shaped by the artists' living their formative years not in the abstraction known to the outside world as "New York," but rather in Fort Greene among upwardly mobile African Americans or in Flatbush among middle-class Jews, or in the constantly shifting ethnic mix of the Lower East Side among recently immigrant Italians or Jews. The four subjects of this study constitute a cross section of very different New York experiences. And as a result, they have become four very different kinds of New York filmmakers.

Despite a general sense of satisfaction that these essays have helped me understand the artists a bit better, the work still remains incomplete, as it must. Even though I am a New Yorker and will remain so even if I never return "home" to live, I'm painfully aware of the fact that I write about these New York neighborhoods as an outsider. This is why I feel chastened. In a perverse way, my very limitations and sense of inadequacy in accomplishing all the objectives of this book really support its central thesis. I am not Jewish, or Italian, or African American. I've never lived on the Lower East Side, in Little Italy, in Flatbush or Fort Greene. It's quite possible that my personal New York experience may have led to several misconceptions and false conclusions about life in their neighborhoods. Yes, it's a weakness of the book, but it proves the point that like me, these directors are really products of vastly different cultures, and even a well-intentioned fellow New Yorker from another clearly defined neighborhood may have difficulty in fully appreciating the insulated small town just a few stops away on the subway. One who attempts this kind of study is like the quintessential New Yorker who proudly advertises his roots by peppering his language with Yiddish, and continually risks getting it wrong. Still, this is a beginning, and perhaps someday, native critics, writing from the inside, will take the project further along.

Orson Welles expressed the conundrum quite well in *Citizen Kane* (1941). At the end of the film, the reporter leaves Xanadu keenly aware of the fact that he had failed to understand the inner workings of Charles Foster Kane. Discovering "Rosebud" painted on the sled really solves nothing for the audience either. The investigation was not fruitless, however. Through his diligent research, the reporter came to know a great deal more about Kane's personal life than he did at the beginning of his quest, and even though he did not solve the ultimate riddle of the man, he did learn quite a bit about him. I hope this book has provoked a similar conclusion: We don't understand everything, but we're better off than when we began.

Notes

Prologue

1. Thomas Schatz, in *The Genius of the System: Hollywood Filmmaking in the Studio Era* (New York: Pantheon, 1988), 5, writes the obituary of auteur criticism in the strongest terms: "Auteurism itself would not be worth bothering with if it hadn't been so influential, effectively stalling film history and criticism in a prolonged state of adolescent romanticism."

Cinema City

1. Marshall McLuhan, *Counterblast* (New York: Harcourt Brace, 1969), 22.

2. Thomas Wolfe, "Only the Dead Know Brooklyn," in *The Complete Short Stories of Thomas Wolfe,* ed. Francis E. Skipp (New York: Scribner's, 1987), 260.

3. Jean Baudrillard, *America,* trans. Chris Turner (London: Verso, 1988), 56.

4. Ibid., 14.

5. Ibid., 15.

6. Ibid., 18.

7. This ambiguity in the perception of the screen image is documented with reference to several theoretical sources in David B. Clarke, ed., *The Cinematic City* (London: Routledge, 1997), 2–3.

8. Roland Barthes, *Camera Lucida: Reflections of Photography,* trans. Richard Howard (New York: Hill and Wang, 1981), 5. Writing in 1980, Barthes did not consider digital enhancement, a development that surely complicates the issue by imposing a third element between the photograph and its referent. The issue has since been treated systematically by Brian Winston, *Claiming the Real: The Documentary Film Revisited* (London: British Film Institute, 1995). In bald terms, he states: "The supposition that any 'actuality' is left after 'creative treatment' can now be seen as being at best naïve and at worst a mark of duplicity" (11). For present purposes, photography and cinema can

be considered as Barthes did, without introducing the added factor of digital enhancement.

9. Barthes, 76–77.

10. In another context, I made a similar book-length argument about religion, maintaining that one can choose whether or not to belong to the Catholic Church, but one cannot choose whether or not to be Catholic any more than one can choose to be Polish or Italian. *Afterimage: The Indelible Catholic Imagination of Six American Filmmakers* (Chicago: Loyola, 2000).

11. James Sanders, in his admirable study of images of New York in film, *Celluloid Skyline: New York and the Movies* (New York: Knopf, 2001), 19–20, points out that the mythical version of New York comes from movies, whereas mythic Paris, for example, arises from painting and London from fiction. Much of the summary of the early film-production history of New York that appears here is paralleled in Sanders. Although Sanders explores the visual elements of his subject matter, the chapters that follow in this work focus on characters and situations, as presented by the directors under discussion. I am indebted to Mr. Sanders for his painstaking organization of this complex subject.

12. Douglas Gomery, *Shared Pleasures: A History of Motion Picture Presentation in the United States* (Madison: University of Wisconsin Press, 1992), 5–7.

13. Robert C. Allen and Douglas Gomery, *Film History: Theory and Practice* (New York: McGraw-Hill 1985), 18–20.

14. Sanders, 25, provides the locations of several of these "factories."

15. Ibid., 34.

16. Sanders, 42, describes the move to Hollywood. He repeats the familiar explanation that producers wanted to be close to the Mexican border in order to avoid the authorities who might be pursuing them for patent infringement during "Edison's Patent Wars." Eileen Bowser, *The Transformation of Cinema: 1907–1918* (Berkeley: University of California Press, 1990), 157–65, provides an alternate analysis of the move. IMP (Independent Motion Pictures) of Fort Lee set up operations in Cuba, and Ammex located operations in San Diego to take advantage of Mexican extras for a film about Pancho Villa. Either locale would have been superior to Los Angeles if escaping the law were a serious consideration. Weather, cheap land, and tax breaks seemed the more significant motivation for the migration to Hollywood.

17. Charles Musser, in *The Emergence of Cinema: The American Screen to 1907* (Berkeley: University of California Press, 1994), 118, explains that the difficulties in importing films from Europe made the move to unite production and exhibition centers as economically desirable.

18. Richard Schickel, *D. W. Griffith: An American Life* (New York: Touchstone, 1985), 91.

19. The documentary attractions of New York are nicely summarized in Sanders, 25–26.

20. Emmanuelle Toulet, *Birth of the Motion Picture*, trans. Susan Emanuel (New York: Harry Abrams, 1994), 16–17.

21. Schickel, 180–81, provides a political context. The mayor, Richard Gaynor, had been criticized for being "soft on crime."

22. Lary May, in *Screening Out the Past: The Birth of Mass Culture and the Motion Picture Industry* (Chicago: University of Chicago Press, 1983), 67–70, ties Griffith's rural background and evangelical religion to his reaction against the threats to the Victorian moral consensus that he perceived in New York.

23. Quoted in ibid., 70.

24. Charles Musser, "To Redream the Dreams of White Playwrights: Reappropriation and Resistance in Oscar Micheaux's *Body and Soul*," *Yale Journal of Criticism* 12, no. 2 (1999): 321–56. Musser presents an extensive analysis of the roots of Micheaux's vision. In "Black Patriarch on the Prairie: National Identity and Black Manhood in the Early Novels of Oscar Micheaux," in *Oscar Micheaux and His Circle: African-American Filmmaking and Race Cinema of the Silent Era*, ed. Pearl Bowser, Jane Gaines, and Charles Musser (Bloomington: Indiana University Press, 2001), 133–35, Jayna Browne explores the frontier myth that Micheaux utilized in his early writings, a pro-rural bias that survives in his later films.

25. Charlene Register, "African-American Press and Race Movies: 1909–1929," in Bowser, Gaines, and Musser, *Oscar Micheaux and His Circle*, 47–48.

26. Richard Slotkin, *Gunfighter Nation: The Myth of the Frontier in Twentieth-century America* (Norman: University of Oklahoma Press, 1997), 11, notes, "Euro-American history begins with the self selection and abstraction of particular European communities from their metropolitan culture, and their transplantation to a wilderness on the other side of the ocean where conditions were generally more primitive than those at home. . . . cycles of *separation* and *regression* were necessary preludes to an improvement in life and fortune."

27. Henry Nash Smith, *Virgin Land: The American West as Symbol and Myth* (Cambridge: Harvard University Press, 1999), 10–11.

28. Colin MacArthur, "Chinese Boxes and Russian Dolls: Tracking the Elusive Cinematic City," in Clarke, *Cinematic City*, 23, indicates that although 90 percent of Americans lived on farms in 1810, the percentage had dropped to 40 percent by 1880 and would continue to plummet until it reached a mere 3 percent in 1980.

29. A point made by Sanders, 227, citing the American historian, Thomas Bender.

30. May, 65.

31. David J. Russo, *American Towns: An Interpretive History* (Chicago: Ivan R. Dee, 2001), 4.

32. Garth Jowett, *Film: The Democratic Art* (Boston: Focus, 1976), 7–8.

33. Bowser, Gaines, and Musser, 162.

34. Sanders, 53.

35. Neal Gabler, *An Empire of Their Own: How the Jews Invented Hollywood* (New York: Anchor, 1989), 6.

36. Allen and Gomery, 100–101, discuss the dismissal of "foreign" films like F. W. Murnau's *Sunrise,* made for Fox in the United States as a film for "pseudo-intellectuals." The film was successful at the box office in New York, but nowhere else.

37. Cited in Sanders, 357.

38. Jane Jacobs, *The Death and Life of Great American Cities* (New York: Vintage, 1992), 56.

39. Sanders, 357.

Lower East Side: Sidney Lumet

1. Robert J. Emery, *The Directors: Take One* (New York: TV Books, 1999), 364. As the author explains in the introduction, 9, the interviews were originally conducted for the television series *The Directors* on the Encore Movie Channel. He reconstructed the print version of the conversation from the unedited tapes.

2. Stephen E. Bowles, *Sidney Lumet: A Guide to References and Resources* (New York: Hall, 1979), 4–6, provides much of the biographical information summarized here.

3. David Desser and Lester D. Friedman, *American-Jewish Filmmakers: Traditions and Trends* (Urbana: University of Illinois Press, 1993), 164–65. Like Bowles, the authors set the date of the Lumets' move to New York as 1926, when Sidney was two years old. Sidney Lumet himself says that he was four. Desser and Friedman provide the outline of Lumet's early career, noting his involvement in plays involving Jewish themes and other social problems.

4. In the 2003 television season, NBC recycled the concept once more as a dramatic series, featuring Debbie Allen, a star of the original film, who puts potential dancers through a harsh regimen as preparation for stardom.

5. Frank R. Cunningham, *Sidney Lumet: Film and Literary Vision,* 2nd ed. (Lexington: University Press of Kentucky, 2001), 17–19, outlines Lumet's work in the theater and his transition to television during the postwar period.

6. Eric Barnouw, *Tube of Plenty: The Evolution of American Television* (New York: Oxford University Press, 1975), 164. Even in the Golden Age of drama, comedy was equally well represented with four entries: *I Love Lucy, You Bet Your Life* (with Groucho Marx), *Jackie Gleason,* and *Bob Hope.* Ed

Sullivan's variety show *Toast of the Town* and the top-rated police drama *Dragnet* completed the top ten.

7. Bowles, 8–10, catalogs Lumet's achievements during his career in television.

8. Steven R. Carter, *Hansberry's Drama: Commitment and Complexity* (Urbana: University of Illinois Press, 1991), 19–20, surveys the reception of the play.

9. Bowles, 13–14, summarizes the state of Lumet's career at this point, including his two poorly received films, his own reaction to them, and his thoughts about moving to Hollywood for *A Raisin in the Sun.*

10. Richard Maltby, *Hollywood Cinema* (Oxford: Blackwell, 2003), 170–73, shows that contrary to popular belief, the decline of the motion picture audience began before the widespread popularity of television. Social factors were at work. After the war, returning servicemen began families, continued their education, and moved to the suburbs. The vast audience of singles in the war industries evaporated as people simply stayed home with their young children. My own father, neither a sociologist nor a film historian but as one who had worked for many movie theater chains from the days of the silents, blamed "installment buying." He maintained that people buying homes and appliances they could not afford to pay cash for simply did not have enough money to hire sitters and have an evening out on a regular basis. Like Richard Maltby, he was skeptical of the simplistic link between television and the decline of the movie audience. He lost his business and his house in the contraction of the industry during this period, but his wisdom deserves at least a footnote.

11. David A. Cook, *A History of the Narrative Film* (New York: Norton, 2004), 509, traces the development of what he calls "small films" or *"Kammerspiel"* from their roots in Italian neorealism and television. He cites *Marty* as a prime example of this "new" trend in the United States.

12. Oddly, I believe, the standard histories treat *On the Waterfront* almost exclusively in terms of its political statement (by Kazan, in light of his dealings with the House Un-American Activities Committee and the prevailing anticommunist hysteria of the time) rather than its New York tabloid-style photography (by Boris Kaufman) or its debt to television or its role in the development of American neorealism. See Gerald Mast and Bruce Kawin, *A Short History of the Movies* (New York: Allyn and Bacon, 2002), 311; Cook, 480; Maltby, 284, 294; and Jack C. Ellis and Virginia Wright Wexman, *A History of Film* (Boston: Allyn and Bacon, 2002), 369. Kristen Thompson and David Bordwell, *Film History: An Introduction* (Boston: McGraw-Hill, 2003), 349, treat it in the context of the New York theater and "Method Acting," as does Maltby, 410.

13. Jeff Young, *Kazan: The Master Director Discusses His Films* (New York:

Newmarket, 1999), 118–21, contains Kazan's own account of his involvement with communism.

14. Emery, 365.

15. Cunningham, 157–87, provides an extensive plot summary and analysis of the film that notes points of comparison and divergence between the script and the Wallant novel.

16. Desser and Friedman, 211–14, offer a remarkably balanced summary of the issues and of the critics who have addressed this emotionally charged issue.

17. Desser and Friedman describe the effects of city living on the Jewish imagination of novelists and filmmakers (6–7) and the attraction of leftist political activism, especially during the Depression (14–17).

18. Ibid., 213–14.

19. Desser and Friedman, 30, describe the theme of the Wandering Jew as a motif in American-Jewish novelists. I suggest here that the concept has application for one possible interpretation of the last scene of *The Pawnbroker.*

20. Cunningham, 211, quotes the Nazerman's entire speech as a response to the implied anti-Semitic basis of Jesus's admiration for him. He further points out that Nazerman is a professor by training and a merchant by accident.

21. Allegations of corruption and cover-up reached even into the mayor's office. As a result, in 1970 Mayor John V. Lindsay appointed Judge Whitman Knapp to chair a committee to hold public hearings on the matter. Sessions of the Knapp Commission were televised, and at least in the New York metropolitan area, they rivaled the popularity of the army-McCarthy hearings of the 1950s and the Watergate hearings that would follow three years later. In 1972 the Knapp Commission released a report highly critical of the department's efforts at controlling corruption. Memories of these hearings were still vivid for the movie-going public when *Serpico* was released.

22. Emery, 378.

23. Desser and Friedman, 182, offer an analysis of Blumenfeld's ultimate failure as an ethical man.

24. Lumet himself had entered into a biracial marriage to Gail Buckley, a daughter of Lena Horne. Desser and Friedman, 181.

25. Sidney Lumet, *Making Movies* (New York: Knopf, 1995), 5, discusses with some humor the presence of a $900-per-week chauffeur supplied by the teamsters union. His main responsibility on the set seemed to be sampling the brunch table.

26. Like many ethnic New Yorkers, Lumet knows less about other groups than he believes. In this, he is like a New York gentile misusing Yiddish expressions to add a hometown flavor to the language. Boston is an archdiocese, so "Bishop" Brophy would begin his tenure in Boston with the title of "archbishop," and according to long-standing tradition, he would have received

the title of cardinal within a few months. Ecclesiastics and their retinues are persnickety in their use of proper titles, even if no one else is. Actor Edward Binns wears the biretta—a square ceremonial cloth cap with three tabs standing upright from the crown—sideways, like a cigar box on his head. This would be the equivalent of having a rabbi appear with his yarmulke poised rakishly over the left eyebrow. Bishops wear the episcopal ring on the right hand, not like a wedding ring on the left, as Brophy does.

27. Sidney Lumet, "Sidney Lumet: Lion on the Left," interview conducted by Gavin Smith, *Film Comment* 24, no. 4 (July–August 1988): 36. Lumet expresses disdain for the radicals of the 1960s for their lack of staying power to implement the reforms they advocated. Gus Winant's character epitomizes the dead end of the movement in Lumet's eyes.

Flatbush: Woody Allen

1. Alexander Bloom, *Prodigal Sons: The New York Intellectuals and Their World* (New York: Oxford University Press, 1986), 25.

2. The trend continues. In 2000, Brooklyn had 2,465,000 residents and Manhattan 1,537,000. To put this in context, this population would make Brooklyn, if independent, the fourth-largest city in the United States, behind New York, Chicago, and Los Angeles, and substantially ahead of Houston and Philadelphia.

3. By way of contrast, the Bronx shares the same north-south avenues with Manhattan, and its east-west streets continue the numeric grid begun in Manhattan. The Harlem River dividing the two boroughs is a modest waterway, more suited to sculls launched from its Columbia University boathouse than to the battleships once berthed in the Brooklyn Navy Yard on the East River. It was rerouted by the Army Corps of Engineers, leaving the Marble Hill section of Manhattan stranded on the Bronx side of the river.

4. David Desser and Lester D. Friedman, *American Jewish Filmmakers: Traditions and Trends* (Urbana: University of Illinois Press, 1993), 41–42, place this characteristic in a context of seeking a substitute for Judaism, not in a quest for social justice but rather for self-fulfillment.

5. Eric Lax, *Woody Allen: A Biography* (New York: Knopf, 1991), 11–16, provides the family history and early biographical information summarized here.

6. Let me explain. I grew up in a resolutely Irish neighborhood, and all my friends went to parochial schools. It was the norm. Years later, I was amazed to discover that some people, hostile and friendly, non-Catholics, Catholics, and ex-Catholics, believe this kind of childhood is something out of the ordinary. One can come from an "observant" family without being terribly self-conscious about it at the time.

7. Lax, 31ff., offers several anecdotes of Allen's childhood schooling.

8. Cited in Graham McCann, *Woody Allen, New Yorker* (London: Polity, 1990), 15.

9. Lax, 19.

10. Cited in Bloom, 27.

11. Richard Schickel, *Woody Allen: A Life in Film* (Chicago: Ivan R. Dee, 2003), 84.

12. Nancy Pogel, *Woody Allen* (Boston: Twayne, 1987), 1–15, introduces this theme, which serves as a starting point for her treatment of the individual films.

13. Annette Wernblad, *Brooklyn Is Not Expanding* (Rutherford, N.J.: Fairleigh Dickinson University Press, 1992), 15–20.

14. Richard A. Blake, *Woody Allen: Profane and Sacred* (Lanham, Md.: Scarecrow, 1995), 3–13, points out that thematic similarities between the theological and nontheological films of Ingmar Bergman provide a useful model for considering the thoroughly secular or "profane" works of Woody Allen.

15. Peter J. Bailey, *The Reluctant Film Art of Woody Allen* (Lexington: University Press of Kentucky, 2001), 3–18, discusses Allen's total immersion in the world of filmmaking as blurring the lines between his biography and his art.

16. Bailey, 11.

17. Julian Fox, *Woody: Movies from Manhattan* (Woodstock, N.Y.: Overlook, 1996), 52, notes that on the basis of his earlier successes, United Artists was willing to give him "absolute control" over his future projects.

18. Fox, 48.

19. Woody Allen, *Four Films of Woody Allen* (New York: Random House, 1996), 9–10. Subsequent references are cited parenthetically in the text.

20. During a prerelease press screening I attended in New York, the critics and reviewers departed from their coldly analytical work to stand in the theater and applaud this sequence with most unprofessional enthusiasm. The only other reaction similar to this in my experience occurred after the baptism sequence at the end of Francis Coppola's *The Godfather* (1972).

21. Woody Allen, *Three Films of Woody Allen* (New York, Vintage, 1987), 107.

22. Ibid., 98.

Little Italy: Martin Scorsese

1. The most valuable source of biographical background of Martin Scorsese comes from the extended monologues of his parents in his documentary *Italianamerican* (1974). Additional information here is provided by Andy Dougan, *Martin Scorsese Close Up: The Making of His Movies* (New York: Thunder's Mouth, 1998), 7–10; and in Mary Pat Kelly, *Martin Scorsese: A*

Journey (New York: Thunder's Mouth, 1991), 15–35, which includes several transcriptions from *Italianamerican.*

2. Martin Scorsese offers the "business" explanation in *Scorsese on Scorsese,* ed. David Thompson and Ian Christie (London: Faber and Faber, 1989), 1, and the "landlord" explanation occurs in an interview with James Lipton, in the television series *Inside the Actors Studio.* In an interview in 1986, cited by Lee Lourdeaux in *Italian and Irish Filmmakers in America* (Philadelphia: Temple University Press, 1990), 220, Scorsese simply says, "I don't quite understand to this day why my parents had to move."

3. This odd tension between cordiality and hostility hits close to home. My high school, Brooklyn Prep, was split down the middle between those of Irish and Italian descent. I recall absolutely no overt hostility between the groups. A smug sense of being somehow different from other boys in our neighborhoods because we attended a selective Catholic, Jesuit-run high school provided a core of unity that outweighed our differences. In the days before political correctness, however, the ethnic humor was crude and at times more than a bit nasty. Years later, while living in Chicago, I was astounded to hear all the old Italian jokes I knew from high school retold as Polish jokes.

4. Peter Occhiogrosso, *Once a Catholic: Prominent Catholics and Ex-Catholics Discuss the Influence of the Church in Their Lives and Works* (Boston: Houghton Mifflin, 1987), 96.

5. Scorsese, in Kelly, 16.

6. Martin Scorsese, *Interviews* (Jackson: University of Mississippi Press, 1999), ed. Peter Brunette, 6. The reference to stickball is interesting because in the interview in *Inside the Actors Studio,* he notes that his asthma prevented him from playing stickball except on rare occasions.

7. Thompson and Christie, 3.

8. Dougan, 14–15.

9. Kelly, 6.

10. Scorsese, in Occhiogrosso, 96–100, explains his relationship to the Catholic Church. The "Easter Duty" refers to a requirement for Catholics to receive the Eucharist at least once during the Easter season, which stretches from Ash Wednesday to Pentecost. Individuals in a "state of sin" are required to receive the sacrament of penance first by making their confession. As one trained in the catechism, Scorsese would have known these obligations and would have considered himself in a "state of sin" because of his divorces.

11. Richard A. Blake, *Afterimage: The Indelible Catholic Imagination of Six American Filmmakers* (Chicago: Loyola, 2000), 25–48, traces much of the influences of residual Catholicism in Scorsese's films.

12. Scorsese, *Interviews,* 5–6.

13. Thompson and Christie, 13. The numbers in Manoogian's class are provided by Dougan, 23.

14. Dougan, 24.

15. Michael Bliss, *The Word Made Flesh: Catholicism and Conflict in the Films of Martin Scorsese* (Lanham, Md.: Scarecrow Press, 1995), xv.

16. Thompson and Christie, 48.

17. Riverdale is an affluent section of the Bronx, overlooking the Hudson River. It looks and feels like Westchester. Although it is technically a part of New York City, to a resident of Lower Manhattan, it would be considered suburban and its citizens easy marks, bereft of street smarts. Michael's embarrassment at being stiffed by two yokels in front of his friends has to be considered in this context.

18. San Gennaro, or Saint Januarius, was the bishop of Beneventum, later Naples, who was beheaded during the persecution of Diocletian around the year 305. According to the stories that grew up in his memory, he survived both an ordeal in a fiery furnace, like Daniel's, and in the Coliseum, where the wild animals did not touch him. Finally beheaded, he was interred in the basilica at Naples, was venerated as the patron of the city, and had many miracles attributed to him, including turning back an eruption from Mt. Vesuvius. On his feast day, traditionally September 19, a vial of his blood is said to liquefy, bringing good luck to the city of Naples for the year. In New York, the festival is naturally centered on Mulberry Street, the Neapolitan section of Little Italy.

19. Martin Scorsese and Nicholas Pileggi, *GoodFellas* (London: Faber and Faber, 1990), ed. David Thompson, 47. Subsequent page references are noted in parentheses in the text.

20. The term *Nativist* is used to designate those Americans who were born in the United States. It adds an ideological note, suggesting their belief in their own superiority and their hostility to immigrants. The term *Native American* would be equally accurate, but at present it is generally used to signify American Indian peoples.

21. Richard Corliss, "*Gangs of New York*," *Time,* December 22, 2002.

22. Scorsese takes liberties with history and falls into a minor anachronism. The prayer to St. Michael was commonly recited at the end of Mass until the liturgical renewal of the 1960s. It was part of what were known as the "Leonine Prayers," after Pope Leo XIII. He composed the prayer in 1884, after what he described as a vision of Satan gathering his forces to destroy the Church. He composed the prayer to St. Michael at that time, nearly forty years after Priest Vallon's using it. By the mid-twentieth century, the prayers were offered "For the Conversion of Russia," whose Communist ideology was then considered "Satanic" in its threat to the survival of the Church.

23. With uncanny accuracy, Boss Tweed foresaw this process of change within Tammany Hall. In fact, he was succeeded as party boss by Honest John Kelly in 1874, who in turn handed the tiller to Richard Croker in 1884, who then was succeeded by Charles Murphy in 1904—a man who furthered the ascendancy of Al Smith as governor and presidential candidate in 1928. In a very short time, Tammany Hall had moved from hostility to the Irish, to patronizing them for their votes, to transforming itself into a symbol of Irish power in New York.

24. Scott Simmon, *The Invention of the Western Film: A Cultural History of the Genre's First Half-Century* (Cambridge: Cambridge University Press, 2003), 189.

25. Paul Schrader, *Taxi Driver* (London: Faber and Faber, 1990), 7.

26. Why would Jake LaMotta ever think of becoming a nightclub comic? Another middleweight contender of the era, Rocky Graziano, became briefly popular on television as the tough-guy comic foil of the comedienne Martha Raye. LaMotta could not duplicate Graziano's success.

27. Martin Scorsese and Jay Cocks, *"The Age of Innocence": Screenplay and Notes* (New York: Newmarket, 1995), 119.

Fort Greene: Spike Lee

1. "Spike Loses Field of Dreams," *New York Post,* June 26, 2004, 2.

2. The factual information provided in this biographical sketch has been compiled from several sources. Where critical comments based on the data appear, they receive individual documentation. The principal sources used were Spike Lee, *Spike Lee Interviews* (Jackson: University of Mississippi Press, 2002), ed. Cynthia Fuchs, especially the editor's chronology, xv–xix; David Breskin, *Inner Views: Filmmakers in Conversation* (New York: Da Capo, 1997), 148–200; and online, Current Biographies, H. W. Wilson, available at http://vnweb.hwwilsonweb.com.

3. Samuel G. Friedman, "Love and Hate in Black and White," *New York Times,* June 2, 1991, Arts and Leisure, 1+.

4. Much of this history of Fort Greene is taken from Nancy Beth Jackson, "Diversity, Culture and Brownstones, Too," *New York Times,* September 1, 2002, section 11, p. 5.

5. Nelson George, "The Foreword," in Spike Lee, *Spike Lee's Gotta Have It: Inside Guerrilla Filmmaking* (New York: Simon and Schuster, 1987), 15.

6. *Spike Lee Interviews* (with Elvis Mitchell), 42.

7. Robert J. Emery, *The Directors: Take One* (New York: TV Books, 1999), 143.

8. Breskin, 184.

9. *Spike Lee's Gotta Have It,* 17. Lee explains his determination to over-

come the obstacles to produce his first commercially distributed film, *She's Gotta Have It.*

10. *Spike Lee Interviews* (with Elvis Mitchell), 54–56.

11. Ibid., 58. This interview took place in 1991, when Lee observed that only Eddie Murphy had the power to green-light films. Since that time, the situation has undoubtedly changed, but Lee's point remains valid for the time in which he made the statement and no doubt contains a certain amount of truth today.

12. Breskin, 188.

13. Spike Lee, *The Films of Spike Lee: Five for Five* (New York: Stewart, Thabori and Chang, 1991), photographs by David Lee. The contributors include Terry McMillan, Toni Cade Bambara, Nelson George, Charles Johnson, and Henry Louis Gates Jr. Melvin Van Peebles provided the foreword, and Spike Lee wrote his own introduction.

14. *Spike Lee Interviews* (with Elvis Mitchell), 58.

15. Breskin, 187–88.

16. *Spike Lee Interviews* (with James Verniere), 82. Among the backers for the film were Oprah Winfrey, Michael Jordan, and Bill Cosby.

17. *Spike Lee's Gotta Have It,* 40.

18. *Spike Lee Interviews* (with Elvis Mitchell), 45, and (with Marlaine Glicksman), 9.

19. *Spike Lee's Gotta Have It,* 302. Subsequent references to the script printed in this volume are provided parenthetically in the text.

20. Terry McMillan, "Thoughts on *She's Gotta Have It,*" in *Films of Spike Lee,* 29.

21. Toni Cade Bambara, "Programming with *School Daze,*" in *Films of Spike Lee,* 52, points to a "disturbing pattern" of misogyny in Lee that becomes apparent when his films are viewed in a series.

22. Emery, 145.

23. George Nelson, "*Do the Right Thing:* Film and Fury," in *Films of Spike Lee,* 79, points out that black and white audiences are likely to have a different perception of these characters.

24. In November 1986, Tawana Brawley was found in upstate New York, covered with dog feces and with racial slurs written on her in charcoal. With three advisors, the Rev. Al Sharpton, Alton Maddux, and C. Vernon Mason, she brought her allegations to court, but the grand jury found her charges not credible and dismissed the case in 1988. In 1989, when *Do the Right Thing* was released, the case was still a delicate matter among many African Americans. Ten years later, Stephen Pagones, one of the white officers, sued the three advisors for defamation, and after a trial that lasted nearly eight months, in July 1998 the jury found in favor of Mr. Pagones and awarded damages of $345,000 to be paid by the defendants.

25. In December 1986, three African American men were driving along the Shore Parkway in Queens on the South Shore of Long Island. Their car broke down in Howard Beach, on Jamaica Bay, an isolated enclave separated from the rest of Queens by the Belt Parkway to the north, JFK Airport to the east, and Spring Creek to the west. Local men taunted the visitors as unwelcome, but they entered a local pizzeria to eat while they waited for help. A crowd gathered, and, armed with baseball bats, they attacked the strangers. In his attempt to escape, Michael Griffith, age twenty-three, ran onto the parkway and was killed. The defense argued that the men had criminal records and one had pulled a knife in defense. They claimed that the defendants were merely defending their neighborhood from undesirable elements. Black leaders made Howard Beach a symbol of segregation in the north. Feelings ran high, but eventually three of the four indicted assailants were convicted of aggravated assault. Two of the indicted had Italian names—Ladrone and Pirone—and Pirone was acquitted. The families and the neighbors of Howard Beach were outraged at the verdict. By 2002 all three convicted assailants had been released from jail after serving lengthy terms. Other than the fact that the interracial incident took place outside a pizzeria, the event had little in common with the fictional violence at Sal's, but in 1989, Howard Beach was still a hot-button issue in the black community.

26. Charles Johnson, "One Meaning of *Mo' Better Blues*," in *Films of Spike Lee*, 119.

27. Breskin, 189.

28. Lee has been criticized as anti-Semitic for his stereotypical portrayal of Josh and Moe Flatbush, a common complaint when any member of an identifiable ethnic group illustrates stereotypical negative traits. Lee does not identify them as Jewish, but Flatbush is a largely Jewish section in Brooklyn. The marker is as clear as giving them Jewish names.

29. The ugliness continued for many years. In 1991, a local man stabbed the Rev. Al Sharpton as he led a protest march through Bensonhurst, and in June 1998, when Keith Mondello, one of the convicted attackers, was released from jail, Sharpton led another protest march and met with jeering from the neighborhood.

30. Flipper is an unusual name, suggesting the lovable dolphin in the children's film on 1963. It makes sense as a child's name that remains in use in the immediate family, but it is highly improbable that the name would be used by a professional architect. It is possible, however, that Lee is making reference to Henry Ossian Flipper (1856–1940), the first African American graduate of West Point. He received a dishonorable discharge when he was blamed for equipment that was missing from the quartermaster's tent and went on to a successful career as a surveyor and civil engineer. It would be an

appropriate name for an architect leaving a firm under unpleasant circumstances. Lieutenant Flipper received a posthumous honorable discharge from an army court of review in 1976 and a pardon from President Clinton in 1999, when review of the case indicated that the punishment was disproportionate to the allegation.

31. Breskin, 155.

32. Friedman, 1+.

33. *Spike Lee Interviews* (with Gary Crowdus and Dan Georgakas), 66, covers much of the long history of the various versions of the script.

34. In *Spike Lee Interviews,* Lee describes his own contributions to the script (Crowdus and Georgakas), 66–67, and explains that James Baldwin's name was removed from the credits at the request of his sister, the literary executor of his estate (Verniere), 84.

35. *Spike Lee Interviews* (with James Verniere), 82–83, covers the financial tug-of-war with Warner Bros.

36. Spike Lee's treatment of Christianity is harsh, which of course is a reflection of Malcolm X's own negative experiences. In an interview, Spike Lee showed himself more cautious about the Nation of Islam, even though he says, "there's no better program in America for black folks to convert drug addicts, alcoholics, criminals, whatever" (*Spike Lee Interviews,* with Crowdus and Georgakas, 74).

37. Ibid., 75.

38. Ibid., 73.

39. *Spike Lee Interviews* (with Elvis Mitchell), 55–56.

Epilogue

1. The pioneering work was Andrew Sarris, "The American Cinema," *Film Culture* 28 (spring 1963). The introductory essay and catalog of directors and their films filled sixty-eight of the special issue's ninety-six pages. Sarris expanded the introduction, updated the catalog, and published *The American Cinema: Directors and Directions, 1929–1968* (New York: Dutton, 1968), a work that lies at the root of auteur criticism for English-speaking academics.

2. The result was *Woody Allen: Profane and Sacred* (Lanham, Md.: Scarecrow Press, 1995).

3. This study was entitled *Afterimage: The Indelible Catholic Imagination of Six American Filmmakers* (Chicago: Loyola, 2000).

Bibliography

Cinema City

Allen, Robert C., and Douglas Gomery. *Film History: Theory and Practice.* New York: McGraw-Hill, 1985.

Barthes, Roland. *Camera Lucida: Reflections on Photography.* Translated by Richard Howard. New York: Hill and Wang, 1981.

Baudrillard, Jean. *America.* Translated by Chris Turner. London: Verso, 1988.

Blake, Richard A. *Afterimage: The Indelible Catholic Imagination of Six American Filmmakers.* Chicago: Loyola, 2000.

Bowser, Eileen. *The Transformation of Cinema: 1907–1918.* Berkeley: University of California, 1990.

Bowser, Pearl, Jane Gaines, and Charles Musser, eds. *Oscar Micheaux and His Circle: African-American Filmmaking and Race Cinema of the Silent Era.* Bloomington: Indiana University Press, 2001.

Brown, Jayna. "Black Patriarch on the Prairie: National Identity and Black Manhood in the Early Novels of Oscar Micheaux." In Bowser, Gaines, and Musser, *Oscar Micheaux and His Circle,* 132–46.

Clarke, David, ed. *The Cinematic City.* London: Routledge, 1997.

Gabler, Neil. *An Empire of Their Own: How the Jews Invented Hollywood.* New York: Anchor, 1989.

Gomery, Douglas. *Shared Pleasures: A History of Movie Presentation in the United States.* Madison: University of Wisconsin Press, 1992.

Jacobs, Jane. *The Death and Life of Great American Cities.* New York: Vintage, 1992.

Jowett, Garth. *Film: The Democratic Art.* Boston: Focus, 1976.

MacArthur, Colin, "Chinese Boxes and Russian Dolls: Tracking the Elusive Cinematic City." In *The Cinematic City,* edited by David Clarke, 19–45. London: Routledge, 1997.

May, Lary. *Screening Out the Past: The Birth of Mass Culture and the Motion Picture Industry.* Chicago: University of Chicago Press, 1983.

McLuhan, Marshall, *Counterblast.* New York: Harcourt Brace, 1969.

Musser, Charles. *The Emergence of Cinema: The American Screen to 1907.* Berkeley: University of California Press, 1994.

———. "To Redream the Dreams of White Playwrights: Reappropriation and Resistance in Oscar Micheaux's *Body and Soul.*" *Yale Journal of Criticism* 12, no. 2 (1999): 321–56.

Register, Charlene. "African American Press and Race Movies." In Bowser, Gaines, and Musser, *Oscar Micheaux and His Circle,* 34–49.

Russo, David J. *American Towns: An Interpretive History.* Chicago: Ivan R. Dee, 2001.

Sanders, James. *The Celluloid Skyline: New York and the Movies.* New York: Knopf, 2001. See also http://www.celluloidskyline.com/main/home.html.

Schickel, Richard. *D. W. Griffith: An American Life.* New York: Touchstone, 1985.

Slotkin, Richard. *Gunfighter Nation: They Myth of the Frontier in Twentieth-century America.* Norman: University of Oklahoma Press, 1997.

Smith, Henry Nash. *Virgin Land: The American West as Symbol and Myth.* Cambridge: Harvard University Press, 1999.

Toulet, Emmanuelle. *Birth of the Motion Picture.* Translated by Susan Emanuel. New York: Harry Abrams, 1994.

Winston, Brian. *Claiming the Real: The Documentary Film Revisited.* London: British Film Institute, 1995.

Wolfe, Thomas. *The Complete Short Stories of Thomas Wolfe.* Edited by Francis E. Skipp. New York: Scribner's, 1987.

Lower East Side: Sidney Lumet

Barnouw, Eric. *Tube of Plenty: The Evolution of American Television.* New York: Oxford University Press, 1975.

Bowles, Stephen E. *Sidney Lumet: A Guide to References and Resources.* New York: Hall, 1979.

Carter, Steven R. *Hansberry's Drama: Commitment and Complexity.* Urbana: University of Illinois Press, 1991.

Cook, David. *A History of the Narrative Film.* New York: Norton, 2004.

Cunningham, Frank R. *Sidney Lumet: Film and Literary Vision.* 2nd ed. Lexington: University Press of Kentucky, 2001.

Desser, David, and Lester D. Friedman. *American Jewish Filmmakers: Traditions and Trends.* Urbana: University of Illinois Press, 1993.

Ellis, Jack C., and Virginia Wright Wexman. *A History of Film.* New York: Allyn and Bacon, 2002

Emery, Robert J. *The Directors: Take One.* New York: TV Books, 1999.

Lumet, Sidney. *Making Movies.* New York: Knopf, 1995

———. "Sidney Lumet: Lion of the Left." Interview conducted by Gavin Smith. *Film Comment* 24, no. 4 (July–August 1988): 32–38.

Maltby, Richard. *Hollywood Cinema*. Oxford: Blackwell, 2003.

Mast, Gerald, and Bruce Kawin. *A Short History of the Movies*. New York: Allyn and Bacon, 2002.

Thompson, Kristen, and David Bordwell. *Film History: An Introduction*. Boston: McGraw-Hill, 2003.

Young, Jeff. *Kazan: The Master Director Discusses His Films*. New York: Newmarket, 1999.

Flatbush: Woody Allen

Allen, Woody. *Four Films of Woody Allen*. New York: Random House, 1982.

———. *Three Films of Woody Allen*. New York: Vintage, 1987.

Bailey, Peter J. *The Reluctant Film Art of Woody Allen*. Lexington: University Press of Kentucky, 2001.

Blake, Richard A. *Woody Allen: Profane and Sacred*. Lanham, Md.: Scarecrow Press, 1995.

Bloom, Alexander. *Prodigal Sons: The New York Intellectuals and Their World*. New York: Oxford University Press, 1986.

Desser, David, and Lester D. Friedman. *American Jewish Filmmakers: Traditions and Trends*. Urbana: University of Illinois Press, 1993.

Fox, Julian. *Woody: Movies from Manhattan*. Woodstock, N.Y.: Overlook, 1996.

Lax, Eric. *Woody Allen: A Biography*. New York: Knopf, 1991.

McCann, Graham. *Woody Allen, New Yorker*. London: Polity, 1990.

Pogel, Nancy. *Woody Allen*. Boston: Twayne, 1987.

Schickel, Richard. *Woody Allen: A Life in Film*. Chicago: Ivan R. Dee, 2003.

Wernblad, Annette. *Brooklyn Is Not Expanding*. Rutherford, N.J.: Fairleigh-Dickinson University Press, 1992.

Little Italy: Martin Scorsese

Blake, Richard A. *Afterimage: The Indelible Catholic Imagination of Six American Filmmakers*. Chicago: Loyola, 2000.

Bliss, Michael. *The Word Made Flesh: Catholicism and Conflict in the Films of Martin Scorsese*. Lanham, Md.: Scarecrow Press, 1995.

Corliss, Richard. "*Gangs of New York*." *Time,* December 22, 2002.

Dougan, Andy. *Martin Scorsese Close Up: The Making of His Movies*. New York: Thunder's Mouth, 1998.

Kelly, Mary Pat. *Martin Scorsese: A Journey*. New York: Thunder's Mouth, 1991.

Lourdeaux, Lee. *Irish and Italian Filmmakers in America*. Philadelphia: Temple University Press, 1990.

Occhiogrosso, Peter. *Once a Catholic: Prominent Catholics and Ex-Catholics Discuss the Influence of the Church on Their Lives and Work.* Boston: Houghton-Mifflin, 1987.

Schrader, Paul. *Taxi Driver.* London: Faber and Faber, 1990.

Scorsese, Martin. *Interviews.* Edited by Peter Brunette. Jackson: University of Mississippi Press, 1999.

———. *Scorsese on Scorsese.* Edited by David Thompson and Ian Christie. London: Faber and Faber, 1989.

Scorsese, Martin, and Jay Cocks. *"The Age of Innocence": Screenplay and Notes.* New York: Newmarket, 1995.

Scorsese, Martin, and David Pileggi. *GoodFellas.* Edited by David Thompson. London: Faber and Faber, 1990.

Simmon, Scott. *The Invention of the Western Film: A Cultural History of the Genre's First Half-Century.* Cambridge: Cambridge University Press, 2003.

Fort Greene: Spike Lee

Bambara, Toni Cade. "Programming with *School Daze.*" In *The Films of Spike Lee,* 47–55.

Breskin, David. *Inner Views: Filmmakers in Conversation.* New York: Da Capo, 1997.

Emery, Robert. *The Directors: Take One.* New York: TV Books, 1999.

Johnson, Charles. "One Meaning of *Mo' Better Blues.*" In *Films of Spike Lee,* 117–24.

Lee, Spike. *The Films of Spike Lee: Five for Five.* New York: Stewart, Thabori and Chang, 1991.

———. *Spike Lee Interviews.* Edited by Cynthia Fuchs. Jackson: University of Mississippi Press, 2002.

———. *Spike Lee's Gotta Have It: Inside Guerrilla Filmmaking.* New York: Simon and Schuster, 1987.

McMillan, Terry. "Thoughts on *She's Gotta Have It.*" In *Films of Spike Lee,* 19–29.

Nelson, George. "*Do the Right Thing:* Film and Fury." In *Films of Spike Lee,* 77–81.

———. "The Foreword." In *Spike Lee's Gotta Have It,* 11–14.

Index

Illustrations follow page 144.
References to illustrations are in italic
and cited by page (for example, *3*).